SELECTED □ FILM CRITICISM 1941-1950 □

edited by
Anthony Slide

THE SCARECROW PRESS, INC.
METUCHEN, N.J., & LONDON
1983

In the same series:

Selected Film Criticism: 1896-1911

Selected Film Criticism: 1912-1920

Selected Film Criticism: 1921-1930

Selected Film Criticism: 1931-1940

Library of Congress Cataloging in Publication Data (Revised)

Main entry under title:

Selected film criticism.

    Bibliography: v. [5], p.
    Contents: [1] 1896-1911 -- [2] 1912-1920 -- [etc.] --
[5] 1941-1950.
    1. Moving-pictures--Reviews. I. Slide, Anthony.
PN1995.S426   1982   791.43'75   81-23344
ISBN 0-8108-1593-1 (v. 5)

This volume is for Herb Sterne--

a good critic and a good friend

□ CONTENTS

Preface

☐ PREFACE

This volume of <u>Selected Film Criticism</u> provides reviews, reprinted in their entirety, of 140 of the most important American-
produced feature films released between 1941 and 1950. For the
majority of the films included here at least two reviews have been
selected from the following periodicals: <u>Cinema</u>, <u>Commonweal</u>, <u>Cue</u>,
<u>Esquire</u>, <u>Family Circle</u>, <u>Films in Review</u>, <u>Fortnight</u>, <u>The Hollywood
Reporter</u>, <u>Hollywood Revue</u>, <u>Hollywood Spectator</u>, <u>New Movies</u>, <u>News-
week</u>, <u>PM</u>, <u>Quick</u>, <u>Rob Wagner's Script</u>, and <u>Variety</u>.

To a certain extent the forties comprised the last decade during which film criticism was kept "in check," reviews ran a reasonable length, and critics had not yet contracted verbal diarrhea. One
could still look to the news magazines, such as <u>Newsweek</u> and <u>Fort-
night</u>, for succinct and intelligent commentaries on the new film releases. <u>The New Yorker</u> critics during this decade were reasonably
short-winded, particularly in comparison with their more recent successors. It is unfortunate that a fair number of the reviews reprinted here were unsigned; one would especially like to give credit
to the reviewer(s) for <u>Fortnight</u>.

The trade papers, here represented by <u>The Hollywood Re-
porter</u>, <u>Hollywood Review</u> and <u>Variety</u>, tended to be somewhat on
the lengthy side in their reviews, and--perhaps naturally--generally
tended to bend over backwards to be kind to the new releases. The
National Board of Review continued its fine tradition of lucid, schol-
arly film reviewing in its forties publication titled <u>New Movies</u>.
Nothing is more disheartening than to compare the writing in <u>New
Movies</u> with the National Board of Review's current publication,
<u>Films in Review</u>, which has steadily declined in the past few years
until it is now at its lowest ebb and shows little likelihood of

improving--or surviving. It is depressing to read the literate reviews of the likes of James Shelley Hamilton, Norbert Lusk, or Arthur Beach in New Movies and then to turn to the current Films in Review, whose writers seem to believe that the English language contains words such as "stringer," "didja" and "flicks."

I am particularly happy and proud to be able to include in this volume many reviews by a much-neglected film critic, Herb Sterne, whose column in Rob Wagner's Script was always a joy to read, a happy amalgam of carefully considered contemporary comment with wistful remembrance of films past. Sterne must surely be the only critic able to make valid comparisons between current releases and those of almost a generation earlier. He writes with humor (sometimes tinged with slight malice) and with intelligence. His farewell to film criticism is reprinted at the conclusion of this volume and serves as a suitable epitaph for this five-volume compilation of Selected Film Criticism.

As with the other volumes, I have tried to avoid reprinting reviews already available in reprint form elsewhere. To direct readers to that "elsewhere," I have also included a bibliography of other critical anthologies.

As usual, I must thank the staffs of various libraries for their cooperation, notably those of the Margaret Herrick Library of the Academy of Motion Picture Arts and Sciences, the Doheny Library of the University of Southern California, and the Literature and History Division of the Los Angeles Central Library. Special thanks also to Elias Savada for checking the copyright status of the various reviews included here.

The reviews from New Movies are reprinted by permission of the National Board of Review. The Newsweek reviews are reprinted through the generosity of that publication. Tichi Wilkerson Miles generously gave permission for me to utilize reviews from The Hollywood Reporter, and all such reviews reprinted here are copyright of that publication. Thanks also to Lisa Bain of Esquire; reviews reprinted from Esquire (January, February, April, and December 1950) are copyright © 1950 by Esquire Publishing, Inc. Edward S. Skillin, publisher of Commonweal, graciously granted

x

permission for my reprinting reviews from that periodical. The review of <u>Meet John Doe</u> by Harry Evans is reprinted by permission of Family Circle, Inc.

Reviews on pages 11, 22, 59, 79, 105, 123, 131, 136, 201, 215, 225, and 232 by John McCarten, Russell Maloney, Philip Hamburger, David Lardner, and John Mosher reprinted by permission; © 1941 or © 1942 or © 1944 or © 1946 or © 1948 or © 1950 or © 1951 The New Yorker Magazine, Inc.

Finally, my thanks to Syd Silverman at <u>Variety</u> for permission not only to reprint reviews here, but also for his generosity towards this entire series.

Anthony Slide

SELECTED FILM CRITICISM:
1941-1950

☐ ADAM'S RIB (M-G-M, 1950)

Although Spencer Tracy and Katharine Hepburn try very hard
to make this a slick, sophisticated farce, their main function is to
fill in until the reel rolls around to Judy Holliday. As a New York
goil booked for the attempted murder of her husband, she is a panic
and good enough reason for going.

--Esquire, Vol. 33, No. 2
(February 1950), page 20.

*   *   *

Unfortunately, on the screen, actors can't wait for laughs.
This is regrettable in Adam's Rib. Your laughter will overlap.
Writers Ruth Gordon and Garson Kanin packed this comedy with the
kind of running wit that will leave you breathless.

It's the old story of the battle of the sexes. Mr. Adam Bonner, assistant district attorney, vs. Mrs. Amanda Bonner, atty.,
who oppose each other in the courtroom and appease each other in
the bedroom. In the case of the latter the censor obviously closed
one eye.

The opponents are Spencer Tracy and Katharine Hepburn.
Tracy as Adam dominates with his particular ponderous masculinity.
Miss Hepburn, as his wife, Amanda, pecks at him with the ferocity
of a mockingbird and excels at being both feminine and feminist.

They are supported with a talent line-up to make any audience
sit up and applaud. Judy Holliday gives out with the charm as a delightful, bemuddled would-be husband assassin whom Amanda defends
and Adam prosecutes. Tom Ewell plays her dour-faced husband.
Jean Hagen is the "other woman," who confesses to wearing black
negligees while talking "business" with the husband and who can't recall where his hands were when the shooting started. David Wayne
steals scene after scene as the nimble-witted composer across the
hall from the Bonner's apartment. Polly Moran comes back after
screen absence of 10 years to do an amusing courtroom scene.
Hope Emerson does a hilarious job as a strong-armed tumbler.

--Fortnight, Vol. 7, No. 11
(November 25, 1949), page 31.

☐ ALL ABOUT EVE (20th Century-Fox, 1950)

This is a somewhat tedious film which happily boasts an
extra-special performance by Bette Davis.   Just to see her with a
part that fits is reason enough for going.   The story is about Eve
Harrington (Anne Baxter) and her rise to stardom on Broadway.
Unfortunately full of stereotypes, from the earnest playwright to the
producer with a thick accent, the film is a half-successful attempt
at defining Broadway and the legitimate stage to moviegoers.   Bette
Davis plays a middle-aged prima donna to the hilt.
                                    --Esquire, Vol. 34, No. 6
                                      (December 1950), page 74.

☐ ALL THAT MONEY CAN BUY (RKO, 1941)

Seldom does fanciful American folklore concern motion picture
makers.   William Dieterle dared to depart from formula in producing
and directing Stephen Vincent Benet's tale of a New Hampshire farmer
who sold his soul to the devil and was given a chance to redeem it
through the eloquence of Daniel Webster.   Benet's original story--
which appeared two years ago in the Saturday Evening Post--was titled
The Devil and Daniel Webster.   For reasons that do not hold water,
RKO has changed this to Here Is a Man, * and the new title is one
strike against the boxoffice success of the picture.

It will take the same high intelligence to sell Here Is a Man
to the public as it took to make it.   Unless the advertising campaigns
are as unusual as the offering itself, a second strike can be marked
against the film's chance of scoring a hit.   Without doubt, this provocative feature deserves place on any list of the year's ten extraordinary pictures.   Whether it also lands among the ten best grossers
depends entirely upon how competently exhibitors create fresh exploitation approaches.   Whatever his picture's fate, Dieterle is to be
congratulated for a masterly realization of a difficult and different
theme.

Neither Edward Arnold nor Walter Huston has ever been seen
to better advantage than as Daniel Webster and the satanic Mr.
Scratch, respectively.   Arnold does not load himself down with make-
up to be a facsimile of Webster.   Rather does he devote himself to
portraying the spirit of the man, and his plea for the return of a
soul is beautifully read to the phantom jury comprising Benedict
Arnold and the shades of 11 other historic dastards.

Huston's Mr. Scratch is performed with a demoniacal glee in

---
*RKO subsequently changed the title again: from Here Is a Man to
All That Money Can Buy.

which the spectator is a participant.   He has a grand time turning
in a grand job that should do much toward putting him right back on
top.   James Craig is perfect as the rugged farmer, Jabez Stone,
who enters into the devilish pact.   He is less assured as the rich
man, but the sum total of his performance is praiseworthy.   Anne
Shirley finds just the right note of appealing simplicity as his young
wife.

Simone Simon's return to the screen is cleverly managed.
Her role of the temptress is deliberately under-played, and registers
solidly.   Jane Darwell is delightful as Ma Stone, as are Gene Lockhart as Squire Slossum, John Qualen as Miser Stevens and a score
of uncredited character actors.   Lindy Wade shows bright talent as
the seven-year-old son, and H. B. Warner makes a brief appearance
as Justice Hawthorne.

Dan Totheroh joined Benet in writing the screenplay.   It is
good writing, almost poetic in numerous passages.   Particularly
well handled are the time lapses under Dieterle's skilled direction.
He does not hesitate to employ the artistic, even at sacrifice of
pace.   For example, the lengthy footage of bringing the mother with
her lantern out of the night to the side of her fallen boy.   Perhaps
there would be some benefit in eliminating nearly a reel from the
finished picture, but this reviewer is glad he saw it exactly as it is.

Technically, the Dieterle production excels in many particulars.
Splendid is the photography by Joseph August, and the wraith effects
something to remember.   Van Nest Polglase and Al Herman accomplished the art direction on a truly lavish scale, the New Hampshire
locale being studio created.   The stunning music was composed and
conducted by Bernard Herrmann, and is outstanding.   Others to share
in the credits are Charles L. Glett as associate producer, Vernon L.
Walker for special effects and Edward Stevenson for the period costumes.

--The Hollywood Reporter,
Vol. 63, No. 49
(July 16, 1941), page 3.

☐ ALL THE KING'S MEN (Columbia, 1949)

It is the honest, violent, and awe-struck story of the rise
and fall of Willie Stark: an all-American, one man juggernaut who
might suddenly start talking politics on your street corner tomorrow.
It is the almost undisguised history of Huey Long.   Broderick Crawford as Willie gives one of the most colorful and sympathetic performances of his (or Hollywood's) career.   A truth-loving crusader
from the farm country carried to power by the "hicks" he hypnotizes
with once-sincere promises, Willie Stark is a Messianic, Humpty-
Dumpty character who becomes fatally corrupt in office.   The private man is little different from the public man as he carries on

two love affairs while alternating care and abuse for his family.
Produced, directed, and written for the screen by Robert Rossen,
All the King's Men is based on the Pulitzer Prize novel by Robert
Penn Warren. Two or three scenes could have been deleted pri-
marily because they needlessly took the spotlight from Willie Stark.
With few exceptions, from hard-boiled (and vaguely motivated) Sadie
Burke (Mercedes McCambridge) to the screaming mobs of non-
professionals, the cast is superb. They are shockingly real as
they focus all eyes on Willie Stark who may come close to having
you, too--in a movie house--chanting "We want Willie!"
                                    --Esquire, Vol. 33, No. 2
                                    (February 1950), page 20.

                              *   *   *

     All the King's Men is a smashing, dramatically-compelling
piece of picture-making revolving around the political scene which
reflects highest credit upon all concerned with its production.
Adapted with keen precision and telling effect from Robert Penn
Warren's Pulitzer Prize novel, it is one of the most gripping films
of the year; certainly it will be one of the most discussed from a
sum-and-substance standpoint. Its appeal, however, is likely to be
limited to more mature audiences, although with strong exploitation
its chances shape up for the more general market.

     The picture primarily is the story of one man, Willie Stark,
an honest man, at first, who starts out trying to put through reforms for the betterment of the people of his southern state. It
is the narrative of his tumultuous political career upward to a
fantastic governorship fashioned undeniably from the Huey Long
regime and the legend and character of Huey himself. Broderick
Crawford in this role delivers one of the most dynamic character
studies the screen has glimpsed, packing the part with power and
passion, asserting himself with a performance which lifts him to a
position of top eminence as a dramatic actor.

     Robert Rossen, who produced and directed from his own
adaptation of the widely-read Warren novel, set a provocative pattern early and cleaved to it faithfully, as a mounting suspense
paces the gradual rise upward of Willie Stark, who ruthlessly
crushes all who oppose him. Audience is actually made to feel
that nothing can come between Willie and his goal, and the action
enlarges constantly upon this premise. Result is a stirring dramatic experience for every spectator. Rossen in his three-way contribution comes through for masterful effect. His creation of the
corrupt political scene and style in which he handles subject generally seldom have been duplicated from a dramatic sense, and his
work bespeaks class throughout.

     Film is filled with outstanding performances, all turned in
by actors who score their respective points decisively. John Ireland as the newspaper reporter who sees Willie through, from the
time he emerges on the public scene until he is assassinated on the

courthouse steps; Mercedes McCambridge, Willie's unmoraled
secretary, who started out against him but was swept up by him
and added to his staff; Joanne Dru, of a fine old southern family,
his devotee; John Derek, his son--these stand out in a large hand-
picked cast. Others who likewise come to attention are Shepherd
Strudwick, Ralph Dumke, Anne Seymour, Raymond Greenleaf, Will
Wright, Walter Burke, Katharine Warren.

Production credits also are highly placed. Burnett Guffey's
camera work is in tune with [the] spirit of the picture; Sturges
Carne's art direction is atmospheric; Al Clark's editing, tight and
realistic; Louis Gruenberg's musical score, vital; Sam Nelson's
work as assistant director is outstanding.

--Daily Variety, Vol. 65, No. 44
(November 4, 1949), pages 3
and 6.

□ ANCHORS AWEIGH (M-G-M, 1945)

Anchors Aweigh is a Technicolor musical that would be
twice as entertaining if sheared to precisely half of its running
time of two hours and twenty-two minutes. As it is, the film contains just about double of everything, including tediousness. Best
sequence: Gene Kelly and Frank Sinatra doing an energetic dance
specialty ... "Those Endearing Young Charms" is quite obviously
designed to be appreciated solely in orphanages where the only other treat besides the showings of such movies is molasses thickly
spread on slices of white bread. Robert Young, Ann Harding and
Laraine Day, I dare say, are very nice people indeed, but they
become most irresistibly irritating as presented by the writers
Chodorov and director Lewis Allen. I would like to report on the
acting debut of one Bill Williams, juvenile. However, the halation
from his very white and very numerous teeth threatened me with
a malady akin to snow blindness, so, in sheer self protection, I
was forced to close my eyes whenever Master Williams appeared
on the screen for any time at all.

--Herb Sterne in Rob Wagner's
Script, Vol. 37, No. 710 (August 11, 1945), page 23.

□ ARSENIC AND OLD LACE (Warner Bros., 1944)

Though Arsenic and Old Lace had a Broadway run sufficiently lengthy to harry Anne Nichols, and more road companies touring
the hinterlands than any play since Uncle Tom's Cabin, the comedy
never seemed quite as hilarious to me as it obviously and understandably did to those who own stock in Forest Lawn, Utter McKin-
ley, Inc., and Pierce Brothers, Ltd.

However, as a play Arsenic and Old Lace had its moments
of satire and sauciness. The film version sharply shears such
saving graces, and in their places one finds frantic farce, and that
particular type of Frank Capra whimsy which many found so ap-
plaudable in Mr. Deeds Goes to Town, Mr. Smith Goes to Washington, and Meet John Doe.

The film transcription builds no bulwarks against the banal.
The opening title reads something like "This transpires in Brooklyn, where anything can happen and usually does."

That's all, brother?

Hardly, for the love interest has been expanded, and now
employs a bridal pair who has to hurdle obstacles before achieving
the privacy which it is hoped will provide delight. Also, there is
one gag which employs a character, carrying corpse, falling down
a flight of cellar steps. This has been provided with a grisley set
of sound effects, and while such antics might well provoke guffaws
at a morticians' convention, it is unlikely to succeed in arousing
merriment in less circumscribed circles.

Under Capra's tutelage, the players comport themselves as
though they were appearing in a Deep South touring troupe of The
Bat. No holds are barred in corning the comedic capers, and poor
Cary Grant has been wheedled into providing a mugfest the likes of
which hasn't affronted a camera since Wally Beery ceased delineat-
ing Swedish serving maids for dear old Essanay.
                              --Herb Sterne in Rob Wagner's
                              Script, Vol. 30, No. 689 (Octo-
                              ber 7, 1944), page 15.

□ THE ASPHALT JUNGLE (M-G-M, 1950)

In The Asphalt Jungle producer Arthur Hornblow presents a
striking study of crime, a film that is almost a classic of its type.
The strong, suspenseful adaptation of W. R. Burnett's novel concentrates its vigorous 113 minutes of running time on a single es-
capade. With almost fanatical detail it records the organization,
consummation and after-effects of a big jewel robbery. Masterly
supervision of the script and meticulous casting characterize Hornblow's work throughout. And the fact that John Huston prowls the
underworld with the understanding of few other directors accounts
for the realistic performances rendered by the hand-picked cast.
Huston forges the script into a breathtaking and suspenseful screen
story which literally has you rooting for the heavies. For sustained drama, few similar sequences pack the same taut excitement
as that Huston achieves in the scene of the robbery.

In two rather important respects The Asphalt Jungle falls
short of its own excellence; namely, in establishing the relationship

of the inevitable boy and girl, Sterling Hayden and Jean Hagen, in making a simple ironic point the only factor that leads to the capture of the mastermind, Sam Jaffe. The casual onlooker, though, will be inclined to forgive these shortcomings in view of the overwhelming entertainment values found throughout the picture. The subject is highly exploitable and, with good reviews and enthusiastic word-of-mouth advertising to nudge it along, it should have little trouble in clearing top grosses, despite a lack of big names.

The story of Asphalt Jungle begins with the release from prison of Jaffe, a bold and painstaking underworld craftsman. He has a plan worked out for a gigantic jewel robbery and goes to Louis Calhern, a crooked lawyer, for financial help. Calhern, seeing in the scheme a way to double-cross Jaffe and get enough money to solve his own pressing financial problems, agrees to help. Actually, stooge Marc Lawrence supplies the cash in Calhern's name. In a fascinating and magnificently professional manner, Jaffe goes about the task of recruiting workers and working out the details. For all the precision of the preparation, the unexpected develops. One of the robbers is killed, and Calhern's scheme backfires. Without a ready market, the jewels have no value except to lead the police to their possessor. One by one the crooks come to a sad end.

The role of trigger man for the job is a fat part for Sterling Hayden, who plays it with enormous authority, the kind of acting that reinstates him in the big leagues. Louis Calhern's smooth and sinister attorney is a well turned characterization. Jean Hagen is a standout as the girl who attaches herself to Hayden. James Whitmore figures impressively in the story as the hunch-backed owner of a dining car who drives the automobile for the robbery. Sam Jaffe, whose infrequent visits to Hollywood always leave behind the feeling of watching a rarely gifted actor at work, again makes a character so completely his own that you forget his own identity. Jaffe is the master strategist, a career thief who is led to his downfall by his one weakness, the ogling of young girls. John McIntire reads conviction and sympathy into his part of a harassed Police Commissioner. Marc Lawrence is a fine choice for the part of the petty racketeer who steps into the big time. Anthony Caruso, playing the safecracker whose quiet home life is as important as his job, is excellent, and Teresa Celli makes her emotional scenes count in the part of his wife. Marilyn Monroe has the simple directness needed for her spot of Calhern's mistress, and Dorothy Tree etches a sharp portrait of the attorney's hypochondriac wife. Brad Dexter is especially good as another Calhern stooge.

Harold Rosson's sharp, semi-documentary style photography is a valuable asset in giving The Asphalt Jungle the realism it needs. Cedric Gibbons and Randall Duell collaborate in a fine art direction credit. Miklos Rozsa's score has power. George Boem-

ler's editing helps sustain the almost incredible suspense.
--The Hollywood Reporter, Vol.
108, No. 49 (May 5, 1950),
pages 3 and 8.

*   *   *

In The Asphalt Jungle John Huston turns his back on major-
league themata like Treasure of the Sierra Madre and returns to
melodramatic tours-de-force like The Maltese Falcon--yet another
Hollywood contribution to the clinical literature on modern crime.

While the Ben Maddow-Huston screenplay does pretend to
deeper significances than the ordinary cops-and-robbers film, it
succeeds only on the level of the super-imposed soundtrack commentary.

Stylistically Huston has achieved a degree of the quality of
our contemporary urban jungles in the harshly lit cinematography
and the impersonal premise. But in its very efforts aimed at that
style, The Asphalt Jungle stifles any spark of three-dimensional
life that may have stirred the film's protagonists.

Huston and Maddow have assembled a gallery of types, all
enmeshed in a single daring plan for a million-dollar robbery.
There is the criminal master-mind (Sam Jaffe) whose brilliant
attainments are warped, the big-time criminal lawyer (Louis Calhern) who lives beyond his means and whose psycho-emotional life
is gravely disjointed. Other threads in the criminal fabric are
the devoted family-man of a safecracker (Anthony Caruso),
the brutish bully-boy who dreams of a lost heritage (Sterling
Hayden) and the criminal coward who turns stool-pigeon (Marc
Lawrence).

Barry Kelley supplies one of the choicer characterizations
as the corrupt police lieutenant, while John McIntire, another capable actor, presents the honorable aspect of the law with quiet
dignity.

The dramatic method herein is classic in its directness, as-
sembling the component elements, interweaving them and finally
dispersing each according to its dramatic desserts. It is disap-
pointing that the resultant drama lacks depth of perception or scope
of understanding.

Notable detail is the harshly effective work of Hayden, the
while both Jaffe and Calhern impress purely as stereotypes. The
women are vaguely motivated and act that way.
--Fortnight, Vol. 8, No. 13
(June 23, 1950), page 32.

☐ BALL OF FIRE (Goldwyn/RKO, 1941)

    Despite all those funny Malapropisms attributed to Sam Gold-
wyn, that producer hasn't recently made a really hilarious comedy.
Sam has a way with dramatic movies, but if you recall Woman
Chases Man, The Cowboy and the Lady (don't, if it will make you
any cheerier), it will be readily understood that his touch is less
deft when he prods the risibilities.

    Ball of Fire is somewhat more successful than his other re-
cent attempts at tripping a light fantastic. It has some capersome
writing by Brackett and Wilder, and the knowing drolleries of the
co-stars, Gary Cooper and Barbara Stanwyck, will pull the wool
over many a spectator's eyes and cozen him into believing he's
witnessing a first-rate frolic. Professor Deeds goes to a nightspot to gather material for a slang section of an encyclopedia.
He meets Sugarpuss O'Shea, takes her home to meet sundry other
scholars, and the colleen plays "Peg O' My Heart" to the tune of
an exaggerated and repetitious colloquial vocabulary. A funny
enough idea, but it's spun to chiffon sheerness.

    Picture might have been more amusing if one could have
seen the action distinctly. Gregg Toland's highly touted low-key
photography is all very well for a Kane or The Little Foxes, but
here it acts as a depressant. Still, Gene Krupa is wonderful at
the drums. Dana Andrews takes another rung up the ladder to
stardom as the fancy-pants killer, and there are other excellent
contributions by Tully Marshall, Richard Haydn, Dan Duryea,
Mary Field, and S. Z. Sakall.

                              --Herb Sterne in Rob Wagner's
                                Script, Vol. 27, No. 619
                                (January 3, 1942), pages 16-17.

☐ BAMBI (Disney/RKO, 1942)

    While we're on the subject of pioneers, Walt Disney has al-
so just turned out a picture based on a book well suited to his
tastes. As you know, he has a leaning toward animals, and he
has chosen Bambi, by Felix Salten, for his latest nature study.
His version of the afternoons of a fawn has a good deal of the appeal that Snow White and Pinocchio had, though not all. The color
and the three-dimensional effect of the scenery are certainly up to
standard, but the characterizations, on the other hand, are slightly
sub. The comedy, for example, is handled by a rabbit who hasn't
nearly as much on the ball as the dwarfs had, or the cricket in
Pinocchio, or even the mouse in Dumbo, who was no panic. And
then there's too much conversation in this piece, as becomes especially noticeable when puberty sets in and all these woodland creatures' voices suddenly change. If a deer's or a rabbit's voice has

got to change, the thing should be handled as unemphatically as
possible. Generally speaking, Bambi is more strictly a children's
picture than its forerunners. One word of warning, though, to
daddies who expect to knock over a little venison when the season
rolls around: the young folks are going to be definitely pro-deer.
                                    --David Lardner in The New
                                        Yorker (August 15, 1942), page
                                        53.

☐ THE BEAUTIFUL BLONDE FROM BASHFUL BEND (20th
    Century-Fox, 1949)

Why 20th feels it must keep Miss Grable's most valuable
assets covered under long skirts, give her as few songs and
dances as possible and expect top results is a major mystery.
Despite the fact that this attempt at horse opera burlesque was
produced by Preston Sturges--a master at sophisticated comedy--
it still doesn't come off. While there are a few fresh twists in
the way of gags most of the show is timeworn slapstick which--to
quote a Hollywood rationalization--will probably "go over great in
the sticks, " but is not good Sturges. The tale deals with a dancing girl (Betty Grable) who shoots up a judge in the gluteal area,
flees to another town where she is mistaken for the schoolteacher.
Lots of gunplay, standard slapstick and a few bright moments.
                                    --Fortnight, Vol. 6, No. 11
                                        (May 27, 1949), page 31.

☐ THE BELLS OF ST. MARY'S (RKO, 1945)

The press and public, almost without exception, invariably
confuse the merits of a film that deals with religion with a religious film, and let a reviewer so much as infer that Ben Hur,
The Sign of the Cross, The Song of Bernadette, The Ten Command-
ments, The King of Kings, One Foot in Heaven, The Servant in the
House and The Passing of the Third Floor Back are somewhat less
than masterworks painted in celluloid by Michelangelo, and he is
immediately bombarded by letters from readers who rant that he is
an enemy of God and all godliness, with no more virtue in his person and private life than Lucifer, Lilith and Adolf Hitler.

Notwithstanding past, and sorry, experiences in such matters,
and the resultant burden to the mailman of toiling up a rugged hill
to my domain, it appears necessary to the peace of my personal
integrity to state that The Bells of St. Mary's is Going My Way,
only in the wrong direction.

The film, which relates the further, if no vastly different
adventures of Bing Crosby's Father O'Malley, is strained and rather

unbecomingly avid for boxoffice gold which it woos by willfully confusing the old hokum bucket with an ecclesiastical fount. It sub-
scribes to the notion that ladies and gentlemen of the Cloth have
no more maturity than Elsie Dinsmore, and that in place of culti-
vating Faith they, one and all, are intent on emulating an athletic
prowess that would put Frank Merriwell, or his brother Dick for
that matter, to positive shame.

The dialogue of Dudley Nichols is so arrantly bobby sox that
one is led to believe those who vow their lives to the Church speak
as though they were more familiar with the Palladium than the pul-
pit, and director Leo McCarey shows no disinclination in encourag-
ing his ecclesiastical characters to conduct themselves in much the
same manner. Several sequences will prove distasteful to those
who consider religion other than material for a cheap charade, and
I am not inordinately touchy on this subject.

Aside from a fetching enactment by Ingrid Bergman, who
manages more adroitly than does Crosby to avoid the pitfalls maneuvered by McCarey and Nichols, there isn't much to recommend
about a picture that finds religion rather resembling a romp.

The Bells of St. Mary's rings a commercial tune that is
blatantly offkey.
                              --Herb Sterne in Rob Wagner's
                                Script, Vol. 32, No. 720
                                (January 5, 1946), pages 14-15.

*   *   *

Leo McCarey's follow-up film to his phenomenal Going My
Way hit of last year is a beautiful picture of great spiritual uplift
that will be balm and ointment to many weary hearts. It is practically certain to do equally as great a business as the other and
audiences will love it equally as much even while they admit that
it cannot hold a candle to the other as entertainment. There are a
great many things wrong with The Bells of St. Mary's production-
wise and while it is never cheap, it is an obvious attempt to catch
on to the other. These factors will be taken up later even though
it would seem to smack of heresy in a picture as truly beautiful
and uplifting as this one.

That The Bells of St. Mary's is the fine picture it is is due
solely and indisputably to the magnificent performance of Ingrid
Bergman as the Sister Superior Benedict. It is probably the single
greatest performance that any actress in motion pictures has ever
given and, as magnificent as she also is in Saratoga Trunk, this
is the jewel that crowns her illustrious career.

It is not the great picture it might have been because there
is a very bad, very hokey performance of the same priest by Bing
Crosby that he played in Going My Way. And because although it
claims to have a screenplay by Dudley Nichols, actually there is

nothing resembling a screenplay and altogether too much of the
film, to its great detriment, has the chill feel of being done im-
promptu on the set and irresponsibly left in the completed picture.
Leaving in Bing's probably unrehearsed and smugly casual low-
down ragtime at the end of the lovely and thrilling singing of "Bells
of St. Mary's" with the nuns was using extremely distasteful bad
judgment. The Crosby performance smacks entirely too much of
the common, is too typically Crosby-ish, and his dialogue is also
typical off-stage Crosby clowning. Instead of continuity, there are
slightly related sequences but so masterful and sure is the Mc-
Carey genius that he actually has strung them together into a
heart-warming and cheering story. Where the Dudley Nichols dialogue has been used, you can spot it in a minute.

        Yet all these faults are as nothing whenever Ingrid Bergman
takes over the screen. The benign beauty of her face is so exquisite and her timing and reading of lines so inspired that she
alone will carry McCarey's new story to the heights that Barry
Fitzgerald did with the other. Not in your life will you see anything ever again so radiant as her smiling face when she finishes
her little Swedish song and looks up to find the priest.

        We will hate ourself when the grosses start coming in from
cities and hamlets and the written and verbal reports from the
little people to whom this inspired film will bring so much cheer.
But we feel that great soul that he is Mr. McCarey needs some
warning that he got off mighty lucky this time in cashing in on his
earlier, greater film. It was his fabulous fortune that David Selznick agreed to lend him Miss Bergman as a co-star. When you
yourself see and play The Bells it will be readily apparent what
the picture would have been without her.

        McCarey takes Father O'Malley this time to St. Mary's
church and school, where the nuns have just caused his prede-
cessor a trip to the hospital. They want a new school to replace
the one that was condemned and repaired and they go after it the
worst way--from prayer to skullduggery. In his inspired handling
of the good these wonderful women do, McCarey's story reaches
its heights, and he tells his message beautifully. By insidious
planting of thoughts in the mind of the man who has got hold of
their erstwhile playgrounds to erect his new office building--and
by their devout faith and prayer--these nuns really do get him to
thinking that his only path to Heaven is in deeding over to them
his bright new building for their school and using their old grounds
for the new playground. There are countless charming sub-plots
such as a triumph of brain over brawn and the redemption of a
Magdalene, and the understanding love of a child. If only they
were as lofty in their execution of writing as they were in their
conception, Mr. McCarey would have in this an even greater
movie than his other one and practically the picture of the century.

        There are two other fine performances to match Miss Berg-
man's triumph. These are an exquisite understanding of the child

by Joan Carroll, the best supporting performance seen so far this
year, and the rich old codger of Henry Travers. Both are price-
lessly understood and superbly directed by McCarey. Not to be
underestimated either is McCarey's own contribution to Miss Bergman's work. Each has found flint in the other's fire. There is
an excellent job by William Gargan of a husband who strayed from
the fold and a finely sympathetic job by Martha Sleeper. Rhys
Williams is immense as the doctor. It is to be doubly regretted
that not in either the Una O'Connor or the Ruth Donnelly assignments did McCarey attempt to develop a counterpart for the Father
Fitzgibbon role in Going My Way. Perhaps that factor is more
lacking than any other in this story development and could have
meant the difference between a hit and a smash. Both these wom-
en are excellent in what little they have to do.

George Barnes is better than he has ever been before in his
photography of the picture and his lighting of Ingrid Bergman is
done with all the artistry of an old master. All the technical ac-
coutrement is superb and the production vastly handsome and in
good taste. The music is brilliantly handled and once an organ
accompaniment underscores the dialogue.

We believe you will forever treasure this fine picture, taking many facets of it, such as the little children's interpretation
of the Christ story, into your imperishable memory books. And
when all the critics have had their says, the public will show by
their love for it that Leo McCarey is now solidly enshrined as the
most human and humane creator of outstanding film entertainment
in our time.

                              --Hollywood Review, Vol. 36,
                                No. 12 (November 26, 1945),
                                pages 1 and 10.

☐ THE BEST YEARS OF OUR LIVES (Goldwyn/RKO, 1946)

The Best Years of Our Lives had an extremely interesting
press. The film became the centre for a deal of international discussion. The British critics were first of all greatly moved by it,
with the exception of a few writers (mostly ex-service) who found
it altogether too emotional. Miss Dilys Powell (Sunday Times) is
a sensitive and serious critic, with a great feeling for the emotional values in a film. After claiming that the film in its plot
does not differ greatly from many similar Hollywood movies on
the same subject, she says:

> "Even now, even with the expected pattern taking
> shape, The Best Years of Our Lives might still have
> been the outstanding film it is claimed to be. Poignant
> to the American public who sees in it the reflection of
> their own maladjustments, it has something to say to a

dozen other publics; for after all soldiers have returned
to more countries than one.   What I regret is that Sherwood, Wyler and Goldwyn (for Samuel Goldwyn "presents") should have preferred to say it in such naive,
really such rockbottom terms.   I have nothing to say
against the choice of the simple, the typical character;
after all The Grapes of Wrath was a film about very
simple characters (so, come to that, was Potemkin).
But for me at any rate, The Best Years of Our Lives
never lifts the simple human being out of the realistic
level into the level of creative imagination.   Not that I
do not recognize in the film several passages dealing
carefully and delicately with a complicated human situation: the passage, for instance, where the cripple ac-
quaints the girl with the facts of his mutilation, or the
airman's reverie, crouched in the nose of the disused,
broken plane.   The settings are honorably lacking in
grandeur; these people live in small houses and apartments in a modest town.   And the camera work (by
Gregg Toland) beautifully underlines the solidity of the
scene.   The piece, in fact is made with all the skill
Hollywood has learned in thirty-odd years of cinema.
But it is made down to its public.   Which is a very different matter from creating popularly within the limits
of a popular art."

Miss Elizabeth Frank (News Chronicle) claims she was unmoved
when she says:

"In the solving of their problems the director uses no
short cuts; nor are there any Hollywood miracles to help
them on their way.   In achieving this end, William Wyler
has left nothing to the imagination.

"The direction is admirable and the acting restrained
and intelligent, at times brilliant.   Yet for all this, the
film left me strangely unmoved."

Miss Lejeune (The Observer) touches the root of the British reaction to this film, in spite of obvious and widespread columns of admiration:

"The Best Years of Our Lives is a beautifully managed
film which is clearly designed, with calculated craftsmanship, for an American audience.   What seems to us over
here like emotional longueurs are incidental to the American style; it is the national trait to exaggerate gaiety, to
press home sentimental points to which we would merely
allude in passing if we could even bring ourselves to mention them.   The emotional candour that was all wrong in
Mrs. Miniver is all right in The Best Years of Our Lives;
it is as much a documentary fact as the square-built
tailoring, the cool glasses of milk in the ice-box, the

pattern of town and highway and railroad seen from a
low-flying airplane.

"This is a picture that no Englishman could have
made, or would have made if he could. In its sentiment, its code of accepted behaviour, and its attitude
toward a job of work done, it is wholly foreign to our
temperament. It would be the greatest mistake to judge
this clever and beautifully acted film by our own standards of decorum, because the people in it happen to
speak our language. The Best Years of Our Lives is
as indigenous as Symphonie Pastorale or Les Enfants du
Paradis; it deserves the clear judgment we should be
prepared to give to any other foreign picture. I do not
hesitate to say that if Fred and Homer and Al had spoken
French, and the lower half of the screen had been cluttered up with sub-titles, the most exigent connoisseurs
would queue in the snow for hours to see it. "

The British and American reactions to each other as revealed in film criticism would offer a useful study for some neutral
sociologist to survey. It may be dawning on Americans that the
old-fashioned trans-Atlantic interpretations of us (a proud, aloof,
haughty race trained through the centuries to be either Dukes or
Butlers or Cockneys) may well have been too specialized to be
true. There is no doubt at all in the mind of this British writer
that the British are reserved about emotional matters (reserved,
not solid or unmoved) and that they find many American films over-
emotional.   What is over-emotional does not move them so profoundly as the emotion that is implied and therefore left to the
imagination.   Hence the British passion for understatement of their
emotions in the best of their films (some of the war films, and
more recently Brief Encounter, are examples). Yet these films,
and more recently still Odd Man Out (directed by Carol Reed, with
James Mason) were for us most emotionally moving experiences.
To carry comparisons further, the emotional values in French films
are different from those in either British or American pictures.
The best that can be said on this subject is that each nation should
be true to itself, making its films as its artists feel they reflect
most sincerely the way their fellow-countrymen behave.   Brief
Encounter will tell America about Britain: The Best Years of Our
Lives will tell Britain about America. The bad films made in both
countries merely serve to confirm all the wrong prejudices.
                              --Roger Manvell in Cinema, Vol.
                    1, No. 1 (June 1947), page 15. *

                         *   *   *

     The Best Years of Our Lives is a magnificent and moving
dramatization of an important theme, dealing with the return of

---

*This piece provides a good overview of the British critical re-
sponse to what was, quintessentially, an American story.

three veterans from overseas and the fitting of their complex in-
dividualities into the jigsaw puzzle of postwar living.   Maturely
contemplative, the film handles the subject with the significance
that it deserves, quite unlike the baldly superficial treatment accorded the problem by other movies.

The absorbing and stirring story of three men who return
to the same home town, Boone City, and find themselves plunged
into a strange new world was originally written in blank verse by
MacKinlay Kantor and titled Glory for Me.   This was adapted by
Pulitzer Prizewinner Robert E. Sherwood into a screenplay for
which Goldwyn recruited Director William Wyler and a big cast
of top-flight actors.

The story opens as the three veterans meet on an Army
plane which is taking them to Boone City.   One is Al Stephenson
(Fredric March), an infantry sergeant returning to his wife (Myrna
Loy) and two children, and the vice-president of Cornbelt Bank.
The other is Homer Parrish (Harold Russell), a young sailor who
lost both hands when his ship was torpedoed at sea.   The third is
Fred Derry (Dana Andrews), a bombardier on his way back to his
beautiful bride (Virginia Mayo).

Their homecomings are as different as their homes.   Homer's parents and his sweetheart Wilma (Cathy O'Donnell) rush out
to greet him, but when he raises his arm in a gesture of farewell
to his new-found comrades he is conscious of the shocked silence
that follows the exposure of his hooks--which he has already learned
to manipulate with considerable dexterity.

Al finds his two children have grown up and he has little in
common with them or his beautiful wife.   Suddenly self-conscious
and embarrassed, he insists that his wife and daughter Peggy
(Teresa Wright) accompany him on a round of the town's night-
spots to celebrate his homecoming.

At one of the bars they meet Homer, escaping from his
over-sympathetic family, and Fred, who is hunting his wife.   The
latter has taken a job in a nightclub, but he is unable to find her.

As time drags on, Homer tries valiantly to adjust himself
to his new life at home, but mistakes Wilma's love for pity and repudiates her efforts to help him.   Fred returns to work in the
drugstore where he had vowed he would never work again, and
gradually awakens to the fact that his wife is unfaithful and bored
with him and their life together.   Al, too, experiences difficulties,
finding himself in the position of a father who misunderstands his
children.

Among the townsfolk of Boone City are some unforgettable
types, acted by such players as Minna Gombell, Hoagy Carmichael,
Gladys George, Ray Collins, Charles Halton and Steve Cochran.
It's a superb cast, and March's interpretation of the ex-sergeant
is a triumph.

Russell is actually a young man who lost both hands during the war when a defective fuse exploded in his grasp. Since his injury he has learned to use the prosthetic hooks so expertly that the War Department featured him in a training film called The Diary of a Sergeant.

The stark realism of the story is well leavened with lighter moments, and though some of the scenes are highly emotional, they are too powerful for tears. Hollywood has finally produced a drama for tomorrow as well as for today.

--Fortnight, Vol. 1, No. 3 (December 2, 1946), page 42.

☐ BEYOND THE FOREST (Warner Bros., 1949)

Bette Davis in the role of a vixen has been a staple box-office commodity for a number of years, and if villainy alone determined financial returns Warners would have no cause to be apprehensive about Beyond the Forest. In this adaptation of the novel by Bruce Engstrand the dramatic actress is the devil incarnate. She totes out every dramatic flourish in the book in a florid attempt to make a character of Rosa Moline, the Wisconsin Madame Bovary. Whether she succeeds or whether at this stage Miss Davis has chosen to become a feminine Corse Payton is a matter that will be discussed throughout the bookings of Beyond the Forest.

For everyone who concludes that Rosa is the nadir of an illustrious career, there are those ready to defend a champion. All, however, are bound to agree that, photographically, Bette Davis has never looked worse; she affects the most grotesque make-up and the strands of stringy black hair hardly belong to a small town belle out to land a man. The actress' performance is bound to stir comment and controversy, an angle that will go a long way toward heightening boxoffice response.

From the viewpoint of a trade paper review, this element can not be overlooked, even while the inescapable facts remain that Beyond the Forest has something of a tragic valedictory about it; that it is an unworthy finale to a studio-star partnership which made artistic and boxoffice history. For Henry Blanke the picture might have been a distinguished production credit. The backgrounds and settings are lovely, and the script and characters hold real interest. But evidently he was given scant support by Miss Davis or director King Vidor, who permitted such Davis conniptions.

The performances are generally good, although essentially the screenplay is a monologue for the star. Joseph Cotten draws sympathy as the doctor, and David Brian is effective as the other man. Ruth Roman comes across splendidly and beautifully as the daughter of a caretaker, who is played effectively by Minor Watson.

Regis Toomey, Sara Selby and Mary Servoss are fine in their bit
parts, while Dona Drake, as an Indian girl and the nearest thing
to comedy relief in the drab proceedings, quite takes the honors
with her individualistic performance.

Robert Burke gets some attractive lake shots in his photog-
raphy, and Robert Haas offers an authentic job of art direction.
Max Steiner's score, using "Chicago" as the theme, is striking.
Rudi Fehr is credited with the editing.

In the story Bette Davis is cast as a small town girl who
has entered into marriage with Joseph Cotten, the local doctor.
Like her French counterpart, she longs for the brighter, gayer
world of the city. And she believes she can find it by ensnaring
the affections of David Brian, a wealthy Chicago business man
whose summer home is on a lake near the town. To achieve her
purpose she resorts to murder, kills her unborn child, and herself comes to death because of throwing herself over a cliff to
get rid of the child.
--The Hollywood Reporter, Vol.
106, No. 9 (October 18, 1949),
page 3.

□ THE BIG SLEEP (Warner Bros., 1946)

Nymphomania, drugs, gats and similar, sundry diversions
are part and package of The Big Sleep, which William Faulkner,
Leigh Brackett and Jules Furthman have concocted for the screen
from Raymond Chandler's novel about nymphomania, drugs, gats
and similar, sundry diversions.

Inflammable, pulp-paper-stuff-with-a-slick-finish it is on
the screen, just as it is between book covers. The dialogue has
the punchy, brass knuckles impact of the original, with the double-
entendre speeches heating the atmosphere to about the same temper-
ature as the greenhouse which figures so prominently and symbolic-
ally in the plot.

Screen mystifiers mystify me completely, even after they
are supposedly solved in the climactic sequences, so don't expect
a detailed account of the hectic goings-on from this page. However, it is possible to report that the occurrences are rapid and
frenetic; that there is the standard and capable delineation of a
shamus from Humphrey Bogart; and that this time Baby Bacall's
projection of a torrid slacks damsel is intriguing. Elisha Cook,
Jr. and Regis Toomey contribute capable support, while Ann Vickers proffers a blue-plate version of Bette Davis, in the role of
Carmen, a lass who has cantharides in her blood.
--Herb Sterne in Rob Wagner's
Script, Vol. 32, No. 739 (Sep-
tember 28, 1946), pages 12-13.

* * *

The Big Sleep follows the Raymond Chandler formula. Mix
one private eye, hard-skulled and honest, with a police blotter full
of murder and mayhem, chiselers, treacherous females, gunfire,
assault and battery, sordid motives and sexual by-play. It comes
up as boxoffice, especially with Humphrey Bogart as Philip Marlowe and Lauren Bacall as his slinky sparring partner. The
Bogart-Bacall team gives off the same kind of sparks that ignited
To Have and Have Not, which Howard Hawks also produced and
directed for Warners.

Rumors around Hollywood had it that The Big Sleep needed
a lot of patching via retakes and cutting, but it comes off as first-
rate melodrama. After a rather slow-paced and talky start, the
film builds up tension as the stack of corpses grows higher, and
ends with a big wallop.

This time out, Philip Marlowe is summoned by an aging
general whose two daughters are running wild. Vivian (played by
Lauren Bacall) is more sedate, being addicted only to high-stake
gambling and drinking highballs at noon, than her kid sister Carmen, who is a coy cuddling psychopath. The general is being
blackmailed for the antics of the latter and wants Marlowe to put
a stop to it.

Marlowe tracks down the blackmailer but latter is shot and
Carmen is planted on the scene, plastered to the hairline and
photographed by another blackmailer, Joe Brody (Louis Jean Heydt).
Marlowe manages to bluff Brody out of the photograph a few minutes before he is knocked off by a confederate of Blackmailer No.
1. Trail leads to a gambler friend of Vivian's who has more
bodyguards and torpedoes than a South American president. Marlowe spars with Vivian, kicks his way through a platoon of assas-
sins and solves the case in a hail of .45 ammunition.

Bogart gives his usual tight-lipped and sardonic touches to
Philip Marlowe and should make audiences believe he's as good as
the script says he is. Lauren Bacall redeems herself from the
memory of Confidential Agent, and, opposite Bogart again, gives a
provocative edge to her play-girl portrayal. Martha Vickers injects
a suggestion of baby-faced evil into her role of the psycho sister.
Charles Waldron is excellent as the aged general. Bob Steele,
Louis Jean Heydt and Elisha Cook, Jr., give a lot of punch to the
supporting cast, and John Ridgely gets into the heavy class for a
change as the suave gambler. Dorothy Malone and Peggy Knudsen
show considerable promise in brief appearances. Same goes for
Joy Barlowe as a bright-eyed taxi driver.

Howard Hawks' technique gets the most out of the script
provided by William Faulkner, Leigh Brackett and Jules Furthman
which closely follows the Chandler story line. Sid Hickox's photography catches the murky mood of same. All other technical credits

are keyed into the production of a Class A mystery film. The Big
Sleep is an excellent mixture of interesting characters, action-
packed melodrama and the maneuvers of Bogart and Bacall.
                                   --Daily Variety, Vol. 52, No. 48
                                   (August 13, 1946), page 3.

☐ BILL AND COO (Republic, 1948)

        Among those recently cited by the Motion Picture Academy
of Arts and Sciences for high-class acting in 1947 were Ronald
Colman, Loretta Young, Celeste Holm, and several live birds.
The birds turned up in town last week in their prize-winning effort, a full-length picture called Bill and Coo, and for my money
their performances are far superior to anything racked up by the
other garlanded actors, even though the material they have to work
with is fairly skimpy. The plot of Bill and Coo has to do with the
efforts of a community of lovebirds to maintain a happy and affectionate civilization, complete with everything from electricity to
saloons, in the face of barbarous assaults by a marauding crow.
This sort of thing with human beings substituted for the birds
would probably have added up to a typical Hollywood confection,
but the parakeets play their roles so shrewdly that even the most
blatantly emotional scenes are toned down to deadpan realism. Of
the participants--besides the birds, there are a couple of kittens,
a few raccoons, some monkeys, and a Chihuahua--the crow is the
outstanding actor, much more menacing than Bogart or Robinson
has ever been.   In fact, he is so frightening that several children
who were around when I saw Bill and Coo stood right up and hol-
lered in trepidation as soon as he appeared. Presumably, they had
been conditioned by a diet of movie cartoons to expect paralyzing
horrors, but, despite their alarm, this picture has none of that uninspired sadism that seems to be the stock in trade of cartoons
nowadays.   It's just as well, I think, that the younger set's knowledge of the animal kingdom should be expanded by a glimpse of
something closer to life than Woody Woodpecker or Bugs Bunny,
two of the more awful scourges of the current cartoons.   There
is, unfortunately, some fierce whimsey in Bill and Coo--puns, for
instance, which run to such lengths as calling a church the Wee
Kirk of the Feather--and I guess once you've seen one bird do
tricks on a trapeze, you've seen them all.   But children ought to
respond to this one, assuming the comic books haven't given them
an insatiable appetite for murder and mayhem.   Incidentally, the
birds were trained by George Burton and the picture was produced
by Ken Murray.
                                   --John McCarten in The New
                                   Yorker (April 10, 1948), page
                                   103.

                    *   *   *

Bill and Coo is outstanding proof that originality, freshness and charm still can be dug up, combined and fashioned into fascinating entertainment. The pic is 61 minutes of grand fun for everybody anywhere. Believe it or not, the whole cast of this epic is composed of birds! It's a feathered fantasy which captures the realism, suspense, humor and anticipation of the good old melodrama plot it follows. Book it as soon as you can.

Bouquets to Ken Murray, for his sense of showman values, courage in breaking traditions and patience in working out a full hour of unusual interest. Ken used his "Burton's Birds" act, from Blackouts, cast Curley, the Crow as the black-hearted villain, and wrote a richly humorous narration.

The screenplay, dreamed up by Royal Foster and Dean Riesner, details the life, loves and tribulations of "Chirpville," a little town somewhere in the Never-Never Land.

Everything is complete, as a town should be. The banker, the lawyer, the firemen--all go to their appointed tasks, step out to a bar at night, live the standard lives of working men all over the nation.

Hero Bill woos his sweetheart, Coo with the brash energy of heroes everywhere. Bill's really a hero. He saves Coo from a burning hotel, puts out the fire, and later saves the whole village from the Crow. Matter of fact, Bill captures the big bully, single handed.

There's also a circus in town. Gad, those trapeze artists, clowns and bareback riders are clever!

Finale, of course, is the marriage of Bill and Coo. He's a bold and forceful lover, that Bill....

Dean Riesner's direction, Murray's clever production elements and the cast itself are grand. Bill and Coo is in line for an Academy Award in the Special Features division.
>   --Hollywood Review, Vol. 38,
>   No. 17 (January 12, 1948),
>   page 5.

□ THE BISHOP'S WIFE (Goldwyn/RKO, 1947)

An angel comes to assist a bishop, yielding a pleasant fairy-tale mid the drab surroundings of the bishop's old-fashioned home and daily drudgery. The bishop was harassed by his wealthy, notably uncharitable parishioners, the worry upsetting his own home. Thus the angel is answer to a prayer, working jaunty little miracles that involve trick photography, and improving the lot of everyone.

For a while the bishop wonders if such a suave angel may not be
an emissary from below. His wife takes great satisfaction in an-
gelic skating parties and intimate suppers. The angel himself
shows more than casual interest in her. But things work out to
perfection in this light-hearted Christmas fantasy. Parish money
has been diverted from empty monuments to foreign relief, an
avowed atheist is very much changed, the bishop's daughter is
happier and the bishop recalls how to love his loyal wife.

                                        --New Movies, Vol. 22, No. 7
                                          (December 1947), page 8.

                          *   *   *

The Bishop's Wife, poor thing, is unhappy. Bishop David
Niven is so distracted trying to get wealthy parishioner Gladys
Cooper to build a cathedral that he has little time left to comfort
wife Loretta Young.

Samuel Goldwyn solves her problem by giving her Cary
Grant for a few days around the house--a therapy that no doubt
might be applied successfully to many another unhappy housewife.
Don't get any wrong ideas, though, for in the film Mr. Grant is--
we blush to say it--an Angel, sent from On High for the relief of
this particular case.

There you have it--a Christmas season fantasy from the
novel by Robert Nathan and a screenplay by Robert Sherwood and
Leonardo Bercovici. Like all fantasies, for full enjoyment this
one requires the willingness to accept the preposterous, and reasonable forbearance in the presence of whimsy. As written, produced and acted, this is not an impossible requirement in this
case, for the film is generously filled with humor as well as the
inevitable sweetness. The Bishop's Wife will probably be one of
the best-loved films of the year.

In stubborn insistence on a quality production, Goldwyn
scrapped the original script, sets, and hundreds of feet of film,
changed directors and started all over after the film had been in
production two weeks. Doubtless the producer knew what he was
doing, even if he did not come to this action until $800,000 was
spent--for the finished product is thoroughly satisfactory. Angel
Cary Grant occupies center stage most of the time, turning in a
delightful performance. In a role that must have tempted him to
display all his familiar tricks of coyness, he plays straightforward-
ly with a minimum of cuteness. It is easily his best work in some
time. Miss Young makes the lady of the piece a decorative and
sympathetic figure, keeping her infatuation for the celestial stranger strictly within the bounds of dignity. Niven, too, is agreeable
in the unusual role of a husband in danger of being cuckolded by an
angel. And, as you might have guessed, Jimmy Gleason is on
hand, puzzled and comical as ever in the presence of the emissary
from Heaven. Henry Koster directed, finally.

                                        --Fortnight, Vol. 3, No. 12 (De-
                                          cember 19, 1947), pages 28-29.

☐ BLOOD AND SAND (20th Century-Fox, 1941)

Visually one of the most imposing productions the screen has
given us in a long time, the pictorial possibilities of Spanish architecture being realized artistically by the art director and the man
behind the Technicolor camera. Not so successful is the color
process with the several mass shots in the picture, the scenes
lacking clear definition, but when only a few individuals are within
the camera range, beautiful effects are obtained. As something
to see, therefore, Blood and Sand is a huge success. And if you
regard bull fighting as good, clean sport, the fact of the story's
being about it becomes another reason why you should see the picture.

I remember Rudolph Valentino's appearance in the same
story, have a photo he autographed for me showing him in the costume he wore, but at the time of its showing the world was peaceful and its mental attitude more receptive than it is now to killing
of any sort purely for the fun of it. In this picture bulls are killed
--off stage, of course--and in the end the hero is killed.

In reviewing a picture one can record only his own reaction
to it. There is little in this one which can be charged with lack
of merit, no fault to be found with direction or acting, but I found
it more depressing than entertaining. The story did not move forward with sufficient acceleration to leave me no time to meditate on
its theme: the heroism of an individual who makes his living killing magnificent looking animals to the applause of multitudes of people who idolize the killer. In each of the combats my sympathy
was wholly with the bull.

But, as I have said, everything is done in a manner which
attains the peak of cinematic skill. The best performance is that
of Rex Downing, who plays Tyrone Power as a boy. It made the
going tough for Ty, who failed to realize in maturity the vividness
and verve Rex made it reasonable for us to expect.
                                        --Welford Beaton in Hollywood
                                          Spectator, Vol. 16, No. 2
                                          (July 1, 1941), pages 11-12.

*   *   *

Despite the fact that the country's employment graph is rising steadily and that defense projects are pouring an unprecedented
number of dollars into the jeans of workingmen, motion picture
theaters are doing deplorable business. The studios are frankly
worried. They would like to discover just what qualities competing
amusements possess, that the movies lack.

Now it seems to Dr. Sterne (the venerable and sage diagnos-
tician) that the symptoms should be clear to even the most fledgling
mail boy employed at the Larry Darmour plant. With its stetho-

scope firmly applied to the public's pulse and its eyes glued to the
celluloid product of the past few seasons, this department is ready
to announce that the lassitude of ticket buyers is occasioned by the
absence of vitamins S-E-X in screen menus.

Frightened by small monasterial cliques in the hinterlands,
Hollywood producers have so caponed motion pictures that they no
longer titillate the average-man-in-the-street. No amount of intelligence, subtlety or ingenuity can compete with the good old hay-
roll as an enticer for prospective patrons. A full revelation of
Marlene Dietrich's charms (as in Morocco), long-shots of Hedy
Lamarr cavorting in the altogether (as in Ecstasy), Mae West's
brash invitations to come up, any time, and view her etchings
(as in She Done Him Wrong) are more substantial bait for a four-
million-dollar gross than George Bernard Shaw's wittiest quips,
the cinematic chess games of Orson Welles, or Stokowski conduct-
ing a full symphony orchestra. The film business was founded
on the undulations of Theda Bara, the navel parades of Mae Murray, and the sooner producers discard decorating celluloid statuary
with an assortment of Anthony Comstock's most enveloping fig-
leaves, the sooner will red ink on the ledgers turn to black. With
world events as they are, it is no small wonder that audiences pre-
fer a shot of straight Bourbon to numberless dishes of weak, luke-
warm tea.

If sex is actually the remedy for boxoffice malnutrition,
Blood and Sand should prove my point. It is as rapturous a piece
of Ostermoor art as the screen has unveiled, and should send
spectators' blood pressure into the upper brackets. Besides this
extremely salable commodity, the film has high romance, hard-
hitting dramatic moments, and a spectacular quantity of visual
beauty.

The picture, of course, is a re-make of Valentino's fabulous
success. The Vicente Blasco Ibáñez novel has been modernized in
background, the feeling is contemporary, but the surging love story
remains the same passional. Rouben Mamoulian has used color to
intensify emotional conflict, to point startling dramatic moments.
He bludgeons the senses through the meditated use of agonizing
oranges, villainous purples, searing scarlets. Again he soothes
with calm blues, placid greens, and dusty grays. There is a definite lyricism in Mamoulian's color field. One has little doubt that
this film may be considered the most astoundingly effective use of
the Kalmus process, to date.

The story is that of Juan, son of a matador, who, from his
youngest years, craves the spectacle and brutal splendor of the bull-
ring. His ambition disturbs his dreams, drives him, as a child,
out of his bed at night to perfect himself in his chosen art. These
early stanzas are magnificently projected, employ a fine young actor, Rex Downing, as the boy. Unlearned, brash, he makes his
way to Madrid, struggles to perfect himself in his profession of
death. As the character matures, Tyrone Power takes over the

assignment. While hardly the ideal Latin type, Power does a fine
characterization of the ambition-driven young bullfighter who, when
he reaches the top, marries lovely Linda Darnell, encounters a
shattering danger in the beautiful, deadly Doña Sol.

Rita Hayworth will probably start an entirely new cycle of
femme fatales as the lady who cared often, if not for long. From
the opening shot, wearing a gown of vicious fuchsia, Rita dominates with a vibrant, frequently breath-taking, display of allure.
Her love scenes are likely to make the lads rise, and cheer, and
the gals will, no doubt, copy her coiffure and come-hither technique. Miss Hayworth's singing is strangely attractive. Not a
beautiful voice, but weirdly magnetic, like that of a peacock herald-
ing the approach of rain. Suggest you particularly attend to the
scene where Rita wanders into the garden, leaving Juan and his
wife to settle their marital scores. Watch, too, for the dance sequence with Anthony Quinn (who gives a great show); it has the
same fire which distinguished the tango routine in The Four Horse-
men.

Nazimova's tragic Señora Augustias is magnificent. Here
is an actress of tremendous tact and resource, an asset to any
film in which she appears. J. Carrol Naish, John Carradine,
Pedro de Cordoba are all splendid. Laird Cregar is properly re-
pellent as Oscar Wilde, turning his attention from the Café Royale
to a critical survey of the more stalwart attractions of Spain's
arenas.

Sets (Richard Day, Joseph Wright), photography (Ernie
Palmer, Ray Rennahan) are superb. Jo Swerling's screenplay is
adroit in capturing the romantic mood and the music of Alfred
Newman, Vincente Gomez, does considerable in heightening the
film's effectiveness.

In Blood and Sand the love spectacle returns to the screen
embellished with a skill that makes it one of the most successful
entertainments in years. Darryl Zanuck, Robert Kane and Rouben
Mamoulian are to be congratulated. They have done a superlative
job that should pay tremendous dividends to Twentieth Century-Fox
stockholders, exhibitors and every type of movie fan.
                                    --Herb Sterne in Rob Wagner's
                                      Script, Vol. 25, No. 602
                                      (May 31, 1941), page 16.

☐ THE BLUE DAHLIA (Paramount, 1946)

The Blue Dahlia, written by Raymond Chandler, becomes
stalwart brass knuckles highjinks once the plot has been established,
and murder has put an end to the exaggerated histrionics of Doris
Dowling. Filled with sufficient pummeling, bludgeonings and general

mayhem to titillate even the more exacting sadists and masochists,
it seems likely that Alan Ladd has little salary in pocket after appearing in such a picture, for his expenditures on arnica, bandages,
etcetc must be tremendous.   Ladd is capable in this typical assignment, and there are two pleasant supporting performances by
Tom Powers and Hugh Beaumont.   At the time Veronica Lake
brushed back her hair to reveal that she possessed a second eye,
it was natural to believe that she had exhausted all possibility for
further surprise.   Here, however, Miss Lake proffers still another, for she demonstrates that if she has not become a good actress, she has at least ceased to be a bad one.

> --Herb Sterne in Rob Wagner's
> Script, Vol. 32, No. 734 (July
> 20, 1946), page 13.

*   *   *

The new type of hard-boiled mystery picture, which the
public cinched with Raymond Chandler's Murder My Sweet early
last year, gets an expert going-over by George Marshall in the
first original Chandler has written directly for the screen, The
Blue Dahlia.   The same author's Big Sleep is on the way from
Warners and MGM, which has completed filming on James Cain's
Postman Always Rings Twice, also plans to film Chandler's Lady
in the Lake.   Mildred Pierce was in the same exciting category
and, to a lesser degree, so was RKO's Cornered.   Exhibitors will
know what to do with it in booking and all they need be told about
Paramount's Blue Dahlia is that it is a fast and mile-a-minute
package of guaranteed excitement.   Also, that it brings back to
them after more than a year's absence from the screen--Alan
Ladd--one of the chosen marquee few whose names never fail to
draw.

The collaboration of writer Chandler and director George
Marshall is one of the happiest events in a long time.   Veteran
showman Marshall gives flint to the other's fire and has inspired
their best performances from an excellent cast in which there is
not one weak job.   In fact, this unbroken chain of fine performances is what really makes the Paramount picture as outstanding
as it is.   Even the bit players catch the mood and spirit of the
drama to enliven the background.   It is one of the strongest credits
Marshall has ever had and, to the best of memory, he has never
had a bad picture under his name.   So you know how much to expect of this.

Everything about the John Houseman production is top grade,
the kind of attraction that cannot fail to rank among the top ten
money pictures of its year.   In cast and sets it is a handsome production, with an authentic ring of characters and places you know.
Marshall in his direction has allowed no posturings nor exaggerated
attitudes but demanded restraint from each of his players, and
Houseman has kept all production dressing in the same key.

Like Double Indemnity, Murder My Sweet and Mildred
Pierce, this hard-boiled thriller is also laid in Los Angeles and
its environs.   A returning war hero walks in on a drunken brawl
at his home and finds his wife in the embrace of a stranger.
Following a scene in which he orders her guests out of the house
and clips her boy-friend on his jaw, the wife reveals that their
child did not die of diphtheria but was killed in an accident while
she was drunk following a party to which she had dragged the baby
along.   With her character thus well-established, there are no
audience regrets when she is found murdered.   Before her death,
however, she has made the acquaintance of one of her husband's
two buddies and he, with her husband and her boyfriend, are the
three leading suspects.   The only other leading character is the
estranged wife of the murdered woman's boy-friend.   Its action all
taking place with 24 hours--in Los Angeles, Hollywood, Malibu and
Beverly Hills--Marshall packs a dizzying pace into his allotted
story time and we defy you to find one dull or wasted moment in
the drama.   With the husband hiding out until he cleans out his
nemesis in one roaring good fight, he returns to confront all the
suspects gathered in one room with the evidence he has obtained
and there is a genuine, surprise ending.   It is Raymond Chandler
writing at his fascinating best, and you know that's good!

Alan Ladd is at his heroic best as the husband and shows
up as well as he ever did in a more spectacular role.   The skillful ease and casual charm with which he dignifies the role are
something pretty special.   It is also pleasant to hail Veronica
Lake for the best work by far that she has ever done on the
screen.   With her quiet and sincere restraint comes a great deal
of the picture's added interest and it is she who forges for the
story much of its quietly believable tenor.   She is also more
beautiful than she has ever appeared.   Hugh Beaumont is excellent
as the cool-headed one of Ladd's two buddies.   This Beaumont chap
has been going along quietly now for two years developing into one
of the finest actors in films.   In spite of the many audience queries
as to "Who is He?" no studio yet has starred him, but his day is
not far off.   William Bendix is great as the suspected buddy after
his chance meeting with the no-account wife.   He draws the story's
most spectacularly hysterical role and plays it to perfection.   Doris
Dowling here gets the chance to prove that her Lost Weekend casting
was her open sesame to stardom.   As the vitriolic, two-timing
wife, she is superb, a portrait etched in crimson.   Tom Powers
makes capital of all his scenes.

Howard da Silva, Will Wright, Frank Faylen, Don Costello,
Howard Freeman and Walter Sande complete the featured cast with
strong jobs that support the main foundation of the drama.   And
you'll delight in a bit choicely performed by the uncredited Mae
Busch.

Lionel Lindon's expert camera marksmanship knocks off a
number of stunning scenes and the process photography, particularly
the Los Angeles backgrounds and the ocean shots, are masterfully

matched with the interiors by Farciot Edouart and Lindon. There
is praise, too, for Victor Young's music and Edith Head's gowns.
                                        --Hollywood Review, Vol. 36,
                                        No. 21 (January 28, 1946),
                                        pages 1 and 2.

□ BODY AND SOUL (Enterprise /United Artists, 1947)

        The more or less standard fight film has added stature in its
1947 version. It's still the little guy forsaking education for the
prize ring and, Cinderella-like, reaching the top. The girl wavers
between love for him and distaste for boxing. The climax comes
within seconds of the big fight's final gong when the gamblers lose
and the pug wins crown and girl. But Body and Soul is written
with more integrity than usual, the sequence of events accents telling sidelights, and James Wong Howe's shrewd camera elicits
more frenzy from the championship bout than newsreels draw from
the real thing.

        Body and Soul is also more than a fight film. As latest
example of the influence of Broadway's more serious talents on
Hollywood it provides an excuse to reconsider that migration of
the mid-thirties. Remember Odets and Irwin Shaw taking their
rough talk to Hollywood, Orson Welles turning from experiments
on stage and radio to the screen? Remember the excitement of
seeing emigrants from the Mercury, Federal and Group theatres
in films--Agnes Moorehead, Joseph Cotten, Ruth Warrick, Franchot
Tone, John Garfield? They were New Yorkers who went to Hollywood with something to say.

        By now their contributions to filmdom are variously assimi-
lated indeed. Cotten wears expensive chaps while Tone runs to
silk pajamas. Orson Welles is deep in Shakespeare and Miss
Moorehead dabbles in murder. Only the Dead End Kids and Garfield are readily recognizable, or the infrequent film which bears
direct traces of the old school. Body and Soul is such a film, its
sternness mellowed by reminder. Here are the gin and tinsel,
squalor and sables of the depression era, less daring than when
first revealed in Dead End or Golden Boy but more valid and mature because shown without sentiment or blur. The old tenement
films with "social significance" had general reform in mind. They
represented a native protest of our social fabric. But Body and
Soul gets deeper into its milieu, makes specific the blame, and
tightens up the conflicts of its cast with logic.

        Johnny Davis (John Garfield) is an East Side Jew whose in-
heritance consists of improper credentials to get a job in depression days. Too proud for charity, too poor for college, the ring
is his only means to money and prestige, and money is the big urge
even at the expense of self-respect. Fighting requires no brains

or ability, only a willingness to parcel himself out to the promoters and fixers on each rung of his ladder to success, and he has
an abundance of this willingness.   The hangers-on are undesirables
too, heedless of law and the boxing commission.   Perhaps they
were thrust down these blind alleys because of unacceptability in
other pursuits.   Certainly Ben (Canada Lee), the colored fighter
with good intentions, is exploited and cast aside because he can
offer no resistance on his own feet.   The conniving of these characters is taut as good theatre should be and seems quite probable.
Again credit is due Mr. Howe for the semblance of life.

A transparent coincidence aligns Polonsky's script with Budd
Schulberg's new novel, The Harder They Fall, on which the film
is not based.   It is just that two sports enthusiasts have known too
well their hobby and been disenchanted.   Both expose with thinly
disguised fiction.   In one case they resort to the same actuality.
It is easier to tell in a book exactly how the fight world got that
way, but the film seems to have more dramatic cohesion.   Two
incidents especially--one suggesting the significance of Johnny
Davis's fight to his East Side neighbors and the other showing Ben's
final eclipse--are resounding.   They have deeper meaning than the
social problem films of the thirties.   The honesty of Body and
Soul is almost unpleasant but its excitement is vivid.   It also has
the enviable grace of being moneyed without being slick.

--Stephen Belcher in New Movies,
Vol. 22, No. 6 (November
1947), pages 9-10.

*   *   *

Body and Soul is a rough, tough melodrama with some exciting fight sequences.

The story has to do with a slugger who fights his way up
from poverty to become the toast of the prize fight mob and then
double-crosses himself in order to regain the respect of his mother, his friends and the girl he loves.   The film betrays an unusual
awareness of certain social problems and challenges anyone to dis-
prove the contention that environment is the force that shapes a
man.

John Garfield does some of the best acting of his career as
the money-mad fighter from New York's lower East Side.   He
tosses aside the "soul" that he really loves (Lilli Palmer) in favor
of a gold-digging "body" (Hazel Brooks) and then pendulums back
again when he sees the light.   Anne Revere is splendid as his
mother.

--Fortnight, Vol. 3, No. 5
(September 12, 1947), page 30.

☐ BORN YESTERDAY (Columbia, 1950)

    Born Yesterday is more fun to watch than anything Holly-
wood has put out this year. And, as far as Judy Holliday is concerned, it is not illogically released for the Academy Award season.

    Garson Kanin's Broadway hit has been reworked to shift
most of the emphasis to the beautiful blonde who starts catching
up rather late on her book learning. And they couldn't have done
a brighter thing. Most of the "political significance" portions of
the stage play have been deleted. These changes have also cut the
role of the successful junk dealer (Broderick Crawford) to what
amounts almost to a supporting role. But what there is of it is
as brash as called for. Happily, the changes have been made to
good advantage, molding every sequence into a form that keeps
running laughter going.

    Minor regrets are some overly sentimental approaches to
democratic government and the fact that some of Miss Holliday's
lines, by very reason of her characterization, are at times not
audible.

    William Holden does well as the bookish young man who dis-
covers blondes while Miss Holliday discovers Thomas Jefferson.
To put the final polish on the cast, Howard St. John is a nicely
restrained lawyer, and Larry Oliver a mild-mannered Congress-
man.
                                    --Fortnight, Vol. 9, No. 13
                                      (December 25, 1950), page 32.

                          *   *   *

    *The hardest problem facing Columbia after the company
bought the screen rights to Born Yesterday was discovering the
right girl for the part of Billie Dawn, the mouse-voiced mistress
of a millionaire junk tycoon. After some 24 aspirants were considered, including Rita Hayworth, Judy Holliday, who had handled
the role on Broadway for more than three years, got the job.

    Despite certain differences in emphasis which time and the
Johnston office have necessarily interjected, Garson Kanin's original comedy about the educability of even the meanest citizen comes
off almost as freshly on the screen as it did on the stage. Paul
Verrall (William Holden), the bespectacled representative of the
Fourth Estate who gets hired to teach Billie about grammar, Washington protocol, and human rights, is no longer identified with a
specific liberal-hued publication. In the role which opened Hollywood to ex-radio announcer Paul Douglas, Broderick Crawford

stretches the gin-rummy playing junk magnate's evil and lack of
social polish to the verge of outright caricature.

The corrupt senator (Larry Oliver) whom Crawford is brib-
ing to legalize an international cartel in scrap iron, and his lawyer
(Howard St. John), an alcoholic has-been who claims he can still
"spot a loophole at twenty paces, " may also seem like evanescent
characters amidst the war clouds of 1951. But the indestructible
if round-heeled Billie and her piercing gashouse inflections go on
forever.

--Newsweek (January 1, 1951),
page 57.

□ CABIN IN THE SKY (M-G-M, 1943)

Some of the standard obtuseness is again in evidence in the
screen transcription of Cabin in the Sky. Behind footlights, the
show was a beguilingly naïf folk tale, simply staged and charged
with the tremendous vitality apparent in every Negro entertainment
I've ever glimpsed. Much of the zing of the original has been
lost between the boards and the Culver City stages, and while the
omission of the superb Katherine Dunham dancers may justly be
blamed, some of the loss must be attached to the studio's over-
elaboration, and fondness for the theatrical geegaws of cliché.

Despite its cumbersome faults, Cabin in the Sky retains
certain salient virtues. Chief among these is Ethel Waters, who
emerges as a vibrant performer, despite the complete camera
mismanagement of Vincente Minnelli. Minnelli has photographed
the film with a preponderance of close-ups, and greatly as this
department admires Miss Waters there is a certain tedium attached
to one hundred minutes of intimacy with the lady's lips, teeth
and the flutterings of her uvula. Eddie Anderson, a competent,
if completely circumscribed comic, plays Little Joe and misses
by miles the virtuosity which Dooley Wilson imparted to the character behind footlights.

Lena Horne, slighted by being assigned only one song and a
meager amount of footage, steals the show as a sweet Georgia
Brown. This gal packs more s. a. dynamite than many of her
paler sisters, and with sagacious casting she could easily become
one of the show world's best bets. One hears the customary nonsense about the difficulty of producing material for such a personality, but there are a number of properties available in which her
talents would glow. Right now this reviewer is willing to put cur-
rency on the line to see Miss Horne appear as the titular character
of the Edward Sheldon-Charles MacArthur play, Lulu Belle, the
passionate Harlem houri of Van Vechten's Nigger Heaven, Thi-Linh
in Harry Hervey's Congaï, or Edna Mouth in a Technicolored version of the Ronald Firbank novel, known variously as Sorrow in
Sunlight and Prancing Nigger.

The preview print of Cabin in the Sky, as exhibited at the
Fairfax Theater, has a thin and gaspy soundtrack, and the syn-
chronization of the songs was disconcertingly awry.   Possibly these
mechanical defects will have been repaired by the time the picture
is ready for commercial release, but this reporter is only able to
report on the version he attended.   Louis Armstrong, on for a
flash in the Hades sequence, is totally wasted as he is not permitted to trumpet or sing.   "Buck" is superb in a brief role, and
Butterfly McQueen makes an insignificant opportunity count.

Cabin in the Sky is recommended, and will undoubtedly prove
more satisfactory to those who are unfamiliar with the superlative
stage version which graced the Philharmonic and Biltmore a season
or so ago.

> --Herb Sterne in Rob Wagner's
> Script, Vol. 29, No. 654 (May
> 15, 1943), page 14.

☐ CASABLANCA (Warner Bros., 1943)

Casablanca is a lineal descendent of the grand old thrillers.
Though it ignores a few such items as the unfortunate gyve to the
sawmill, and the matahari heroine who is such a lulu that the
pubescent soldier turns his rifle upon himself rather than execute
the charmer, the piece has plenty of lush and succulent sequences
which will endear it to all with a taste for derring-do.

Most of Casablanca is laid in a nightspot in the city of the
same name.   It is a veritable Exiles' Club, frequented by desperate
characters to whom lawlessness is the only law.   And behind each
brazen mask are splintered dreams.   Tears well in the eyes of the
protagonists during the playing of a tune steeped in memories, and
out of the night drift the damndest collection of people, all disastrously reckless, all intentionally bent on Hell--or is it Heaven?
The drama has all the subtlety of a three-alarm fire, but the blaze
is attractive, the situations cozy, and those who don't enjoy such
scenes as the love tryst between Humphrey Bogart and Ingrid Bergman, while the doom of cannonades sounds ever closer to beleaguered
Paris, deserve nothing better than the literary creation of Herr Hitler, come next Christmas.

Humphrey Bogart sponsors one of the best shows of his career as Rick, Ingrid Bergman is her very excellent self as the
lady who is practically sundered between two loyalties and Paul Hen-
ried, after that deplorable lapse in Now, Voyager, is pleasantly
natural again in the role of the leader of Europe's underground movement.   'Fact is, the entire cast--Conrad Veidt, Claude Raines,
Sidney Greenstreet, Peter Lorre, S. Z. Sakall, Dooley Wilson--
deserves deep salaams.   And the screenplay of the Epstein brothers
and Howard Koch, the direction of Michael Curtiz, and the senti-

mental music score, by Max Steiner, all add to the satisfaction of
a film that is all movie and miles long.

--Herb Sterne in Rob Wagner's
Script, Vol. 29, No. 647
(February 6, 1943), page 24.

*   *   *

It has taken only a fast few weeks to change this picture
from contemporary to historical romance. It's something a bit
more than mere romance if you are attuned to take it that way--
it moves on the two levels of adventure-love story and of what one
likes to think of as eternal verities, and a story that moves on
more than one level multiplies its interest and its audience. There
are few people who like movies at all who won't enjoy Casablanca,
whether they are looking for romance, thrills or just human beings.

Warner Bros. have been dipping into contemporary affairs
for story material this long time, and with a practiced hand.
They even give contemporary overtones to historical themes.
Sometimes they are ahead of their audiences: Confessions of a
Nazi Spy stands out as a notable example because for the last
year we have been paying the price of not having learned in time
a lesson that picture tried, well in advance, to make us face.
There have been others about more local but highly important problems.

Casablanca isn't any "problem" picture, and is contemporary
only in happening to be located in a place that has popped dramatically into the headlines--just as Algiers would be if it had come
along a few weeks instead of a few years ago. It is the Casablanca
where people with money enough to go to swanky gambling clubs
all go to Rick's, and where refugees with enough money to flee in
expensive ways from Hitler's Gestapo sometimes pause on their
way to Lisbon. All this in our pre-war days. Rick's is run by
an American of mysterious background, smart enough to hold his
own in brisk competition with other rascals, maybe a rascal himself. Hard-boiled, anyway, avowedly looking out for no one but
himself, and apparently a man without a country. But unobtrusively little things reveal likeable things about him--the people who
work for him, for instance: the Negro singer and piano player
(enacted in beautiful fashion by Dooley Wilson), the waiter, the
bartender. The decent people who adore him and the rascals who
respect him combine to give him glamor.

To Rick's come a dubious little fellow just ahead of somebody's gun (enough to say he is Peter Lorre), a lovely lady named
Ilsa (and lovely she is: she is Ingrid Bergman) and her husband,
the leader of an underground freedom movement (Paul Henreid).
And expertly on their heels, Conrad Veidt in one of his masterly
cold-blooded Gestapo parts. Among the more or less permanent
residents are Claude Rains--a Vichy official of no detectable

scruples--and Sidney Greenstreet, keeper of a rival joint who en-
joys using a fly-swatter.

   All of these people, against a lively background of local
color, are involved in an adventurous chase, and the romance
arises from Rick's having been in love with Ilsa in Paris in the
days when the Germans were marching on the city. What separ-
ated them? What about her husband, a fellow with a fine streak
of heroism and nobility in him?

   No one who is going to see the picture wants to be told how
it ends. The ending is satisfactory enough, if a bit hasty and arbitrary. Up to then it is superb melodrama, so expert that it almost gives the illusion of character creating events instead of a
plot-spinner skillfully manipulating his puppets. That they never
seem like puppets is due to the first-rate workmanship that a fine
cast, fine direction, and a dramatic camera instinct put into the
picture, with the anonymous help of the people who build the scenes
and set the lights.

   And somehow there comes out of it a conviction that people, in these times, cannot run away from the decency that is in
them, not even at Rick's, in Casablanca.

--James Shelley Hamilton in
New Movies, Vol. 18, No. 1
(January 1943), pages 10-11.

□ THE CAT PEOPLE (RKO, 1942)

   Cat People is a terror titbit which converts one's spine into
a column of icecubes. The dark, inferential horror it evokes is
comparable to that which pervades the pages of Arthur Machen,
Ambrose Bierce and Algernon Blackwood, and only the most stalwart will retire to his cot without a reassuring peek beneath, after
viewing this tale of werecaterie.

   DeWitt Bodeen's screenplay has imagination, wit and a
singularly felicitous stealth in its approach to the career of a damsel who is a damned descendant of a long line of mousers of males.
Sex (the Hays Office insists it be a kiss) is the lever which prongs
the animal in the lady to destroy, and as she doesn't relish her
attributes any more than those who are the victims of her teeth
and claws, there is a certain curious poignancy to the fate of this
unwilling dispenser of doom. Bodeen wisely constructs a mundane
atmosphere at the beginning of the piece and seeps slowly into the
shadowy implications of the metaphysical, with the latter gaining
considerable impact through the counterpoint of the everyday. There
have been few screen sequences to match the chill engendered by
the scenes in the draughting room when a T-square is employed as
a crucifix, and those of the darkened swimming plunge, with a
panther prowling its edge.

Editing of the photoplay is irritatingly inexpert, and the director, Jacques Tourneur, sloughs a number of the important dramatic points of the piece. The pivotal statue of King John means little through a lack of photographic-stress, and the entire museum stanza loses orientation because of Tourneur's failure to focus attention upon the salient figure of Bast, feline-headed goddess of Bubastis.

Simone Simon essays Irene with a seemingly confused idea of what the part is about, and reads her dialogue in a language that sounds like anything but English. Kent Smith definitely establishes himself as marquee material, and there is a wonderful bit by Elizabeth Russell, as an uncanny cat creature. Atmospheric aspects of the lensing are a credit to Nicholas Musuraca, considering these shoot-and-run deals, and soundman John Cass deserves a deep salaam for the aural effects he obtained during the pool moments.

--Herb Sterne in Rob Wagner's
Script, Vol. 27, No. 642
(November 21, 1942), page 18.

* * *

Imagination and care have made of this a fine horror film. The cleverly told story has its heroine, when in the grip of strong emotion--jealousy, anger, love--turn into a great murderous cat. Played by Simone Simon with sincerity and restraint, she becomes a pathetically tortured creature, as terrifying to herself as to others. A most sensitive handling of light and sound, including the score, builds up a supporting atmosphere of supernatural evil seldom achieved in these tales.

--New Movies, Vol. 18, No. 1
(January 1943), page 13.

□ CHAMPION (Screen Plays/United Artists, 1949)

The emotional impact left by a picture like Champion is such as to send the reviewer scurrying through the dictionary for a suitable description when he knows full well the only accurate word is "great." Champion adapted from Ring Lardner's memorable story about a prize-fighter who is a hero to his fans and a heel to his family and friends, bursts on the current crop of celluloid efforts like a flash of lightning from a cloudy sky. It was turned out for something more than half a million, but its grossing potential is several times that amount. It is compelling, moving entertainment, made so by the artful combination of terrific story, enterprising production, forceful performances and imaginative direction. Stanley Kramer and his associate Robert Stillman, who fought the show through to completion, are to be commended not merely for turning out a boxoffice winner but for producing a film of some artistic

stature--a drama whose virility and excitement will long be remembered. Mark Robson's direction moves <u>Champion</u> through its paces
to its ironic conclusion with masterful finesse. While he concentrates on the enormously interesting characterizations, he cleverly
makes the camera implement his story with angles and tricks which
subtly contribute to the mood and gripping pace.

Kirk Douglas is Lardner's immortal character, the fighter
whose story is picked up on the night of his greatest triumph, the
occasion when the people hail him as the great sportsman of the
ring. His own life, however, is quite a different story and in
flashback, it is recounted. He turns to the ring after a shotgun
marriage to Ruth Roman whom he leaves directly after the ceremony. He puts himself under the management of Paul Stewart and
with the latter's careful tutelage rises to the top. He refuses to
go for a "fix" and wins a fight against the current champion despite
the advice of the gambling overlords. This is the feat that makes
him a public idol. But the promoters drop him like a hot potato
and in order to continue fighting he is obliged to make a deal with
them. This means dropping Stewart. With no qualm of conscience
he makes the change and continues on his meteoric career. While
his wife waits for him in the Chicago home of his mother he uses
Marilyn Maxwell and then Lola Albright to further his insatiable
ambitions. Finally his brother, Arthur Kennedy, is his victim
when Douglas steps in, at the last moment, and breaks up a chance
of happiness between Kennedy and the unhappy Miss Roman. Tragedy finally stalks him on the night of his big fight when he dies of
a brain injury. To the world he is a greater hero for it, because
the people whose lives he has affected so bitterly are decent enough
to keep their silence.

Kirk Douglas, who has been edging himself rapidly up the
stellar ladder, completes the climb with his performance of "The
Champion." Here is a vigorous, manly, exciting actor whose personality, torso, and skilfull histrionic talent give his every second
on the screen conviction and authority. Marilyn Maxwell, a beautiful blonde, deftly plays the gal who lives on the outskirts of the
sporting and gambling world. Arthur Kennedy's sensitivity makes
a touching portrait of the crippled brother. Paul Stewart's manager is a masterpiece of subtle, restrained playing, and Ruth
Roman's wife is hauntingly lovely. Lola Albright, a show girl who
has found a way of life with a wealthy, older man, is excellent.
The quiet dignity of Luis Van Rooten, who sacrifices a small fortune to keep her affections, is a performance worth noting. Harry
Shannon, John Day, Ralph Sanford, and Esther Howard make up
the remaining and excellent supporting cast.

Frank Planer's photography has much drama as the script
as it begins to tell the story right under the titles and continues
compellingly on its course through the grim, relentless narrative.
Rudolph Sternad accomplishes an arresting production design, and
the editing of Harry Gerstad is smooth throughout. Dimitri Tiomkin

accomplishes a brilliant job of musical composition and direction.
                              --The Hollywood Reporter, Vol.
                              103, No. 6 (March 14, 1949),
                              page 3.

                    *   *   *

     Ever since cameras started grinding out dramas about pugil-
ists, practically every fight film has been identical with the last.
This year, two have defied the ancient formula (The Set-Up and
Champion) and now, ironically, the producers are at swords' points,
complaining that they are similar.

     Champion is taken from Ring Lardner's famous short story,
now almost a classic--a tough, uncompromising study of a miser-
able young fighter who works his vicious way to the championship,
all the while being built up as a clean-living youth who might well
be a model for youngsters to emulate. Adapter Carl Foreman expanded and altered the original story, but he was honest enough to
go easy on the expurgation. He slighted the hero-worship buildup
which gave the story its ironic impact, but still the film remains
a mordant study of a first-rate heel.

     Champion was well directed by Mark Robson, is a welcome
fresh treatment of a dramatic subject that has become too stereo-
typed. In the leading role Kirk Douglas achieves mixed results--
Hong Kong exercises undoubtedly would increase his effectiveness.
                              --Fortnight, Vol. 6, No. 8
                              (April 15, 1949), page 31.

☐ CINDERELLA (Disney/RKO, 1950)

     Cinderella's simple moral of the happy transformation from
rags to riches continues to have sufficient universal appeal to survive even the atomic era though I suspect that in 1950 it is more
the favorite of the pre-adolescent girl than of the contemporary
little boy equipped with flashlight gun, baseball glove and gaudy
comic book.

     Disney's Cinderella is a good deal more elaborate than the
customary version one reads to one's children. Not only does he
give a quick account of Cinderella's happy childhood with her devoted father and some insight into her stepmother's and stepsisters' jealousy, but a lot of explaining is done at the Prince's end
of it too. One learns that the King wants grandchildren badly and
therefore bullies his chief courtier into arranging a ball for the
Prince to meet all eligible women in the kingdom. The relation
between the King and the Grand Duke is very much that of a comedy team on the Abbott & Costello level. Even the fairy godmother
is made more ordinary in the sense that she is not a dazzling
beauty, but a homey motherly kind of woman who is absent-minded

enough to misplace her magic wand. These elaborations make the
action more explicable and realistic to a twentieth-century audience,
but except for the lovely Disney touch of having the helpful animals
responsible for the happy ending of Cinderella's story, they manage
at the same time to take away from the fantasy.

Animated pictures, after all, offer almost limitless possibilities for suggesting the magic of fantasy. By their very nature,
they are unreal. Not that live-action movies do not effectively
suggest fantasy and magic, but by and large as photographs they
cannot avoid the limitations of the actual, whereas animated pictures are limited only by the imagination of their creator.

I mention this difference in the two kinds of visual media
because Disney is most successful when he departs from the confines of a legend and improvises his own characters and situations.
His people are substanceless imitations of real people. Cinderella
herself is a sister to Snow White. Both have a willowy floating
two-dimensional quality; both are fated to spend the rest of their
lives with the most unvirile Princes imaginable. Cinderella's stepmother with her grande dame manner will not scare children the
way that Snow White's stepmother terrified when she became a
witch. She is so unformidable one feels that Cinderella could have
outwitted her, had she made the effort.

Where Disney really creates interesting and appealing characters in Cinderella is precisely where he leaves the humans and
shows the mice who live in the interior of the palace, and the
barnyard animals. And this is where the contemporary little boy,
with memories of Mickey Mouse and Donald Duck and Jiminy
Cricket in Pinocchio and all the wonderful animals of Dumbo, sits
up eagerly in his chair. And the rest of us too become more ab-
sorbed in the mice skirmishing with the cat Lucifer than with
Cinderella's run-ins with her stepsisters, and we enjoy the secret
passageways of the mice through the old castle more than the elegant interiors Cinderella cleans so industriously. Disney's inventiveness is at its best in the elaborate devices the mice and the
birds concoct to sew a party-dress for Cinderella. And to prove
that he can be charming without being insipid, Disney mirrors
Cinderella in many-colored bubbles of all sizes that float above
her as she scrubs the floor and the little reflected Cinderellas
join in singing with her in tiny bubbly voices.

On the whole, an air of caution and a lack of originality
pervades the film. The mice and other creatures, though positive
in comparison to the humans, lack the vigorous spontaneous endearing qualities of Mickey Mouse, Donald Duck and the early Pluto.
Cinderella presents a crystallization of the sentimentality of Snow
White, while losing some of its freshness. The songs in Snow
White were charming, but Cinderella's musical score is disap-
pointingly mediocre and one of the picture's weakest points. Let
us hope that with the forthcoming Alice in Wonderland, Disney's

great imaginative talents will be rekindled.
                    --Elspeth Burke Chapin in Films
                       in Review, Vol. 1, No. 3 (Ap-
                       ril 1950), pages 27-29.

                            *   *   *

    If you want to spend a delightful evening, be sure and see
Walt Disney's Cinderella. This production climaxes Disney's development in the cartoon arts. The animation is unbelievably
smooth and the characterizations are wonderfully drawn and warmly sympathetic.

    Disney has created a group of animal characters which are
to Cinderella what the Seven Dwarfs were to Snow White. One
mouse is a sort of Humphrey-like character and another looks like
a hep little Mortimer Snerd. All the animal sequences are true
Disney at his best.

    The story of Cinderella is too familiar to concern us here.
But to give a brief idea how tremendously appealing the film is:
at the conclusion of the sequence wherein the fairy godmother created Cinderella's gown and coach, the preview audience (never
notably sympathetic) spontaneously applauded. The fairy godmother
looks a little like Mary Worth of the comic strips.

    There is little to say about this picture other than real
praise for the painstaking work which went into its making. Adults
will enjoy it fully as much as children. There'd better be many
prints made of this one--it is destined to be around for a long time.
Highly recommended.
                    --Fortnight, Vol. 8, No. 5
                       (March 3, 1950), page 31.

☐ CITIZEN KANE (RKO, 1941)

    When it was announced that RKO had given Orson Welles a
contract to write, direct, act in and produce a number of pictures,
the Spectator (May 27, 1939) characterized the transaction as a
folly the studio would regret. Entrusting the expenditure of a million dollars to a man who never had written, directed, acted in or
produced a motion picture did not conform to the Spectator's conception of good business procedure. Some weeks later Orson and I
had lunch together and in the Spectator which followed I wrote that
if anyone could accomplish the impossible, he could.

    Well, I am just back from seeing Citizen Kane. During the
first half-hour of the showing my attention was held by the Welles
technique, by his revolutionary use of the camera, by the startling
but always artistically satisfying grouping of characters, by a dozen

other touches which combine to make the picture one which all Hollywood and students of screen technique could study to their advantage.
But after the first half-hour I began to wonder what the story was
all about. From there on, I was more bored than entertained.

Having had William Randolph Hearst as its pre-press agent
and Orson Welles's fame as a publicity factor, Citizen Kane will
attract early audiences, but published reviews, word-of-mouth
condemnation and its lack of even one established picture name in
its cast will keep it from having the extended runs which would
make it the financial success which alone would justify RKO's action in giving its producer such a contract. A display of new screen
technique will not entertain audiences. The public demands stories,
and Citizen Kane is a biography, not a story; the biography of a
man it does not make interesting.

Much footage is devoted to Kane's efforts to force his wife
on the public as a grand opera star. She can neither sing nor act
with sufficient skill to entertain audiences; she lacks the personality which makes for popularity, and the many scenes in which she
appears are without story values.

It was not until we were driving home that I found out what
the story was about. Kane as a child had a sleigh with its name
painted on it--"Rosebud. " The opening scene shows him--an old
man--dying. His last word is "Rosebud. " Newspapers spend
much energy and money in trying to discover the significance of
this last word. They agree it must mean a woman--but what
woman? Does it signify a love affair which never was made public, as was every other happening in the great man's life?

The closing scene shows the sleigh being thrown on a fire.
The flames light up its name. The story significance is that the
last thought of the doer of great things was of the sleigh he owned
as a child, and that does not strike me as important enough to
justify all the fuss and footage devoted to it. I did not catch it,
nor did any other reviewer I have read. On the way home Mrs.
Spectator told me about the name on the burning sleigh.

                                    --Welford Beaton in Hollywood
                                       Spectator, Vol. 15, No. 7
                                       (May 1, 1941), pages 6-7.

                          *   *   *

Hollywood, home of the potboiler, lover of formula, worshiper
of the tried-and-untrue, has a vast suspicion of iconoclasts. Not
"Is it worthy?" but "Has it been done before?" is the standard
measuring rod, and le bon Dieu help the pure in heart who attempt
innovations.

When Orson Welles arrived on the Coast with an acting-
writing-directing-producing contract in his pocket, the local gentry
greeted him with three lusty jeers. He was young. Tsk, tsk!

He had never made a movie.   Tsk, tsk, tsk!!   That he had made
worthy contributions to other fields of dramatic art made no difference.   Orson held his peace, seemed utterly undisturbed that
his name became the jibe of the day for many a long month.   When
Uncle Carl was head of Universal the standard wheeze ran that a
big hotel was being built on the back lot--to house all the rumors.
The same bad pun could well have been resurrected for the Welles
unit at R.K.O.   First came "Welles will never make a picture."
Then, "It's a flop," "It will never be finished."   Finally, when
Citizen Kane was completed, the Hearst agitation commenced and
it was reported (with great glee) that the effort would never be
released.   Well, Citizen Kane was finally previewed last week and
Hollywood packed its sneers away, trotted forth its best adjectives.
B'gosh, hadn't Hollywood always known the kid had it in him?

Citizen Kane is a magnificent picture.   Nothing like it has
been seen since the good old days when movies were still a fluid
medium and craftsmen were more interested in the picture in production than whether time-and-a-half was being paid for overtime.
Citizen Kane shows unmistakable signs of loving care, unswerving
devotion, endless hours of planning, complete enwrapment by the
subject at hand.   There are no indications whatsoever of a med-
dling supervisor, the triple threat of budget, box office and time
clock.   Inventive, stimulating and forceful, the work is a complete
triumph for Welles, a total vindication of that minority which con-
tends that what motion pictures need are one-man visualization,
new blood, and enthusiasm hitched to imagination.

Citizen Kane is a highly personalized effort.   To those who
are familiar with Welles' personality and career, it is at once apparent that he dominated every phase of every frame.   As it
stands, the picture has a pervading autobiographical tone; it reveals much more of its creator than it does of one William Randolph Hearst.   However, it seems unlikely that Orson will sue himself for violation of privacy.

Welles has made use of rhythmics, once so potent in silent
films.   He harks back to the dictatorial days of D. W. Griffith and
Erich von Stroheim (the latter, you will recall, also acted in his
one-man shows, besides writing, producing and directing them) in
his careful attention to detail.   There is an extraordinary simplicity in the composition of individual scenes, a thoroughly new sense
of sound perspective.   It's not a picture for the lazy spectator.
Citizen Kane demands all-out attention, for the plot is intricately
woven and resembles a carefully planned mosaic.   If one piece is
missed by an observer, the other parts fail to form a coherent
whole.   The story is related through the eyes and words of those
who intimately knew Kane.   Direct sequence is avoided, numerous
viewpoints of the central character are projected.   In this respect
the film borrows from Bromfield's The Strange Case of Miss Annie
Spragg and various Joseph Conrad novels.   Being a cerebral work,
the film requires agile wits.   The spectator (again, as in the silent
masterpieces) must supply as well as receive.   It bludgeons like

nothing that has been produced since <u>Intolerance</u> and <u>Greed</u>. At
the final fade-out one is left with a sense of having been pummeled
by a rare and exciting experience.

The fact that the picture contains no "heart" will prevent
wide popularity. Its appeal will likely be greatest to craftsmen
capable of appreciating its technique. Those who rate their shadow fare by the customary boy-and-girl romances are likely to be
disconcertingly puzzled and little pleased. Welles has always been
able to conjure suspense, terror and interest. He has never displayed a knack or understanding for what is usually considered
emotion. When he has attempted the more tender reactions, the
effect was as false and rococo as the betrayed-maiden melodramas
of the early years of this century.

Since the advent of sound it has become a ritual to accompany the main titles by thumpings of an insistent brass band. The
louder the blast, the more expectancy (supposedly) was engendered.
Welles reverses the procedure and the opening title ("A Mercury
Production by Orson Welles") is heralded by a most eloquent silence which continues through the announcement of screen-filling
<u>Citizen Kane</u>. Welles takes all the bows, dispenses with all other
credits. Now this department is more than willing to place a good
many laurels on the Wellesian brow. However, this neglect of his
co-workers is as complete a piece of presumptuousness as has
been unveiled since Sam Taylor insisted on receiving co-credit for
the dialogue of the Pickford-Fairbanks version of <u>The Taming of
the Shrew</u>. If Welles is a genius then there is little doubt that
photographer Gregg Toland is the co-genius of <u>Citizen Kane</u>. The
camera work adds no small amount to the feature. That goes,
too, for the sets (Polglase-Ferguson), the musical score (Bernard
Herrman), costumes (Edward Stevenson), the make-up of the central character (Maurice Seiderman), Herman Mankiewicz, who had
a hand in the scripting, and film editor Robert Wise. The cast,
drawn primarily from the stage, is also consigned to anonymity;
and that despite many fresh faces, so many new and unfamiliar
talents. Joseph Cotten, Everett Sloane (he plays Bernstein;
Welles' real-life guardian had the same name), Agnes Moorhead
and Dorothy Comingore acquit themselves in remarkable fashion.
As an actor Orson gives one of the best performances the camera
has ever registered. In the early sequences he is acutely magnetic and the transition to age is managed so convincingly that one
seems to be living the years with the man. Even the eyes become
rheumy, lose the sparkle of youth.

Citizen Kane is an achievement. Those who are interested
in the cinema's best will have themselves a time.
                                        --Herb Sterne in <u>Rob Wagner's
                                        Script</u>, Vol. 25, No. 596
                                        (April 19, 1941), page 16.

☐ COVER GIRL (Columbia, 1944)

Big time from the word go, Cover Girl deserves to stand
among the best filmusicals of all times. The Arthur Schwartz
production for Columbia puts to splendid use seven new hit tunes
by Jerome Kern and Ira Gershwin; the dancing by Rita Hayworth
and Gene Kelly is superb; it is the show for which Phil Silvers
has been waiting; the flash of the fifteen cover beauties recruited
for the entertainment gives just the necessary touch to pay off at
the boxoffice; and the whole affair is cleverly put together under
the smart direction of Charles Vidor, from a swell script, and
photographed for a Technicolor fare-thee-well by Rudolph Mate and
Allen M. Davey. All of these statements of facts leave a reviewer
slightly breathless. But that's the way Cover Girl leaves an audience. It is a great attraction for anybody's theatre, extensively
exploited and showmanly pre-sold for maximum results in its play-
dates.

A character named Danny McGuire is running a tiny nightclub in Brooklyn when the story opens. Two of his dancing girls
decided to enter a magazine contest for a cover girl, and one of
them awakens enough interest on the part of the editor to have her
bring the publisher to Brooklyn to scout the lovely. To her surprise, he chooses the second girl, with whom Danny is in love.
The reason is that she is the granddaughter of a theatrical charmer
at Tony Pastor's during the publisher's youth, a girl whom he loved
and lost. By sponsoring the granddaughter, he hopes to take her
out of her cheap environment, as he was unable to do for her
grandmother. But the course of true love has its way.

Twice during the proceedings, highly imaginative street
dances are staged, each time to stop the show cold. The first
has Hayworth, Kelly and Silvers stepping high, wide and handsome
to the Kern-Gershwin hit, "Make Way for Tomorrow," on their
way home following an unsuccessful search for a "poil" at Joe's
"erster" bar--this being Brooklyn. The second street dance is a
solo performed by Kelly in step with the shadow of his conscience
when he is plagued by the thought of losing the girl. Nothing finer
in the way of a dance routine has ever been filmed.

Miss Hayworth's performance matches her attainments in
singing and dancing by being gloriously alive. She doubles for her
grandmother in the two flashbacks of Tony Pastor days, on one
occasion warbling the devastating "Poor John" to wash up her
romance with the rich man. This "Poor John" song is by Fred
Leigh and Henry E. Pether. For staging and dance numbers, Val
Raset and Seymour Felix divide lavish credit, and M. W. Stoloff
served as musical director.

Kelly has an appeal entirely his own, and his stock will soar
as the result of this appearance. Silvers has never socked over a
better job, and he, too, will benefit materially from his part in

Cover Girl. Eve Arden is invaluable as the wise-cracking editor,
a role she takes to town as only she can, and Otto Kruger is swell
as the aging publisher. It is a slick idea that has Jess Barker
playing the same role in grandma's times.

Lee Bowman makes the most of what could have been a
thankless assignment as Miss Hayworth's Park Avenue suitor.
Leslie Brooks shows to excellent advantage as a jealous chorine,
and Ed Brophy scores in his part of Joe, the "erster" man. Curt
Bois is in for a chef bit, Thurston Hall does Tony Pastor, and
there are only walk-ons for Jinx Falkenburg and Anita Colby as
cover girls, but what walk-ons.

The fifteen winners of national cover girl contests decorate
the waiting room for models in an early sequence, then make an
appearance that counts in a spectacular revue number which celebrates them. John Hoffman is credited with the montage presentation of the number, which he and Robert Coburn created.

There are many spots where Vidor's direction might have
faltered, but never does. He keeps the story on a plane of equal
interest to the spectacular dance investitures, which, in itself,
is no mean achievement, for Technicolor has seldom been called
on for more magnificence than is demanded by the cameras of
Mate and Davey. Natalie Kalmus, with Morgan Padelford as associate, was Technicolor director, and Lionel Banks and Cary
Odell did the gorgeous art direction. For gowns, no less artists
than Travis Banton, Gwen Wakeling and Muriel King were called
upon; for hats, Kenneth Hopkins.

Schwartz found his knowledge of music standing him in superior stead in this filmusical smash, his production debut. Norman Deming shares his acclaim and is named on the screen as
assistant to the producer.

> --The Hollywood Reporter, Vol.
> 77, No. 23 (March 2, 1944),
> pages 3 and 20.

☐ DR. JEKYLL AND MR. HYDE (M-G-M, 1941)

After viewing the latest edition of Dr. Jekyll and Mr. Hyde,
the critical gentry along our eastern seaboard unleashed cleavers
and saws, promptly fricasseed Spencer Tracy's delineations, ran
the actor through their columnar meat grinders. The august tribe
intolerantly hooted, "Ham!" quite forgetting that any actor who ab-
stained from chewing scenery in the dual role would, ipso facto,
invite audiences to expire of entertainment malnutrition. Now, I
am not attempting to hail the Tracy characterizations as marvels
of restraint. But it seems only fair to the gentleman to remind his
traducers that he plays Hyde with fully six sets of teeth less than did

Freddie March, and with considerably fewer hirsute adornments
than Jack Barrymore utilized.

As a shocker, this still shocks with high-powered voltage.
My grouse is not with the "old-fashioned" aspects of the Stevenson
piece, but, quite contrariwise, with its alleged improvements. The
new carbolic fumes of humanitarianism are distracted and the
Freudian implications add nothing but a needless pretentiousness.

There is a beautifully hysteric performance of Ivy, by Ingrid Bergman. Gone is her stolid quality, and the unfortunate girl
is a triumph of variations in mood. The portraiture (credit Jo
Ruttenberg for this as well as for the magnificent shots of the
lamplighted, fog-bound London streets) evokes a soft, fleshly quality in Bergman that will harpoon numerous new admirers for the
actress. Lana Turner is miscast as a Victorian maid, but there
are worthy contributions by Donald Crisp, Sara (Whisht!) Allgood
and Billy Bevan.

Those who share my enthusiasm for the illustrious Ingrid
will consider the movie a "must. "

> --Herb Sterne in Rob Wagner's
> Script, Vol. 26, No. 611
> (September 13, 1941), pages
> 14-15.

☐ DOUBLE INDEMNITY (Paramount, 1944)

Billy Wilder--and it is nice to note that he hasn't become
"William" because he has become successful--lands the season's
most impactful melodramatic wallop with Double Indemnity. By
those who take their whisky straight and rationally demand a Tom
Collins without sweetening, it is likely to be considered something
definitely exhilarating in the way of entertainment.

Wilder, you will recall, is the lad who contributed to
Ninotchka, The Major and the Minor, and Five Graves to Cairo.
On this film, he served as director and co-writer, and the work
clearly displays his distinctive intelligence and craftsmanship.

Double Indemnity is tough. It aims its dramatic punches
at the solar plexis, sometimes at the groin, and quite definitely,
is nothing for admirers of E. P. Roe and Lloyd C. Douglas.
Based on a story by James Cain, the screen version has retained
the potency that is the brand of Cain. The saga of chicanery and
death is told with all the relish of a Hearst reporter, sans the
sentimentality, and with considerably more art. All of the sexual
implications are there, and you'll recognize the people as people by
their authentic language, the way they act and react.

Barbara Stanwyck is a shade too brassy, too strictly from
a burlesque runway to convince and convey that her character's
background ever included the rigours involved in becoming a trained
nurse. If one accepts her rag-and-bone-and-hank-of-hair conception, Miss Stanwyck is excellent. About Fred MacMurray's Walter
Neff there is nothing to dispute, for he is distinctly first-rate as
the chap who outlines the design for death.   Edward G. Robinson
forms the third member of the starring trio and holds his own in
fast histrionic company.

Double Indemnity at no time makes compromise with an
adult approach to drama.   Both Wilder and Paramount are to be
congratulated for having the courage to prepare and present such
a photoplay.

--Herb Sterne in Rob Wagner's
Script, Vol. 30, No. 686
(August 26, 1944), page 10.

☐ A DOUBLE LIFE (Kanin/Universal-International, 1947)

The instant Ronald Colman is identified as a popular Broadway actor of the historic Empire Theatre, and is surrounded solely by people of the stage, his calling and his life made evident
from the start of this carefully made picture, we know that we
shall not be concerned with poised, self-contained human beings
intent on telling us they are involved in emotions and relationships
common to us all. Instead, we know we are in a world of over-
wrought men and women given to sudden joy and as sudden depression, whose reactions are close to the surface and, by the very
nature of the milieu in which they live and work, must find easy
expression.   For this is theatre.   If this extreme emotional sug-
gestibility brings grief to its possessors, and sometimes destroys
them, that is theatre too.

Thus it is no surprise that something strong is in store for
the debonair though moody Anthony John as personified by Mr.
Colman.   Are we not given to understand that his roles take hold
of him until he believes he is the character he is acting? If not
entirely then partly.   That, in short, he lives his roles though
happily we are spared hearing it put so tritely.   We see him airy,
flippant, jaunty off stage when acting drawing-room comedy.   What
will his forthcoming role do to him? It is heavy, it is big, it is
passionate.   It is Othello! His former wife, whom he still loves,
will be his Desdemona.

In the course of an incredibly long run (for Othello) the actor loses control of himself in simulating jealousy and nearly
strangles Desdemona to death.   Panic ensues backstage and a doctor is called to treat the bruised actress.   Actual jealousy soon
grips Anthony John, jealousy of the fancied attentions of the com-

pany's press agent to his ex-wife. Brooding over this, he meets a waitress and finds solace in an unworthy affair. After many months of Othello his mind becomes deranged and he strangles the girl without cause. The remainder of the picture is given over to devices that trace the murderer and bring about his suicide on the stage.

This story written by actress Ruth Gordon and her husband, Garson Kanin, who knows the theatre as well as she, and the screen better, is said by some to be shallow and contrived. It seems to me that all stories on the screen are contrived else they would never get there unless, as was the case with D. W. Griffith and Erich von Stroheim, they exist not on paper but in the head of the director. What is meant, of course, is that a film to which a critic cannot respond is apt invidiously to be called "contrived." There is no doubt of this being a planned work full of effects calculated by Director George Cukor, the authors and all contributors. Some of these effects are the Empire Theatre reproduced to the least detail, and the authentic atmosphere and activity backstage during a performance; another is the sight and sound of a play coming to life from its first halting rehearsal to its first exciting performance. One of the effects overdone is the exuberance of an audience aroused to a pitch of excitement only possible from "dress extras" rehearsed to applaud wildly, all together now! at an assistant director's signal. The second year of Othello on Broadway, with a promised third, must be looked upon as exuberance of another kind, since the theatre repudiates any such phenomenon. However, the picture's entertainment quotient is higher than average to the susceptible and overshadows these lapses.

Mr. Colman's performance of the tragic scene in Desdemona's chamber is earnest, his appearance striking, the excerpts from Othello staged with imagination. Shakespeareans might question him in the entire play, but his part in the story proper is long and dominant, yielding transitions enough to make it the showiest and perhaps best character he has attempted, excluding Sydney Carton. Interesting because especially intelligent is Signe Hasso, and Shelley Winters is sharply effective as the unfortunate waitress who is a "massoose" in her spare time and intent at all times on making "contacts."

> --Norbert Lusk in New Movies,
> Vol. 23, No. 2 (February-
> March 1948), pages 7-8.

*   *   *

The team of Garson and Ruth (Gordon) Kanin (writers) and Michael Kanin (producer) have turned out an extraordinarily interesting film for their initial offering--a showy piece with full-bodied characterizations, heady atmosphere and superb staging.

Largely a backstage story of a popular acting team, A Double Life reproduces the atmosphere of the theatre in a way that puts

most backstage movies to shame.   Its characters are recognizable
stage folk--temperamental actors, harried directors, short-tempered
stage managers and frantic publicists.   When you watch the lengthy
sequences from the last act of Othello, you have the conviction that
this is a performance actually being witnessed by a live audience
as well as by the camera.

George Cukor deserves much credit for the effectiveness of
the film, for his fluid staging neatly blends sharply detailed realism with hallucination.   Milton Krasner's artful camera work is
of tremendous assistance, as is Miklos Rozsa's score.

As for the acting, it is largely Ronald Colman's show--one,
incidentally, in which he celebrates a record 25 years as a motion
picture star.   In portraying an actor who lives his roles so intensely that he becomes psychopathic, Colman has gotten away from
his recent, mannered style and achieved a fully believable characterization.   The role is enormously complex, a triumph of writing.
Required to picture convincingly the narrow line between sanity and
dementia, Colman accomplishes this assignment subtly and impressively.   His stage Othello can be argued about--but we see only
fragments of it, so it is hardly fair to judge it.   His Anthony John,
the actor, is completely authoritative.

Signe Hasso's effectiveness in the opposite role is marred
by her unfortunate accent and by an inclination to overact.   But
Shelley Winters stands out strikingly in a smaller role, and Edmond O'Brien gives a workmanlike performance.
                                                --Fortnight, Vol. 4, No. 2
                                                (January 16, 1948), page 25.

□ DUEL IN THE SUN (Selznick/United Artists, 1946)

$7,000,000 is the sum David O. Selznick proudly proclaims
he spent on the production and exploitation of Duel in the Sun.
Now, this department is an ardent champion of the rights of the
individual.   As a matter of fact, over our work desk and typewriter hangs a sampler stitched with the motto, "Chacun à son goût."
If Mr. Selznick wishes to spend $7,000,000 on a gamey celluloid
memorial to the techniques of the defunct David Belasco and the
artistically defunct Cecil B. DeMille, he is certainly entitled to
do so.   However, the spectator is equally entitled to point out
that Josef von Sternberg made a memorable and aesthetically interesting motion picture, The Salvation Hunters, some years ago
for the sum of $6,000.

The rise in production costs since von Sternberg's venture
has something, but really not so very much, to do with the difference in budget between his sensitive minor masterpiece and Selznick's colossal sex peep show.   More pertinent is the fact that in

recent years Selznick has come to confuse extravagance with quality and no matter what subject he selects to film, it is couched in
terms of the Ringling Brothers and staged to suit the visual requirements of the type of amphitheater Vespasian most admired and
the intellectual and emotional level of the subscribers to the New
York Mirror.   Gone with the wind are the days when Selznick was
content to sponsor such normal-length and intelligently entertaining
productions as A Bill of Divorcement, What Price Hollywood? and
Nothing Sacred.   Today, it would appear, he is not interested in
filming any story that does not permit him, one way or another,
to burn down the city of Atlanta.

Duel in the Sun is a lengthy, brawling western, filmed in
flaming Technicolor and liberally emblazoned with sex situations
so tawdry and lewd as to make The Outlaw, by contrast, seem but
another episode in the adventures of Elsie Dinsmore.   The screenplay, credited to Selznick, is a sprawling work, without dramatic
contour but with some of the most banal dialogue to be heard in
several seasons.   Blatant and tasteless, the situations are just so
many animated covers from the pulp-paper sex and other action
magazines.

The main story line concerns one Pearl Chavez, the torrid
pelvised daughter of a squaw and a squawman who, after a series
of rapes and a drastic pommeling by her cowpoke lover, decides
that his death will be her only happiness.   It is doubtful whether
the entire female star list once under contract to Charles Frohman
could have done very much with this assignment, and Jennifer
Jones in the role seems completely baffled by it.   As though the
plot weren't raucous enough, the sound-effects department has gone
to work with a will on racing hoofbeats, explosions, screeches and
gunfire, all of which blast the ears while the visual histrionics
blast the eyes.   Over all is a musical score that is so insistently
obvious that when one closes one's eyes there still isn't the slightest doubt as to the action transpiring on the screen.

In the midst of all this din and Technicolor glare, the quiet,
gentle performance of Lillian Gish is a particularly exquisite thing.
The writing of this character, like that of all the others, is never
very clear, but Miss Gish surmounts this lack with a fragile and
tender performance which culminates in a death scene as lovely,
as touching, as the one she played once before for director King
Vidor in La Bohème.   Lionel Barrymore, sheared of his more exasperating mannerisms, is exceptionally good as the overbearing
land baron, and Walter Huston is excellent, too, in the flashy role
of the revivalist.   Gregory Peck is the oyster-geared bad man, and
Joseph Cotten plays straight and well as the virtuous brother.

The picture has moments of pictorial grandeur in the
scenes on the range and in the lush fiesta sequences.   In its
entirety, the photography is woefully uneven, which isn't surprising as the credit sheet reveals that a quintet of lensmen did the
camera work.   There are times when the photoplay courts interest.

There are times when it courts disdainful laughter. In the latter
category one may place, among others, the amorous rendezvous by the swimming hole, which seemed pretty silly when
Norma Talmadge and Conrad Nagel went through much the same
maneuvers in Du Barry, Woman of Passion (1930); the climax in
which the lovers shoot each other, and then, perforated and
hideously bleeding, crawl across the desert to die in each other's arms, much in the same manner as the climax of Rene-
gades, which Myrna Loy and Warner Baxter made for the old Fox
company in 1930.

By reason of its cheap sensationalism, Duel in the Sun will
probably net several millions above its exorbitant budget. However, to give it critical recommendation would be as ridiculous as
if a Nobel prize were to be bestowed upon the Police Gazette.

                         --Herb Sterne in Rob Wagner's
                         Script, Vol. 33, No. 747
                         (January 18, 1947), pages 14-
                         15.

                    *   *   *

The biggest and emptiest thing since the Grand Canyon is
sprawling this week across the screens of 50 theaters in the metropolitan area. Bolstered by a budget said to exceed $6,000,000;
ballyhooed for two years at the cost of another $2,000,000; pro-
duced by David O. Selznick with the aid of 59 foreman-technicians
and an army of assistants; and glamorized by a star-studded cast
of 25 Movie Names and 2500 extras--the lavish, lush and inordinately expensive Technicolored Duel in the Sun turns out to be
the biggest cinematic molehill ever puffed up to mountain size in
or out of Hollywood.

In simplest outline Duel, based on Niven Busch's novel of
Texas in the 1880's, is the aphrodisiacal tale of a sexy, low-
boiling-point, half-breed Indian girl (Jennifer Jones) and her high-
fevered "primitive passion" for a reckless and murderous cowhand
(Gregory Peck); and of the pure love for her that burned in the
breast of the cowboy's brother, an honest, conscientious and somewhat naive young lawyer (Joseph Cotten). The turbulent, episodic,
sensation-mongering Duel is probably the poorest example of literature to attain the prestige of nationwide screening since Salome
Where She Danced and Diary of a Chambermaid. At no time does
this highly touted picture have validity--either in plot, development,
characterization or performance. The whole absurdly overblown
emotional steam bath is frequently and comically reminiscent of the
1890 school of panting passion and asthmatic melodrama. Its pop-
eyed, hard-breathing innuendoes are aimed directly and without sub-
terfuge at the peanut-munching, gum-chewing level of movie-goers
--and will undoubtedly pay off heavily in proportion.

Aside from its titillating tale of illicit love in bedroom,
bushes and among the desert boulders (so heavily pre-censored that

fade-outs draw many a modest veil across its sexier scenes), Duel
also dances around the edge of a gun-popping story about the perennial battle between the open-range baronial cattlemen and the rail-
roads that encroached upon their vast empire. For the most part,
however, the film concentrates upon super-heated sex and sin in
the blazing desert, winding up in a bloody double-ambush wherein
the hasty lovers pistol each other to death in the battle that gives
the film its title.

        In seeking something in this opulent production to praise,
one returns inevitably to the magnificent outdoor photography. God
made Texas--and not even Mr. Selznick can take the credit away
from Him; although it is on record that he tried, having chosen to
recreate Texas in Arizona.   Mr. Selznick took full advantage of
God's generous gift to Technicolor: the rolling Western grasslands,
the flaming crimson Texas (or Arizona) sunsets, the sky-piercing
gray and purple mountains on the rim of the shimmering golden
desert, the breathless sweep of blue sky, and the mighty panorama of thousands of cattle stampeding through the valleys and the
passes and across the western plains.   The background music by
Dimitri Tiomkin is impressive, and there are occasional touches in
King Vidor's direction that are technically intriguing, even if a bit
too obviously symbolic.

        Cost has been no object in the making of this 129-minute
magnum opus.   And so such ranking players as Sidney Blackmer,
Tilly Losch, Herbert Marshall, Harry Carey, Otto Kruger, Charles
Bickford and Joan Tetzel are tossed into the film for only a few
minutes.   Walter Huston, in the role of the ranting, preaching "Sin
Killer, " appears for only a little longer.   Miss Jones as the "hero-
ine" of the piece frequently overacts in her role of passion's pawn;
Gregory Peck is effective enough as a cow-wrangling desert Don
Juan, working under the handicap of some pretty silly scenes; and
only Joseph Cotten in the role of the discarded suitor contributes
a straightforward, believable performance.   Once more, Lionel
Barrymore as a snarling cattle baron is inclined to ham it--in
sharp contrast to the modest and competent performance of wife
Lillian Gish.

                                    --Jesse Zunser in Cue (May 10,
                              1947), page 11.

□ DUMBO (Disney/RKO, 1941)

        At a time when the best of all Christmas gifts is the oppor-
tunity to flee woes and worries, along comes Santa Walt Disney
with Dumbo in his pack.   Of all the joyous presents which have
come from the Disney plant, this feature-length three-ring circus
is the best yet.

        If there has ever been any doubt about the fact that Disney
produces the finest cartoon movies in the whole world, Dumbo will

silence such tittletattle forevermore. It is prankish, entirely delightful, and quite sensibly realizes when it has said its piece at
the end of sixty-five minutes. There is none of the padding which
most films deem so necessary. Disney has simplified his attack
and his work has improved thereby. This is a return to the
single-thread idea which was so consummately employed in his
early cartoons and, as hero, Walt has evolved a baby elephant
that is certain to give Mickey and Donald mighty competition. The
reality Dumbo possesses is remarkable. He is a pathetic little
fella, with all the whimsey, pathos, hopes and fears that Chaplin
implants in his tramp figure. Like the chap with the derby, cane,
and shuffling gait, Dumbo is a misfit, a target for jibes and assorted misfortunes.

It is suggested that you watch for such innovations as the
successful psychological use of color, the superb cutting and
"angles, " and the amusing satire on "abstract" films (so dear to
the hearts of devotees of l'art moderne de cinema)--the Pink Elephant Ballet. The opening sequence of the storm and the squadron
of storks delivering blessed events via parachute is one of the funniest ever glimpsed. I would like to thank each person named on
the three pages of production credits of Dumbo for furnishing
laughter and cheer just when we need them most. A most Merry
Christmas to Walt and all his boys and girls!

--Herb Sterne in Rob Wagner's
Script, Vol. 26, No. 618
(December 20, 1941), page 14.

*   *   *

Dumbo is the nicest, kindest Disney yet. It has the most
heart, taste, beauty, compassion, skill, restraint. It marks a
return to Disney first principles, the animal kingdom--that happy
land where Disney workers turn into artists; where their imagination, playfulness, ingenuity, daring flourish freest; where, in short,
they're home.

Dumbo's the most enchanting and endearing of their output,
maybe because it's the least pretentious of their works, the least
self-conscious. It tries only to be a wonderful example of a form
they themselves created--the fable expressing universal human
truths in animal guise. This particular one is the most tempered
of any the Disney studio has told. It will frighten no little children, no adults either. Though it has the usual Disney sequence
of destructive violence, of Nihilism almost--this time it's not violence for violence's sake, it's not the usual orgy of devastation that
usually bemuses Disneys, and from which they can scarcely tear
themselves away--but a sequence necessary to the motivation of the
story, swiftly done and swiftly gotten over with. Indeed, there's
not a notion in Dumbo that lingers a moment past its fullest usefulness.

From the moment the story opens until it ends far too soon,
it is a constant delight, spilling over with entrancing details, nail-

on-the-head "touches, " splashed on a canvas whose color is always
graceful, and occasionally even Art.

It's peopled (or maybe it should be "animaled") with rich,
unforgettable personalities, Dumbo himself, his mother Mrs. Jum-
bo, his friend and champion, Timothy Mouse. It's got ideals: it
venerates mother love; it believes people are essentially good; it
preaches sympathy, not derision, for Nature's slip-ups. It does
its good and noble and utterly enjoyable job with more camera
angles than Citizen Kane, with every bit as much subtle, and also
obvious, suggestion.

Its sheer professional competence alone makes it noteworthy,
but it is also heart-warming, appealing, suspenseful entertainment.
This makes it a treat that's coming to you, whoever you are.
                                  --Cecelia Ager in PM (October 24,
                                  1941), page 23.

☐ FANTASIA (Disney/RKO, 1941)

Walt Disney, the screen's greatest genius, ascends to new
heights in his creation of Fantasia. In all its aspects it is an
extraordinary accomplishment. View it materially: He spent
nearly three million dollars in making it; add to that what his other product would have earned if he had not abandoned it to concentrate on Fantasia, and we find he risked around five million
dollars in blazing a new cinematic trail of which no other producer
ever dreamed, and which had no precedent by which to estimate the
chances of success. Only an adventurer with the daring of Walt
Disney would have staked so much on his confidence in himself,
and only he could achieve such brilliant results.

I have no technical knowledge of music as an art. I judge
what I hear solely by my emotional reaction to it. That gives me
a place, I believe, among the great majority of people upon whose
patronage Disney must depend to make his artistic triumph a financial success. My comments on the production, therefore, are for
such people, not for those with technical knowledge of the art.

For its entire length Fantasia thrilled me, moved me profoundly, which makes it, for me, superb entertainment. It gave
me a new impression of symphonic music. I have heard great
orchestras play here and abroad, considered my time well spent,
but never could grasp what the composers were endeavoring to
express. I was given nothing to look at except the physical exer-
tions of the conductors and the musicians they were leading, movements suggesting nothing to enlighten me as to what themes the
composer had in mind.

Disney gives us something to look at. He standardizes the
stories the music is telling, gives them meaning, makes symphonic

music mean something definite.   And yet Fantasia is only a start
in that direction, only Walt's first effort.   To what heights will he
climb?   What further triumphs will be his?

Hereafter when we hear the Nutcracker Suite we will see the
Dewdrop Fairies, Hop Low and the Mushroom Dancers, the Blossom Ballet; when we hear again the selections of which Fantasia is
composed we will see Walt Disney's pictorial mounting of them.
Let me quote from the opening night's printed program:

> "Writing of the Pastoral Symphony, Beethoven said,
> 'It is feeling rather than tone-painting ... I leave it to
> the listener to discover the situations for himself....
> Anyone with a notion of country life will imagine the
> composer's intentions.' Walt Disney has taken Beethoven
> at his word.   He has imagined the situations for him-
> self.   But with a fine disregard for the obvious, Disney's
> imagination has leaped nine thousand feet upward to the
> summit of Mount Olympus and thousands backward into
> mythology, remaining faithful, however, to the Pastoral
> spirit.   The music itself, of course, is performed just
> as Beethoven wrote it."

From a purely motion picture standpoint, Fantasia is an
amazing production.   Never before has color been used so effectively.   In short, the whole film makes excellent entertainment,
which, in addition to the esthetic pleasure the music gives, has a
generous mixture of comedy and a succession of the most beautiful
scenes ever presented on a screen.

--Welford Beaton in Hollywood
Spectator, Vol. 15, No. 4
(February 15, 1941), page 13.

*   *   *

Fantasia is a rare treat.   If you live in one of the twelve
lucky cities in which it is playing and if you want a new esthetic
thrill, you'd better hurry over for a ticket.   It is unusual cinema
in the first place, because the music came first.   Leopold Stokowski led the Philadelphia Orchestra in the recording of compositions
by Tchaikovsky, Bach, Stravinsky, Schubert--eight in all, covering
a wide range of musical tastes.   Then Walt Disney and his staff
listened again and again until they were able to capture for the
screen the colored pictures that the music suggested.   The result
is Fantasia--a synchronized rhythm of sight and sound that is
neither an ordinary animated cartoon nor a high brow interpretation of music.

The theatre is darkened.   You see on the screen the men
of the orchestra taking their places.   You don't exactly see them so
much as their silhouettes.   You hear their instruments being tuned.
Deems Taylor, who acts as commentator before each composition,
appears, explains that Fantasia is the designs and stories that

might pass through your mind as you listen to this music. Mr.
Stokowski rises, lifts his arms and the concert starts. As the
tone patterns of Bach's Toccata and Fugue in D Minor fill the
theatre, you see the famous Stokowski hands, the shadowy orchestra playing, colors forming vague arrangements and designs that
change with this abstract music. Next comes the Nutcracker
Suite, and Disney is at his best with Dewdrop Fairies making
beautiful sparkles; Mushroom Dancers, in a few unbelievably de-
licious moments that bring a round of applause, doing the Chinese
Dance and little Hop Low having a terrible time keeping up with
them; the Blossom Ballet turning and swirling; the Thistles and
Orchids dancing in a riot of color; pollen becoming the lovely
Milkweed Ballet as Autumn Fairies release them from their pods;
Snowflake Fairies skating gracefully on a frozen pond.

Then our old friend Mickey turns up as the Sorcerer's Ap-
prentice. While you hear Dukas's music, you see Mickey Mouse
trying his hand at magic that runs away with him. This is conventional stuff for Disney, and though charming is soon forgotten
when the orchestra blares into Stravinsky and the violent Rite of
Spring takes us back a couple of billion years to planets whirling
through space, the first growths of life (from blobs and amoebas
to amphibians and dinosaurs), and earthquakes, flowing lava and
floods. This is probably the most exciting and daring interpretation of the whole program; and incidentally it teaches almost as
much Historical Geology as does a whole school semester in that
subject. The least successful item in the series is the mythologi-
cal setting for Beethoven's Pastoral Symphony, in which prudish
prettiness, love-sick centaurs, coy centaurettes and a burlesque
Bacchus are only made acceptable by mischievous fauns, lightning-
tossing Zeus and a Disneyish family of Pegasi.

A delightful note of humor is introduced into Fantasia when
Deems Taylor persuades the visualized sound track to react to
various instruments. But the most hilarious number on the program is the exceedingly funny parody inspired by Ponchinelli's
Dance of the Hours. Ballet is kidded unmercifully when Ostriches
try to be graceful as the early hours, Hyacinth Hippo and her hand-
maidens portray the languors of the day, elephants get coquettish
with bubbles in twilight, alligators leap about in sinister night, and
the tout ensemble carry on vile in the finale. The closing numbers
of the concert are a picturization of struggle between profane and
sacred. Moussorgsky's shrieking Night on Bald Mountain becomes
doubly effective with a mad Walpurgis Night dance of demons, skele-
tons and ghastly riotous figures under the prince of Evil. A bell
tolls. Death and Despair return to their graves. A long line of
hooded figures wind their way with lighted tapers through a cathe-
dralesque forest as you hear Schubert's Ave Maria. "Fantasound,"
the new system of reproduction for the excellent recording used
throughout, swells the auditorium with a glorious music that comes
from all parts of the theatre. Fantasia may have its faults (it is
too long and some of it is too loud, for one thing), and it will no
doubt be improved upon next time it is done, but to Walt Disney

now should go fresh laurels for giving us a new artistic experience
of great beauty--another milestone in the motion picture.

> --Philip T. Hartung in The Com-
> monweal (November 29, 1940),
> pages 152-153.

□ FATHER OF THE BRIDE (M-G-M, 1950)

Father of the Bride is a confection at heart, although a
shrewd amount of salty commentaries have been sprinkled throughout the piece.   Starring that dark-eyed beauty, Elizabeth Taylor,
and apparently timed to coincide with some real-life nuptials,
Father of the Bride owes its entertainment potential chiefly to the
urbane wit of screenplay and direction.

The Frances Goodrich-Albert Hackett script stretches a
good gag probably to its limits, but it is accomplished with enough
style and balance to make that gag palatable for 90-odd minutes.
Vincente Minnelli's direction is deft and sharp, and in the hands of
a veteran acting company, Father of the Bride registers some good
laughs and sustains an infectious spirit of fun-poking.

Carrying the mildly satiric load is Spencer Tracy, who is
Miss Taylor's cinematic papa.   It is through him that the entire
gamut of conventions surrounding the institution of weddings is lovingly lampooned.   From the moment Tracy hears the news that his
little daughter has betrothed herself to a young man he cannot single
out from a host of boy-friends, he is beset by these conventions.

Tracy carries through the entire film with his familiar side-
of-the-mouth observations.   Before he is through, every parent of
every bride will have chuckled at some common experience: mock
battles fought over guest lists, over the wedding cake, the bride's
mother laying siege to the bride's father's pocketbook, etc.   It is
a tribute to the writing and direction that these frothy proceedings
seem quite natural and humorous.

Satire is dropped unceremoniously for a few stilled minutes
at the actual wedding, but is merrily picked up for the reception.
Miss Taylor is arrestingly beautiful and a credible young bride,
and Tracy is familiarly competent.   Joan Bennett comes through
with a poised characterization as the mother, a charming bit of
work.   Top comedy moments involve the embarrassments of the
first meeting between the young couple's parents, and the picture
itself has been polished to a high gloss technically.

> --Fortnight, Vol. 8, No. 12
> (June 9, 1950), page 31.

*   *   *

In Father of the Bride, an adaptation of a sort of documentary novel by Edward Streeter, there are several jokes. There is
the joke about the man who fixes a lot of Martinis for a party and
then discovers that his guests want practically every known drink
except a Martini.   There is also the joke about the man who tries
on his old cutaway after twenty years and finds that it looks very
comical.   And there is the joke about the caterer who visits a
customer's house and considers everything about it beneath contempt.   These jokes, I'm afraid, are rather wheezy, and they certainly don't do much to speed up the picture.   Since the plot consists simply of outlining the difficulties of putting on a wedding,
including, of course, the damnable expense of it all, it grows a
little tiresome after a half hour or so.   Spencer Tracy participates
as the father, Joan Bennett as the mother, and Elizabeth Taylor
and Don Taylor as the pair who are about to get hitched.   At one
point, the film runs through a wedding service from beginning to
end.   This may fetch some susceptible ladies in the crowd, but I
think it will be hard on everybody else.

--John McCarten in The New
Yorker (May 27, 1950), page
63.

□ FIVE GRAVES TO CAIRO (Paramount, 1943)

Five Graves to Cairo, which poses the possibility of Field
Marshall Rommel's route in North Africa, has been passed by the
actual march of events in that region, but, nonetheless, it remains
an unusually intriguing thrilldrama.   Atmospherically directed by
Billy Wilder, and produced with considerable discrimination by
Charles Brackett, the film is founded on a well-contrived script
written by the pair--which makes the production something in the
nature of a two-man triumph for the versatile team.

Five Graves to Cairo wisely makes the North African background an active participant in the plot.   The camera of John Seitz,
and the canny production design, dramatize the hot, brash sunlight
and the dense velvet shadows of the country to the point where the
spectator breaks into a factual perspiration and feels his sinuses
tantalized by the dust of desert sands.   Through the heat storms a
romantic plot of derring-do, with Franchot Tone imparting full justice to his assignment as the sole survivor of a British tank unit
in the fateful days following the fall of Tobruk to the Germans.
Anne Baxter is impressive as the Alsatian girl, and admirably
manages an accent that never falters, slips, or sounds absurd.
Miss Baxter is an actress worth watching, and may accomplish
notable things if she is able to avoid the pitfalls of the makeup and
directorial divisions which threaten her individuality at 20th Century-Fox.   As witness: Crash Dive.

Akim Tamiroff, Peter Van Eyck and Fortunio Bonanova essay

an interesting trio of characters, but the hit of the piece is Erich von Stroheim, as the aggressive and supercilious Rommel.   Von Stroheim is as great a director as he is an actor, and this department is looking forward to the day when some astute producer will again permit this brilliant maestro a free hand at making motion picture masterpieces.

Five Graves to Cairo is sparkling and exciting melodramatic fare, garnished with witty and observant dialogue.   The ending is weak and mawkish, but the reels that precede it are eminently enjoyable.

> --Herb Sterne in Rob Wagner's
> Script, Vol. 29, No. 656 (June
> 12, 1943), page 14.

□ FOR WHOM THE BELL TOLLS (Paramount, 1943)

Technicolor and its harsh hues and troublesome tints imbues any film which employs the process with a devastating unreality. This quality, which enhances a musical and blends quite genially with the blatant artificialities of Cecil B. DeMille's revels in bumptiousness, automatically rapes a serious subject of its fundamental virtue.

Pouring Easter-egg dyes over Hemingway's For Whom the Bell Tolls is as aesthetically sensible as turning Donatello's "David" over to Jack Dawn and Max Factor for embellishment. Beyond inflating the budget, and thus giving Paramount's sales division the opportunity of boasting about the fact that it is one of the most expensive photoplays ever made, the tinting achieves nothing but the further emasculation of a property which suffers sufficiently through political pussyfooting that prevents a Fascist from being named just that, and the sacrosanctimonious Joe Breen office which proclaims that a handclasp and a fleeting kiss be the utmost culminations of love.   How an artist of the integrity of William Cameron Menzies was ever prevailed upon to lend his time and talent to such polychromatic fiesta is just another fantastic facet of a medium that is indigenously an art, but strives so hard and successfully to be nothing more than an industry.

As a novel, For Whom the Bell Tolls is an infinitely prolonged political tract, passionate in its revilement of dictatorship and cumbersome in the unfoldment of the personalized passages of the story.   The film avoids the ideological issue, which for some curious reason it considers inflammable, and slavishly follows the pompous format of Hemingway's exposition of the characters for three mortally lengthy hours.   The guts of the original have been decorously disemboweled and hidden, so as not to offend Isolationists, Bundists, P. T. A. and the shade of Anthony Comstock--with result that the drama, both political and sexual, bears little more

relationship to the brutal realities of the world in which we live
than do the cavortings of Rudolf Rassendyl in the kingdom of Ruritania.

The bulk of the action of the Hemingway book transpires
either in retrospect or in a sleepingbag, and Dudley Nichols, faced
with complicated dramatic and restrictional hurdles, managed a
screen-play of craftsmanship that, understandably, eschews further
editing than was forced upon him before he placed typewriter to
paper.   Instead of adapting the novel to the requirements of another
medium, Nichols attempts a literal transposition of the original's
plot, with the result that the structural faults of the novel are repeated in the film.

Sam Wood's direction indicates that he was in awe of his
material, and his guidance prefers the ponderous to the pithy, the
circuitous to the simple.   Despite this approach, the screen leaps
into life on occasion, particularly when the camera and microphone
are focused on Katina Paxinou, who contributes the most distinguished performance of the year as Pilar.   Here is dynamic histrionic force tethered to intelligence, and the actress evokes an
impressive performance of stature, soul and force.   She storms
the spectator in the sequence in which she explains what it means
to a woman to have been born ugly, and it is regrettable that the
speech which vividly recreates the taking of a town was not permitted
to carry the scene, and was needlessly augmented by visual action.
Paxinou impales sufficient attention with her majestic voice, and
needs none of the montaged tricks which the customary photoplay
performer would require to fire such a barrage of emotion.

Ingrid Bergman is a disturbing and lovely Maria, and though
the character has been looted of pivotal psychological explanation,
it is emblazoned with a warm, earthy naturalness that has life despite a lack of perspective.   Gary Cooper's Robert Jordan is Gary
Cooper, which is precisely what Hemingway wrote.   The cast, with
the exception of Cooper, is a veritable Tower of Babel, and there
is a certain comic confusion in listening to Greek, Swedish,
Russian, Roumanian, Italian, Mexican and Spanish accents all
struggling for dialectical supremacy in depicting Spanish characters.

Despite its faults, For Whom the Bell Tolls deserves to be
viewed.   However, this department advocates taking along a high-
grade pneumatic cushion, for three hours is a long, long time to
spend perched on an ordinary theater seat.

                                        --Herb Sterne in Rob Wagner's
                                        Script, Vol. 29, No. 661 (Au-
                                        gust 28, 1943), page 14.

☐ THE GANG'S ALL HERE (20th Century-Fox, 1943)

    Sumptuous is the word for The Gang's All Here. Nothing
quite so lavishly routined for a maximum of stunning effects or so
vividly splashed with the magnificences of Technicolor has ever
been offered in a screen song and dance spectacle. The ending is
sheer camera magic, a kaleidoscopic creation by Busby Berkeley
who stages a startling departure in finales with intricate turntable
and mirrored devices which would have overtaxed the skill of an
any less gifted craftsman than photographer Edward Cronjager.

    Long noted for innovations that demanded camera mastery,
Berkeley was obviously given full reign by astute producer William
LeBaron. Even though there is no precedent for some of the fabulous abstractions created, the imaginative results are undeniably
stimulating to the visual senses. And LeBaron has carefully provided a wealth of star names, headed by Alice Faye, Carmen Miranda, the surefire Benny Goodman orchestra and strong supporting
talent, to draw audiences to the theatres. To help the exploitation
of the attraction, there are seven new hit songs from Leo Robin
and Harry Warren. By almost every analysis, The Gang's All
Here indicates smash boxoffice.

    But it is true that the extraordinary camera wizardry which
amazes the eye has a tendency to slight the already slight story
content of the picture. The plot is a mere trifle about a soldier
who marches away to war, leaving two girls believing themselves
engaged to him. When these two girls meet, as inevitably they
must to unwind the tangle, one tries to conceal her heartbreak
until it is learned that her rival prefers to follow a career.

    Miss Faye, arrestingly and beautifully photographed, plays
a nightclub chorine on her way to stardom. She distinctively handles two grand Robin-Warren ballads, "No Love, No Nothing"--the
show's enduring hit--and "A Journey to a Star." In contrast to
her haunting delivery of these melodies are the Miranda bombshell
tactics to put over "The Lady in the Tutti Frutti Hat" and "You
Discover You're in New York," the opening number. She does put
them across in her own certain style, then joins Benny Goodman
in singing a novelty ditty called "Paducah." This and a topical
swing lyric, "Minnie's in the Money," mark Goodman's first film
vocalizing. It calls for more of the same. "The Polka Dot Polka"
is the catchy Robin-Warren offering used for the finale in which
all join.

    Berkeley directed the story and created and directed the
dancing. He sends Cronjager's camera on wondrous journeys of
traveling and zoom shots, of hedge-hopping and roller-coaster
tricks. The photographic movement is continuous and strikingly
varied. In addition to the kaleidoscope divertissement, there are
such resourceful bits of business as the rainbow water curtain, and
the staging of the "Tutti Frutti Hat" routine atop that hat with a

large group of Berkeley lovelies forming symmetrical patterns with
the fruit. His creations refuse to acknowledge any limitations in
the medium of the screen, nor does he have to when met with the
technical artistry of Cronjager, faultless Technicolor direction by
Natalie Kalmus, art direction by James Basevi and Joseph C.
Wright, and special effects by Fred Sersen.

James Ellison has small chance as the soldier who drifts in
and out of proceedings. Sheila Ryan is the rival to Miss Faye for
his affections, and surprises by her partnership with Tony De Marco in a pleasing dance. Eugene Pallette, Charlotte Greenwood and
Edward Everett Horton amuse as assorted parents of Ellison and
Miss Ryan, yet it is La Miranda's hilarious garbling of the English
language which scores the majority of the laughs.

Phil Baker, a performer whose name value has increased
since he started emceeing "Take It or Leave It" on the radio, gets
third billing despite the fact that there is little left of his role in
the picture. He is eliminated before reaching the $64 question.
Specialty dances are provided by De Marco, Miriam Lavelle and
Charles Saggau. The chorus beauties are glamorized by the costumes of Yvonne Wood, and Alfred Newman and Charles Henderson
divide the credit for musical direction of the sumptuous LeBaron
production.

--The Hollywood Reporter, Vol.
76, No. 4 (November 26, 1943),
page 3.

□ GASLIGHT (M-G-M, 1944)

Gaslight is a film adaptation of the English shocker that appeared here at the Hollywood Playhouse, with Judith Evelyn as the
much put-upon heroine, before it safaried east for a highly successful stint on Broadway. This type of psychological melodrama
is played to greater suspense in the theater, where it benefits by
the compactness of a single set, and the tenseness lent situations
by the unbroken, up-sweep of live performers who are able to build
and contour emotion without the interference of mechanical effects.

The screen version, although it lacks the sharp, nerve-
shattering tension of the original, is an excellent thriller. George
Cukor has endowed it with a pleasant Victorianism, furthered by
florid acting that artfully matches the décor. Cukor ingeniously
uses the camera to heighten the highlights, and cannily counterpoints
sound with silence during several of the more dire situations.

Handsomely mounted, spiritedly performed, Gaslight is deft
movie. If it never lashes the spectator to the convulsive state of
jitters engendered by the stage play, mark that down to the physical
disqualifications of the two central performers. Ingrid Bergman

has a robustious quality that implies her quite capable, if ever
really tired of Charles Boyer's iniquities, of launching a haymaker
destined to knock the actor right into the middle of what is frequently termed next week.

> --Herb Sterne in Rob Wagner's
> Script, Vol. 30, No. 683 (July
> 15, 1944), page 24.

☐ GENTLEMAN'S AGREEMENT (20th Century-Fox, 1947)

Here is an important picture. With a rare combination of
passion and truth it focuses and turns to the light, in a succession
of salient episodes, most of those common or garden aspects of
anti-Semitism practiced in America today. Not by violent and
dreadful people like Hitler and his gang, but by nice, very nice,
people. Let me suggest by people like you and me (if we happen,
that is, not to be Jews ourselves). By people who belong to clubs
to which no Jews are admitted, by those of us who live in "restricted areas" where there is a "gentleman's agreement" that
Jews shall not also live. By people who go to hotels from which
Jews are habitually turned away. By those who give jobs to
Greens but not to Greenbergs, and by others whose children sometimes call the little Rosens and Adlers "dirty kikes." By many
who are often heard to say that they have no prejudice against
Jews, that indeed some of them are their best friends. It is because we, the "nice," the unprejudiced, well-placed Americans
are somehow shown to be implicated in these un-American attitudes, that this simply stated and forthright picture is as eloquent
and excellent a sermon as I have heard delivered (truthfully and
justly, without undue excitement, but with obvious and inescapable
integrity) to the American people in a long, long time.

Basing his picture on Laura Z. Hobson's novel, Moss Hart
has contributed an excellent and telling script. A young writer,
accompanied by his son and mother, arrives from the Pacific Coast
to work on a large New York weekly. He is assigned to write a
series of articles on anti-Semitism as it exists in this country.
The writer hits on an idea. His name is Green: he will assume
the name of Greenberg and thus be in a position to discover at first
hand something about the manner in which Jews are treated.

He doesn't have to wait long to learn all about it. He finds
himself at once running up against all the familiar attitudes--the
prejudices, the ostracisms, the clichés. In a variety of scenes
brilliantly wrought into the story they are all displayed to him.
But as the drama must of course revolve around a love affair, we
keep our eyes upon the young woman he has fallen for, and who
might be you or me or any nice non-Jewish girl caught almost unaware into the trap that has been set for her. She is much in love
with her young man and declares that she is enthusiastic about the

clever ruse he has thought out for getting information for his articles.   Unfortunately, she finds she hasn't quite got the courage to
buck the actual showdowns as they begin to present themselves to
her.   She considers his singleness of purpose, his passion and
integrity a little on the zealot's side.   He is exasperating and excessive.   She can't see why he has to go for it with such intensity.
Why can't he understand that it is natural that her family shouldn't
think him a Jew?   They have a very stormy time of it.   On these
issues he is not inclined to let her off.

Presently her position towards the whole business is unhap-
pily exposed when she refuses to make available a house in a
"restricted" community to his great friend David, a young Jew
just back from overseas and impatient to set up housekeeping with
his wife.   She does her best to explain to her young man all this
"restricted area" business, but it doesn't go down with him and
they break their relationship over the issue.

However, David manages to heal the breach between them
and she is ready to capitulate.   He shall have his house, and she
will fight the good fight along with her young man--a conclusion
considerably too slick for my own taste.   But let us not cavil with
so serious and thought-provoking a picture, one which would do
everyone capable of honest thought a great deal of good to see.

The principal actors, Dorothy McGuire as the girl, Gregory
Peck as the writer, and John Garfield as the Jewish friend, act
their parts with competence and move through sets and scenes of
unimaginable elegance and unreality.   But let us not cavil with that
either.   "The play's the thing."   And here is an important and
serious picture.

Darryl F. Zanuck has done a service to his company, to the
screen, and to the American spirit in producing this sane, this
responsible, this telling analysis of intolerance.   He need not fear
how our democracy will stand before the world if we are represented abroad by a picture such as this courageous producer has
given us here.

> --Mary Britton Miller in New
> Movies, Vol. 22, No. 7 (De-
> cember 1947), pages 4-5.

*   *   *

Gentleman's Agreement is the second film this year to speak
out against a subject heretofore taboo in films: anti-Semitism.
Crossfire, which put across its message in terms of melodrama,
was a forceful document, sickening in its implications.   The present film is equally forceful and even more frank.   It is films like
these two, which treat important themes in adult, cogent fashion,
that make one realize what a powerful social force films could be--
and seldom are.

No Gentile, probably, can fully appreciate the foothold anti-Semitism has in present-day society.   To get a fuller insight into the problem, reporter Phil Green (Gregory Peck) posed as a Jew to document some articles he was preparing.   This brief experiment brought vividly to him--and will to you--the daily indignities and humiliations, the cruel hypocrisy, the senseless bigotry that people are subjected to through accident of birth.   And before Green reverted to his own place in society, he and his friends pledged themselves never again to let baseless prejudice pass unattacked.

All this, of course, can be called preachment.   But surely it is preachment in the cause of the best principles, and it has the advantage of being presented as thumping good entertainment.   Gregory Peck plays his rewarding role with all the expertness at his command, proving once more that he is one of our most persuasive actors.   It is no new thing, either, for Dorothy McGuire to demonstrate how skillful an actress she is.   And if you have never before given much notice to Celeste Holm, you will discover here that she is an actress to watch.   They are all fine, and so are the rest of the cast.   Elia Kazan directed, from a screenplay by Moss Hart based on Laura Z. Hobson's novel.   Hollywood can be proud of this film.

--Fortnight, Vol. 3, No. 12
(December 19, 1947), page 28.

☐   GILDA (Columbia, 1946)

Gilda is a jewelled production and an always fascinating picture about whose entertainment quality there will be widely divergent schools of thought.   All will revel in Rita Hayworth's sultry beauty, and admire Glenn Ford's acting and the film's magnificent Buenos Aires sets and background.   But not all will find things to admire in its hard to follow and often cheaply melodramatic and theatrical story.   Showmen booking it will find crowds waiting that first day to pay for the privilege of seeing Rita Hayworth and attracted by the sensationally lurid advertising provided in the press book.   If difference of opinion causes boxoffice then Gilda will be a natural.

To divine what is wrong with the picture, one starts at the first.   Its whole approach to its subject is miserably wrong.   Not until its final scene does one begin to feel the least bit of sympathy for hero or heroine and no picture yet was very successful in which romantic leads were so badly written that audiences didn't feel one emotion or another for them.   The picture, even at this release date, cries for just one establishing shot near the opening to let us know what makes the characters act the way they do toward each other, to let us know that the girl is fundamentally good and not the lovely monster that we know her as through the boy's eyes.   This would allow us to feel some particle of sympathy for either or both

of them. As it stands assembled now, not even when it is over do
we know what inspired the morbid love-hate affair that propels the
plot. Virginia Van Upp is guilty of a cardinal sin in allowing the
script to go to production in its present form. Granted its present
form does build the suspense, mystery and intrigue of the story--
and establishes some wonderful dark moods--no movie yet has
pleased many people (nor has one ever been attempted) in which you
hate all the leading characters.

This is a screenplay by Marion Parsonnet from an adaptation
by Jo Eisinger of a story by E. A. Ellington. And some of its
plot structure and much of its dialogue is indisputably Van Upp.
The dialogue--all of it--is brilliant. Its biting retorts, bitterly
cynical speeches, bon mots, epigrams and idioms more than once
touch greatness of writing. So is its story premise sound and
evilly interesting and it comes excitingly to life under Charles Vidor's direction. It is peopled with extraordinarily fascinating men
and a woman but one watches their actions only to see that they
come to the foul end they deserve. The happy ending is such an
unexpected and abrupt change of character for hero and heroine that
it almost makes you wonder what it was you liked about the rest of
it in retrospect. What the film is, is much to be admired; what
it might have been and isn't, is to be bitterly regretted. One
senses even the urgency of getting the script pages from producer's
office to the sound stages.

When his life is saved by a mysterious but important looking
man, the boy of the story, footloose and equally mysterious, throws
in his lot with the man, leader of Buenos Aires' gambling life and
a sinister international figure. He rises to a position of trust,
second in command. Soon the man of mystery goes away for a
while but returns with a beautiful and cynical young bride. The
boy and the young wife are antagonistic from the instant of their
meeting and what the audience suspects is soon revealed in their
constant hatred of one another. Each has been to the other the
cause of their present calloused behavior. Soon again it is revealed
that our man of mystery controls a vast cartel and German agents
close in on him at the same time he interrupts his wife and the boy
about to spend their mutual passion, although the boy still hates this
girl. When the man's escape plane is seen to crash, believing him
dead the boy marries the girl in order to exact still further, sweet-
er revenge on her for what he imagines she has meant in wrecking
his life. In the unconsummated marriage, the girl almost goes
crazy, runs away and dances again for her living. Thwarted by
his stooges at every turn, she returns to beg him to release her
from his hold on her. Then the husband of mystery returns and
the star-crossed lovers are finally sure of each other after he has
most definitely been done to death this time.

In the radiant beauty of Rita Hayworth is all this picture's
strength. Without her it would be the merest drivel. Hers is the
kind of fatal fascination, however, that does drive men to deeds
such as this preposterous story presents. Sex comes into its own

again on the screen--sex, such as never has been presented before
--in Miss Hayworth's two dance numbers. She is voluptuous and
she is exciting. Best of all, she is an actress in the story's moments of legitimate drama. Vidor is terrific in his handling of her
and wise in his making her the picture's pivot. Glenn Ford is
great in his presentation of the boy's warped and wretched mind.
He gives it intense study and redeeming fire. In physical appearance, however, Ford is not at his best in this second of his films
since he returned from the war, and it is hoped that Warners'
cameramen did better with him than his own studio's have done.
Ford is one of our finest actors, has always been, and he must be
treated right. But comes steam baths for him now. George Macready is in command of every scene in which he appears, no matter who shares it with him. He is superb as the man of mystery.
There are more brilliant supporting roles in this than any one film
has a right to have and winning fresh acclaim in them are Steven
Geray, Joseph Calleia, Joe Sawyer and S. Z. Martel. Robert
Scott is excellent as one of the young wife's pick-ups and distinguishes his role.

Rita Hayworth is breathtaking in her Jean Louis gowns and
the camera of Rudy Mate is her most devoted swain as it lavishes
its greatest gifts upon her and she upon it. The art direction is a
thrilling accomplishment for Stephen Goosson and Van Nest Polglase
and the music one equally as fine by M. W. Stoloff and Marlin
Skiles.

Virginia Van Upp's production makes up on all counts in excitement what it lacks in story integrity. If the principals may still
be recalled for that added scene of love and angry parting in which
a motive will be established for the story's whole being, then she
will also show Columbia and the film industry how great a boxoffice
success can be.

--Hollywood Review, Vol. 37, No.
2 (March 19, 1946), pages 3 and
17.

* * *

Practically all the s. a. habiliments of the femme fatale have
been mustered for Gilda, and when things get trite and frequently
far-fetched, somehow, at the drop of a shoulder strap, there is always Rita Hayworth to excite the filmgoer. When story interest
lags, she's certain to shrug a bare shoulder, toss her tawny hair in
an intimately revealing closeup, or saunter teasingly through the celluloid. She dissipates the theories, if any, that sex has its shortcomings as a popular commodity. Miss Hayworth will do business.

The story is a confusion of gambling, international intrigue
and a triangle that links two gamblers and the wife of one of them.
The setting is Buenos Aires. Sneaking in somehow is the subplot
of a tungsten cartel operated by the husband, who also runs a swank
gambling casino. A couple of Nazis are thrown in also.

It seems that the younger gambler and the wife had been sweethearts before her rebound marriage, but now they hate each other oh-so-much. For some reason the scripters don't reveal the cause of this hate. When the husband apparently suicides in an ocean plane crash, after his cartel machinations are found out by the police, the younger man and the wife marry in what looks like a patchup of their feud. But no. He's still mad. He's married her only to get even. And there she is wearing gowns down to here and waiting futilely for him every night. And looking oh-so-beautiful! And never more beautiful than in her hapless plight. Just a lot of impractical madness.

Of course, they finally get together. A cop who wends his philosophical way through the picture breaks down the guy's resistance. That's where the pic really winds up on its cartel.

Miss Hayworth is photographed most beguilingly, an undoubted envy for the femmes and an excitement for the men. The producers have created nothing subtle in the projection of her s.a., and that's probably been wise.

Glenn Ford is the vis-à-vis, in his first picture part in several years, after his release from service. He's a far better actor than the tale permits. And there are times, despite the script, when he's able to give a particularly creditable performance. George Macready plays the older gambler with some plausibility, and Steven Geray believably portrays the casino attendant.

There are a couple of songs ostensibly sung by Miss Hayworth, and one of them, "Put the Blame on Mame," piques the interest because of its intriguing, low-down quality.

Gilda is obviously an expensive production--and shows it. The direction is static, but that's more the fault of the writers. But this is another pic where the professional critics--those guys with passes--can't do enough to detour the paying public.
--"Kahn" in Variety, Vol. 162,
No. 2 (March 20, 1946), page 8.

☐ GOING MY WAY (Paramount, 1944)

Going My Way is as smooth an example of the audience picture as you are likely to witness. Its Hibernian humor and drama stroke the heartstrings with frankness, skill and an unashamed schmaltz that should rocket the reels into one of the biggest box-office bonanzas of all time.

Nothing has been omitted to make the opus sure-fire. Religion, sacerdotal music, Tin Pan Alley tunes, young love, grand opera, a mortgage, an elderly cleric who wanders disconsolately

into the night and a rainstorm feeling he has outlived his usefulness, mother love, frequent references to ould Ireland in brogues
as thick as Liffey mud, drama out of Dion Boucicault, jokes out of
Joe O'Miller's manual, and sundry other stand-bys of the bestseller theatricals that have been with us since the first Irishman
toddled across a stage, clay pipe in mouth and red bandana trailing
from a rear pocket of his pantaloons, to great applause in the theater and to queues at the boxoffice outside.

Mind you, Going My Way is persuasive. It has an easy,
palsy-walsy performance by Bing Crosby as a Catholic priest, one
so right that one stops to wonder and marvel that this is the same
personality glimpsed in such an agony of selfconsciousness in College Humor and We're Not Dressing. Barry Fitzgerald, really
bringing to the camera for the first time that arrogant art and
blatant personality which was wont to blast us from the boards of
the Abbey Theater Players, gives so dynamic a show that the
shades of Theodore Roberts, Cyril Maude, George Fawcett and
Claude Gillingwater must be three shades of white paler in pure,
uncelestial envy at the effrontery and success of his attack.

Leo McCarey has taken most of heart throbs of Make Way
for Tomorrow, and many of the gags from The Milky Way, colored
them à la St. Patrick's Day carnations, garnished them with four-
leaf shamrocks--and they are served with a side order of Irish
stew for extra attraction.

It is noticeable that while such of the lesser help as Gene
Lockhart, Anita Bolster and several of the small-fry are excellent,
McCarey has permitted James Brown to be a hero who is all gleam-
ing teeth and broad shoulders, and condones the heroine of Jean
Heather in being so goddamned girlish as to make the late June
Caprice, by comparison, seem like one of the Four Horsewomen
of the Algonquin.

> --Herb Sterne in Rob Wagner's
> Script, Vol. 30, No. 686 (Au-
> gust 26, 1944), pages 10-11.

*   *   *

This is a picture the director obviously enjoyed making: Leo
McCarey had a story of his own devising to work with, and his affection for it seems to warm it all the way through. It is no great
wonder for plot, being hardly more than an unpretentious and distant
relative of The Passing of the Third Floor Back, brought nearer
home by being set in a run-down parish among the poor in New
York City. But its rather makeshift narrative is enlivened by good
will and good humor, and two fine actors make the whole thing bub-
ble with human interest.

It is not the habitual kind of Bing Crosby picture, though it
won't be any great surprise to people who have pleasant memories
of Sing You Sinners, and it is certainly no jolt to see Bing playing a

young priest.   Mr. Harry Lillis Crosby, dubbed crooner in the beginning, has been jogging along so many years, casually making millions of friends who always hunt up whatever new picture he appears in, that he has seemed more an amiable institution than an actor.   Songs and easy-going comedy, always a pretty good show, with other people never being pushed around or crowded out by the star--that's what we expect and get from a Crosby movie.   But all this time he has been mellowing into an excellent actor, so deft and unspectacular in craftsmanship that he always seems to be just his natural self--the fellow we think of as Bing--and at the same time whatever character he is temporarily assuming.   Which, after all, is what acting really is.

Going My Way tells of young Father O'Malley arriving at the eastside parish of St. Dominic's, ostensibly to be the assistant of old Father Fitzgibbon, actually to supersede him and put new life into the church and its activities--it has been running into debt, a mortgage is threatening it, and the aging pastor, whose vigorous work built it up originally, seems to be losing his grip.   The idea is to get the job done without hurting the old man's feelings.

And done the job is--Father O'Malley (whose friends call him "Chuck," and who hasn't forgotten the boyhood when he played baseball in East St. Louis) isn't what the neighborhood is used to in his methods, but before he is through, and without sermonizing or pious talk, he has steered the ringleader of a gang of hoodlums into paths of more social usefulness and changed the gang itself into a choir; he has rescued a girl from night-club singing and helped smooth the way for her into the safe harbor of matrimony; he has lifted the mortgage on the old church and so softened the heart of the financier that a new mortgage for a new church is in the offing. And this job finished, he is finally being sent to do likewise in another needy parish.

It is all as simple and artless as The Old Homestead, and the new songs Bing has to sing are about on a level with the plot. But the characters of the two priests, as they are written and acted, create something way above plot manoeuverings--a humanity of tremendous and universal appeal, which is also art of the finest kind.   Barry Fitzgerald at last has a part in the movies that gives scope for the gifts he has had no chance to show since his days with the Abbey Theatre: his Father Fitzgibbon is a masterpiece. No such finely wrought picture of old age has ever come to our screen before.   But its richness and variety should not obscure the performance of Bing Crosby, which in its different, quieter style is just as much of an achievement.   The two are magnificent foils for each other.

--James Shelley Hamilton in New
Movies, Vol. 19, No. 3-4
(April-May 1944), pages 5-6.

☐ HAIL THE CONQUERING HERO (Paramount, 1944)

Laughter, that one gift the gods gave Man to distinguish him
from all animals save the hyena, has a pluperfect practitioner in
Preston Sturges.

Through sundry cinemas Sturges has proved that he possesses
a very special and rare talent for lallapalooza lampooning.   The
gent has a muscular literary arm capable of unloosing strong, sardonic shafts that strike hard at the rumpish heart of human folly.
And in satirically tracing the curiously pathological and pathetic
pattern formed by the combination of the minute mind tethered to
cardiac hypertrophy, Sturges, in celluloid, has several times
equalled those trenchant poison-pen portraits of the American scene
limned some years ago by H. L. Mencken.

However, there have been ominous indications that, besides
being a wit and scholar, our Mr. Sturges is also a showman.   Having no taste for commercial martyrdom, he has frequently masqued
his cinematic caprices and criticisms in garb so guileful that the
multitude is neither afrighted nor incensed by his nose-thumbings
at current social conceits.   As a matter of record, the gentleman
can be so subtle, so adroit, that such a film as The Miracle of
Morgan's Creek, in which he slaughters an entire stockyard of sacred cows, becomes as lucrative a length of celluloid as anything
to be adapted from the works of Lloyd C. Douglas, Eleanor H.
Porter and Channing Pollock.   Sturges' audacity in that film has
been completely, and no doubt providentially, misunderstood, and
it will require whatever peace years the future holds, before a
proper evaluation may be publicly placed on its brilliant impropri-
eties.

There is small doubt that Sturges realizes the narrow squeak
he had with popular prejudice and its retaliatory tar-and-feathers in
The Miracle of Morgan's Creek, and there is certainly an indication
in his latest comedy, Hail the Conquering Hero of a determination
to play more gently with Mr., Mrs. and the younkers Grundy.

True, the subject matter satirizes still another national predilection, the indiscriminate apotheoses of such stuntsfolk as first
trans-oceanic flyers, Kiki Roberts, first trans-channel swimmers,
Peaches Browning, flagpole sitters, consumers of live goldfish,
marathon dancers etcetcetc.   And it also takes a tilt or two at the
supernal halo that unitedstatesers allege descends about any female
the very second she conceives, and proves herself sufficiently fe-
cund to contribute that Wonder--an addition to the human race.

In his current cinematic caper, Sturges' roguish jig-steps
are too greatly interspersed with a sentimental waltz routine, done
to a schmaltzy hofbrau orchestra droning a Sigmund Romberg med-
ley.   I don't for a moment believe that Sturges has been in the
least swayed by tabloid and tradepaper savants who have frequently

lamented that he has no "heart"; neither is it likely that his cul-
tured contempt and contumely have suddenly become corroded by
the philosophical piffle of Will Carleton and/or Edgar Guest.   However, there is a pretty good chance that Sturges felt that tempting
Providence twice in a row would be really tempting Providence.
There is an equally good chance that the writer-director is becoming somewhat more conscious of the boxoffice than this admirer believes is good for his professional soul, and, too, there seems to
be a hearkening, in this latest opus, to what passes as popular
"taste."

Hail the Conquering Hero is an inventive film, and in many
ways a brilliant one.   It suffers, somewhat, by so closely following
the impeccable Miracle of Morgan's Creek into release, for the current work's lightnings and thunderclaps are less brilliant and resounding.   The fabrics of both pictures are too similar.   The re-
appearance of Eddie Bracken and William Demarest, in pivotal
roles, although they are again both excellent, does nothing to contribute needed notes of variety and contrast in the Sturges style.

Sturges' genius for reflective and satirical high jinks should
not be permitted to gravitate to a thematic groove.   His gifts are
too great to permit needless repetition and such withdrawals as are
here to be detected.   Fresh faces, a glib change of genre, material drawn from such rich archives as Evelyn Waugh or Ronald
Firbank, and a completely casual disregard for the demands of audiences and auditors will best serve in continuing to give the screen
the full potency of this creator's striking powers.

--Herb Sterne in Rob Wagner's
Script, Vol. 30, No. 688
(September 23, 1944), page 20.

*   *   *

It is too bad that the expression "the human comedy" can't
be freshly invented, with no left-over connotations hanging to it
from other uses it has undergone.   For nothing else comes easily
to mind for an apt description of the kind of movie Preston Sturges
has brought to top heights in Hail the Conquering Hero.   All the
other films of this dynamic director, from The Great McGinty to
The Miracle of Morgan's Creek, seem to be practice exercises for
this latest release of his, which has the vitalizing, seasoned sureness of a creative hand with all its tools in order and sharpened to
their utmost effectiveness, applied to the execution of a design that
mind and feeling have plotted for all the highest values within its
scope.

Whether deliberately or just following natural inclination,
Sturges--at least up to the present--has given the comic spirit free
rein in his pictures.   Maybe he made a sort of confession in Sullivan's Travels, where he sent his hero to probing the sorrows of
the world and brought him back with the conviction that laughter was
just about the world's greatest blessing.   If only from the evidence

of the Sullivan film, Sturges is aware enough, and keenly, of the
darker side of life, and he could obviously make stark tragedies
with the best of them.   But he seems more bent on holding up his
mirror so that its reflections highlight things that have laughable
aspects.   Usually it has been the follies and weaknesses of the
American human that he has picked out for fun-poking, which has
made a lot of people call him a satirist.   But less and less does
he seem to indulge in the kind of reformatory attack that is the
essence of satire, and more and more there emerges a mellow
kind of understanding that mingles sympathy with laughter and takes
the edge off ridicule.   If he has decided that life, so far as he is
going to put it on the screen, is a comedy, he has perfected a
method of tickling the laugh muscles with warmth and fellow-feeling,
with all the emphasis on the human nature of our daily living, not
holding it up to derision but giving us a chance to laugh comfortably at ourselves and the kind of people we know.   Though he avoids
plumbing depths and exploring strong passions he never seems to
be dealing fundamentally with shallows and froth.   He gets his situations out of his characters, and he pictures his characters--with
however sharp an eye to their foolishness and sentimentalities--
without distorting them with any sloppiness or sentimentality of his
own.

It would be no addition to anyone's delight in Hail the Conquering Hero to know in advance what happens in it.   It is about a
soldier who through an unlucky physical misfortune lost any chance
to be heroic but comes home to a town eager to hail him as a
hero.   Hero worship, "Mom" idolatry, small-town politics and
plain ordinary human nature, all in a humorous aspect but touched
with a surprising amount of sympathetic tenderness, have their
part in the complications, and an undercurrent of heart-warming
feeling mingles with the constant stream of laughter.   As usual,
Sturges gets the best out of his actors, particularly Eddie Bracken,
William Demarest and Franklin Pangborn.

> --James Shelley Hamilton in New
> Movies, Vol. 19, No. 6 (Octo-
> ber 1944), page 5.

☐ HARVEY (Universal-International, 1950)

The lovable animal who charmed so many theatre audiences
for so long, has arrived on the screen with whimsy in full bloom.

This sort of thing is either a delight or a bore according to
your view, but if it's your dish, you'll find Harvey fairly intact
with the exception of a few scenes which have been somewhat
lengthened or spread thin to suit the medium.

Harvey's friend in this case, Jimmy Stewart, is nicely at
home with his "pooka," and if his lanky, boyish frame doesn't quite

fit the role as Frank Fay played it, his completely believable characterization certainly makes up for this discrepancy.

Josephine Hull (and Stewart does seem a little young to be
her brother) exhibits for the screen the talents which have long
since established her as among the best stage players, and she is
in turn firm, confused, horrified and sentimental concerning her
brother's companion.

There are many weaknesses in the plot itself. For instance,
the little romantic byplay with Nurse Peggy Dow and Doctor Robert
Drake appears to hang too heavily on the arts of Harvey's charms.
But then, you have to be willing to take whimsy undiluted to be
thoroughly enchanted.

Pixyish as it all is, some reviewers didn't even see the
rabbit.

--Fortnight, Vol. 9, No. 13
(December 25, 1950), page 32.

*   *   *

*Mary Chase's comedy about a pooka named Harvey opened
on Broadway in 1944, won the Pulitzer Prize the following year,
and subsequently spread the titular rabbit's fame to the four corners
of the globe.   Having paid a record $1,000,000 (against one-third
of the profits) for the screen rights, Universal sensibly brings the
play to the screen almost intact.   Further, producer John Beck has
provided Josephine Hull and Jesse White of the original company
plus James Stewart, who followed Frank Fay briefly in the role of
Elwood P. Dowd.

Elwood, of course, is the gentle, perpetually squiffed philos-
opher who is aware that a pooka, according to Irish folklore, is a
mischievous specter that often takes the form of a horse but could
just as well materialize as a rabbit.   Elwood met Harvey one night
after one of his elbow-bending soirees at Charlie's place.   He was
walking home and minding his own business when someone called:
"Hello, Elwood."   Turning, Elwood saw this unusually tall rabbit
(say, 6 feet $1\frac{1}{2}$ inches in his padded paws) leaning against the lamp-
post.   As Elwood explains later, he wasn't so surprised as you
might think, because in a small town everyone knows everyone
else's name.

By this time Elwood's gracious relationship with his not-
quite-visible chum and his encounter with the eminent psychiatrist
(Cecil Kellaway) who runs Chumley's Rest Home should be available
as international folklore.   Director Henry Koster and Oscar Brodney,
who worked on the adaptation with the Denver playwright and news-

paperwoman, carefully maintain the fantasy and the comic stance that made Harvey one of the decade's most enjoyable evenings in the theater.

Although Stewart lacks the precision timing and the delicately deranged humor that Frank Fay brought to the original Elwood, his amiable, gregarious eccentric is a very satisfactory substitute. Peggy Dow, Charles Drake, Victoria Horne, Wallace Ford, and William Lynn round out a supporting cast that draws its chief strength from Josephine Hull's completely delightful re-creation of a daft and harried sister Veta, who toddles bemused in brother Elwood's wake.

> --Newsweek (December 25, 1950),
> page 64.

☐ THE HEIRESS (Paramount, 1949)

For years, if you were a proper aesthete, you insisted that film was film and play was play and the twain met altogether too often. Of course you admitted that both told stories and both used actors, but you held that the essence of each was unique, the essence of drama being the word, of film the individual shot. Hence, you concluded, the best film material was derived not from the drama at all (or the novel, for that matter), but from original inspiration conceived in terms of the screen. Occasionally a picture like Henry the Fifth or The Long Voyage Home came along to confound you, but you admired them as exceptions and stood your ground. The principle was right, therefore the evidence must be wrong.

Now it is time to admit that the film outgrew the simplicity of such aesthetics when it learned to talk; for the talking film wedded two arts as surely as opera brought music and drama together in uneasy marriage. When speech was added to silent film, the intricacy of the artist's job was multiplied by infinity. He was forced to satisfy new demands of character development and dramatic progression without abandoning older claims of the peripatetic camera. To the extent that dialogue demanded repose, he had to inhibit motion. Yet he could never forget the restless eye of the audience, nor the fact that his principal source of emotional power was still --as it had been in silent film--the significant juxtaposition of individual shots. No wonder the aesthetes wept for the purity of the lost art, and still weep at times.

It takes a film of such quality as The Heiress to revive the old issue of play into motion picture. For producer-director William Wyler is that rarest of craftsmen who can take such a drama as this, already completely fulfilled in theatre terms, and convert it to film without ever permitting the play-form to dominate the screen. What he did so successfully with The Little Foxes he has repeated with increment in The Heiress.

The story which Ruth and Augustus Goetz derived from Henry
James, first for Broadway and now for the screen, tells of the
heiress whose father finds her dull and unlovely in comparison with
the image he cherishes of his dead wife.   When Catherine Sloper
falls in love with the first young man who has proffered himself as
a suitor, her father sets out to prevent their marriage on the pre-
text that Morris Townsend is a fortune-hunter, as indeed he is
proved to be.   The father succeeds, and in doing so condemns his
daughter to a lonely and bitter life whose greatest triumph is an
empty revenge on her former suitor.

As Dr. Sloper and his daughter Catherine, Ralph Richardson
and Olivia de Havilland have roles that are boldly presented and
rich in suggestion.   Dr. Sloper, in particular, with his splendid
presence, his charm so devastating to a charmless child and his
undercurrent of cruelty, is a role for Richardson to turn with elegance and precision of timing.   Miss de Havilland is at her best in
the early sequences, where she catches in delightfully mobile features and telling gestures the anguish of the inept young heiress.
Under Wyler's tutelage, she leads in and out of her lines with a
change of expression, a shift of stance, that inform and expand the
meaning of every phrase.   If, in the latter half of the film, she is
not fully up to the tragic implications of the role, she has found
how to lower her voice, to mold her face to a mask, and to move
with cold and considered gestures that give a suitable outward form
to the tragedy.   Miriam Hopkins as a well-meaning aunt is pleasantly foolish, and only Montgomery Clift as the suitor appears unable
either to speak or to move or to wear his clothes in the fashion of
the eighteen-fifties.

Except for a few new exterior scenes, notably the ball at
which Catherine and Morris meet, the script has held firm in spirit
and pattern to the Broadway original, confining the major part of
its action inside the walls of the doctor's house on Washington
Square.   Even within these limits there is sufficient potential for
movement for the director who knows, as Wyler does, where to look.
Shrewdly he pivots his action around the central staircase that leads
up two flights to Catherine's room, marking her emotional changes
in the way she moves up and down the stairs.   The vista of rooms
end to end in these narrow houses along the Square provides many
variations for the camera, and when their limit is reached there
are mirrors to extend the view.   In such a setting, with the aid of
the long-focus camera the director can deploy his actors for dialogue without appearing to hold the scene in static composition.   If
the large sliding doors which divide the parlor floor of the mansion
are opened and closed a little too often, punctuating the scene in a
way to remind us that the theatre is not far away after all, this is
only a minor flaw in a visualization which, for all its repose, is
almost endlessly beguiling to the eye.

Aaron Copland has provided The Heiress with a literate score
which, translated, means that he has borrowed from excellent
sources (notably his own Appalachian Spring).   He has used the

French chanson, "Plaisir d'Amour," as a leitmotif without pressing
it to the point of obviousness, and has only once (in his scoring for
the doctor's discovery of his impending death) approached the banal.
With this exception, the music, like everything else in this admirable film, is conceived with taste and executed with style.

--Hermine Rich Isaacs in Films
in Review, Vol. 1, No. 1
(February 1950), pages 25-27.

*   *   *

The thought of Henry James in Hollywood version is enough
to strike terror into the heart of any James admirer. An adaptation of his Washington Square, however, has already been seen over
theatre footlights and it was a comforting sight. While James himself failed cataclysmically at the playwright's art, Ruth and Augustus
Goetz did very well by their dramatization of his novel.

They have done just as well by their screenplay. The Heiress ("suggested" by Washington Square) gives reason to expect more
James on film within the next years, though it would be folly to expect the successors to live up to this first venture. But the James
revival (or "fad," say the antagonists) is now rounding a decade--
time for Hollywood to jump in.

James' sensitive morality, his fine perceptions of good and
evil and their play upon the minds and hearts of his characters,
particularly his heroines, are all here in The Heiress. The title,
though not his, is a touch James would probably approve. It refers
not only to Catherine Sloper's 30,000 pounds-a-year legacy but to
another inheritance: the ultimate pride and too-great strength of
character of the father she learned to hate.

It is this legacy which, despite her rebellion before his
death, stays with her to shape her final action. As the door of
her home in Washington Square is bolted and the frantic blows and
calls of fortune-seeking Morris Townsend fall against it unheeded,
as Catherine slowly climbs the stairs to her room, she is most
fully her father's heiress.

In her first film since The Snake Pit, Olivia de Havilland
makes a fine, richly understood Catherine. Ralph Richardson,
though one might quibble over his accent as not quite that of a
New Yorker of 100 years ago, is excellent as Dr. Sloper. As
Lavinia Penniman, the sprightly, loquacious parson's widow who
does her best to further the cause of Morris' and Catherine's
romance, Miriam Hopkins is at her best. With such a well-selected
cast, the quality of the rest of the production could hardly be other
than it is.

Montgomery Clift, the improvident fortune-hunter who returns
a second time to ask Catherine's love as well as her legacy, provides the right mixed note of good-for-nothing candor and lovable-

ness.   His over-careless diction seems out-of-place for a New
York gentleman of the 1840's who spent his income in Paris, then
returned to America's salons of the day to re-enforce his resources, but probably few will quarrel with this casting.

> There are few better films around these days than this one.
> --Fortnight, Vol. 7, No. 10
> (November 11, 1949), page 47.

☐ HELLZAPOPPIN' (Universal, 1942)

Hellzapoppin', the ear-splittin', thigh-slappin' musical which
recently concluded a meager four-year run on Broadway, has now
been filmed by Universal, for the edification of the undertraveled
members of this democracy's corn belt.   The same studio that has
grilled this reviewer's workanight existence (and enhanced its own
bank balance) by productions starring Abbott and Costello, drafted
Olsen and Johnson to recreate their mad buffooneries for the camera.   Although mine be a solitary voice crying in the wilderness of
tumultuous approval, I'd like to venture a sotto voce "Hohum!"

The banal insanities still include the gent who endeavors to
deliver the ever-growing tree, the demoiselle periodically screech-
ing her search for "Oscar!", the magazine addict who reads his
way through the entire show.   Incidentally, the latter is not a bad
idea for those who are able to concentrate amidst pandemonium.
A saving grace of the flicker version is that the actors bear the
brunt of the wear and tear.   Not that the cataclysmic activities are
one whit less wild, but as audience participation is impossible in
the movies, the spectator is exempt from having cakes of ice and
live fowl deposited in his lap, while "spiders" are tumbled down
his neck.

> --Herb Sterne in Rob Wagner's
> Script, Vol. 27, No. 622
> (February 14, 1942), page 14.

☐ HERE COMES MR. JORDAN (Columbia, 1941)

Only curmudgeons will not like Here Comes Mr. Jordan,
Robert Montgomery's latest.   Not that the curmudgeons couldn't
make a couple of telling points against this scatterbrained fantasy:
the plot, even in terms of fantasy, is pretty hard to swallow, the
boy-gets-girl theme is too toilsomely pursued, and there is a touch
too much metaphysical gab.   But the hell with that, as Ernest Hemingway would say.   Here Comes Mr. Jordan is one of the brightest
comedies of the year, and you'd do well to see it.

This tale is based on the premise, somehow not unlikely, that things get just as mixed up in Heaven as they do down here. The soul of Joe Pendleton, a promising contender for the heavyweight championship, arrives in the Hereafter fifty years before his appointed time, through the overzealousness of Heavenly Messenger 7013, who has snatched him from an airplane crash that he was supposed to survive. The problem of getting Joe back in a garment of mortal flesh, so that he can win the championship as predicted in the heavenly ledger, is so acute that it is personally taken over by Mr. Jordan, a high executive on the Other Side.

Robert Montgomery, whose willingness to tackle unorthodox movie roles must have won him a good many admirers besides me, does a neat job as the ghost whose only wish is to get inside a well-conditioned male body (about 190 pounds, say, with a good reach) and have a crack at the title. Edward Everett Horton is the Messenger, who, because he is new to the work, has been started at the bottom, in a place called New Jersey. James Gleason has a fine part, too, as a prizefighter's manager. But my loudest huzzas are saved for Claude Rains, who plays Mr. Jordan. Mr. Rains' acting is the kind that makes the term "ham" a word of endearment, and I mean that for a compliment. He manages to put a sort of sinister gloss over the character of Mr. Jordan, leading one to speculate on the possibility of his being in some sort of heavenly racket, like smuggling Chinese. Did I tell you to be sure to see <u>Mr. Jordan</u>? Well, see that you do.

--Russell Maloney in <u>The New Yorker</u> (August 16, 1941), page 52.

☐ HOW GREEN WAS MY VALLEY (20th Century-Fox, 1942)

When members of the working press were ushered into Darryl Zanuck's private projection sanctorum for the preview of <u>How Green Was My Valley</u>, it was at once apparent that 20th Century-Fox believed it had something very special in the way of a cinematic item. Now this department has long been accustomed to the drumpoundings of studio publicists, the enthusiasms that are so often false dawns, the tintinnabulary hopes so infrequently justified. In sheer self-defense, a reviewer learns to harden his heart against the cozenings of million-dollar budgets, champagne suppers, highly-touted artisans, pyrotechnical junkets that end in the unveiling of strips of very ordinary celluloid at such recherché spots as the Everglades, Santa Anita, and Noah's Ark. Having garnered, through bitter (ha!) experience, that the better the Scotch at previews, the worse the movie usually proves to be, my skepticism as to a film's worth is immediately aroused by undue preliminary highjinks. However, at the end of two hours, the studio's evaluation of <u>How Green Was My Valley</u> proved not one whit too optimistic, for the John Ford effort is one of the most meritorious motion pictures to reach the screen.

This tale of a coal-mining town in Wales and the engulfment
of its people in a tide of commercialism, has the careful documentation and detail found in the better Victorian novels.   The adult
Huw is never seen; then, as the last of his line prepares to leave
the valley, he reviews his life through the eyes of youth.   An entire era is recreated in what occurs to the Morgan family and the
disintegration of faith, simplicity and beauty is depicted with a
shattering emotional quality.

John Ford has endowed the treatment with idyllic grandeur.
His work has a deep, poetic cadence and, for the first time in his
long and representative career, the director has captured the basic
nature of all true art, the poignancy of humanity.   With infinite
pity he reveals the aspirations, the struggles, the small triumphs
and harrowing defeats of Little People, and his personal concern
with the fates of his characters breeds a lyricism that is all too
rare in an era of the machine-made photoplay.   Compassion is the
keynote, even in the natural, human comedy, and the talking screen
has given us few sequences to match the emotional tug engendered
by the sons' departure from home and their eventual return.

Ford utilizes the tableau for dramatic effect, bases his faith
on a complete visualization of story threads, relates the most telling scenes in terms of pantomime.   The magnificent choral work of
the Welsh Singers, the unusually effective musical score of Alfred
Newman, blend with the action in an unprecedented manner and project a mood that dialogue could not hope to attain.   The sparse
speech employed has an authentic Cymric lilt and augments, never
seeks to replace, the most august protagonist of any motion picture:
the camera.

The cast performs with the integration of a superlative symphonic group; each individual performance blends into a smooth ensemble and no attempt has been made to accent romance for the
sake of Mammon.   Sara Allgood and Donald Crisp give the most
consummate performances, and sharing their triumphs are Roddy
McDowall, Anna Lee, John Loder, Walter Pidgeon, Barry Fitzgerald, Patrick Knowles, and Maureen O'Hara.   Earning equal commendation are the photography of Arthur Miller, the script by Philip
Dunne, the editing of James B. Clark.

Although not given to prognostications, it seems to me that
How Green Was My Valley will, in time, be regarded as a classic
and that future years will see it often revived as an example of the
best in screen literature.   Congratulations, Commander John Ford
and Lieutenant Colonel Darryl Zanuck!
                              --Herb Sterne in Rob Wagner's
                                Script, Vol. 27, No. 620
                                (January 17, 1942), page 16.

                         *   *   *

The same sort of solid enjoyment, enrichment and communi-
cation between author and audience that comes from reading a good

book, awaits you in How Green Was My Valley, director John
Ford's new picture which opened gala at the Rivoli last night.

This is a film conceived and executed with dignity, honesty,
thoroughness and superlative competence. It is a full-bodied work.
It has stature and completeness; a maximum of cinematic skill, the
minimum of movie trickery. It does what it sets out to do. And
so it commands, and holds, your respect; it compels your serious
consideration.

Its subject is a man's memories of his boyhood. The man
happened to be the youngest son of a Welsh coal miner, but his experiences, his perception of the world about him, his relationship
to his family, his taking his place in the community, his gradual
awareness that growing up means encountering insecurity, changes,
sorrows, as well as developing the strength to combat them--are
universal experiences.

He remembers his childhood, and because his emotions and
reactions are true and real, we remember ours. They differ only
in detail, and evoke a remembrance that is good and heart-warming.

Since this is a story of looking backward, some of it is an
idyll seen through a mist, and some of it is the exaggerated night-
mare of evil that a good lad would properly remember. The forces
of good--his father and mother, his brothers and sister, the minister, his brother's beautiful wife, his home--these are gleaming
Biblical pictures; the forces of evil--the schoolmaster, his sister's
rich husband who takes her away, the bigoted in church, the gossips
--these are screaming caricatures. They are all blended in a
movie that flows and moves, whose sequences surge gently to their
climaxes, when it's a moment of tenderness they're relating; which
pound up to them, when it's anguish they're concerned with.

Most of the work is done by the camera and score. The
camera watches their emotions; the score intensifies them. The
dialogue is held down, as becomes inarticulate people, and articulate directors.

How Green Was My Valley is a long picture, and leisurely,
yet it retains its hold. If it loses you for a spell in the middle, it
snatches you back again. It dwells in the Russian manner on the
strength and character and beauty in the faces of people. It does
not, however, in the Russian manner also concern itself deeply with
the economic causes that etched their faces with such picturesque
lines of sorrow. There's a mine in the movie, and consequent
mine disasters and unemployment, but gently, for pictorial effect--
not for analysis and the answer.

This is a movie with no stars (unless it's the magnificent
singing of its male Welsh chorus) and fine acting. The boy is
played by Roddy McDowall, a likable lad because mostly he stands
silently by and watches, and learns. Donald Crisp, who plays his

father, and Sara Allgood, his mother, and Maureen O'Hara, his
sister, are as real and dear as your own. So, too, the family
group; so, too, their home.

> --Cecelia Ager in PM (October
> 29, 1941), page 23.

☐ HUMORESQUE (Warner Bros., 1947)

To learn that a wicked woman exists at all in Humoresque
will come as something of a surprise to those who recall the Fannie
Hurst story of mother love, tears and marinated herring, and the
film version thereof which brought fame to Vera Gordon in 1920.
Only a strand or so of the original plot remains in this adaptation,
but from my orchestra chair I find little to regret.

The current Humoresque is a plushy, febrile romance of
passion and music. It has been directed with more trickery than
Orson Welles employed in sawing Rita Hayworth in half, and its
transitional devices appear to have been supervised by the shade of
the late F. W. Murnau. The music is exciting, and it has been
cannily employed to emblazon the polychrome plot of a violin virtu-
oso from the New York ghetto who becomes entangled in the bed
and boredom of a neurotic socialite. A concerto arranged from the
Carmen themes, and a highly emotionalized rendition of the Tristan
and Isolde music make the evening seem as though one were reading
Cosmopolitan magazine with the radio going full blast.

In the cantharides cutie, Joan Crawford has a part that is a
lineal descendant of Diana of Our Dancing Daughters, of Billie of
Our Modern Maidens. Helen Wright is very much what those chits
could have become two decades later, and with the aid of twenty-one
stylish wardrobe changes by Bernard Newman, Miss Crawford proffers a titillating personality performance that is right down the star's
own glister alley. Superbly photographed by Ernest Haller, and
with her hair untouched by the sadistic fingers of Sidney Guilaroff,
Miss Crawford is more entrapping than she has been for years,
mostly because she eschews "acting" and concentrates on being
magnetic, a quality she can certainly manage.

For the rest, John Garfield again is a frustrated genius,
and Oscar Levant again makes bold to hold the title of "The Beard-
less Monty Woolley" against all comers. Some, perhaps, will
register a complaint or two about the way the Jewish family has
been Gentiled-up. But, possibly, Warner Brothers figures that
Semites are not fashionable at the box office of the postwar world,
and it is only fair to recognize that a studio must make a living,
too.

> --Herb Sterne in Rob Wagner's
> Script, Vol. 33, No. 746
> (January 4, 1947), page 12.

*   *   *

The habit movies have of playing follow-the-leader has been
paying off lately to the cash customers.   For one studio (Columbia)
discovered Music not long ago, and--presto--every studio has found
fine music latent within its gates and has made haste to offer it to
the public.

There have been some splendid instances lately of musical
films which depend for their box-office appeal on beautiful music
instead of beautiful legs.   Not the least of them is this production
which stars Joan Crawford and John Garfield.   The story, like an
old lady with her hair retouched and dressed in gay young clothes,
might have been exciting a number of years ago, but is lacking in
emotional stimulus today, despite its brittle dialogue, its swank
settings and the glamorous clothes worn by the heroine.

Miss Crawford lives up to the standards she has set herself
as an actress in her portrayal of the wealthy woman who tries to
forget her failure in marriage in two ways--by sponsoring young
and unrecognized talent and by drinking to excess.   Garfield, a
violinist whose career is furthered through her efforts, falls in love
with her, although their personalities clash and her continual drinking irritates him.

Ruth Nelson, as his mother, gives a splendid performance
as she foresees the harm which threatens him through his association with this woman of the world and tries to reunite him with his
childhood sweetheart (Joan Chandler).   Oscar Levant, as Garfield's
close friend and frequent accompanist, contributes light touches to
the drama by his cynical wisecracks and is well cast.   J. Carrol
Naish has the role of Garfield's father, and Craig Stevens is the
man about town who escorts Joan Crawford on some of her drinking
sprees.

The story ends, appropriately enough, on the notes of Tristan und Isolde, as Garfield makes his debut with the Philharmonic
following a successful tour.

Isaac Stern is one of the many talented soloists to be heard
in the picture, and much of the music was recorded with full symphony.   Among the several outstanding musical numbers is a viola
concerto which uses three melodies from Carmen.
                                   --Fortnight, Vol. 1, No. 5
                                   (December 30, 1946), page 42.

☐ I MARRIED A WITCH (Paramount/United Artists, 1942)

Warlocks, sorceresses and assorted abracadabra are taken
for a satirical ride on their own broomsticks in René Clair's sly

diversion, I Married a Witch.   Caviar comedy it is, chuckleful and
enchanting,   and the screen has not had a more intriguing figure
than modern Jennifer, 290, 000-year-old descendant of a thaumatur-
gical family acknowledgedly responsible for Pompeii's demolition,
Rome's fall and, possibly, not inactive in the more iniquitous activities of Atlantis, Sodom and Gomorrah.   Veronica Lake's wraithlike
charm admirably suits the bewitching witch, and Fredric March, as
her victim from Puritan days on, has a role quite as congenial as
the high comedy assignments he played so convulsingly in the nos-
talgically remembered Nothing Sacred and Laughter.   Cecil Kellaway, too, is proficient as the wizard whose prowess fails under the
regime of the Daemon Rum.

Clair surveys the contemporary American scene with wit and
wisdom, twits us gently for our moralistic rituals, governmental
foibles and passion for the practicalities of life.   The scene in
which the malevolent maid yearns to relinquish her Powers--for
love--and wants to be just a simple girl who can light a fire with
a match instead of a rune, and the sequences building the gubernatorial campaign are as brilliant examples of cinematic humour as
the camera and sound track have captured.   I Married a Witch
casts a comedic spell all its own, and is recommended to all who
have ears, eyes and heart for an imaginative peregrination.
                              --Herb Sterne in Rob Wagner's
                                Script, Vol. 27, No. 644 (De-
                                cember 19, 1942), page 22.

                    *   *   *

A happy meeting of sympathetic talents is responsible for the
movie of I Married a Witch.   The late Thorne Smith, whose Topper
stories set a style in movie fantasy, wrote the book, which he
called The Passionate Witch.   It is an adult fairy tale about a New
England gubernatorial candidate who is suddenly visited by a witch.
The beautiful and malicious creature turns his smug existence upside down till she's caught and weds her victim.

Preston Sturges, Hollywood's most successful pixie, produced the film; René Clair, French satirist who created Sous les
Tois de Paris and The Ghost Goes West, directed it.   Marc Con-
nelly, author of the stage fantasy Beggar on Horseback, wrote
the script.   And, for perfect casting, Veronica Lake is the
witch.

The sum of their individual achievements is the sprightliest,
most original movie story of the season.
                              --Louise Levitas in PM (Novem-
                                ber 1, 1942), page 29.

☐ I REMEMBER MAMA (RKO, 1948)

    *This department saw John van Druten's I Remember Mama
several times on Broadway, and again, including rehearsals, as a
Little Theater production in Wilton, Conn. Ordinarily, it should be
somewhat tedious to sit through it once more as a film, particularly
as van Druten's dramatization of Kathryn Forbes's best seller,
Mama's Bank Account, is not easily susceptible to the movie medium.   Fortunately, George Stevens's expert direction and a fine cast
overcome any difficulties involved, and Mama and the rest of the
Hansons are welcome back.

    DeWitt Bodeen's sympathetic screen adaptation naturally gets
this Norwegian-American family outdoors a bit more in San Francisco of 1910 and, just as reasonably, adds a touch of sentiment
that might be classified as corn by those who saw Mama on the
stage. But otherwise this is the same warm, honest, and tenderly
amusing play that van Druten wrote and directed in 1944 as if he
had all the time in the world and didn't mind talking about the Hansons indefinitely.

    If you want to be captious about it, Mama does skip from
one anticlimax to another before it settles down. But so much the
better, as long as the Hansons are with us. Irene Dunne, wearing
a blond wig and conjuring up an acceptable accent, does a fine job
as Mama, who bolsters her family with a fairy story about their
fictional bank account. Mama, as you remember, has four children,
an appreciative husband (Philip Dorn), three sisters with minor
emotional problems, and an Uncle Chris (Oscar Homolka) who has
a heart of gold, a brassy voice, a mistress (the film has him married to the girl), and a rugged capacity for alcohol.

    Mama reaches for the coffeepot when the situation is strained
and is given to saying "Is good" whenever she feels it psychological-
ly useful. In fact, Mama is altogether a wonderful person who can
take any family crisis in her stride with understanding and a matri-
archal tolerance.

    Barbara Bel Geddes is charming as the eldest daughter who
narrates Mama's story in a series of flashbacks, and Cedric Hardwicke appears impressively, if briefly, as an impecunious boarder
who departs hastily, paying off the Hansons with a bad check and
his contribution to their ultimate literacy. Possibly for the benefit
of the matinee masses, Rudy Vallee is cast as a bearded doctor
and Edgar Bergen as a timid mortician who wants to marry into
the family. There is no nonsense about their roles, and both are
quite good. But, next to Miss Dunne's Mama, this film belongs
to Homolka, who can draw that slender line between hamming and

acting, and is the same blustering, bibulous Uncle Chris that he
was when he created the role on Broadway.

--Newsweek (March 29, 1948),
page 80.

*   *   *

Once in a while a gem of a film comes along to warm the
heart and confirm one's faith in the movies as rewarding entertainment. Such a film was Going My Way. Another was Life with
Father. Such a one is the new RKO film called I Remember Mama.

In its several phases--as New Yorker sketches by Kathryn
Forbes, in book form, as a play by John van Druten, finally as a
motion picture--Mama has proved to contain the sort of homely humor that goes straight to the heart. Its Norwegian-Americans,
with their naivete and their good heartedness, are exceptionally
lovable characters.

There is not much to describe in the way of plot, for Mama
is merely a set of loosely connected reminiscences about a San
Francisco family's domestic crises and humors, and an affectionate
portrait of the matriarch of the family.

This altogether delightful material has been adapted for filming with conspicuous skill. Carefully avoiding either mawkishness
or bathos, George Stevens, executive producer and director, staged
it like a man who must have had a mother himself. Actress Irene
Dunne, who surpassed herself in Life with Father, does a still finer job here. You will not soon forget her Mama, nor Barbara Bel
Geddes' Daughter Katrin, nor Oscar Homolka's Uncle Cris. The
entire cast of this enchanting film performs with sensitivity--making
I Remember Mama a film experience you must certainly treat yourself to.

--Fortnight, Vol. 4, No. 8 (April
9, 1948), page 30.

☐ IT'S A WONDERFUL LIFE (Liberty/RKO, 1946)

It's a Wonderful Life is a wonderful title for a motion picture
about which practically everyone who sees it will agree that it's
wonderful entertainment. The film marks Frank Capra's first production since his return from distinguished war service, and he has
invested it with the tremendous heart that always stamps his offer-
ings as above average. This couldn't be other than a Capra picture,
the humanness of its story the dominant factor at every turn of situation. His direction of the individual characterizations delivered is
also distinctively his, and the performances, from the starring roles
of James Stewart and Donna Reed down to the smallest bit, are
magnificent. When Capra is at his best, no one can top him.

The story opens imaginatively upon Heavenly constellations that are twinkling and conversing. They are talking about a fellow down on earth who requires some guidance. To provide him the help he needs, a neophyte angel, still in the process of earning his wings, is dispatched to take over the case of George Bailey. But before he starts he has to know considerable about George's early life.

When he was merely a youth, George jumped into a lake to save his brother from drowning. This act brought partial deafness to George, a disability that kept him out of the army when World War II came along. Meanwhile he had married his childhood sweetheart and was raising a little family of his own in a typically American small-town community, called Bedford Falls. He had taken over the management of the building and loan association and was bucking a local Scrooge who had jockeyed him into a position where he could be dealt misery. All these troubles came to a head during a Christmas season.

It was then that George, in a moment of weakness, wished he had never been born. The fellow from Heaven, named Clarence, who was assigned to watch out for him, granted that wish. In the fantastic events that follow George is brought to a realization of how much his apparently aimless existence has meant to others and he retracts his wish. For showing him the futility of feeling futile, Clarence is rewarded with a beautiful pair of wings. Capra's trick rests in the fulsome manner in which he allows a motion picture audience to share in the glory.

The musical score to accompany this story was written and directed by Dimitri Tiomkin and its value to the narrative is frequently out of this world. You will look far to find a finer score for a dramatic film. The photography by Joseph Walker, the credit for its completion shared by operative cameraman Joseph Biroc, is superior on all counts. So is the small-town atmosphere captured by the art direction and other technical aids. This is indeed a superb start for the company that calls itself Liberty Films and is headed by Capra, George Stevens, William Wyler and Samuel J. Briskin.

James Stewart is distinctively Jimmy Stewart as George Bailey, his initial role in Hollywood after five years in the armed forces. He gives Capra everything that is asked for, and he does it with the real authority of understatement. Donna Reed lends lovable personality to the childhood sweetheart he marries, ever a typical American wife and mother. No one could have bettered Henry Travers in the richly amusing part of the angel, Clarence.

Then there is Lionel Barrymore making the town banker even more of a Scrooge than anyone else could have. Thomas Mitchell is a splendid drunken Uncle Billy and Beulah Bondi a glorious mother for George. The kid brother is tellingly played by Todd Karns, of whom more will be heard, and the girl who is his ro-

mance is neatly portrayed by Virginia Patton.   Performing the girl
who has been given a bad name in town, Gloria Grahame will win
a lot of personal attention.

Small-town characters are brought to vivid life by Frank
Faylen, Ward Bond, H. B. Warner, Frank Albertson, Charles Williams, Mary Treen and Sarah Edwards.   A stunning gem is that of
a bartender by Sheldon Leonard.   The roles of the central characters as children are sharply done by Bobbie Anderson, Ronnie
Ralph, Jean Gale and Jeanine Ann Roose.   George Bailey's children are respectively Carol Coomes, Karolyn Grimes, Larry Simms
and Jimmy Hawkins, and are all excellent.

--Jack D. Grant in The Hollywood
Reporter, Vol. 91, No. 36
(December 19, 1946), page 3.

*   *   *

The prewar movie-hit team of ex-Col. James Stewart,
USAAF, and director ex-Col. Frank Capra, USASC, have rejoined
forces to produce another boxoffice hit.   Their third joint effort,
It's a Wonderful Life (others: You Can't Take It with You, Mr.
Smith Goes to Washington), is in this pair's familiar high-entertain-
ment vein--a grand and heart-warming film as American as apple
pie--overflowing with bright comedy, gentle humor, chuckling
homey philosophies and poignant drama.   Characteristically, it
has a moral.   Once more Capra and Stewart extol the democratic
idea, praise and poke good-natured fun at the Common Man--
picturing his courtship and marriage, his happiness and misery,
and bringing him perilously close to disaster before allowing him
to win his inevitable victory over public enemies Greed, Corruption
and Selfishness.

David smiting Goliath in the common good has long been a
favored Capra theme.   In his Mr. Deeds Goes to Town the small-
town yokel emerges triumphant over big city temptations and the
menace of sudden wealth.   In Meet John Doe Capra's minor league
baseball player-turned-crusader in pitched battle slays the demon of
embryonic fascism.   In Mr. Smith Goes to Washington Capra-Stewart
pictured the desperate but inevitable victory when a finally aroused
citizen single-handedly fights political corruption in high places.
And in It's a Wonderful Life the same team proves to every man's
satisfaction that the life of one poor man who does good is of far
greater value--to himself, his family and his community, to society
in general and to God in particular--than the existences of all the
money grubbers who live only to attain success in a worldly sense.
The rewards that accrue to the man of good will, say Messrs.
Capra and Stewart, are beyond measure.

In making Wonderful Life, four-time Academy Award winner
Capra abandoned one long-time film habit, kept another.   For years
he has filmed two endings to every picture, choosing finally the one
favored by sneak preview audiences.   This time the film's original

ending--fantastic as it is--remains unaltered. Every Capra film
includes a torrential rainstorm or blizzard. Wonderful Life is no
exception. Just as Cecil DeMille's bathtub scenes are his trade-
mark and Hitchcock's brief appearances in his films his, so Capra's is a heavy snow or rain ("It lends emphasis to the dramatic
value of a scene"). Refusing old-fashioned cornflakes for his big
snow scene in Wonderful Life, Capra employed a new device that
sprays chemicals through nozzles under high pressure, forming
fluffy flakes in the best imitation-snow tradition. For real Winter
scenes filmed at the gigantic RKO-Studio ranch, Capra also used
3,000 tons of shaved ice, 300 tons of "limestone" snow, and 50
tons of "white plaster" snow.

In the course of the comedy-drama which marks the return
of Stewart and Capra to Hollywood seemingly hopeless frustration
is turned into success. Stewart, in the role of a small town citizen whose whole life has been a record of worldly failure, discovers in time that actually he has achieved far more than most
men ever do. As a boy he lost part of his hearing while rescuing
his younger brother from drowning; as a young man he surrendered
his dreams of world travel to stay home and help support the family
his father had left unprovided for. Later he gave up college to
work in a tottering building loan society, and helped save the homes
of people who had depended upon his father for help. He worked
nights to finance his younger brother's college career; he gave up
his freedom and hopes of ever leaving his one-horse town when he
found himself suddenly married and soon burdened with children,
debts, obligations, and commitments unending. Finally, faced by
jail for a crime he did not commit, but responsibility for which he
assumes to shield another, he rebels and wishes he had never been
born. In a fantasy, now, he sees what his town might have been
like had he never been born--and it is not good. He sees how much
misery he had prevented, in one fashion or another, and how much
happiness he had brought to many people; how many lives, unknow-
ingly, he had been the instrument of saving. He sees how no man
lives for himself alone, and how every man's life touches the fate
of more people than he can ever know.

Aside from the obvious moralizing, It's a Wonderful Life is
excellent drama, fine comedy, filled with the warm and sympathetic
directorial touch of Capra and the catalytic ingratiating performance
of Stewart. The supporting players are no less competent: Donna
Reed as the girl he loves, playing with him two of the funniest
courtin' scenes the screen has seen; uncle Thomas Mitchell, father
Samuel S. Hinds, druggist H. B. Warner, mother Beulah Bondi and
Lionel Barrymore.

                              --Cue (December 21, 1946) pages
                                16-17.

☐ JANE EYRE (20th Century-Fox, 1944)

Although there is neither credit nor reference made to David
Selznick's pre-production preparation on Jane Eyre, the film bears
that gentleman's unmistakable signature.   The mark of his congenital
good taste, sense of beauty, and literate regard for a literary work
is there, and the filmic transcription of the Charlotte Brontë novel
should prove a satisfaction even to the more rabid devotées of the
Victorian scrivener.

Exquisitely designed by William Periera, the photoplay soars
through a series of sets that provides precisely the right atmosphere for the low-key love story, and the poetic and superbly penned
screenplay by Aldous Huxley, Robert Stevenson and John Houseman
condenses, contours and dramatizes the novel without in any way
outraging the fundamentals of the original.

Even though one could fuse the descriptive passages of the
heroine in the written work, and have a sculptor model the words,
there could not possibly be a more perfect result than that evoked
by Joan Fontaine.   She mirrors the text as flawlessly as one could
expect or wish, and her performance, at all times, is a gracious
and moving thing.   However, Orson Welles's Rochester is obviously
the product of faulty casting.   The actor, feeling his inadequacies
in a romantic role, has italicized the macabre measures of the
character, and fashioned a performance so completely operatic that
the spectator is continuously amazed that dialogue, rather than a
Verdi aria, escapes from his lips.

Peggy Ann Garner, a diminutive Lillian Gish, is a delight,
and there are other portraits of excellence from Agnes Moorehead,
Henry Daniell, Mae Marsh, and "The Divine Sara" Allgood.

Only Hillary Brooke strikes a discordant note, somewhat
confusing her assignment as Blanche Ingram with that of an Earl
Carroll cutie descending that white satin spiral stairway currently
being featured in "V for Venus."

--Herb Sterne in Rob Wagner's
Script, Vol. 30, No. 673
(February 19, 1944), page 18.

*   *   *

There is no disputing this is an "arty" hit.   It is production
achievement all the way.   That kind that rears its beautiful head for
Academy Award nomination--in production finesse, directorial fine
points, characterizations supreme.

But Jane Eyre is cruel enough to be drab in many spots.   It
savors a bit too strongly of "the theatre" to be as cherished by the
masses in this day and age.

As for characterizations, it is almost entirely Orson Welles' show. A perfect vehicle for his histrionics--as we have come to know him on screen, stage and radio. This is said in no disparagement. His delineation of Rochester is as near perfection as could be imagined.

[Jane Eyre] depends mainly upon the building up of sympathy--first, for Jane as a child and then as the governess in love with her master. Yet, somehow, the sympathy for the master takes over and the audience is induced to hope that she'll stick with him. As for general satisfaction, however, the main elements are left to the appreciation of production and direction quality--and the performances of the entire cast, from Welles to Ethel Griffies, the keeper of the insane wife.

A juvenile artist, Peggy Ann Garner, who portrays Jane as a child, is used to set the performance pace--and what a pace. She does such a remarkable job that there is little doubt that the characterization of the same role later by Joan Fontaine is somewhat dimmed. Not that Miss Fontaine faltered even slightly. She is magnificent. But there was no chance of topping that performance of her kid days by little Peggy Ann.

Then, too, the handicap for Miss Fontaine, of playing "up" to Mr. Welles, who is by character the center of attraction whenever he is on scene. And, you may rest assured, Mr. Welles was consistently in the center of that spotlight through sheer artistry.

And another moppet, the very clever Margaret O'Brien, is in there pitching a grand job as Adele, the adopted child of Rochester. But, grand as her performance is, comparison with that of Peggy Ann Garner again had the dimming effect.

Great trouping by Sara Allgood as housekeeper Bessie, Agnes Moorehead as Aunt Reed, Henry Daniell as the cruel Brocklehurst, and John Sutton as the good Dr. Rivers, top the balance of the featured players.

In the supporting players, it is John Abbott as the brother of the insane wife who knew the castle's secret that steals most of the honors, but Aubrey Mather, Edith Barrett, Hilary Brooke, Barbara Everest and Ethel Griffies all come in for spotlight briefs.

--Hollywood Motion Picture Review,
Vol. 30, No. 4 (February 7,
1944), page 6.

□ JOAN OF ARC (Sierra/RKO, 1948)

Nearly $5,000,000 was spent by producer Walter Wanger on this gigantic Technicolor drama of France's great savior-saint--and

the picture shows every penny of it. The splendor of the pageantry
is overwhelming, the settings are stupendous, and the overall effect
--awesome, reverential, almost idolatrous--is overpowering.

Certainly, there is high drama inherent in the story of Joan
--a country girl who, in two crowded years, led an army, crowned
a king, conquered the English invaders, became the idol of her people, and died a martyr at the stake. But--even with the incomparable Ingrid Bergman in the title role--the enormous weight of
Wanger's gargantuan production frequently overshadows the drama
of the simple shepherd girl, while the involved and tedious pro-
cesses of the Church trials that condemned her to death consume
an unconscionable length of time and film--slowing down the last
hour of the picture to a snail's pace.

The screenplay by Maxwell Anderson and Andrew Solt is a
workmanlike job. But it bears no resemblance to Anderson's stage
play Joan of Lorraine, in which Miss Bergman had such a triumph
and never does it approach Bernard Shaw's Saint Joan, with its
brilliant and incisive interpretation of the vast forces that combined
to raise Joan to her great eminence and then destroy her. As presented, this Joan of Arc is a colossal and colorful historical pag-
eant--an eye-filling procession of scenes picturing the chain of
known events in Joan's life, from the day in February 1429 when
she first appeals to Robert de Baudricourt to take her to the Dauphin, until, two years later when, fallen and in disgrace, she is ex-
communicated by the Church at Rouen, and burned as a heretic.

There has been some attempt to forestall history here by in-
dicating that the French Bishop of Beauvais, who betrayed Joan to
the English and the stake, did not act with the sanction of Rome.
The Church's claim to infallibility is not subjected to question since
the Bishop, as a minor cleric, could have been and was (as the
Church later maintained) in error. A quarter of a century later
Joan was officially vindicated and five hundred years later she was
canonized. Thus the Church publicly atoned for its error, if any.
But the film is, nevertheless, careful to state pointedly that the
iniquitous Bishop acted on his own in persuading the judges of the
University of Paris and the prosecutor of the Holy Inquisition to
agree with his point of view regarding Joan and her "voices."

Although Joan of Arc may wander from the path of historical
accuracy, as straight film entertainment the picture is a tremendous
and impressive spectacle. Its elaborate authenticity in costume,
setting and period detail is nothing short of amazing. The battle
scenes are an unsurpassed photographic and directorial achievement.
Perhaps never before have such breathtaking sequences been filmed
as those involving the massed army assault upon the fortresses surrounding Orleans. They picture the march of the opposing French
and English armies, with banners flying, with armored knights upon
prancing horses, with foot-soldiers as far as the eye can see; the
bombardment by the earliest cannon used in European wars; the advance of the French bowmen behind barn-door-sized shields mounted

on huge wheels, the raising of the assault ladders against the but-
tressed stone forts; the use of catapults, flaming arrows, swinging
sword, and mace, and pike-staff.   The pomp and panoply and medi-
eval beauty of the Dauphin's court and the wondrous splendor and
magnificence of Charles' coronation in the Cathedral at Rheims are
awe-inspiring.

All this is the stirring stuff of motion picture spectacle.   It
is only to be regretted that the story had not been treated more
like the drama it is and less like the adoration of a saint.   The
reverential hush with which the picture was made, under the direction of Victor Fleming (Gone with the Wind), has a blanketing effect
upon the performance of Miss Bergman.   Even so, she triumphs
over the difficult assignment of picturing a shepherd girl, general,
king-maker, martyr and saint all rolled into one, and makes of this
complex character a completely believable, real and ingratiating
personality.

The rest of a notable cast (4000 players, of whom 248 have
speaking parts) gives Miss Bergman and the production fine support.
Among them: José Ferrer, splendid as the Dauphin, J. Carrol
Naish, Francis L. Sullivan, Ward Bond, John Emery, George Coulouris and many more.

--Cue (November 13, 1948), page
20.

*   *   *

Most overwhelming picture of the year from the point of view
of pageantry is Sierra Pictures' (Walter Wanger, Victor Fleming,
Ingrid Bergman) Joan of Arc.   Photographed in Technicolor and
staged on a grand scale, Joan has all those spectacular filmic qualities that used to be termed "colossal."

Aside from its pageantry, though, the current Joan is not a
very memorable film.   But it has its points.   Maxwell Anderson
and Andrew Solt have written a studious screenplay, whose greatest
virtue is that it makes of historical, semi-legendary characters
lifelike personalities.   And producer Walter Wanger and director
Victor Fleming, both experienced in mounting large-scale cinematic
undertakings, have made Joan big and pretty.   The "big" scenes are
the best; intimate sequences, such as those at the beginning, call
for acceleration.   And the final reels dwell so laboriously on Joan's
trial, they become, frankly, tiresome.

Miss Bergman, of course, dominates the film.   Every scene
testifies to her sensitivity as an artist and to her effortless technique.   Few actresses can project such glowing sincerity.   But her
concept of the character is another matter.   Hers is a sweet, modest, girlish Joan, a peaches-and-cream Joan, well-scrubbed in the
midst of battle, primly distressed by her rough surroundings.   The
Maid of history must have been a more forceful personality, if a
less decorative one.

The cast is so large and so uniformly good that it is unfair to single out names for mention--except for one. José Ferrer, in his first role in pictures, does a fascinating piece of work with the complex character of the Dauphin. He deserves to be heard from again.

--Fortnight, Vol. 5, No. 13
(December 17, 1948), page 31.

*   *   *

In an inspired performance, Ingrid Bergman portrays the last three years in the earthly life of Saint Joan. It is not difficult to believe that the heroine of the beautifully made movie, Joan of Arc, was a saint; what is more difficult to believe as one watches reel after reel of this handsome film is that this Joan was also a real flesh-and-blood girl. At times Bergman moves as if in a trance; she is actually hearing the voices from heaven that told her she must drive the English from French soil; but we can't help wishing that we could also be made to believe that she heard and faced the temptations of everyday life--that she had a few of the earthly troubles that most of us have to meet. It is true that in the big scene in which she finally submits to her judges ("I would rather abjure than be burned") Joan is human; her fear of fire drives her to deny the voices. But later Joan the saint, admitting her mistake in abjuring, realizes that to live without faith is more terrible than the fire, more terrible than dying young.

Because Joan is practically always portrayed as a saint, it is difficult for us to project ourselves into the film. We are naturally interested in Joan and we watch her with fascination as she goes through the familiar episodes from Domremy with her family, to Vaucouleurs, where she wins the governor (George Coulouris) to her cause, to the court at Chinon, where the tricky Dauphin (expertly played by José Ferrer) is finally convinced of her mission. The picture takes on even greater interest as we see Joan with her captains, commanding her army and in battle.

The scenes of the trial and the burning are by far the most interesting, although the whole picture deserves praise for its magnificent pageantry and handsome Technicolor that brings out the beauty of the regal and clerical apparel. Perhaps what intensifies the fascination of the trial episodes is our realization that in spite of Cauchon's determination to find Joan guilty of heresy, the trial itself was conducted with more fairness than most trials of its day. While the prisoner was by no means treated with dignity or even decency as a person, she was allowed her say; and Joan handled herself well.

The script, written by Maxwell Anderson and Andrew Solt, should be credited for using as many of the accepted Joan quotations as possible. The main trouble with this script, as well as with the direction of Victor Fleming, is that the film makers were overawed by their subject. If possible in telling the story of Joan (and maybe

this cannot be done), the entire piece should be kept on simple, unpretentious terms.   While Walter Wanger merits praise for the
beauty of his production, one wishes he had stressed realism more
than splendor and that Joan's armor were not so shining or so
white.   But in spite of this armor (which too strongly recalls Ten-
nyson's Galahad), Saint Joan shines through Bergman's performance
and we can still hear her ringing speech to her army: "Our strength
is in our faith. . . .   We can win only if we become God's army--
only if we purge ourselves of sin. "

> --Philip T. Hartung in The Com-
> monweal (November 19, 1948),
> page 143.

☐ JOHNNY BELINDA (Warner Bros. , 1948)

Johnny Belinda might almost have been thought to be impossible movie material, considering the restrictions that are imposed
on film-makers.   For Elmer Harris' play was a violent drama in
which rape and murder figured strong.

Working with this original, scenarists Irmgard von Cube and
Allen Vincent, producer Jerry Wald, director Jean Negulesco and
photographer Ted McCord have fashioned a touching film that still
has raw ingredients but is characterized by such excellent taste and
restraint that it is one of the most compelling films so far shown
this year.

Johnny Belinda is the story of a deaf mute, played most appealingly in pantomime by Jane Wyman.   She is a shy, sensitive girl
who has never known affection.   Into the Cape Breton Island village
where Belinda lives comes an idealistic doctor (Lew Ayres), under
whose guidance the girl learns sign language.   Her life takes on
richness.   Then tragedy strikes: a drunken boor rapes her, and
she bears his child.   When her seducer attempts to steal the baby,
Belinda shoots him.

With such lurid material to deal with, it is horrible to think
what might have evolved.   But Johnny Belinda has been made with
tenderness.   The sombre little story has been given enormous poignancy and yet has been told with just the right restraint, so that it
is neither crude melodrama nor shameless tear-jerker, rather a
warm, intensely human, impassioned tragedy.

Jane Wyman's handling of her role is splendidly simple and
sincere.   Her expressive eyes tell more than any actress's since
Garbo, and she is all gentle grace and sweetness.   Lew Ayres delivers another of his fine performances, earnest and persuasive.
And Charles Bickford and Agnes Moorehead are superlative as Belinda's father and aunt.

> --Fortnight, Vol. 5, No. 9
> (October 22, 1948), page 29.

* * *

*In recent years Jane Wyman has deserted comedy for
straight drama with considerable success, notably in such films as
The Lost Weekend, and The Yearling. But in Johnny Belinda she
attempts the most exacting role of her career, and with her moving
portrayal of the drab, deaf-and-dumb slavey, Belinda McDonald,
converts a potentially turgid melodrama into an absorbing story of
simple folk in an isolated Cape Breton Island village.

Until the arrival of the young and idealistic Dr. Richardson
(Lew Ayres), Belinda is called "the dummy" by the townsfolk and
regarded as little better than a tractable animal by her embittered
father (Charles Bickford) and her frosty aunt (Agnes Moorehead).
But Richardson, who recognizes the girl's intelligence, undertakes
to teach her sign language. Then, as a new world unfolds, Fate
resumes dealing from the bottom of the deck.

Belinda is raped by a drunken Lothario (Stephen McNally)
and bears his child (the Johnny Belinda of the title). Her father
is murdered by the same lout who, in turn, is shot dead by Belinda
when he establishes a legal claim to her baby. That Belinda's or-
deal--a trial scene included--is finally crowned with a happy ending
is something of a miracle; but so is the fact that Direct Jean Negulesco, and Irmgard von Cube and Allen Vincent, who adapted the
Elmer Harris play, were able to avoid the mawkish. The rest is
Miss Wyman's delicate pantomime, and the intelligent playing of a
first-rate cast.

                              --Newsweek (October 4, 1948),
                                page 85.

☐ THE JOLSON STORY (Columbia, 1946)

Here is showmanship at its best, a film which tells a story,
an interesting story, through musical numbers. Usually filmusicals
are woven around a hackneyed, unbelievable plot and have little to
offer save lavish costumes, a few enchanting melodies, and pretty
girls.

This one is different. Based on the life of the mammy-
singer, it catches the spirit of Jolson and what he stood for in the
entertainment world. The story is simple, picking up Al (Larry
Parks) as a youngster in Washington, D. C., when he sings in the
gallery of a music hall and thereby gets his first taste of the theatre. From this moment, Jolson knows that his destiny lies behind
the footlights, and he joins a touring vaudeville act. This leads to

Broadway, where he meets his bride-to-be (Evelyn Keyes), and following their marriage, goes with her to Hollywood.

Produced by Sidney Skolsky, whose familiarity with show
business is far-famed, the plot serves as a showcase for many of
Jolson's famous melodies, sung by the mammy-singer himself and
dubbed in for Larry Parks to portray. Parks undoubtedly will win
an Academy nomination for his delineation of the character, for he
has all of Jolson's movements down pat, both while singing and in
his acting. Among the numbers you'll hear are such favorites as
"Mammy," "I'm Sitting on Top of the World," "You Made Me Love
You," "Swanee," "April Showers," and "Liza," all of which are
used to motivate the drama enacted on the screen. The color photography is exquisite. Alfred Green directed and the cast, without
exception, is well-chosen.

--Fortnight, Vol. 1, No. 1
(November 4, 1946), page 42.

*   *   *

This romantic, sentimental fabrication of Al Jolson's life will
please or displease according to one's stomach for the kind of thing
that the Jazz Singer stood for in the world of entertainment. It is
an unabashed record of his adventures in that world, lengthy with
incident and loaded with the easy, oversimplified, vulgar emotions
that brought him fame and fortune and made a fabulous, brassy
epoch in the history of the Broadway theatre. The adventures in
the film do not necessarily record the facts of Mr. Jolson's life,
they are undoubtedly sweetened up according to the accepted canons
of screen biography, the kind of nil nisi bonum rule that spotlights
the genius and the heart of gold, that draws its conflict from guileless misunderstandings and rigidly blacks out the scandalous, the
unpleasant, the awkward incidents. The Jolson of the story is always motivated by generous impulses, the happiness of his married
life (only one is mentioned) is marred only by the driving impetus
of his talent (he is always singing), his wife leaves him because
she feels herself to be an inadequate audience for him sitting at the
homey fireside. This line of kindness in this sort of film invariably reduces the hero to the mental status of a generous, talented,
heedless child, leaves the story writers with a namby pamby plot
to bite their nails over but saves many a burnt finger and a trodden
toe. In spite of these hazards The Jolson Story fares much better
than other recent biographies on celluloid. It does reflect the spirit
of his time, his flamboyant personality and the showmanship that
captured the applause of his generation. In doing this the picture
for all its sugar and spice, its amiable judgments, its facile mixture of the true, the near-true and the frankly invented, creates a
colorful, song crammed panorama of show business from one night
stands and minstrel shows to Broadway and finally to the sound
stages of Hollywood.

Mr. Jolson's story begins in a burlesque house in Washington
where he attracts the attention of a trouper by singing "On the Banks

of the Wabash. " The trouper persuades his parents to let little
Asa go on the stage and a career is launched that takes our hero
from a kid whistling in the gallery to an artistically grayed oldster
applauded into song in a Hollywood nightclub.   In the interim he
plays blackface for Lew Dockstader's minstrels, learns about jazz
in a "blues session" in New Orleans, hits the jackpot in Shubert's
Winter Garden, meets the girl of his dreams on Mr. Ziegfeld's
arm (in the film you spell it Julie Benson instead of Ruby Keeler),
makes the first talkie picture and retires into nervous boredom in
one of those modest little farms outside Hollywood.   All this takes
a couple of hours to tell so it is happily lashed with almost all the
songs Al made his own, with pleasant pictures of Cantor Yoelson's
family life, including a very effective episode in the synagogue and
snippets of theatrical life both high and low.   Thus freighted and
lapped in handsome Technicolor The Jolson Story makes an entertaining show, tuneful, clean and mildly informative, long on footage
and deep in hokum but stamped with the image of its hero.

    Larry Parks is a prettier Al than Al.   He is also an aston-
ishingly capable mimic.   And consanguine with his image is the
great Jolson voice, a voice whose dynamics seem to have lost nothing through the withering years.   Mr. Parks' skill and the magic
of movie technique have made possible an astounding fusion of two
people to create a memorable portrait.   Even Al Jolson should be
pleased with The Jolson Story.

                              --Arthur Beach in New Movies,
                                Vol. 21, No. 11-12 (November-
                                December 1946), pages 5-6.

☐ KEY LARGO (Warner Bros. , 1948)

    Key Largo is a moody and intense gangster drama--a sweep-
ing, exciting narrative that carries the spectator along in a fascin-
ated manner from its provocative opening to its suspenseful conclusion.   The Maxwell Anderson play on which it is based has some
psychological overtones, but these are not emphasized to the point
of minimizing the physical conflict and gunplay.   Rather both elements are adroitly blended to form a tense and vigorous drama that
is inevitably headed for a leading position on Warners' list of top
grossers this year.

    Jerry Wald contributes a really outstanding production job.
His supervision of all the elements, ranging from the screenplay
through the technical points and casting, helps make Key Largo the
excellent and unusual show that it is--an underworld piece with
class.   John Huston's direction, accomplished in terse, taut style,
has an intimacy about that gets deep inside the various characters.
The effect makes for electrifying melodrama.

    Key Largo is one of the Key Islands off the coast of Florida
--a sparsely-settled, little-known outpost where Indians live in tribes

and where the nearest thing to activity is the fishing facilities for
sportsmen.   Lionel Barrymore is the proprietor of a sporting lodge
that is surprised by the off-season visit of Edward G. Robinson,
accompanied by a group of men.   Another visitor is Humphrey Bogart, ex-army officer who has come to see Barrymore and tell the
old man about the death of his son.   Eventually Robinson's identity
as a gangster is revealed, as is the purpose of his stay--to sell a
stack of counterfeit bills which he has imported from Cuba.   A
battle of wits ensues between Bogart and Robinson--a battle that
brings death to two Indians and kills off Robinson's henchmen before
the army man finally disposes of the evildoer.

Humphrey Bogart, looking more like a human being than he
has in some of his recent characterizations, gives his usual strong
performance of the soldier.   It is an excellent portrayal that gains
stature because of the absence of overdone heroics.   Edward G.
Robinson is impressive as the gangster--a familiar part for him
which he plays with broad, punchy gestures.   Lauren Bacall, the
widow of Bogart's buddy, gives a most charming account of herself
in a part singularly free of artifices and affectations.   Lionel Barrymore is his most excellent self as the crusty innkeeper.   As for
Claire Trevor, her performance as a dipso and Robinson's moll is
one of those superlative jobs of acting that comes from this performer whenever she is given the opportunity.   It is played thoughtfully and intelligently, and reaches heights of pathos in the sequence
wherein she tries to recapture the days of her singing career.
Thomas Gomez, Harry Lewis, John Rodney and Marc Lawrence
bring fine characterizations to the supporting cast.

Karl Freund's photography is distinguished by his artful use
of the close-up for dramatic effect.   Leo K. Futer's art direction
is in the mood of the locale and the drama itself.   Max Steiner contributes a vivid musical score, and Rudi Fehr's editing is a first
rate job.

                                        --The Hollywood Reporter, Vol.
                                        99, No. 30 (July 7, 1948),
                                        pages 3 and 4.

                              *   *   *

Time was, in the movies anyway, when gangsters were pretty
hot stuff.   But time passes.   Now it's the FBI man who is the popular hero.   Public enemies have come to be regarded as just that.

However, crime is still with us, and in Key Largo, a screenplay by Richard Brooks and John Huston freely adapted from a Maxwell Anderson play, the question is asked: What is the individual
to do about it?   When faced with a criminal element can one say it
is not his problem, or does a time arrive when the individual must
take a stand?

A tentative answer is arrived at in Key Largo when Humphrey
Bogart, as a disillusioned veteran (again!), finally concludes that as

long as there is evil anywhere, there is danger everywhere--and the individual must face it if he is to keep his conscience as a man. It is no new conclusion; the mystic John Donne noted in the 17th Century that no man is an island unto himself. But it is a principle that bears restating now and then.

Key Largo's setting is a Florida hotel, where Edward G. Robinson's gang is waiting to transfer counterfeit money. They have as virtual prisoners the hotel owner (Lionel Barrymore), his widowed daughter-in-law (Lauren Bacall), the dead son's war buddy (Bogart). There is a great deal of talk as these people, representing respectable society, exchange insults with the mob, and in the nature of things this makes for static melodrama. But Huston's direction furnishes mobility whenever possible. Toward the end the action finally moves outdoors, affording some slight relief.

On the whole, the picture rambles endlessly--and unavoidably --and is not very exciting. There are, though, some quite effective scenes. Besides Robinson, who is in top form, Barrymore excels himself, and Thomas Gomez and Claire Trevor impress favorably.

> --Fortnight, Vol. 5, No. 3
> (July 30, 1948), page 30.

☐ THE KEYS OF THE KINGDOM (20th Century-Fox, 1944)

The difficulties of making a religious picture seem to be almost insurmountable. The films that have been made with this in view within the freshness of memory have merely used the mechanics of religion. They have recorded the surface of piety. They have masqueraded in the habiliments of the church. For the most part if the religious furniture had been left out the films would very probably be just as effective as tales of good people. The movie maker has yet to realize, with any flavor of truth on the screen, the meaning of holiness. The possible exceptions are passages in The Song of Bernadette and even there a heavy hand often smudges the image. Going My Way is notable not because it has a church background or because its principal players wear cassocks but because it is a superbly executed human document. The stars could have played doctors in a struggling clinic without detracting very much from the film in entertainment, quality or message.

And that precisely is what is wrong with The Keys of the Kingdom when viewed as a religious picture. The Keys of the Kingdom is the story of a good man who works hard and sacrifices much to help people to a better, healthier, more enlightened life. In the prosecution of his vocation he has all the virtues to help him, humility, fortitude, temperance, justice, faith, hope and charity. He tends the sick, feeds and clothes the poor, teaches the ignorant. But all these things the philanthropist does. They are

not the primary duties of a priest. Nor are they primary constitu-
ents of what the Gospel calls "the more abundant life" in the realization of which religion resides. There are implications of this
realization in The Keys but they are far and away subordinated to
the kindly philanthropism by which the actions and labors of Father
Chisholm are explicitly characterized. In its accidentals only can
The Keys be termed a "religious" film or a Christian film. Of the
three most admirable people in it just one is a religious man, the
others are a pagan mandarin and an atheist doctor. The priest is
prompted to his heroism by the love of God, the mandarin is moved
by his sense of honor and the atheist by his humanity. All three
meet on the common ground of natural goodness. To contrast this
aspect of the film with the authentic religious qualities of Bernadette: Bernadette can meet none of her contemporaries except on
the plane of supernatural goodness. Not that she lacks the homely
every day virtues that one finds in Father Chisholm, but rather
that the point of view of the film is focused on her supernatural
life, on her dedication to God.

Setting aside The Keys as a religious film we can talk about
it on its proper level. The picture is static, most of the characters are types to be foils for the central figure, some of the scenes
raise the suspicion of artistic insincerity. The incidents, the actions of other characters are always pivotal to the missionary; he
is always in the focus of the camera; it is his personality that gives
the film its life, its power to move with emotion, its meaning.
Emerging from this concentration is a powerful, heart warming
delineation of a noble man. Contrastingly, the parts of the doctor,
the bishop, the two monsignori, the reverend mother, the mandarin
and the Chinese mission boy are only sketched in outline. Each
might be characterized by an abstract noun such as humanity, understanding, pretentiousness, officialism, dedication, generosity and
faithfulness. What color and life the roles have come out of the
personalities and creativeness of the performers.

Some of the mechanics of the plot and at times the straining
after emotional effect are disturbing and unfortunate. As a boy
Francis' parents are killed, the result of local bigotry in Scotland.
As a young man at school he stays away from his girl so long that
she loses her grip, gets in trouble and dies in illegitimate child-
birth. That, together with kindly pressure from a clerical friend
of his sends him into a seminary whence he emerges to an unsuccessful career as a curate in several parishes in Scotland. Pretty
much of a failure, his old mentor at school, now a bishop, urges
him to go to China as a missionary. He consents, and, after some
hard going, makes a success of his mission. Finally, an old man,
Father Chisholm is recalled to Scotland and threatened with retirement from his village church by reason of poor administration and
odd doctrine. Most of the sequences are good in themselves but
they are hinged together by the most obvious contrivance. The violent episode in his childhood is no more necessary for his impulse
to piety than is needed the sad and not wholly understandable de-
struction of his love affair to push him into Holy Orders. His ca-

reer is a series of dragged-in vexations: faithless converts, unsympathetic mission nuns, pompous clerical superiors, revolutions,
fires, loss of friends, rival missionaries; and the only thing they
do is extend the story and bring out the virtues with which the beset man is endowed.

On the credit side you have a superb cast, good production
and artfully emotional direction to create an illusion of life and
feeling that covers up quite amazingly the flaws of construction and
characterization in the script.   Gregory Peck as Father Chisholm
brings a restraint, simplicity and beauty to his part that illumines
the screen.   The other players make the most of their smaller and
more arid roles.   But probably it is in the Chinese that the more
authentic feeling in the film lies.   With a surpassing sense of form
and mobility they give distinction to the scenes in the picture in
which they take part.

> --Arthur Beach in New Movies,
> Vol. 20, No. 1 (January-
> February 1945), pages 5-6.

☐ THE KILLERS (Mark Hellinger/Universal, 1946)

Ernest Hemingway's superb short story, The Killers, forms
only the prologue to the film of the same title.   From the murder
of Swede, Anthony Veiller capably carries the tale back to the motivations behind the murder.   In the main, it is a good job of match-
ing moods and manner.

Director Robert Siodmak and Cameraman Woody Bredell have
collaborated to fine effect in stiffening the elongated story line, and
the result is worth one's evening in the theater.   Tough, rough and
sordid, the film never compromises with its subject matter.

One of the major surprises of this or any other year is
Vince Barnett's appearance in a dramatic role.   Known heretofore
as a low comic, both in private and professional life, one is inclined to wonder at, and disinclined to pry into, the thaumaturgy
(black?) used by Siodmak to obtain this transformation for Barnett.
Edmond O'Brien, Queenie Smith, Phil Brown, and newcomer Burt
Lancaster all give impressive accounts of themselves.

> --Herb Sterne in Rob Wagner's
> Script, Vol. 32, No. 739
> (September 28, 1946), page 13.

☐ KINGS ROW (Warner Bros. , 1942)

As a novel, Kings Row pompously pretends to be a definitive
depiction of life in an American Midwestern hamlet.   Actually, the

author has performed a literary shotgun wedding between Zona Gale
and Baron Richard von Krafft-Ebing, the offspring being somewhat
of a bastard, combining the depressing traits of both parents.
Henry Bellamann, beckoning attention with a calculating finger, obviously employed wholesale sexual delinquencies in the not abtruse
conviction that any fictional work that combines incest, nymphomania, homosexuality, sadism and dementia praecox will send the
prurient-in-heart to the nearest bookseller, in droves.   Mania is
piled upon mania, excess upon excess, with the cumulative result
courting derisive laughter, rather than the titillation the scrivener
hoped to confect.

The film version of the tome, of course, has been somewhat
fumigated by the Hays' Production Code, but enough of the emotional oddities remain to furnish two harrowing hours in the theater.
Small-town life is surveyed in a distorting mirror: the "people"
are devoid of natural instincts and seem to find malformed tragedy
a normal habitat.   Wallowing in misery, the tale covers a multitude
of years, clutches its characters in an embrace as loving, as comfortable, as that of Torquemada's Iron Maid.   It's hell on the audience, too.

Technically, the photoplay is superb.   Casey Robinson has
maneuvered a literate transcription, which is cautiously dialogued,
imaginative in its transitional devices.   The screenplay is ably
abetted by Sam Wood's sensitive direction, Bill Menzies' singularly
effective production design.   A pity these substantial talents were
harnessed to a vehicle so festively morose, so frenetically depressing.

Ann Sheridan surprises by her comprehensive depiction of the
lass from the wrong side of the tracks.   She has added a new, human quality to her personality, convinces that she is no mere
oomph strawgirl, but is well on the way to becoming an actress of
understanding and tact.   Claude Rains, the pretty Kaaren Verne and
Nancy Coleman are effective, while Ronald Reagan again proves
himself one of the screen's most personable personalities.   Betty
Field pitches her performance in one wild-eyed key; as that is what
the assignment demands, Miss Field can nowise be condemned.
Robert Cummings, marcelled and otherwise ludicrously beautified,
performs a strenuous dramatic role as though he were appearing in
the front chorus line of the fourth touring company of "Oui, Oui,
Ouida!"

Kings Row is a cozy little chamber of horrors.   Shudder
fans, and those with a recherché sense of humor, may find it worth
their time.

                                        --Herb Sterne in Rob Wagner's
                                          Script, Vol. 27, No. 626 (April
                                          11, 1942), page 18.

*   *   *

Kings Row will give you that rare glow which comes from seeing a job done crisply, competently, and with confidence. It has such distinction that it is plainly too good for the shoddy fellowship of the "ten best pictures of the year." Let us simply record that in February 1942, Warner Brothers produced a good movie.

People who live in small towns really don't know any more about their friends and neighbors than do people who live in cities; the very fact that they see them every day, sitting on their front porches or strolling down to the village, prevents it. In these terms, growth or degeneration is imperceptible, and a catastrophe which is inevitable seems, when it finally occurs, merely inexplicable. (Pinch me, somebody; I'm talking this way about a movie.) This is the theme of the violent, chaotic novel by Henry Bellamann on which Kings Row is based. Casey Robinson, who did the adaptation, has done much to clarify the story and nothing to prettify it. He has gracefully dodged a good many censorship taboos; when he came up against a taboo too big to dodge--specifically, the one against incest--he left the problem to Sam Wood, the director, who found a perfectly adequate solution.

At Gone with the Wind, I got a severe attack of the bends before they had even finished fighting the War Between the States, so it is high praise when I say that Kings Row, which runs two hours and seven minutes, left me as fresh as a daisy. I wish I could understand the mechanics of the picture--how they combined dialogue, costuming, and set design to convey the variety of the social structure in an American town of the nineteen-hundreds, at the same time never forgetting its spot-on-the-map unimportance. Anyway, they did it. Of course, every movie has faults; in the case of Kings Row, the worst fault is the musical background, which telegraphs all the punches.

The cast includes Betty Field, Judith Anderson, Ouspenskaya, Claude Rains, Charles Coburn, Ronald Reagan, ROBERT CUMMINGS, and ANN SHERIDAN (Warner Brothers' billing). ANN SHERIDAN is completely convincing as a good-natured slut from the wrong side of the tracks, and ROBERT CUMMINGS, as the boy through whose eyes the story is seen, does well with a difficult sort of role. The Messrs. Coburn and Rains impersonate as psychopathic a pair of physicians as you'd find walking around outside of an asylum. It is the peculiar pleasure of Dr. Gordon (Mr. Coburn) to perform amputations without anesthetics, and Dr. Tower (Mr. Rains), no less peculiarly, keeps his daughter Cassandra (Betty Field) shut up in his house, away from the young men. Ronald Reagan capably breezes through the part of the town sport who becomes a victim of Dr. Gordon, and Judith Anderson will make your blood run cold with her account of the awful thing that happened when the deceased Dr. Gordon was laid out in his parlor.

--Russell Maloney in The New
Yorker (February 7, 1942), page
56.

☐ KITTY (Paramount, 1946)

    Kitty would like to appear a direct descendant of Amber St. Clare for purposes of boxoffice pelf, but it is also to be judged that she has a blood relationship to Liza Doolittle. The writing, I hurry to relate, is closer to the Winsor hovel than it is to the Shaw castle.

    This pageant of 18th-Century London is a handsome, slow and somewhat amusing movie of a wench no-better-than-she-should-be, who, praise be!, never receives her come-uppance, unless one subscribes to the Bolshevik belief that marrying a title and a fortune constitutes catastrophe.

    Paulette Goddard at no time has difficulty appearing beautiful, conniving, brittle and carnal, no more than which Kitty demands. Ray Milland has little to do beyond being arch, and trying not to look silly in hats that only the astounding style of Hedda Hopper could save from looking silly. Sara Allgood, all done up in a La Frochard makeup as a mistress of a Houndsditch stew, gives a wonderfully traditional performance, as does Constance Collier, portraying an aging damsel who spends most of her time on lost weekends.

                             --Herb Sterne in Rob Wagner's
                               Script, Vol. 32, No. 729 (May
                               11, 1946), page 23.

          *   *   *

    Kitty is a fascinating picture and one of beauty beyond words. Look at the technical credits listed above. For every man and woman artist and technician who had a finger in it, it is the finest screen work they have ever accomplished and redounds to their everlasting glory in this industry. There is pomp and splendor and pageantry in the superlative Leisen production investiture but it is a picture without a heart. We'd like to think that it was going to go out into release and become a thumping financial success just so that all its artisans who labored so magnificently over it could spread their fame the width of the world. But we cannot because we fear it is more a triumph of instruments and artistry than it is of emotional entertainment.

    It is not pleasant to say but the fault almost beyond question lies in the casting of Ray Milland as the hero. He is peculiarly cold and lifeless in a role that demanded to be clothed in all the warmth he could muster for it. Costume dramas are notoriously cold to begin with with their settings in a bygone day. Paulette Goddard is wonderfully warm and real as the dirty little urchin who rises to become the Duchess of Malmunster (her finest film work bar none) but the fire of her performing never serves to melt the icicle frigidity of Milland.

It was our great pleasure in a recent issue of this journal to herald the shining artistry and perfection of Ray Milland's performance in The Lost Weekend. That will always stand. With all humility and constructive criticism in mind, we must deplore the sullenness with which he attacks a rich and colorful role now in Kitty. Milland actually seems to be sulking his way through the entire film, unhappy in his casting, and it lies like a blight over the whole picture. He takes one back, in fact, to the unhappiness of his early work opposite Dorothy Lamour in such vehicles as Jungle Princess. Admitted it is a rather thankless role, nevertheless there was the opportunity to distinguish it in his inimitable style.

Besides the rich mimicry and deep understanding which Paulette Goddard brings to her little guttersnipe, the beauty of her face casts rich shadows over this story. She is wonderfully good as the Pygmalion creature created by the English nobleman so that he can marry off her beauty to someone of wealth and thus reap to pay his financial losses. She, of course, falls in love with him but lets him talk her into two marriages--one of gain and one of state--so that he may restore his standing in society. The Rosamond Marshall novel was a fascinating story and it has been given flavorsome film body by Karl Tunberg and the late Darrell Ware in their screenplay. The urchin character is fully rounded in her transition to great lady and it achieves its full measure of legitimacy in Goddard's playing and study of it. After she has borne her second husband, the Duke, his son and heir and he has died of age, the woman the urchin has become feels that now she has surely discharged her debt to the man who made her and that the way is clear for her to confess her love for him if he is so blind himself. This she does. Spurned, she finds something approximating love with his friend, the Earl of Carstairs. In what seems like a particularly vile trick, knowing now he is deeply in love with her and knowing she is more a true lady than many of noble birth, her creator brings in the old strumpet to whom the girl was bonded in the beginning. Trumping his ace card like the fine person she is, Kitty is kind to the old drunk, saves face with her Earl and turns tables on her creator. It ends wisely happily.

Many are the excellent performances Mitchell Leisen has extracted from his formidable cast. Miss Goddard's leads all but there is solid worth in the rich harridan of Constance Collier, the feeble old Duke of Reginald Owen, the Gainsborough of Cecil Kellaway, the Earl of Patric Knowles, Kitty's first husband by Dennis Hoey and Sara Allgood's old strumpet. Michael Dyne impresses favorably and strong as H. R. H. The Prince of Wales and there is a pathetic and excellently done bit by Heather Wilde.

The splendid individual scenes created by Leisen are without number so many are there. Daniel Fapp's absorbingly interesting camera has legs as Leisen takes it almost the entire length of a sound stage, up and down stairs, to follow the old Duke to the birth of his heir and his slow and faltering procession to his death. Gor-

geously staged is the scene in which the Duchess breaks her strand
of pearls and lapses into the forbidden Cockney of her birth with the
rich "Lor' lu'me, me beads!" In many, many ways this is an im-
maculately directed job and it is a monumental triumph for the sensitivity which always enriches Leisen's creations.

The real stars of this jeweled and brocaded Tunberg-Ware
production are the artists Leisen has selected to help him weave it
into the glowing tapestry it has become. To put one above the other would be most unfair but sharing large and importantly are Raoul
Pene du Bois, Daniel L. Fapp, Victor Young, Hans Dreier and
Walter Tyler, Ray Moyer and the other gentleman of the set decorations whose name is on the screen but not on the credit sheet;
Alma Macrorie, Gordon Jennings and Farciot Edouart, Madame
Karinska and Billy Daniels. A study of the intrinsic values that
have gone into the making of this brilliant production will prove to
you how important were the men and women behind the scenes.

But it is for these reasons that we fear its fate at the boxoffice. As a triumph of picture-making, to Hollywood and the industry it is without an equal. The public, not being appreciative
of the talents that make it so splendid, may wonder at its curious
lack of emotional warmth when they come to warm their hands before its high-powered star names and sensational advertising.
Mitchell Leisen's Kitty is Mitchell Leisen's Frenchman's Creek
without the Technicolor; it is Mitchell Leisen's Lady in the Dark
without the chi-chi and gingerbread and more substantially human.
And in these comparisons perhaps one may take heart when one
remembers that practically the same criticisms were hurled at
them. They cleaned up and were properly rewarded for their artistry when the public thronged to see their wonders. But they were
not too long remembered.

Kitty will be long remembered. She is a glowing creature
in Paulette Goddard's knowing hands. Women will love and understand her and, by exhibitor reckoning, that is all that counts. But
how it counts.

--Hollywood Review, Vol. 36, No.
5 (October 8, 1945), pages 3
and 20.

☐ THE LADY EVE (Paramount, 1941)

An amusing, well mounted, expertly written and brilliantly
directed Paramount picture. In estimating the values of a picture,
a reviewer has no way of knowing how praise should be distributed
between writer and director when record is being made of the
merits of the production. No such difficulty arises here; the writer
directed his own story, the third upon which he has done double
duty. Seems to me Preston Sturges is destined to gain recognition

as one of Hollywood's real geniuses.   Already established as a
writer of ability when he took on direction as an additional outlet
for his mental energy, in this, his third directorial venture, he
reveals a sureness, a sense of values and an eye for pictorial effect that any veteran director in the business would do well to
study.

Outstanding is Sturges's flair for a mobile camera, for
smoothly flowing visual motion to give emphasis to spoken lines.
He is not afraid to have characters speak when their backs are
turned to the camera.   He makes notable use of background action
to keep scenes alive when lines are being read in the foreground.
An example: when the principal characters are carrying the story
in dialogue spoken in close-ups in scenes on the deck of a steamer,
we have the lively chatter of a group of children playing outside
the camera lines.

Another feature of The Lady Eve which adds greatly to its
entertainment value, is the use of music as a story-telling element,
the manner in which it is woven into the action to become a part
of it.   The same can be said of the noise of a train which is rushing through the night.   It is a loud noise, but as it is just the
noise you hear when travelling in a Pullman at night, it does not
offend your ears.   The only jarring sound in the picture is the
voice of William Demarest, who shouts his lines.   That is the only
flaw in the direction, as Demarest can give a director anything the
latter wants.   The whole picture is mounted handsomely, the settings provided by Hans Drier and Ernst Fegte being notable examples of skilled designing.   Photography is up to the high standard
Victor Milner long since established for himself.   Paul Jones, producer of the picture, is to be commended for the fine job he made
of it.

The Lady Eve is a picture you should see, one which stu-
dents of the screen should study.   All performances are excellent.
Heading the cast are Barbara Stanwyck and Henry Fonda; in sup-
port are Charles Coburn, Eugene Pallette, William Demarest, Eric
Blore, Melville Cooper, Robert Greig, Martha O'Driscoll, Janet
Beecher, Dora Clement, Luis Alberni.

--Welford Beaton in Hollywood
Spectator, Vol. 15, No. 6
(March 15, 1941), pages 14-15.

*   *   *

When Christmas in July was previewed some months ago,
this department found cause to stand on its critical ear and chant
the praises of Preston Sturges.   It is a pleasure to record that the
writer-director's latest production, The Lady Eve, is every frame
as good.

This departs from the homespun standards to which Sturges
adhered in his first two pictures.   The Lady Eve is a glamour

comedy, handsomely mounted, sumptuously set.   From this it is
not to be deduced that the current frolic suffers from its opulent
mounting.   It is as gay, as debonair, as anything that's ever been
run through a projector.   Sturges continues his pursuit of originality in approach and procedure.   He has provided a picture that will
make you forget that you've just paid your income tax.

Henry Fonda, long entrapped in serious roles, dons romantic
make-up again and sails down the comedic fairway like a full-sailed
skiff in a stiff breeze.   He portrays a young ophiologist, who has
spent a year up the Amazon, away from all female society.   When
he encounters Barbara Stanwyck aboard an ocean liner, his methods
are so direct that she has cause to murmur, "I'm glad you weren't
up the Amazon two years!"   The plot doesn't matter much, but the
way Sturges constructs his comedy emphatically does.

Sturges piles gag upon gag with lightning rapidity.   Just
about the time one feels that he has heaped laughter as high as
possible, he adds a topper.   And the edifice still stands and doesn't
tumble into the debris of anti-climax!

Hank Fonda takes pratfalls, chinfalls and assorted tumbles
precisely as though he'd never heard of Tom Joad and Abe Lincoln.
The chap's an ace funster and here's hoping that he'll be assigned
more lightweight fare.   Barbara Stanwyck, for the second time this
week, proves delightful.   Charles Coburn gives another grand show
and there is assorted praise for Eric Blore, Eugene Pallette and
William Demarest.

I won't dwell on the intricacies of humor, Sturges' neat
combinations of silence and sound, the wonderful effects achieved
by quick shots in the train sequences.   Why detain you with a review when you can be on your way to the nearest film emporium
showing The Lady Eve?

> --Herb Sterne in Rob Wagner's
> Script, Vol. 25, No. 592
> (March 22, 1941), page 16.

☐   LADY FROM SHANGHAI (Columbia, 1948)

It has not yet been recorded that anyone ever fell asleep at
an Orson Welles movie.   Mr. Welles is lavish in the dispensing of
his varied talents: his rich imagination, his colorful performances,
the daring and frequently revolutionary uses to which he puts his
camera and soundtrack.

In The Lady from Shanghai Welles strikes a new level of excitement.   The picture itself is as phony as the distortion mirrors
he introduces in one hair-raising sequence; but it is presented with
a carefully calculated illusion of realism and hammer-blow impacts

that are magnificent tributes to the skill of the writer-star-producer-director, superb performances by a fine supporting cast, and the dynamic photography of Charles Lawton, Jr.

The plot of this nightmarish film revolves around a crazy and crooked romance between a naive young Irish-American sailor and a topaze-blonde lady of uncertain ancestry and no uncertain morals, who is married to a crippled and unbelievably evil criminal lawyer. All three, in one fashion or another, are entangled in the machinations of the husband's partner, an utterly loathsome perversion of a man. The key characters are as unpleasant a lot as you'd never care to meet on or off the screen; and by picture's end they have raced through most of the sins on the calendar--winding up in three, maybe four, murders, and a heart-clutching climax.

Welles, never keeping his camera quiet, aims it at a rapid succession of strikingly effective scenes--a hold-up in Central Park; a rowdy, beery conference in the hiring hall of the maritime union's headquarters in New York; menace-filled sequences aboard a yacht lazying about in the Gulf of Mexico; a prodigious day-and-night picnic in Acapulco; a lover's meeting in the dim corridors of San Francisco's Aquarium, plunk in front of a glass tank containing the ugliest deep-sea monsters dredged out of the seven seas; a murder down by the Sausalito waterfront; one of the most thrilling courtroom trials ever filmed; a manhunt in San Francisco's famed Chinese Mandarin Theatre; and, as a rousing climax, a breathtaking gunfight in the Crazy House of an oceanside amusement park.

This is visual entertainment at its exciting best, although a great deal of it is akin to Mr. Welles' sleight-of-hand tricks ("Now you see it, now you don't"). And this, aside from the exciting but frequently illogical story that spins do dizzily it's almost impossible to follow, is the entertainment essence of Welles' film. The star's performance is in the bravura tradition, marred from time to time by an exaggerated sing-song brogue so fragrant you can almost smell the peat-bogs of Ireland in it. Rita Hayworth as the evil lady of the case is glamorous and inscrutable in the fashion of movie ladies of mystery. Everett Sloane and Glenn Anders, as husband and friend, are thoroughly and satisfactorily repulsive--theatrical exclamation points punctuating Mr. Welles' snorting melodrama.

--Cue (June 12, 1948), page 20.

*   *   *

That bad boy of the arts, that latter-day Barnum from whom we have learned to expect almost anything--Orson Welles--is offering another film which he has written, produced, presumably directed, and acted. A few other people are employed in it, but that does not keep it from being distinctly a Welles show.

By now we have almost come to know what to expect of a "Welles show," but one is never positive. This time it is an intricately webbed drama of hate and intrigue with sinister undercurrents and violent grotesqueries. The characters of Welles' film are an unscrupulous band of human sharks who feed upon and are consumed by their own evil. Caught in the eddy of this whirlpool of evil are Welles, as a sailor of fortune, and Rita Hayworth, as a lady of mystery.

It can hardly be said that this infinitely detailed study of the multiple double-cross will please audiences looking for innocuous, relaxing entertainment. But there is no doubt that the film will have occasional fascination for some moviegoers who are more interested in the technique than the substance. For, as always, Welles has produced a flashy, bold, moody, uneven, unconventional show. Even if there is nothing at all here of lasting interest, it is often an intriguing show to watch.

--Fortnight, Vol. 4, No. 9
(April 23, 1948), page 30.

☐ LAURA (20th Century-Fox, 1944)

Laura is one of the best melodramas to flicker across a screen this season. The whodunit has been contrived with care, mood and style, and should rate high on the list of films one makes an effort to see.

Unlike most mystery photoplays, this accents atmosphere and character, which is all to the good in fabricating a passing reality that, for the time being, makes the spectator believe what he sees. Producer-director Otto Preminger subordinates the plot to people, and so generates an interest in the protagonists that is rare in such endeavors.

Dana Andrews filches top honors as the gent on the homicide squad. As an actor, Andrews has gained in veracity, and this performance is his best screen work despite the fact that he has groomed the man as though he were Philo Vance instead of a routine New York flatfoot. Gene Tierney, a beauty if I've ever seen one, has little difficulty in meeting the verbal glamour build-up given her by the opening reels of the plot, and Bonnie Cashin has gowned the damsel in some striking outfits that make Gene about the best dressed woman of this movie year. Judith Anderson is superb as a lady with no illusions, and Vincent Price, as her vis-à-vis, contributes his customary characterization of Francis X. Bushman to a part which, for once, requires precisely that quality. Clifton Webb makes an auspicious camera debut, though one is never quite able to shake off the eery feeling that one is really watching Monty Woolley bereft and bereaved of a beard. The excellent score by David Raksin is a sound reason to visit Laura, who is an intriguing gal, even though some of the "sophisticated" chatter sounds

as though it had been lifted from a column hatched by Katherine
T. Von Blon.

--Herb Sterne in Rob Wagner's
Script, Vol. 30, No. 693 (December 2, 1944), page 15.

*   *   *

Rarely does a serious crime drama get such sound and brilliant professional treatment on the screen as is the case with
Laura. Working with an exciting and consistently developed script
by Jay Dratler, Samuel Hoffstein and Betty Reinhardt, from Vera
Caspary's novel, Otto Preminger scores an extraordinary success
both as director and producer.

The performances are top-notch, credible, fascinating,
guided by logical behavior. The air of threatening reality which
Preminger [imparts is] supported further by contributions from
every technical department. It's a top-flight offering which should
get handsome returns.

The story is developed from the viewpoint of a young police
detective, Dana Andrews, assigned to uncover the mysterious murder of a young woman of prominence in a sophisticated professional
group. The dead girl is presumed to be a business woman, Gene
Tierney, whose career has been furthered by a strangely interested
newspaper columnist, Clifton Webb.

In the course of his investigations, the young detective falls
in love with her, posthumously, as he reads her love letters to
other men and haunts her apartment, alive with her personality.
Then, shockingly, the girl returns--from a period of retreat in the
country, not from the dead. The dead girl is a pretty and provocative model, of whom the other had every reason to be jealous because she had been making a play for the latter's fiancé. She had
been shot by mistake. So the mystery design is set, and in its
unravelment the detective finds fulfillment of his strangely begun
love.

Much of the tale is told in the glib narrative by Clifton Webb,
the columnist, who turns in an elegant role as one of the suspects,
glittering in characterization and crisp in dialog to make the part
memorable. Gene Tierney projects probably her most mature part
as the attractive, ambitious protégée of the vitriolic columnist, in
whom she incites a psychopathic possessiveness. Dana Andrews
skillfully holds his detective's character under restraint, managing
power and authority in his dealings with all the other principals.
Vincent Price leaves a vivid impression as the vacillating ne'er-do-
well who, in his way, loves and tries to protect the girl. Judith
Anderson, an older woman, pitches for Price and [embellishes the
part of the] loyal maid.

Laura is a crime story connoisseur's dish which has much

to sell as absorbing entertainment.

--Daily Variety, Vol. 45, No. 26
(October 11, 1944), page 3.

☐ LETTER FROM AN UNKNOWN WOMAN (Rampart/Universal-
International, 1948)

Letter from an Unknown Woman is one of those old-fashioned,
sentimental, lavender-cased pieces which have no particular resemblance to life, but which once had a great vogue in the theatre. It
belongs to the East Lynne era, when women were gentle creatures,
ruled by sentiment, easily seduced and betrayed, but, through it all,
bravely loyal.

Such tearful goings-on seem remote indeed in this more in-
delicate age, and it is questionable how much popular interest a film
like this can have today.   But there are always romanticists among
us and for them Letter is a field day; they will have a lovely time
dabbing away at tears as they watch beautiful Joan Fontaine suffer
her wistful passion for dashing Louis Jourdan, knowing these two
can never meet for a final blissful embrace.

--Fortnight, Vol. 4, No. 11
(May 21, 1948), page 30.

☐ A LETTER TO THREE WIVES (20th Century-Fox, 1949)

Because so much of Johnny Belinda was shot in Nova Scotia,
the picture seemed a bit more real than it should have.   In the
same way, the Hudson River and its towns and picnic spots help a
new film from Twentieth Century-Fox that would still seem fresh
and plausible without such reality.

The Fox picture, taken from John Klempner's novel A Letter
to Five Wives, belies Hollywood's reputation for megalomania; for,
though they used to say that our film-makers would cast a Biblical
picture with twenty-four apostles, Director-writer Joseph Mankiewicz
has reduced the title--along with the cast--to A Letter to Three
Wives. His screenplay makes the most of a suspenseful situation.
As three women leave to chaperon a children's picnic, they receive
a letter from a bitchy friend announcing that she is leaving town
with one of their husbands.   While they watch over the picnickers,
their minds and the screen go back to episodes in the past that show
why they may suspect their husbands of being just a little too ready
to fall for the blandishments of a classy and queenly dame named
Addie Ross.   This particular afternoon each husband had gone away
on some plausible excuse, and thus each wife returns to her home
with an apprehension shared by the film's audience.   Mankiewicz

has worked out the climax of the picture with even more skill than he gives to the individual flashbacks.   By cutting down the five wives to three, he has made Klempner's story more manageable and effective, without losing much of real value.

A Letter to Three Wives is bitter and truthful without risking the complete reality of the Italian pictures.   Occasionally Mankiewicz goes a bit overboard in comic exaggeration after the good old fashion of our popular cinema--probably under the misapprehension that the basic material of the story is not effective enough to insure big audiences.   For the greater part of the film, however, Mankiewicz is true to the realism in the novel, and he goes out of his way to say some cogent things about teachers and teaching.

The wives are excellently cast in Jeanne Crain, Linda Darnell, and Ann Sothern; the husbands, too, in Jeffrey Lynn, Kirk Douglas, and Paul Douglas.   The latter--snatched from his brilliant performance in Broadway's Born Yesterday--is outstanding as the bounding tycoon who is forced into marriage by old Mother Nature and a girl from across the tracks.   Hollywood seldom does better in either acting, writing, or direction than A Letter to Three Wives. Italy seems to have done so six times.

--Kenneth MacGowan in Script,
(March 1949), pages 46-47.

*   *   *

A Letter to Three Wives is a most ingenious job of moviemaking.   Its cleverly contrived screenplay concerns three suburban matrons whose husbands have been intrigued to various degrees by a temptress who is never shown in the film.   While they are on an excursion one day word comes to the wives that the female menace has run away with one of the husbands; which one is a matter for suspense.   This is the motivation for a succession of skillfully mounted flashbacks which picture certain domestic crises that might have induced all three of the husbands to bolt the marital yoke.

Jeanne Crain is an ex-farm girl, painfully sensitive, dreadfully unsure of herself in the circle of her wealthy husband's sophisticated friends.   Ann Sothern's husband is a high-minded, low-paid schoolteacher.   To increase their income Miss Sothern has taken to writing remunerative soap operas for radio until it is a question of who is supporting whom and whose work is more important.   Linda Darnell is an ex-shopgirl who schemed deliberately to marry her boss for his money.

The point of the script is that these are good, reasonably happy marriages.   And yet you can see that each of the girls has cause to worry.   The smooth way in which scenarist-director Joseph Mankiewicz manipulated his triple-flashback, maintaining sharp interest throughout, borders on magic.   He has accomplished the rare feat of making a very contrived drama seem a very convincing one, and of making his characters seem thoroughly real.

All three actresses perform expertly. The husbands are
Jeffrey Lynn, Kirk Douglas and an interesting recruit from the
stage, Paul Douglas.

--Fortnight, Vol. 6, No. 3
(February 4, 1949), page 31.

□ LIFE WITH FATHER (Warner Bros. , 1947)

Just as the Howard Lindsay-Russel Crouse play, Life with
Father, wrote an unprecedented chapter in the annals of the American theatre, so will its celluloid counterpart score a triumph in
the world's motion picture market.   For this Robert Buckner production, so warmly and sensitively directed by Michael Curtiz, is
an example of Hollywood craftsmanship at its very finest.   This
bright, entertaining bit of Americana is beautiful to look upon, acted
with consummate artistry by a hand-picked cast, and generally put
together with such meticulousness that there is no mistaking its
enormous boxoffice potentialities.   Here is a motion picture which,
like its legitimate theatre original, will play on and on, and come
back for repeat engagements both on Broadway and Main Street.

The screen version is a vast improvement over the play;
first, because the broad canvas covered by the camera allows a
more colorful picture of life and customs at the turn of the century.
Secondly, and infinitely more important, is the fact that Father Day
has been humanized.   Still bombastic, ever the terror of his family, always the bickering overlord, one nevertheless understands
him as a man who loves his wife and children in his own peculiar
fashion.   A scene here and there, a touch in the direction, and the
inflection in the reading of a line are the factors which do the trick.
Otherwise the story hews close to the original in its account of the
Day family with the ever-changing servants, the visiting relatives,
and mother's insistence on leading father to the altar for a belated
baptismal ceremony.

In the title role William Powell is just wonderful.   There is
no other word to describe his vigorous, zestful performance.   And
it is because Powell plays him so beautifully and with such thorough
understanding that Father's human qualities are apparent for the first
time.

Irene Dunne is Vinnie and a happier choice for the assignment
would be difficult to imagine.   Miss Dunne, stunning in the period
costumes, etches a rich warm, portrait of an American mother
whose grace and charm are born of forbearance and tolerance.

In the coordination of the elements which have gone into the
making of Life with Father, producer Robert Buckner combines
taste, showmanship and superlative craftsmanship.   His supervision
of story elements and the technical departments is evident throughout.

The direction by Michael Curtiz is another outstanding accomplishment by a man whose appreciation of American foibles and
the American scene is delightfully witty and as perceptive as it is
affectionate.   Curtiz moves his story along at a fast tempo, but
when he finds a scene such as that in the church where mother
passes a whispered "hush" down to father by way of their four sons,
the director has the sensitivity to sacrifice tempo for charm.

The supporting cast is a perfect assemblage of players, with
Elizabeth Taylor particularly appealing as the visitor who falls in
love with the oldest Day boy.   As played by Jimmy Lydon, Clarence Jr. is an amusing picture of frenzied adolescence in a frenzied
household.   Edmund Gwenn is excellent as the minister and ZaSu
Pitts has her innings as Cousin Cora.   Others who stand out are
Emma Dunn, Elisabeth Risdon, Clara Blandick and Derek Scott.

Peverell Marley and William V. Skall share the photography
credit and, with the cooperation of associate Technicolor director
Monroe W. Burbank, they have caught every mood and every detail.
Max Steiner's music, arranged by Murray Cutter and directed by
Leo Forbstein, is a distinguished contribution.   Particularly impressive is the art direction by Robert Haas.   George Amy in the capacity of editor must be singled out for special praise in view of the
fluidity he has achieved in a somewhat episodic story.

> --The Hollywood Reporter, Vol.
> 95, No. 3 (August 15, 1947),
> page 3.

*   *   *

Life with Father is really no longer a book, a play or a
movie, but an institution.   A Spanish-language production is prosper-
ing in Buenos Aires and the Royal Dramatic Theatre version is a
sellout in Stockholm.   Contracts have also been signed for productions in Norway, Denmark and Finland.   Victor Francen, leading
actor of the French theatre, has completed negotiations for a production in Paris which he will direct and in which he will play the
lead.   The only place where Father hasn't prospered is London.

In the New York production and road shows of the stage play
nine actors have played Father, eight actresses have played his
wife and 70 boys with dyed red hair have played the Day children.
Up from the ranks of the play casts have come such players as
Teresa Wright, Richard Ney, Andrea King and Cathy O'Donnell.

The comedy has had many strange and wonderful experiences
since the night of August 14, 1939, when it first saw the footlights
in a summer theatre at Skowhegan, Maine.   November 8, 1939, it
opened on Broadway, garnered rave reviews, was a sellout for
years.   It was a longer-run hit than Abie's Irish Rose, or Lightnin',
two of the greatest theatrical successes of all time; and it out-
grossed Tobacco Road.   Howard Lindsay and his wife, Dorothy
Stickney, played the starring roles for five consecutive seasons on
Broadway, to a total audience of more than 6,000,000 persons.

The classic of family life, however, began with a sketch
written by Clarence Day, Jr., in 1917, called "Father Trains a
Dog." Several years later, there appeared in Harper's a new
sketch called "Father and His Pet Rug." These concerned Clarence Day, Sr., his wife and four sons who lived at 420 Madison
Ave., New York. Here was a family that owed its very life to the
fact that nothing ever happened to its members--except that they
were uninhibitedly themselves within the handsomely paneled walls
of an absolutely conventional world in New York of the 1880's.

Although Day never intended the brief chronicles of his family life to take on such proportions, the years built up a great following for Father, until the New Yorker magazine began running
them regularly in 1931. They became too voluminous for one book
to hold, so they emerged in three books, Life with Father, Life
with Mother and God and My Father.

The author always intended to write a play himself, but he
never accomplished this. One evening in the middle '30's a Broadway playwright was reading a book to his actress wife. The playwright was also an actor. "This," said the actor-author, "would
make a great show for us together."

Howard Lindsay phoned his collaborator, Russel Crouse.
Seventeen months later they completed the play and received permission from Clarence Day's widow to produce it.

A host of top stars from Mary Pickford down to the current
crop of favorites were tested for the various roles in the film production. Michael Curtiz finally took over the directorial reins, his
72nd picture during his 20 years with Warners.

Ace art director Robert Haas was assigned to reproduce the
family background and the various New York landmarks and submitted for approval a total of 400 detailed sketches, the largest
amount of pre-production art work in studio history. For instead
of the one-set combination of parlor-dining room which has become
so familiar to playgoers throughout the country, the movie shows
interior and exterior scenes of 1880 New York. Recreating the
famed Delmonico's was the designer's worst headache. Since there
were no actual plans in existence, Haas designed the restaurant
from old photographs. McCreery's was the largest Technicolor interior ever built on the Warner lot--an authentic reproduction of the
store when it was on 11th and Broadway in lower Manhattan.

The movie cast, like the Broadway players, had to have their
hair dyed red; the routine during production included two shampoos
and one rinse regularly every week. All the hair required constant
toning up to keep it the same shade under the hot Technicolor lights.
The cast was ordered to stay away from the direct rays of the sun
and out of swimming pools during the shooting of the picture, for
the chlorine of the pools would turn their hair green.

Martin Milner, the second Day son, had never set foot on a sound stage until the day he was tested. He presented unusual wardrobe problems for he had to have an entirely new wardrobe because of his growth from the time of his original tests to the third month of filming. The scene in which he leaves for dinner at Delmonico's and the scene of his return were shot three months apart; in the short space of time consumed by Sunday dinner he grew two inches.

Johnny Calkins, the 11-year-old third son, also presented problems in growth. Near the end of the filming Irene Dunne and Bill Powell stood on wooden blocks to make him appear as short as he was in earlier scenes. The youngest son was portrayed by six-year-old Derek Scott, who, early in production, lost his baby teeth and had to wear "falsies" through most of the picture. His pranks were a headache for Curtiz and the cast. He would smile broadly into the camera lens in the middle of a "take" and reveal the fact that he had purposely forgotten to put in his two front false teeth.

Life with Father is certain to be one of the outstanding contenders for Academy Award honors. Implausible though it may seem to the 6,000,000 theatregoers who were convulsed by this family classic, the screen play is even funnier than the Broadway production.

Superlatives will no doubt be lavished on the performances of the four boys, Jimmy Lydon, Derek Scott, Johnny Calkins, and Martin Milner, who play the roles of the four sons; and Elizabeth Taylor is touching and pretty as Mary. William Powell has one of the most taxing parts of his entire career as the mercurially tempered Father and he does beautifully with it. His performance is well matched by that of Irene Dunne, graciously expert as the impetuous and charming Vinnie.

There are also sound and pleasant performances by ZaSu Pitts, Edmund Gwenn and Frank Elliott. Director Michael Curtiz has captured the style and tempo of the original stories and the stage production and has added new values to every chuckle and sentimental touch in the play. And Peverell Marley's photography displays real genius.

--Fortnight, Vol. 3, No. 5
(September 12, 1947), pages 29-
30.

☐ LIFEBOAT (20th Century-Fox, 1944)

If 1944 reveals a more exemplary example of the photoplay than Lifeboat, this department will be considerably surprised. A film that can well be compared with the best the screen has ever offered, the work has the advantage of the discriminating production

guidance of Kenneth Macgowan, Alfred Hitchcock's sensitive and
restrained direction, a literate and literary original by John Steinbeck, an incisively dramatic screenplay by Jo Swerling, and acting
performances that both individually and collectively, are just about
precisely right.

      Lifeboat is not only an extraordinary film, it is also an
extraordinary Hitchcock film.   Here, he has expanded his mathe-
matical formula of mere suspense until it fully exploits the human
equation, veers always towards reality, and employs a pathos that
never becomes sleek or slick.   Despite the fact that only nine characters carry the action which is laid entirely within the confines of
a life-craft, there is no strain in the development, no sense of the
mechanical ingenuity necessary to keep the events taut and moving.
The characters are dimensional, fresh and human, all quite
free of the formula quality with which Hollywood habitually en-
dows a collection of antitheticals in group-dramas ranging from
Grand Hotel to Lost Horizon.

      Tallulah Bankhead, a lady who can crisp an epigram like no
one else in the history of histrionics, is superb as the sophisticate
who finds the war and the world just so much grist for her typewriter.   The rest of the cast--Walter Slezak, Mary Anderson,
Heather Angel, John Hodiak, Hume Cronyn, Henry Hull, and William Bendix--would be difficult to improve upon.   However, it is
Canada Lee who made the most indelible impression upon this observer with the single line of dialogue, "Do I get to vote, too?,"
which he managed to invest with the inference of an entire lifetime
of injustice, terror and despair.

                              --Herb Sterne in Rob Wagner's
                                Script, Vol. 30, No. 671 (Janu-
                                ary 22, 1944), page 14.

                       *   *   *

      Lifeboat looks like a big grosser.   John Steinbeck's devastat-
ing indictment of the nature of Nazi bestiality, at times an almost
clinical, dissecting room analysis, though it is always carried along
for strong audience values under the impetus of exciting narrative,
emerges as powerful adult motion picture fare.

      This is one of the first films to deal with the problem of the
people of Germany.   It is not a problem picture, however, and its
sociological implications are neatly and expertly fictionized.   Neither
is there any effort to solve any problem.   Yet a provocative issue
is raised, one of a kind calculated to stir theatregoers throughout
the country.   The question Steinbeck poses is, "What can you do
with people like that?" meaning the Germans.

      The picture is based on an original idea of director Alfred
Hitchcock's.   Hitchcock, from accounts, first asked Steinbeck to
write the piece for book publication, figuring that if it turned out a
big seller the exploitation value for film purposes would be greatly

enhanced. The author, however, would not undertake the more ambitious assignment and wrote the story for screen purposes only,
with Jo Swerling handling the adaptation.

Patterned along one of the simplest, most elementary forms
of dramatic narration, the action opens and closes on a lifeboat.
It's a lusty, robust story about a group of survivors from a ship
sunk by a U-boat. One by one the survivors find precarious refuge
on the lifeboat. Finally they pick up a survivor from the German
U-boat. Despite the fierce hatred of the suspicious Kovac (John
Hodiak), an American of Czech descent, the majority vote against
killing the Nazi. He is first tolerated and then welcomed into their
midst. They share their food and water with the Nazi. And in the
end he repays their trust and confidence with murderous treachery.

The Nazi, who turns out to be the captain of the submarine
which sunk the ship originally, hoards vitamin-food and water while
the others go hungry and thirsty. He steers the lifeboat off its
course, heading it straight for German waters. He torments the
suffering group with extravagant boasts of Nazi "master race" superiority. And when he is finally disposed of there is a momentary
sense of loss among the survivors, as if "the motor is gone."
Yet, when the group of Americans and Britishers is confronted later
with another Nazi whom they rescue from the sea, they appear likely
to repeat their first mistake. Have they so soon forgotten Willie,
the first Nazi? Maybe not, but as humans they cannot murder
another defenseless human in cold blood.

Walter Slezak, as the fat, greasy, conceited German, comes
through with a terrific delineation. Henry Hull as the millionaire,
William Bendix as the mariner with a jitterbug complex who loses
a leg, John Hodiak as the tough, bitter, Nazi-hater, and Canada
Lee as the colored steward, deliver excellent characterizations.

Tallulah Bankhead, as Mrs. Porter, a cynical newspaper
writer, is not photogenically acceptable in the brief, fiercely romantic interludes with Hodiak. The camera treats her unkindly
throughout, except in one or two instances.

While the film has no top picture names, it is a production
that holds first-rate exploitation possibilities.

Hitchcock has piloted the piece skillfully, ingenuously developing suspense and action. Despite that it's a slow starter, the
picture, from the beginning, leaves a strong impact and, before
too long, develops into the type of suspenseful product with which
Hitchcock has always been identified.

                                    --"Mori" in Variety, Vol. 153,
                                    No. 5 (January 12, 1944), page
                                    24.

☐ LITTLE WOMEN (M-G-M, 1949)

A remake of the Louisa May Alcott classic at this date is
hardly anything that might contribute to the advancement of the
cinema.   But never mind that.   Certainly it is better to revive an
old story than to fuss with some of the new material that is submitted for the screen.

Another thing about reviving 19th-Century classics: one is
struck once again by their quality. Little Women, for example,
reminds us that besides sentimentality it possesses sensitivity and
delicacy, humor and robustness.

The story, of course, requires careful casting for effectiveness, for its characters are well-known and loved.   Mervyn LeRoy
could hardly have chosen better for his prettily Technicolored production: June Allyson for tomboy Jo; Elizabeth Taylor as high-
strung Amy; Janet Leigh, common-sensible Meg; Margaret O'Brien
for delicate Beth.   It is just the show for Easter.

                              --Fortnight, Vol. 6, No. 8 (April
                              15, 1949), page 31.

                    *   *   *

*The severest critics of Little Women will be the moviegoers
who delighted in the 1933 screen version of the Louisa May Alcott
classic and in Katharine Hepburn's unforgettable performance as Jo
March.   Considered solely on its own merits, the current remake
is properly respectful to the novel and generally successful both as
a period piece and a sentimental Technicolored Valentine.

There should be no serious complaints about the actors producer-director Mervyn LeRoy has chosen to impersonate the March
family and their neighbors.   June Allyson is appealing as the purposeful, tomboyish Jo who dominates the temporarily fatherless
household and valiantly resists growing up.   Janet Leigh is charming as Meg; Elizabeth Taylor is appropriately trivial and attractive
as Amy and, except at the very end, Margaret O'Brien is nicely
restrained as the soulful, doomed Beth.

The Italian actor Rossano Brazzi (Furia) is pleasant, if some-
what miscast, as Jo's Professor Bhaer, but Mary Astor's Marmee,
Lucille Watson's Aunt March, the late Sir C. Aubrey Smith's Mr.
Laurence, and Peter Lawford's Laurie are sound characterizations.

The core of the film, however, is the performances of the
actresses playing Jo and her beloved sisters, and these vary with
the vagaries of the screen play.   Although Victor Heerman and his

wife, Sarah Y. Mason, were responsible for the earlier adaptation, their present chore (in collaboration with Andrew Solt) fails to achieve a sustained mood.

In the beginning, as Marmee and her brood carry on bravely while Father is away at war, Little Women is gay and sentimental in the proper proportions. But in the latter sequences, when growing pains and sorrow trouble the Marches, the film topples its delicate balance in a determined effort to twang the heartstrings. This isn't fatal, but it is owing chiefly to Miss Alcott that the Marches retain their perennial charm.

> --Newsweek (March 28, 1949),
> page 84.

☐ THE LODGER (20th Century-Fox, 1944)

The Lodger is an average scare-'em, given a certain distinction by John Brahm's sense of light, shadow and photographic values. The film has less to do with the Mrs. Belloc Lowndes novel than it has with every other celluloid fable about a psychopathic killer, but if the preceding ones have pleased you, there is no particular reason why this should fail.

Laird Cregar is given the opportunity to have a perpetual banquet on the scenery, and his appetite is profound. Lady Korda (Merle Oberon) displays a handsome set of gams, a pleasant personality, but as a singer of Parisian music hall songs she is neither a Lucienne Boyer nor an Irene Bordini. Actually, the lighting, lensing and atmosphere are the stars of the piece, and they are quite worth viewing.

> --Herb Sterne in Rob Wagner's
> Script, Vol. 30, No. 672 (February 5, 1944), page 11.

*   *   *

In the new screen version of Mrs. Belloc Lowndes' The Lodger, the actor cast as the man who doesn't like girls to go on the stage and who does what he can to deter them with a shiny knife is Laird Cregar, who is probably a reasonably good choice. He is big and powerful-looking and an intelligent performer. If the picture were made over into a perfect job, which it isn't now, he might still belong in it, though he might have to be revamped and made a more forceful character. Somehow, he would have to manage to give off menace without the aid of a baby spot hanging around his eyes and upper cheekbones, a device which is frequently used in scary pictures and which is singularly ineffective. It is also used, sometimes, on glamour ladies in other kinds of pictures, to give their faces a luminous quality. In all cases, it just makes the subject look as though he or she were standing in a strong light and would probably wind up with a case of eyestrain.

Other members of the cast of The Lodger are Merle Oberon,
George Sanders, Sir Cedric Hardwicke, and Sara Allgood.   Sir Cedric and Miss Allgood play the couple who rent rooms to a mild-
mannered medical gentleman who pays cash in advance and doesn't
turn out until later to be Jack the Ripper on the side, Mr.
Sanders plays the male romantic lead from Scotland Yard, and Miss Oberon
plays opposite him as the niece of the house, who sings and dances
in music halls and is consequently on the lodger's black list.   As
you can see if you read the book, there have been some changes
made.   The main one is the invention of the niece, and it's too bad
that the girl had to be built up as a popular variety artist, because
Miss Oberon, though alluringly clad in a cancan outfit, isn't quite
the type for the part, being unable, in the first place, to do much
singing or dancing.

Mr. Cregar or the director or the author or all three have
decided to make the main character a rather diffident and sensitive
maniac, a bit more given to apology than I remember the one in
the book to have been.   This is perfectly all right with me, but I
thought I'd mention it.   They may well have studied up on homicidal
loonies and found this one to be a common type.   However, the
book had a good deal of suspense, whereas the picture has rather
little.   More trick stuff than solid work has been used to establish
atmosphere, and if it weren't for weird lighting and some trumped-
up fog, there wouldn't be much to intimidate you.   All the picture
has it owes to the original story, and where it has struck out on
its own it has come to no good.

--David Lardner in The New Yorker, (January 22, 1944), pages
46-47.

☐   THE LOST WEEKEND (Paramount, 1945)

The Lost Weekend is enthusiastically endorsed for all film
devotées who do not confine their definition of diversion to Technicolored closeups of The Grable's gams.   Charles Jackson's clinical
novel of an alcoholic has been transposed to celluloid with a rather
remarkable integrity, and a pleasing dexterity in avoiding the oubli-
ettes of the obvious.   At no time does the film confuse its thesis
with that of Ten Nights in a Barroom, and such deviations as the
photoplay makes from the novel in order to placate the censors and
their taboos do little or nothing to impair the dramatic fabric.   The
ending, which pretends to be "happy," is to be really more rationally interpreted as sardonic, and the main theme is no less arresting
for changing a subsidiary character, Bim, from a follower of Hema-
phroditus to an admirer of the Marquis de Sade.

It will be interesting to observe audience response to this
film which pulls all the emotional stops in a crescendo-study of one
binge in the life of a man whose life is a series of binges.   For a

number of years now, audiences have been conditioned to the superficial, the trivial and adolescent by the domestic photoplay. It has
long been the mode to avoid climaxes in plot, acting and treatment,
and whether the average patron will be able to readjust himself to
this abrupt departure from the "shall-we-dance?" style is problematical. Fans, it is to be feared, will be embarrassed into a cack-
ling, moronic reaction by the sudden return of the film to a full
bodied technique of emotionalism for which they are unprepared.

Billy Wilder and Charles Brackett have formulated an admirable two-man show. Between them they are accountable for the
screenplay, the direction and the producer credit, and the result is
an incisive photoplay that commands, and certainly deserves, attention.

No punches are pulled in depicting the plight of Don Birnham,
an egocentric whose nature demands star billing. He flees the frus-
trations of the would-be creator via the bottle, fearing the gamble
that creation entails. Drunk, the man is a success to himself.
He is unable to face the rigours of the typewriter, the stern self-
discipline and courage demanded of the creative person before he is
able to achieve personal freedom through personal expression.
Birnham seeks salvation in rye whiskey. Alcohol is the key which
unfetters the man from the everyday, the dreary treadmill of the
routine. Alcohol provides the fantasy of achievement without the
seering struggle that attainment requires in reality. Birnham pretends that he is refusing to sell out to life, refusing to cheapen his
objectives and dazzling demands from existence. But in this bogus
refusal to barter himself on a retail basis, he eventually sells out
wholesale. To obtain liquor with which to sustain the illusion of
self-respect, the man relinquishes every vestige of decency. He
lies, steals, betrays others and, worst of all, betrays himself to
obtain liquor. Eventually, he even turns prostitute, and sells himself to a clipjoint cutie for the purchase price of drink.

The film pummels the nerves and the emotions. The sequences in the alcoholic ward, and the subsequent scenes of delirium
tremens in Birnham's apartment are shattering. There are times
when the observer suffers almost as does the screen character, and
the final fadeout left this spectator exhausted. In addition, I was
parched, and forthwith hiked from the Paramount projection room
to Lucey's across the street, where I promptly downed several
double shots of bourbon, happy in the realization that, unlike Jackson's protagonist, I wasn't a rye man, so that it can't happen here.

For Ray Milland, the film is pretty much of a strenuous
soliloquy, and under Wilder's guidance he meets most of the reasonable demands made by the characterization. In the early stanzas,
there are certain loutellegenisms, but as the photoplay progresses,
the performance gains in believability. As the brother, Phil Terry
is quite excellent, and the easy naturalness and quiet normality of
his work proclaim his theory of Thespian art to be antithetical to
that cherished and practiced by his wife, Joan Crawford. In support

are Jane Wyman, Howard DaSilva, Frank Faylen and Doris Dowling,
all of whom proffer people who fit perfectly into a picture that has
a completely encompassing, and frightening, reality.

--Herb Sterne in Rob Wagner's
Script, Vol. 31, No. 719 (December 15, 1945), page 14.

*   *   *

You hear complaints fairly often about how much drinking is
done in the movies, but surely never has so much liquor flowed out
of bottles on the screen as in this film.   Anyone who has read
Charles Jackson's painful and frightening novel about a man's weekend drunk might wonder how Hollywood came to be interested in it
at all--Hollywood, which customarily either makes drinking as casual a social habit amid its moneyed characters as taking a cup of
tea in an English setting, or uses it as a comic element, here suddenly letting its hero be a dipsomaniac with no comic intent whatever.   The reader of the novel, surprised that the picture should
have been made at all, will be even more amazed at how faithfully
the novel has been followed--right up to but not including the end.
And no one need fear that Don Birnam and his weekend bout will
lead others along his alcoholic path.

Charles Brackett and Billy Wilder, working together as producer and director and collaborating on the script, have gone at
their material seriously and with understanding, as well as with
their special gifts as a producing team, and they have done a stunning job--in any sense of that word.   Also, the photography and the
musical score with which they are assisted are both notably effective.

The story is an almost clinical study of an alcoholic, a writer who has never lived up to what his friends have expected of him,
and who is always running away from his typewriter to escape from
reality and hard work in bemused, drink-nourished fantasies.   Were
anyone but Ray Milland playing this part it might easily have turned
out an utterly unsympathetic character: why bother about such a
weakling, why do his brother and his girl want so earnestly, even
so passionately, to save him, what is there worth-while about him
that an audience should care whether he lands permanently in the
gutter or not?   What, after all, was that early promise whose un-
fulfillment we are asked to believe so tragic?   Was his contem-
plated novel, to be called The Bottle, so important?

What we see of this young man, mostly, are his efforts to
get by himself and get drunk, during a weekend which his brother
and his fiancée want him to spend healthily in the country.   To accomplish this he uses up enough ingenuity and energy to win a minor
battle, and with a ruthless lack of scruples.   He lies, steals, begs
abjectly, wears himself out completely, solely to get a few dollars
to buy himself another bottle or two, to land eventually in a terrifying attack of DTs.

Yet, from the way the part is written and acted, this man is made a sympathetic and even pitiable person. In one scene he tries to explain himself to his sweetheart and convince her he is not worth her devotion and care, and it's a scene of deeply stirring power which somehow justifies the girl, in spite of all it reveals about himself, and anyone who has at all experienced a similar case will be wracked with sympathy for them both.

For this is a man with a sickness, psychic, physical--whatever it might be called--which involves far more than good resolves and will-power. Ray Milland has illuminated the presentation of such a character with countless bits of expression, voice and gesture that convince as both outer and inner truth.

No cure is suggested, though few knowing people will believe that something outside himself isn't needed for the reformation of such a man. Merely, in the utter exhaustion at the bout's end, to say "Never again!" is usual enough, but there is always an "again." The book was more truthful in its ending--the man was left slyly hiding away ammunition for the next attack which he knew perfectly well would come eventually. The picture--rather half-heartedly, as if it didn't really believe in its solution--tries to leave the impression that the "Never again!" is emphatically final, and that Don Birnam will live soberly, work hard, marry happily, and sublimate all his inner chaos in a fine and successful novel--to be called, still, The Bottle. Thus, on the screen, ultimate tragedy is shoved out of sight.

In spite of this lapse from truth for the illusion of a happy ending, the film is singularly powerful as well as unusual. The plight of the alcoholic may not seem one of the most important of the world's problems, but there are plenty of people who have encountered it, and here it is presented not only with surprising force and understanding, but with expert cinematic skill. The leading actors--Jane Wyman, Philip Terry, Howard da Silva, Doris Dowling, Frank Faylen--back up Ray Milland's incomparable performance splendidly, and there is an almost documentary background of New York scenes and population. Someone made the playful crack, "Isn't it just like Hollywood, always enlarging things, to change Second Avenue to Third Avenue?" But that is about the only amusing thing that can be said of The Lost Weekend. It is stern stuff, and far from unimportant.

--James Shelley Hamilton in New
Movies, Vol. 20, No. 7 (October, 1945), pages 4-5.

☐ LOUISIANA STORY (Flaherty/Lopert, 1948)

The writers for the silent screen were learning some of the free-ranging powers of the moving picture when the talkies stopped

them dead in their tracks. Then, in a sense, they went underground; what they had learned of the special technique of building
emotion and idea from the relationships of things seen, was pre-
served in the documentary film which Robert Flaherty made of the
silent picture, and John Grierson perfected by adding narration.

That sort of picture is no complete expression of the screen.
You sense that when you see Flaherty's new Louisiana Story. This
story of a bayou boy, partnered by alligators and oil wells, is told
with the sensitiveness and beauty which Flaherty has always com-
manded--though not with the complete success of Nanook of the
North or Moana--yet for all that, it remains a surface story.
Flaherty's pictorial pattern does not carry us far enough into the
special province of the screen, the swift, clear expression of spiritual and physical relationships. He uses dialog, but not to dig
deep into emotion and conviction.

--Kenneth MacGowan in Script
(September 1948), page 43.

*   *   *

Choice of this and several fortnights is this extraordinarily
attractive film by the great documentarian, Robert Flaherty.

Louisiana Story was commissioned by Standard Oil Company
of New Jersey but is in no sense a commercial film. In fact, the
name of the company is never mentioned. But Flaherty found long
ago that his approach to film-making differs from Hollywood's and
he prefers to work with this sort of subsidy.

This documentary film pictures idyllically the unspoiled existence in the Bayou country not far from New Orleans. It focusses
on a 13-year-old boy who paddles his little boat through the moss-
hung swamps, stops now and then to fish, goes trapping, fights alligators, makes friends of birds and animals. Into this peaceful
byway oil drillers come one day to sink a well. The boy's fascin-
ated amazement is caught as he watches the strange machinery put
to work. Eventually the oil men move away and the boy resumes
his uncomplicated life.

It is that simple a story, narrated and photographed with
great beauty. For his small cast Flaherty used people of the local-
ity, who, untrained, come vividly to life because of their lack of
artifice.

It is a lovely film, constantly absorbing, beautifully back-
grounded with a musical score by Virgil Thomson--most certainly
a picture to be seen and treasured.

--Fortnight, Vol. 6, No. 1 (January 7, 1949), page 31.

☐ MACBETH (Mercury/Republic, 1948)

It is axiomatic that no playwright ever has endured more
humiliating interpretations of his work than the greatest of them
all, William Shakespeare.   The magnificence of his plays, however,
has kept alive the artistry of the Bard down through the centuries.
And, happily, Shakespeare will continue to be a vivid element in
theatrical culture long after the Orson Welles version of Macbeth
is forgotten as one of the most disastrous of motion picture enter-
prises.

It is insufficient apology for its inadequacies to point out that
Welles sought to accomplish the almost impossible by shooting
Macbeth in 21 days (to say nothing of the nights) and on a comparatively low budget.   Time and money had nothing to do with the
ridiculous manner in which Welles has edited the text.   It is utterly lacking in continuity and dramatic compulsion.   What once was
the stellar vehicle of Lady Macbeth, a fascinating and cunning con-
spirator, is now a display of the posturing and strutting of Orson
Welles in the title role.   The costumes, ostensibly authentic, make
for a drab, dirty production which never fulfills the traditional
Shakespearean promise of color, pageantry, and genuine theatrical
excitement.   Surely budget played no part in the Welles decision to
use thick Scottish accents which render the first 40 minutes of the
film unintelligible.   The latter half is spoken with less accent, in-
dicating that the Republic authorities stepped in after listening to
some of the rushes.

Macbeth is slow, dull and monotonous.   It is made so as
much by the direction of Welles as his gloomy, shabby production.
It is photographed against a background of smoky haze.   The characters appear from nowhere, speak their lines, and then depart into
the mist.   One is barely distinguishable from the other, thanks to
their hideous make-ups and the aborted text.   Welles even imple-
ments Shakespeare by forming a composite of several characters
and calling him a holy Father.   The fellow, incidentally, played by
Alan Napier, gives the nearest thing to a legitimate performance in
the entire film.

As for the others they can be no better than their director.
Jeanette Nolan, as Lady Macbeth, is obliged to characterize the
sexiness of the ambitious Scottish woman by appearing in the opening scene as though setting the stage for "Diamond Lil."   Roddy
McDowall, as Malcolm; Dan O'Herlihy, as Macduff; and Edgar Barrier, in the part of Banquo, are to be congratulated for speaking a
brand of English that can be understood by others than Orson Welles.
As for the witches of Brainerd Duffield, Lurene Tuttle, and Peggy
Webber they sound like a Disney Donald Duck cartoon played backwards.

The final disfigurement of Macbeth is contributed by the
Welles performance of the character which is completely devoid of

thoughtfulness or intelligence.   It is big, broad and blustering--a
booming elocutionary display that taxes the ear drums and never
touches the heart.

Macbeth, the film, and Macbeth, the character, are two of
a kind--dramatic abstractions with neither rhyme nor reason, lacking in artistic and entertainment values and woefully inadequate in
the matter of boxoffice elements.

> --The Hollywood Reporter, Vol.
> 100, No. 47 (October 11, 1948),
> page 3.

* * *

There is no doubt that Orson Welles is gifted with colossal
ingenuity and resourcefulness.   It would take colossal ingenuity to
make so great a bore of Shakespeare as he has done in this outrageously poor production of Macbeth.

It is a production that surpasses description, for practically
everything about it is unbelievably bad.   Most blatant fault is the
absolute absence of clarity--in narration, characterization, dialogue.
The lines are almost unintelligible, mouthed in a curious burr with
no regard for metre or meaning.

Welles' Macbeth is certainly not Shakespeare's.   The role is
played for introspection, not impulse.   Instead of the Bard's easily
fired character, Welles offers a sluggish, blankly staring figure,
mooning through countless close-ups with mouth open, eyes expres-
sionless.   Lady Macbeth, one of the great characters of dramatic
literature, is played by Jeanette Nolan in painful deadpan, her reading and accent even more obscure than Welles'.

It is pointless to detail the ineptitude of the rest of the cast,
the butchery of the text, the weird costuming, the production boners,
and the poor sound.   Welles is said to have thrown this film together in 21 days of shooting, at a cost of only $300,000.   Even
so, it was a waste of time and money and an insult to artistry.

> --Fortnight, Vol. 5, No. 10
> (November 5, 1948), page 31.

☐   MAD WEDNESDAY (California/RKO, 1950)*

What happens when a clean-cut, ambitious American boy
graduates from college, sets his foot on the bottom rung of the

---

*Mad Wednesday began life as a 1947 production, The Sin of Harold
Diddlebock.   Because of a dispute between its director and its producer, Howard Hughes, the film was not released until 1950.

ladder to success--and then stays on that rung for 20 dull years?
One answer appears when Harold Lloyd, back in his first film since
the early 1930s, plays this part.   As any old Lloyd admirer knows,
the lower Lloyd's fortunes get, the higher he'll bounce.

   The fun starts when Lloyd is fired after his 20 years at the
foot of the ladder and takes the first drink of his life.   Thereafter
a whole lost weekend is crowded into one Mad Wednesday.   Lloyd,
master of silent-film comedy, retains all his old genius for preposterous situations and hairbreadth escapes.   And, of course,
there's a happy ending.

   All told, Lloyd and writer-director Preston Sturges make
Mad Wednesday one of the best comedies in years.
                                --Quick (January 15, 1951), page
                                  53.

                    *   *   *

   In Mad Wednesday, Harold Lloyd attempts to regenerate a
comic figure who flourished in silent pictures a quarter of a century
ago.   Once again, he plays the incredible innocent who peers wistfully at the world through tortoise-shell glasses and smiles foolish-
ly every time fate deals him a rotten hand.   When Mr. Lloyd was
a youth, he was able to make this character a rather engaging type,
but in Mad Wednesday the perennial dupe isn't very entertaining
company.   This, I think, is due largely to the fact that Mr. Lloyd
in his middle years is quite a stern-looking fellow, with a voice
so full of rich authority that it's hard to associate it with anyone
less austere than, say, an Imperial Potentate of the Nobles of the
Mystic Shrine.   In addition to this handicap, the comedian has very
little in the way of material to assist him.   As written and directed
by Preston Sturges, Mad Wednesday is a hopeless mélange of wheezy
routines, which range from Mr. Lloyd's old business of teetering on
the ledge of a skyscraper to the conversation of a talking horse.
Beginning with some footage from The Freshman, which was made
in 1923, the film goes on to describe how the freshman, whose
name is Harold Diddlebock and who believes in all the platitudes
about hard work and success, spends twenty years crouched over
a ledger and is then fired by a boss who doesn't like to see his
assistants settling down into a rut.   Equipped with two thousand
dollars, his life's savings, our hero goes on the first spree of his
career, makes a killing on a horse, and wakes up the possessor of
a prosperous circus.   The devices that keep this one laboring along,
such as having Mr. Lloyd lead a lion through crowded streets,
aren't particularly original.   Among the other actors who struggle
with the story are Jimmy Conlin, Raymond Walburn, Edgar Kennedy, and Franklin Pangborn.
                                --John McCarten in The New York-
                                  er (February 3, 1951), page 86.

                    *   *   *

Mad Wednesday takes up where The Freshman and Harold
Lloyd left off a good many years ago, and will surely attract those
who delighted then in the Lloyd brand of guffaws and those who are
curious to see just what all the shouts of laughter were about.

Those who used to roar at the young clown will find that he
is still in the same business, that maturing has altered his pattern
but slightly.   He maintains his ability to get caught up in zany situ-
ations--inevitably hanging, finally, from a window sill with a dizzying drop below him--and yet to make it seem more funny than silly.

Slapstick is usually good for more hearty laughter than almost any good sophisticated comedy line, but just how much of it
you enjoy is a personal matter.   However, if you've never watched
Lloyd in action, this big day of madness is probably an event you'll
want to attend.

--Fortnight, Vol. 9, No. 12
(December 11, 1950), page 32.

☐   THE MAGNIFICENT AMBERSONS (RKO, 1942)

If the hostility and bewilderment of the local critical gentry,
following the studio unveiling of Orson Welles' The Magnificent Ambersons, may be used as a gauge of its reception by the laity, the
film will lose even more money for R. K. O. than did Citizen Kane.
The dogmatists who insist that photoplays be as simple as their own
minds and react to dramatic experimentation with vertigo and emotional colic will probably damn the venture.   Fortunately, the
volume of anserine abuse vouchsafed a film does not distort its intrinsic worth and many a worthy celluloid bloom has languished and
withered on the altars of popular approval; one has only to recall
the wholesale apathy that greeted D. W. Griffith's Abraham Lincoln
and Isn't Life Wonderful, Vidor's The Crowd, Slim, Trouble for
Two, Clair's The Flame of New Orleans, Nazimova's Salome, von
Sternberg's Scarlet Empress and The Devil Is a Woman.

Welles has taken Tarkington's tale of a small, mid-western
American town, at the turn of the century and treated this transitional period with an oblique, searching, stylized realism.   Disdain-
ing the catch-penny nostalgia with which less trenchant minds would
have frosted the piece, the director-author-producer turns an ironic,
somber and frequently witty gaze upon the near-past.   There will,
without doubt, be caterwaulings from those who contend that the approach ravishes the spirit of the Tarkington tome, just as there
were bitter complaints, a few seasons back, when Welles produced
his bizarre version of Macbeth with a Negro cast, and Julius Caesar
in modern dress.   Those who make a ritual of starting the day with
toast and honey are likely to be startled and affronted by the sudden
substitution of a mango.

The Magnificent Ambersons shows a noteworthy progress in Welles' grasp of motion picture technique. The current film is more compact than Citizen Kane, its investigations of rhythmics more successful, and there is a taut, emotional quality which his debut effort lamentably lacked. There is less of the arrogantly cerebral, more of the fluently human note in this brooding study of a wealthy home which houses a family of strangers. The speech of the people is flavorsomely idiomatic, and the evocations of the ponderous architecture, the heavy hangings, the bulky furnishings of gas-lighted America are as important and as articulate as the actors. Snobbery is satirized with marked skill, stupidities admirably ridiculed, and a dour, ominous threat of inevitable catastrophe is projected by the leit-motif of low-key camerawork. Unfortunately, in his preoccupation with the characters, Welles disregards the necessary historical background. The inception and development of the mechanical age and its effect on the pattern of small town existence is the true story, and this is only unsatisfactorily materialized. Too, the closing portions are hurried--possibly due to editing--the fall of George is never clearly conveyed, nor does his rehabilitation ever become anything but obscure.

Welles repeats many of his mannerisms, such as the main title unaccompanied by the customary musical fury, and intermittent narration. He again borrows the "quick-shot" from D. W. Griffith with vast success, and this time, too, makes use of the gauzed-edge photography which was a factor in all the Old Master's films. Such exhumations Welles makes his own by literate utilization, and he even resurrects the "iris-out" for a superb optical moment.

Welles' actors proffer dimensional performances and there is a total lack of the conventional in the contributions of lovely-as-ever Dolores Costello, Joseph Cotten, Ray Collins, Anne Baxter, Tim Holt and Richard Bennett. An astonishing delineation is that of Agnes Moorehead as the frustrated spinster. Her work is completely of the period, and its elements of flamboyant hysteria form striking contrast to the repressions of the other characters. Fact is, there hasn't been such a complete depiction of emotional distortion on the screen since von Stroheim directed Dale Fuller, Malvina Polo and Caesare Gravina in a series of macabre portraits.

The Magnificent Ambersons is sinister, disturbing; as pungent, as stimulating, as pernod. For those who aren't averse to expending concentration and imagination in the theater, it should prove provocative photodrama.

--Herb Sterne in Rob Wagner's
Script, Vol. 27, No. 632 (July
4, 1942), page 24.

*   *   *

Orson Welles gives the film industry a second lesson in his new celluloid technic--but this time the boxoffice story is going to be far different than was the reaction to Citizen Kane. In The

Magnificent Ambersons, without stars and with much gloom, Welles
has a picture that's distinctly not attuned to the times and probably
will be just as dismal at the b.o. as the story is on the screen.

Although within 88 minutes, this emotional downbeat appears
to be endless.   On top of the slow and constant jerking on the audience's feeling for hatred, the focal point of that emotion is so in-
consequential as to be ludicrous.   With a world in flame, nations
shattered, populations in rags, with massacres and bombings, Welles
devotes 9,000 feet of film to a spoiled brat who grows up as a
spoiled, spiteful young man.   It's something of a Little Foxes, but
without the same dynamic power of story, acting and social preachment, a single moment of contrast; it piles on and on a tale of woe,
but without once striking at least a true chord of sentimentality.

Like Kane, although this time via photographer Stanley Cortez
instead of Gregg Toland, Welles utilizes an original method of un-
folding his story.   Though not in the visual cast this time, Welles
serves as the offstage commentator in introducing the characters and
the plot.

The central character is Tim Holt, son of Jack Holt, who is
portrayed first as the spoiled, curley-haired darling of the town's
richest family, and then for the major portion as a conceited, power-
conscious, insufferable youth.   It's brought out that his mother,
Dolores Costello, had originally been in love with Joseph Cotten,
but instead married the more social Don Dillaway.   Cotten, an auto
inventor, returns to the town a widower with an attractive daughter,
Anne Baxter, who attracts young Holt.   When the latter's father dies
and Cotten again attempts to cotton up to the brat's mother, Holt
steps between them.   He breaks off with Miss Baxter when she insists that he choose a career other than that of an idle gentleman,
and then he and his mother go on a trip.   Meanwhile, Cotten's auto
factory prospers while the Ambersons' wealth melts away.   Miss
Costello suffers a heart attack in Paris and is brought home dying,
but her son denies her last wish of again seeing Cotten.   Then the
autocratic grandpa Amberson, played by Richard Bennett, dies virtually impoverished and Holt finds himself on his uppers.   It's in-
ferred at the finish, however, that Cotten accepts him as a son-in-
law.

Thus is the woe piled up, but in Welles' artistic fashion of
keeping characters on the move, photography focussed so that it
appears third-dimensional with sets almost constantly in the dark.

Welles comes up with a few more tricks in the direction of
the dialog.   He plays heavily on the dramatic impact of a whisper,
and on the threatened or actual hysterics of a frustrated woman as
played by Agnes Moorehead, an excellent actress here portraying
Holt's maiden aunt and long secretly in love with Cotten.   However,
she's hysterical too often for the film's good.   Introducing a story
point via the mouths of bystanders is another trick Welles utilizes
here.

Of the original Mercury Theatre group in Kane, only Cotten, Miss Moorehead, Ray Collins, playing an uncle of Holt, and Erskine Sanford, who is the bystander always hoping young Holt will get his final due, are included in Ambersons. They give fine performances. Welles' screenplay is far from good, being slow-moving and completely actionless. The dialog at times sounds childish.

With the exception of Miss Moorehead, Welles evidently strove for the non-theatrical in performance. Hence Cotten works like a man on the street; ditto Miss Costello, Ray Collins, who is one of the few in the cast who smile, and Richard Bennett. The latter evidences none of the scenery-chewing for which he was once known. Miss Baxter, a cute, personable and fine little actress, is another on the more cheerful side. Don Dillaway isn't seen much, but furnishes one of the picture's two deaths, the other being that of Miss Costello. She's still very attractive and does as good an acting job as possible in a stilted role.

Cameraman Cortez, evidently following Welles' orders, filmed the picture virtually entirely in dark and shade. It's sombre and unattractive.

At the finale, Welles' offstage voice re-introduces the players, a closeup of each flashing on the screen, and then speaks the credits for cameraman, etc., finally winding up with a personal bow for his own triple-threat job of scenarist, production and direction. He actually has very little to be proud of, nor has Booth Tarkington, who wrote the best-selling novel on which this film is based.

--"Scho" in Variety, Vol. 147,
No. 4 (July 1, 1942), page 8.

☐ THE MALTESE FALCON (Warner Bros., 1941)

Dashiell Hammett, who gave the movies The Thin Man, rates the first curtain call for The Maltese Falcon. After that, applaud the movie-wise imagination of the director, John Huston (who also adapted the screen play) and his co-operative cast.

For The Maltese Falcon, like the first Thin Man, cuts away from the established murder mystery routine and rediscovers the wonderful art of story-telling, an art that keeps an audience uncertain to the very last scene. Filmed once, in 1931, it certainly bears re-telling.

Its suspense is based on characterization. Its most absorbing question is not so much who killed who as what's going to happen to these people?--a rich assortment of scoundrels, such as you rarely meet in a movie, each trying to outsmart the others for possession of the gem-studded falcon. They're not the polite penthouse

crowd of The Thin Man; they all carry guns, and for good reason.
There are Humphrey Bogart, a tough, iron-willed private detective,
perhaps a little too clever to be credible; Mary Astor, adventuress
with a string of aliases, best of all "Brigid O'Shaughnessy"; Peter
Lorre, an effeminate rogue with a gardenia-scented calling card;
Sidney Greenstreet (in an auspicious movie debut), a grossly fat and
elegant crook; Elisha Cook, Jr. , his chicken-hearted gunman.

All of them, and even the bit players, have polished their
roles to a shiny perfection. (One bit player, incidentally, you'll
recognize as Walter Huston, appearing so briefly in his son's
movie that he doesn't even get screen credit.) But it's John Huston who wrote the screen lines they speak and whose camera ideas
enhance these performances.

The Maltese Falcon is his first movie, and though it leaves
a few loose threads ungathered at its finish, it's good enough to
make the next John Huston picture something to look forward to.
                                    --Louise Levitas in PM (October
                                       5, 1941), page 19.

                        *   *   *

Spasms of moral reformation never weaken the course of
Dashiell Hammett's plots. His Maltese Falcon now turns up with
a substantial cast of actors who can be tough on occasion (Mary
Astor, Gladys George, Humphrey Bogart, Peter Lorre, and that
rotund expert in villainies, Sidney Greenstreet) and who here live
up to the strictest Hammett standards. Such an airy release from
the normal human hesitancies and repugnances as the Hammett
stories provoke--the quick adjustment of nerves to murder at a
moment's notice--give something breezy and comical to all Hammett's works. You probably recall this particular novel of a few
years back and remember how the mysterious porcelain image from
the days of the Crusaders brought about a series of fast shootings
and considerable intrigue in modern San Francisco. A beautiful
Miss O'Shaughnessy calls upon Sam Spade, private detective, asks
his aid, and begins to fib and fib. Then, quickly enough, come
the shootings. There is, indeed, such a delirium of fibbing and
killing and passion that we spectators, humdrum at heart after all,
are never quite entirely sure what is happening, or that it makes
any sense or is ever made tidy by logic. The delirium is sufficient, however, and somehow the effect is nicely refreshing, the
wilder the better.
                                    --John Mosher in The New Yorker
                                       (October 4, 1941), pages 63-64.

☐ MEET JOHN DOE (Warner Bros. , 1941)

One hour ago I saw "The End" fade in on the screen to signify my meeting with John Doe was over. I think it is too soon for

me to comment on this Frank Capra production, but this Spectator is waiting for what I have to say about it, and I have no choice. The reason I say it may be too soon to review it is the doubt I feel now that any picture could be as near perfection as I think this one is.   If fate ordained that you could see only one drama during the next decade, I unhesitatingly would recommend that you see Meet John Doe at once, as the chances are remote that during the decade you will have an opportunity to see another even as good. It is by long odds the best thing Capra has done; it raises him to greater heights, gives him new importance, gives the screen new dignity.

There is a lesson in Meet John Doe as universal as humanity itself, a lesson driven home by great screen writing, great direction, great acting.   For two hours it will hold you in its grip, thrill you with its power, melt you with its humanness, leave you speechless when it ends.   It is one of the greatest arguments for right living ever presented by any medium.   And still it is superb entertainment.

For those who can appreciate film craftsmanship on its own account the picture will be an intellectual delight.   No other offering since screen entertainment was born has achieved greater technical perfection.   You have learned to anticipate brilliant direction when you see a Capra picture, but you scarcely can anticipate such a degree of perfection as distinguishes this one.   It is a creation every student of the screen must see, one which teaches Hollywood how talking pictures should be made.   He will find here a group of people in various walks of life, working out their problems without once reminding him they are actors playing parts, ordinary people who converse with one another and do not declaim lines in the loud tones which mar so many motion pictures.

Capra makes marvelous use of his camera as his chief story-telling medium, and relegates the microphone to its rightful secondary status.   He keeps his screen alive with smoothly flowing movement and weights every foot of film with its share of the story burden.   Robert Riskin's screen play, based on a story by Richard Connell and Robert Presnell, is a brilliant achievement.   Settings by Stephen Goosson, photography by George Barnes, and all other technical contributions reflect screen craftsmanship at the peak of its perfection.

Only superb performances could be the result of such masterly direction.   Not one person in the long and distinguished cast ever gave a performance to match in excellence the one we have here. Gary Cooper reveals powers he never previously had more than hinted at; Barbara Stanwyck rises to emotional heights she never before had reached.   Edward Arnold, Walter Brennan, James Gleason, Spring Byington, Gene Lockhart distinguish themselves in important roles.   Rod La Rocque, Irving Bacon and Regis Toomey make valuable contributions to the feast of fine acting.   But it is impossible in the time at my command to make adequate acknowledg-

ment of the many perfect contributions to this perfect whole. Nor
can you who read what I have written get more than a hint of the
treat in store for you when you meet John Doe.

--Welford Beaton in Hollywood
Spectator, Vol. 15, No. 6
(March 15, 1941), page 13.

*   *   *

In Meet John Doe, Frank Capra and Robert Riskin have provided an "inspirational" anthem, aimed at the more emotional members of the country's corn belt. Its rhythms proffer the intellectual
stimulus of an Aimee Semple McPherson camp meeting, plus the
added delights of such civilized bons mots as one encounters at a
gathering of the International Ladies Garment Workers' Union. All
stops are pulled out in sentimentalizing the bucolic viewpoint, and
the considerable din fondly hopes to be mistaken for a sublime orchestration of democracy.

A number of years ago, King Vidor produced The Crowd, an
admirable, sincere and thoroughly literate glorification of the Average Man. It made a heart-rending appeal for social equality, struck
its roots deep in American simplicity and flowered as a photoplay
of integrity and worth. But Meet John Doe employs trivial hokum
in an effort to achieve the same results. Outside of the warm and
inventive comedy of its early reels, the picture is completely formula and makes still another trip to the well from which came the rich
rewards of Mr. Deeds Goes to Town and Mr. Smith Goes to Washington. Again we are treated to the young hayseed who finally out-
smarts the urban rats, the worldly wench who turns heroine under
the persuasions of True Love, etc., etc.

Mr. Deeds and Mr. Smith were simple chaps, but John Doe
suffers from delusions of grandeur. First he dons the robes of a
modern messiah for sheer gain. Then, like the central figures of
The Miracle Man, The Angel of Broadway and The Sorcerer's Ap-
prentice, he becomes obsessed with the conviction that he is the
symbol of an arbitrary truth. The local newspapers have devoted
numerous columns to the discussion as to whether or no John Doe
should have met a tragic end to justify the faith he aroused. The
pundits of print have made no mention as to the plausibility of the
man arousing faith in the first place. This department has a deep
belief that the average American is not a dunce, that he is not carried away by pap and piffle. I sincerely suspect that my neighbors
are a mite too logical to think that a slap on the back (or any other
part of the anatomy, for that matter) can cure the ills of an ailing
world. To believe that they would up and follow a small-time baseball player because of an obvious, mumbled speech heard over the
radio, amounts to declaring that they are eligible for the nearest
boobyhatch. There are those, indeed, who are inflamed by George
M. Cohan flag-waving, exalted by the works of Dale Carnegie and
Lloyd C. Douglas. But to state that such citizens are in the majority is a direct and consummate libel.

Capra knows the art of picture making. It is apparent in every foot of film he shoots; and this is all the more reason to be indignant that he has chosen to aim at the lowest common denominator. Under his guidance, Gary Cooper gives the most superlative performance of his career; Barbara Stanwyck gains a new, feminine charm and has acquired a becoming warmth of manner. Walter Brennan, as the individualist to whom a train whistle is the sirens' song, is a completely believable character. No sheep is Walter; and neither is the American man-in-the-street. Edward Arnold, restrained and flexible, scores as the would-be Fascist President. James Gleason and Regis Toomey are excellent, despite the maudlin "big scenes" they are handed. Rod LaRocque returns to the screen as the second heavy of the piece; it's good to see him back.

You are going to hear about <u>Meet John Doe</u>. You may want to see <u>Meet John Doe</u>. And I'd very much like to eavesdrop on your comments when you exit from the theater.

--Herb Sterne in <u>Rob Wagner's</u>
<u>Script</u>, Vol. 25, No. 592
(March 22, 1941), page 16.

*   *   *

*SITUATION--Barbara Stanwyck loses her job as reporter when her newspaper changes management. To give the new owner a headache, she composes a fake letter and puts it in her final column. The letter states that the writer, who is unemployed, has been made so unhappy by the misery and injustice in the world caused by man's inhumanity to man that life has become intolerable. The writer realizes the hopelessness of raising his lone voice against the powers of corruption, and so he is going to make a final gesture to arouse the public. He says that he is going to jump off the top of the highest building in the city on Christmas Eve. Thus will he proclaim, through an act which will be shouted round the world: "I protest!" The letter is signed "John Doe."

The effect of the message exceeds Barbara's fondest hopes. The contents are brought to the attention of the governor. Civic organizations swoop down on the mayor. They will not stand for this man's killing himself. The newspaper is really on a spot. Everyone is asking "Who is this John Doe?" The newspaper sends out an appeal for the writer of the letter to call at its offices immediately. There is no need for him to consider suicide. There is a good job awaiting him. Then the editor, James Gleason, who fired Barbara, sends for her. When she tells him the letter was a fake, that there is no John Doe, he's fit for a strait jacket. The newspaper will be held up to ridicule; it will lose prestige--and circulation.

At this moment, in answer to the paper's appeal, a mob of
ragged men swarm into the building. Each claims he wrote the
letter. The editor is about to drive them all out when Barbara
springs her big idea. It's this: Why not select a John Doe from
among the gang of men in the outer office claiming to be the John
Doe? Pick out the one who looks most like the typical American.
Give him a publicity build-up, then run articles in the paper signed
by John Doe--articles attacking everything of which the newspaper
disapproves. They'll use him as the Common Man through whom
they can air their own grievances. "I protest against this abuse
in distributing relief money! I protest against this or that tax! I
protest ... --signed, John Doe."

Editor Gleason falls for the stunt. They look over the phony
John Does. Among them is a tall, lean hobo (Gary Cooper). He
admits his name is not John Doe. John Willoughby is the name--
Long John to the guys he used to play baseball with. Yeah. Bush-
league pitcher. He'd had a chance to go to the big leagues, but
then his arm went bad.

Barbara and the editor explain the setup, and Gary agrees
to co-operate. So the hoax starts rolling--like a snowball downhill.
The climax is a radio speech by John Doe. The speech, written
by Barbara, is based on notes from her father's diary. He had
been a doctor--a great humanitarian who was always helping others.
And he died penniless. So Barbara puts the thoughts of her fine
dad into the mouth of her fake John Doe. The speech is a sensa-
tion. But Long John becomes frightened at the stir he has caused
and runs away. But there is no escaping. The thing has become
too big. John Doe Clubs have sprung up everywhere. The owner
of the newspaper, Edward Arnold, has John apprehended. Then
Arnold and Barbara explain to Gary that he has become the voice
of the common people. Everywhere folks are taking the advice he
gave over the radio--going back to the Golden Rule, tearing down
their spite fences, getting to know and love their neighbors.

The people in the small town where John was tracked down
stage a demonstration in his honor, and he realizes the amazing
influence for good he is creating. So he goes back on the radio
and makes lecture tours. Soon he has so many followers that one
fact is clear: John Doe and the John Doe Clubs control enough votes
to swing a national election. Particularly aware of this fact is
ruthless, powerful, ambitious capitalist Edward Arnold, who has
built up the whole movement with one idea in mind. When the time
is ripe, he will have his stooge John Doe make a radio speech in
which he will tell the public that at last he has found the one man
who has all of the fine qualities which he and his army of followers
demand in their candidate for the Presidency of the United States--
Edward Arnold.

Comes the day selected by Arnold. Through his newspaper
he has had John Doe representatives from all over the country
brought to attend a mass meeting in his city. Arnold dictates his

speech and demands that John deliver it to his assembled followers.
He refuses.   So Arnold goes before the meeting and exposes John
Doe as a fake.   He makes John admit that he is not John Doe,
that he did not write the original letter, and that he had no intention of jumping off a building on Christmas Eve as a protest against
injustice.   Then, when John attempts to explain his position, Arnold's hoodlums cut the cables and silence the loudspeakers, while
other Arnold hirelings incite the crowd against their former hero.
The crowd turns on the poor fellow, and he has to be escorted
away by police to escape violence.

And so in a few minutes John Doe becomes the most despised
man in America--forced to hide his face, avoid recognition.   But
one thought is with him always: He cannot--he will not--let die all
the good he has started.   So he makes his decision.   There is one
way in which he can definitely convince his followers that he was
honest and sincere, despite the deception through which he became
their leader.   He will carry out the threat of that fictitious John
Doe.   He will jump off the top of the highest building in the city on
Christmas Eve!   What happens next will be revealed when you see
the film.

COMMENT--A critic could no more advise people against
seeing Meet John Doe than he could advise them against believing
in the Golden Rule.   That's what the film is--a superbly produced,
wonderfully acted, beautifully written motion picture based on the
simple theme that everything would be sweetness and light if we
would make an effort to know one another better.   It comes at a
time when the country is hungry for such homely, down-to-earth
sentiment.   It will cause Parent-Teachers' Associations to get out
bulletins of endorsement, civic clubs to proclaim their approval,
censorship boards to throw away their scissors.   Neighbors who
haven't spoken since one's little boy kicked the other's little boy in
the teeth will, after listening to evangelist John Doe, walk out of
the theatre with their arms around each other.

To give credit properly, let's start with producer-director
Frank Capra.   I have become convinced that Mr. Capra either owns
a piece of the Golden Rule or holds the exclusive motion picture
rights to the idea.   Mr. Capra apparently loves to think that everybody is a right guy and all's for the best.   A few days before this
review was written, I lunched with Mr. Capra at a race track.
From the look of understanding on his face when the horse finished
10th, you would have thought that Mr. Capra just knew that the
poor horse couldn't do any better because it was worried about
things at home.

In Mr. Capra's films there are no really bad people.   Search
as you will, after the final fade-out you cannot point to a real heel
in the cast.   Well, maybe a heel but never a louse.   No matter
how much of a no-good so-and-so one of Mr. Capra's characters
may be for eight or nine reels, Mr. Capra will clean him up--even
if he has to do it in the last 10 feet of film (as he does in this one).

But let me express my disapproval of this minor item before
it slips my mind.   There is so much to commend in Meet John Doe
that you are likely to forget the straws of imperfection at which you
must grasp in order to gripe.   And here is my complaint.   Edward
Arnold not only represents rich, unscrupulous vested interests; he's
also the protagonist of some sort of ism.   In one of his speeches
he mentions a "new order," and he even has his own private police.
Gathered around him, in one scene, are other powerful figures in
industry, politics, and labor--all approving his nasty scheme to use
John Doe as a means of becoming President of the United States.
The labor power, obviously a disorganizer and troublemaker, okays
the plan, then adds, "But don't forget to cut me in," or something
to that effect.   In other words, Mr. Arnold's pals represent the
rotten side of capital and labor.   And he's their boss.

The final chapter of the film, as outlined, deals with the
suicide angle.   Mr. Arnold and a group of his henchmen go to the
top of the building mentioned in the original fake John Doe letter.
After exposing John Doe, they have dared him to jump, and they're
afraid he might.   So their plan is to prevent the suicide.   But when
John Doe appears on the tower and walks over toward the railing,
Mr. Arnold, who is hidden, makes no move.   He even holds out his
hand to restrain one man who starts forward.   He then allows John
to walk all the way to the railing, meditate for a few moments, and
start to climb over the railing before he, Arnold, says, "I wouldn't
do that."   He had every chance to seize Doe and hold him when he
first appeared, but once John had reached the railing, Mr. Arnold
had no power other than his words to prevent the suicide.   Of
course, it was necessary to allow John Doe to go to the railing to
give the scene added suspense.   But Mr. Arnold's actions, or lack
of them, come under the head of criminal negligence in my book.

Before this scene ends, Mr. Arnold makes a gesture which
would indicate that he has experienced a complete change of heart--
in the space of but a few minutes.   He quietly orders one of his
men to reprint John Doe's farewell letter on the front page of his
newspaper.   I respectfully ask you readers who see this film to
remember this point and see if you do not agree that the producer
should have let Mr. Arnold remain the villain rather than attempt
to clean him up with one line of dialogue.

Gary Cooper as John Doe offers what I believe is the best
performance of his screen career.   He is (as are all of Mr. Capra's characters) someone you might know in your own town.   And
that first radio speech he makes is something you will carry away
from the theatre with you.   Listen for the hush (and I mean just
that) which will undoubtedly come over the audience in which you
are sitting when he ends his speech, his voice dropping until it
almost trails away on the words, "Wake up, John Doe.   You are
the hope of the world."   In praising Gary Cooper on this score, we
automatically praise another man.   The change of mood effected by
those last lines are typical of the great human understanding which
makes Mr. Capra a figure apart in his own field of producing and

directing. He is a great student of the human heart, this Frank
Capra.

Now you can just repeat that first line about Gary but insert
the name of Barbara Stanwyck. In the early moments of the film
she handles swift-moving comedy with deft authority. In the final
moments her emotional scenes are genuinely moving. Our sincere
congratulations, Miss Stanwyck.

And now, just to cross up our readers completely, I will
say that the finest acting bit in the film is contributed by neither
Miss Stanwyck nor Mr. Cooper. The palm goes to Jimmy Gleason
for his magnificent pretending during the scene in the bar when he
tells Gary how Edward Arnold is trying to use him. Jimmy starts
the conversation on a note which a few years ago would have been
pointed to by critics as flag-waving hokum. Well, it's not hokum
today; it never was hokum. Not as Mr. Gleason offers it, with a
quiet sincerity which projects from the screen with every syllable
and hits you right where Mr. Gleason says the "Star-spangled Banner" hits him--somewhere between the heart and the stomach.
Yes, Mr. Gleason says that. He also says, "I'm a sucker for this
country," and, "Nobody's going to take my liberty away from me,"
and, "When they play the 'Star-spangled Banner,' it hits me here,"
pointing to his solar plexus. And to this last remark, Mr. Cooper
nods and replies, "Yes, I know. It always hits me here"--and he
gives himself a quick rabbit punch on the back of the neck. In that
short scene Mr. Gleason expresses practically all the sentiments
that have been going through the minds of Americans in recent
months. It might be called "Patriotism--in one easy lesson." I
can't wait to see Jimmy Gleason to tell him so.

It has always seemed to me that most directors give us too
much moving with a movie camera. While two persons are talking,
the camera shows one face, then the other. Then close-ups and
profiles and anything else they can possibly throw in to do it the
hard way, change setups, take up time, spend money, and make it
seem difficult. But just notice how Mr. Capra leaves his camera
alone when he gets a good scene going, such as this one between
Mr. Gleason and Mr. Cooper. And that long speech earlier in the
film delivered by the soda jerker. Which is another fine bit,
thanks to that greatly neglected actor Regis Toomey. The average
director would have had his camera everywhere except in Mr.
Toomey's hip pocket during his lengthy address.

(By the way, Frank, I would have done without old Mrs.
Delaney's kissing Gary's hand at the end of Toomey's scene. And
say: Remember what we were saying about background music that
day at Santa Anita--you and Gregory Ratoff and I? Well, now,
mister, please explain to me why in one scene between Barbara
and Gary they used Cole Porter's "Begin the Beguine" for atmospheric music?)

Walter Brennan as the Professor (always warning Gary not
to accumulate money or he'll become one of the heelots--all rich

folks to the Professor being a lot of heels); Edward Arnold as the
scheming capitalist; Rod LaRocque as Mr. Arnold's equally crafty
nephew (and why don't we see more of him?); Spring Byington as
Barbara's mother--every member of the enormous cast, in fact,
rates a bow.

Also bouquets for Production Designer William Cameron
Menzies and Cameraman George Barnes.

Which brings us to Mr. Capra's other self--his companion,
guide, advisor, friend, utility infielder, and pinch hitter--Robert
Riskin.   In addition to these chores, Mr. Riskin is Mr. Capra's
scenarist and word-weaver.   If Mr. Capra suddenly composes a
new piece of business in a scene, Bob steps in and supplies the
lyrics.   If Frank dreams up a new character, five minutes later
Bob's got him talking.   When it comes to dialogue, Bob does everything except talk in Mr. Capra's sleep.

As a director-writer team these two gents have given us
such entertainment as It Happened One Night, Mr. Deeds Goes to
Town, and You Can't Take It with You.   And now this fine, timely,
inspiring film.   It's a pleasure to pay tribute to creators of such
superior entertainment, especially when they happen to be just as
likable when they're being themselves as they are admirable when
they're being geniuses.

OPINION--Worth its weight in dramatic goose bumps, patriotic spine chills, and intelligent, wholesome entertainment.   Plus
a timely reminder of the great American ideal which made this
country possible: Give your neighbor a break.

(P. S. to Frank and Bob: Which of you birds thought up the
cute business on the freight car when Walter Brennan makes those
drum noises before the start of his duet with Gary?   I made a bet
with Fred Astaire that it was Bob.)

(P. P. S. to Gary: You are wonderful, fellow.   But baseball
players will never believe you ever were a pitcher.   In the bushes
or anywhere else.   Not with that delivery.   The wind-up is okay,
but the finish-un-uh.   I wouldn't bring it up, but I used to be a
bush-league pitcher myself.)

                                        --Harry Evans in Family Circle
                                        (April 11, 1941), pages 15,
                                        16 and 19.

☐   MEET ME IN ST. LOUIS (M-G-M, 1945)

It is likely that everybody but the Warner frères will be delighted by Meet Me in St. Louis.

The movie adaptation of the Sally Benson stories is very much the Day family moved west and set to music, and MGM has so festooned the material that there will be very little that is novel left about Life with Father when that play, which the Warners recently purchased from Oscar Serlin at a husky price, finally reaches the screen.

Set against a nostalgic period in America's age of innocence --the precise years are 1903-04--Meet Me in St. Louis contrives to make the era appear uniformly picturesque and pleasant in a way remindful of Ruritania. Instead of Rudolph Rassendyll and the Princess Flavia, the central protagonists are here named Smith, but, nevertheless, they possess all the shimmer and sham and sunny dispositions of mythical kingdom characters.

The sets and Technicolor photography set a captivating mood, and director Vincente Minnelli has paced the piece for a leisurely and wholly encompassing charm. The costumes, by Irene and Sharaff, are wonderfully decorative, and aid to provide a pleasure no other musical film has so successfully managed since Cover Girl.

Judy Garland, both pert and pretty, again proves that she is a persuasive performer, as well as one of the screen's top purveyors of popular tunes. Judy is heard to best advantage with "The Boy Next Door," even though it is "The Trolley Song" which is heard most frequently on the juke boxes of laager emporiums. Mary Astor, one of the most lovely ladies to face a camera, is excellent, as usual, and there are certain other competent contributions from Lucille Bremer, Marjorie Main and June Lockhart.

In the matter of Margaret O'Brien, this department admits complete prejudice. For something over a quarter of a century the antics of such cinematic half-pints as Baby Marie Osborne, Little Thelma Salter, Jane and Katherine Lee, Jane Withers, Baby Peggy, Shirley Temple, Little Mary McCallister, Mary Louise Miller and sundry other exponents of the bum-freezer-frocks coterie of cuteness have drawn from this scrivener but one reaction, that of violent nausea. In the pursuit of complete honesty, I am forced to report that the O'Brien fragment seems to me to be no whit less like histrionic ipecacuanha than her many, many mite predecessors.

--Herb Sterne in Rob Wagner's Script, Vol. 31, No. 395 (January 6, 1945), page 22.

☐ MIGHTY JOE YOUNG (Arko/RKO, 1949)

Mighty Joe Young is a stop action novelty film whose special effects, trick photography and spectacle of a giant gorilla terrorizing a huge city form intriguing exploitation angles. It has been some

time since the screen has seen such a wide-eyed adventure drama,
and a whole new generation has grown up since the memorable
King Kong.   This gives Mighty Joe Young a mighty advantage at the
boxoffice.   The enterprising exhibitor who capitalizes on its unusual-
ness and who circuses his publicity campaign will find the results
profitable.   The attraction is particularly well suited to the action
and juvenile trade.

As a story Mighty Joe Young leaves much to be desired.   It
is little more than footage strung together by a plot that rarely
makes sense.   But there's no denying that the piece has everything
in the book--wild animals escaping from their cages, a drunken
gorilla, heavies, and a fire (done in red) in which the gorilla saves
school children from the burning building.   You may laugh at
Mighty Joe Young but you won't be bored.

Story has Robert Armstrong as a publicity hound theatrical
producer who makes a safari to Africa to bring back animals for
the new cafe he is opening in Hollywood.   He comes back with a
prize, a huge gorilla owned by Terry Moore, who has cared for
the animal and trained him since he was a baby.   The opening sequences, in which the gorilla is bought by a child, are, by the
way, extremely clever.   From the moment of the gorilla's arrival
in New York the story takes a pat course.   The animal escapes
and frightens everyone nearly to death.   The police decide to shoot
him.   Armstrong, Miss Moore, and her sweetheart Ben Johnson
set out for the harbor to get him on a ship.   En route the fire
breaks out and the gorilla becomes quite a hero.

Terry Moore is excellent as the girl who knows and understands the huge monster.   Ben Johnson, lean and lanky, is charming as the rodeo rider who succumbs to the charms of both Miss
Moore and her strange pet.   It's good to see Robert Armstrong in
a glib, high-powered role again.   Frank McHugh's few comedy
scenes are done with usual zany style.   Supporting cast is uniformly good.

John Ford and Merian C. Cooper, plainly, had their tongues
in their cheeks when this was shot.   Their show is wild, woolly
and entertaining.   Director Ernest B. Schoedsack offers a directorial job that highlights the action scenes and rather ignores the
story.   Technician Willis O'Brien, photographer J. Roy Hunt and
Harold Stine and Bert Willis who supply the photographic effects are
to be commended for interesting and imaginative work.   Linwood
Dunn supplies the excellent optical photography.   James Basevi's
art direction is craftsmanlike.   Roy Webb's musical score has excitement.   Ted Cheesman is credited with the editing.

                              --The Hollywood Reporter, Vol.
                              104, No. 7 (May 24, 1949),
                              page 3.

□   MILDRED PIERCE (Warner Bros. , 1945)

        Miss Crawford returns to the screen after an all-too-long
absence playing, with polish and restraint, a mother who lavishes
love and indulgences on a revoltingly selfish daughter.   Her first
marriage has been a failure so she sets out to make a way for her
two children after shedding her feckless husband, and does famous-
ly with a string of restaurants that she establishes.   But money
doesn't satisfy her unscrupulous kid.   She wants social standing,
so the mother marries a bounder with plenty of blue blood and no
money.   Things grow rather sticky from then out, until someone
murders the second husband and Mildred finds herself explaining
things to the district attorney.   In the film Miss Crawford shows
an increasingly mature and subtle technique in her acting and insight into character.   Jack Carson plays an earthy real estate
agent with style and force.   Zachary Scott does a fine job with the
broken-down socialite.   And Ann Blyth interprets the role of the
nasty daughter with a brattishness that would get up anyone's dan-
der.   The production of this study in fulsome maternalism is
smooth and handsome and very movie-wise.
                              --New Movies, Vol. 20, No. 7
                              (October 1945), page 18.

                    *   *   *

        It is not until Mildred Pierce has ended and you have had
the first chance to get your breath since its start, that you realize
what a truly great motion picture it is; what a disturbing emotional
experience; what a brilliantly distinguished production.   Then you
realize what a powerful woman's drama it is and what a wallop it
plants on the minds of men, and you start thinking about its boxoffice chances.   The Wald production can hardly fail to pass practically all Warner Bros. money hits that have preceded it, for it
is so laden with every single factor that goes to make a popular
success that it is almost without an equal as the perfect example
of motion picture entertainment.

        Mildred Pierce has everything.   A great star name in her
most dazzling brilliance, a screenplay that bares emotion and then
turns the screws on it, direction that never once fails to wring you
limp and a production that not only welds these creative elements
superbly together but is breathlessly beautiful on the physical side.

        The mature mentality which is splashed prodigiously over the
screen gives heart to those who would have their screen grow with
the times.   So Mildred Pierce is a laying of their trump cards on
the table for Michael Curtiz, who was never so completely the master of power and passion as he is in it; for Jerry Wald, who has
evolved from fine writer alone to a shrewd trader in the mart where
people pay for emotional thrills; for Joan Crawford, who wears the
mantle of actress with an assurance and distinction not many of her
contemporaries can even claim; for Ranald MacDougall, whose screen-

play has probed into all the twisted byways of human behavior and
found the souls of his men and his women. These four talents
blaze upon the screen with warmth and with lustre, ripe and full-
bodied, with intelligence of a new order that proudly speaks the
harmony with which they labored to create this magnificent pas-
sionel.

The story of Mildred Pierce may be told in a few sentences.
It is in the developing of the characters by MacDougall and the
manner in which Curtiz strips them of outward appearances to bare
their emotions that the picture has its major lusty strength. Mildred was the wife of a struggling real estate salesman. She slaved
to give her daughters all the things she never had at the cost of
her husband's love. When he leaves her she becomes a waitress
by day and a cook for the restaurant by night. When the brat of
an elder daughter taunts her with her past, she takes the plunge
into the business world that sets her up as the success of successes
among businesswomen. Side-stepping the predatory advances of her
husband's ex-partner, she uses his business head well but has
picked up a new love along the way, a down-on-his-luck playboy
who gives her life the glamour she always wanted. The pampered,
spoiled daughter gets into one mess after another, with her mother
always buying her out of them, until finally she leaves home and
her mother sees her next making a spectacle of herself in a cheap
night spot. The entire film is told most skilfully in flashback. It
opens with a murder under intriguingly written and staged mysterious circumstances. The story unfolds as Mildred tells it to the
intelligently written police officer character. Mildred has married
the playboy finally to win her daughter back to a kind of home the
girl wants, although the kept toy he has since become allows her
no chance to love him. The identity of his murderer is kept a
well-written secret until the very end and you will be hard put to
remember even one second in which your interest is allowed to
waver from the telling of this absorbing drama as Curtiz has staged
it.

Joan Crawford, ever a star among stars, plays Mildred with
unerring artistry, shading it with passion and tenderness to make it
rank close to the top among all the memorable roles she has created for the screen. She is as radiantly lovely as she has ever
been for Ernest Haller's masterfully directed camera but it is an
inner rather than outward strength that reveals how Miss Crawford
has pulled this role up to her superb measure. She feels it with
enormous vitality and projects the love of an artist for a role that
challenges her.

Ann Blyth sparks Miss Crawford in the role of her daughter
and provides the flint that draws her fire. You will be spellbound
at the several scenes in which the two square off for a dramatic
match of the century. This Blyth child is exquisite in her understanding of one of the most difficult roles ever written. Only the
undeniable genius that has made Joan Crawford the great popular
star she long since became enables her to keep Ann Blyth from
running off with the film.

Every role is given all the footage it needs, however, and
therein is another facet of its strength.   Curtiz, wise man that he
is, pits all his players against the other until one watches with
bated breath for the explosion that is latent under the surface emotions they hide.   So Zachary Scott is allowed to make of his assignment one of his most distinguished performances, a scoundrel
so polished in his interpretation that he makes you feel pity for
him.   His is great acting.   Jack Carson, too, is allowed to find
sympathy for his mountebank and makes his strong support an important factor in the drama.   In many respects, this is about as
fine a job as Carson has ever done and he has done a great many.

Nor will any gainsay what a romp Eve Arden makes of the
comedy lead.   With some richly racy dialogue from the agile Mac-
Dougall pen, she takes a back seat to none when she is on the
screen, which is fortunately often.   Bruce Bennett is awfully good
in the script's only colorless role, and it must be admitted that
its very colorlessness is a spoke in the wheel that turns its staggering drama.   Moroni Olsen, Manart Kippen, Barbara Brown,
Butterfly McQueen, Jo Ann Marlowe and John Compton are really
excellent.

Mildred Pierce is a picture consummately produced.   There
is no single line of dialogue that is wasted, no gesture that is unnecessary.   It is as tight and beautifully put together a picture as
has ever come forth from this industry.   It is the example--at last
--of what the films can do with adult drama, proving beyond question that even such novels as James Cain's can be invested with
sympathy for their strong characters and clothed in the glamour
that movie fans have always deemed uppermost in their entertainments.

It is thus you will find Haller's camera gilding everything it
touches and making even the drab attractive.   You will find Anton
Grot at the peak of his artistry still again, giving you a cottage
which you can see the girl wanting to get out of, or the beach house
which you can see the playboy tenaciously hanging on to.   The set
decorations by George James Hopkins also are understandingly put
in their places.   Accomplished editing means a credit to David
Weisbart that sets him a little apart in his craft.   Max Steiner's
music is mood and magic as it underlines emotion or crashes upon
the senses.   The orchestral arrangements were in the capable hands
of Hugo Friedhofer and the musical direction in Leo Forbstein's.

The release of this new Jerry Wald production on the heels
of his record-breaking Pride of the Marines is another proud day
for Warner Brothers.   Whether they were in the business for the
prestige or the money, it opens the door wide for both.   Mildred
Pierce is going to be that kind of popular hit which have been so
few in this industry's 50 years that you can safely count them on
the fingers of both hands.

                              --Hollywood Review, Vol. 36, No.
                              4 (October 1, 1945), pages 1
                              and 6.

☐ THE MIRACLE OF MORGAN'S CREEK (Paramount, 1944)

Satire, that pertinent evaluation of the commonplace, is a
rare entrant in the realm of the motion picture. With but a few
salubrious exceptions, the Hollywood photoplay condemns itself to
emblazoning the spurious, flattering banality and defending a complete lack of discrimination.

Chaplin, both in his comedies and his irreverently ironic
drama, A Woman of Paris, skillfully annotated the pages of that
present when the films were made. Ben Hecht, with the assistance
of Charles MacArthur in The Scoundrel, and alone in Nothing Sacred, discerningly dissertated on a way of life and living. Lowell
Sherman's What Price Hollywood? was an adroit passage of arms
with certain standards, and the salty asides linger in memory, despite a lapse of years. Erich von Stroheim in Greed, Foolish
Wives and The Merry Widow used his wit as a scalpel to dissect
folly and frailty. Ernst Lubitsch, too, in the early films he made
in America, was pungently observant.

However, with these and a few other sparse exceptions, the
Hollywood film prefers to survey life with the complete relish a
parlourmaid bestows upon the novels of Mrs. Georgie Sheldon.

Satire requires a highly personalized stance, and it is perhaps for this reason it is so infrequently encountered in the average film--which is more of a collaboration and a series of concessions than it is a creation. Since satire, fundamentally, is a one-
man show, its successful exercise in the motion picture medium
means that the artist must also be no mean exponent of pugilism,
one who is willing and capable of battling the stupidities of the
studios, exhibitors and "the public."

Preston Sturges must not only be cerebrally muscular to
have coerced a celluloid factory into permitting him to make The
Great McGinty and Christmas in July, but his prowess with his
dukes must certainly rival that of Joe Louis. And now comes
Sturges with The Miracle of Morgan's Creek, a photoplay so witty
and so wise that he no doubt had to battle the Front Office like a
combination Firpo-Carpentier-Dempsey-Sullivan-Tunney in order to
project it on the screen in its present state of perfection.

The Miracle of Morgan's Creek is not only Sturges' major
cinematic effort, but it is also one of my favorite motion pictures.
It is so brilliant and blithe that it is likely to keep the eclectic
patron out of the picture emporiums for a full twelvemonth after
its unveiling, because of the fear that anything seen thereafter, by
contrast, is likely to seem vapid, inane and dull. As writer and
director of this photoplay, Sturges appears in the role of the artist-
commentator, discoursing on the ways and waverings of our fellow
citizens, and his running narration on the American scene can only
be compared with the best of the essays H. L. Mencken contributed
on the subject some years back.

The film is no less noteworthy than the accomplishments of
that literary poltergeist in its acute observation, dislike and ability
to cause discomfort to Mrs. Grundy and her multitudinous brood.
Sturges touches lightly but disastrously on such widely divergent
topics as Jive, Jingoism, The Movies, Soft Beverages, Hard Liq-
uor, The Viciousness of Virtue, The Stupidity of Sin, The USO,
Wedlock, True Love, The Law, Justice, The Wiles of Women,
Motherhood, The Foolishness of Men, Politics, Honest Toil, The
Armed Forces of World War I, The Armed Forces of World War
II, and sundry other subjects of moment.   And through it all run
Trudy Kockenlocker and Norval Jones, such a heroine and such a
hero as you have never seen before in the realm of the cinema.

The comedy spins like a pinwheel, races like a high-powered
launch, and on occasion, capers like a kitten on a catnip jag.   Certain of my confrères have seriously informed me: (a.) "The work
lacks 'good taste'..."; (b.) "It is an insult to American Woman-
hood..."; (c.) "It is a subversive gnawing at the very roots of
Democracy...".   Still, I am afraid, I found it one of the wittiest
and most enjoyable celluloid strips ever to run through a projection
machine, and one of the rare films that may be unreservedly recommended to one's friends.

Thanks very much, Preston Sturges, for providing The Miracle of Morgan's Creek, which is as provocative, amusing and di-
verting as anything one has glimpsed in a motion picture theater.
Scripters with the correctly shaped craniums and funnybones--it's
all yours!

> --Herb Sterne in Rob Wagner's
> Script, Vol. 30, No. 673 (Feb-
> ruary 19, 1944), page 18.

☐ MIRACLE ON 34th STREET (20th Century-Fox, 1947)

When someone calling himself Kris Kringle, and offering
every evidence except reindeer of being that gentleman, officiates
at Macy's Christmas activities, the wave of good will that floods the
big store and its competitor causes a merchandising revolution.
In the complications that follow, his champions are forced to prove
the Kris is not an imposter, and no less authorities than the New
York Supreme Court, the United States post office, and the city's
children take a hand in the matter.   It's as entertaining and appealing a film as has appeared in many a day, done without the
taint of cuteness, the actuality of its New York settings and the
logic of its approach making heretofore legendary figures like Santa
Claus and Mr. Macy and Mr. Gimbel as real as any of us.

> --New Movies, Vol. 22, No. 4
> (Summer 1947), page 25.

*   *   *

Miracle on 34th Street is one of the finest pictures of the season, with a tender story, charmingly told, of Santa Claus on trial. This movie, which will be known in the industry as a "sleeper" because it cost comparatively little and will be shown without advance fanfare, has a warmly human feeling and a simplicity of treatment that will please every member of the family.

The story begins on Thanksgiving Day in New York, when a plump little man with a white beard and pink cheeks, the resident of an old folks' home, who actually believes he is Kris Kringle, takes part in the annual parade staged by a department store. Complications ensue and the old fellow gets sent to Bellevue. Finally a stern superior court judge is called upon to decide whether or not there really is a Santa Claus--and whether the old man named Kris Kringle really is who he claims to be.

Though there's a supplementary romance between Maureen O'Hara and John Payne (who defends the old man), the film belongs to Edmund Gwenn; from beginning to end, he breathes real life into the role of Santa. Gene Lockhart is superb as the judge, and both Natalie Wood and William Frawley offer fine supporting characterizations.

Don't miss this!

--Fortnight, Vol. 2, No. 11
(June 2, 1947), page 28.

☐ MISSION TO MOSCOW (Warner Bros. , 1943)

Comrade Jack L. Warner raises a loving cup of borscht to Soviet ideology in Mission to Moscow, but completely in capitalistic tradition, the "executive producer" expects America's theater patrons to pay for the beets and sour cream of his enthusiastic toast.

This bottoms-up to the Bolsheviki is as entertaining as a union soirée, and detours the altars of Maat as frequently as do the editorials in the Peoples' World. The Warner Brothers studio obviously feels about our Russian brethren as Bill Saroyan does about all Mankind, and it scrubs, fumigates and polishes them quite beyond nature and recognition for their appearance in this photoplay. Truth is bound, gagged and sterilized, and the complete composure with which one is expected to believe that the only fundamental difference between the peoples of the U.S.A. and the U.S.S.R. is that one prefers jitterbug Terpsichore while the other relishes the kazotsky, is a smugly cynical and idiotic computation of the reasoning powers of the average American citizen.

Joe Stalin comes as close to being characterized via a white light, in the manner of Ben Hur, as is possible, and the film tours Russia with the same perspicacity and intelligence to be found in the

collected works of Eleanor H. Porter.   The residential sections of
the country, as seen through Burbank eyes, show not the slightest
deviation from the more exclusive sections of Park Avenue, and
while outland Europe resembles the less biased accounts of Siberia,
once the Russian border is crossed the country takes on all the attributes of a travelogue prepared on California by its own Chamber
of Commerce.   The opening shot of Moscow embraces a church
steeple, and lingeringly and lovingly traces its architectural design
in hopes that the sight will pacify and placate our Bible Belt, and
there are canny glimpses of a cosmetic factory to assure American
damsels that Communism holds the lipstick as holy as does Democracy.   Such attempts at hornswoggling top roselytize for the hagio-
latrous cult of Lenin, Stalin and Karl Marx may possibly take in
the mite-patrons of Saturday matinees, but that's about all.   The
dialogic attempts at palsywalsyism founder in the morasses of
cliché, and the language placed in the mouths of politicians is so
hilariously trite as to make the worthies appear never to have gone
beyond the pages of McGuffey's Reader.

When the film occasionally stops anointing the ears of the
Kremlin with hosannas, and drops salty comment on those in the
democracies who sealed their eyes with complacency when the
blaze started by Hitler first swept through Europe, it is excellently
impactful.   When it blubbers its indiscriminate admiration for all
things Russian and gazes with school-girl rapture at the Hammer
and Sickle, the effort defeats its patient purpose through anserine
silliness.   The depiction of the purge trials is as tricky a whitewash job as has occurred since Sam Clemens penned Tom Sawyer,
and there is more than hint and rumor that the Ogpu is really
nothing more frightening than a frat organization.

On its local opening night Mission to Moscow engendered a
verbal and fistic brawl at Warner's Hollywood Theater.   And the
first won't be the last, for the enterprise attempts a job of salesmanship for a brand of Red-herring that has never had a wide
market over here.   The Mads and the Glads are likely to have
even more violent tussles when the picture moves into the neighborhood houses and--but this department has to go now, a Hedy
Lamarr movie is being shown around the corner.
--Herb Sterne in Rob Wagner's
Script, Vol. 29, No. 655 (May
29, 1943), page 14.

*   *   *

Sent as ambassador to Soviet Russia by President Roosevelt
with, we are told, particular instructions to report on conditions
there from the viewpoint of an open-minded, open-eyed, intelligent
American business man and lawyer, Mr. Davies wrote a book about
his experiences and conclusions which is pictured in this film with
his approval and assistance, although not with complete faithfulness.
As an attempt to present and clarify urgent contemporary affairs
for the mass audience the film represents a new and most com-

mendable trend in movie making, an enterprise of enormous difficulties which, to be completely successful, would call for supernatural wisdom and ability.   Mr. Davies was greatly impressed
with Russia's military and industrial strength, and came to like and
admire the Russian people and many of their important men.   The
picture, in its representation of actual people and events, ranges
from the impressive to the absurd.   Its general effect is to show
everything about Russia in the best possible light and to create sympathetic understanding of a great ally.   Reinforced by many scenes
from newsreels it gives the impression of being all fact, whereas
it is actually one man's opinion and judgment, presented with a
good deal of after-the-event astuteness and many misleading implications and falsifications.   If it creates controversy and further
examination of the facts involved it will do a great service.   With
non-dramatic material, much of it only to be expressed in talk and
argument, it manages to have a surprising lot of cinematic movement.   Walter Huston makes Mr. Davies a likeable and admirable
person, and many of the other personages--notably Litvinov and
Kalinin--are re-created with impressive and persuasive effect.   As
a forerunner of serious films about contemporary history--a kind
of thing fraught with danger and difficulty--it is an extremely important picture.

                              --New Movies, Vol. 18, No. 6
                              (October 1943), page 23.

                    *   *   *

     When Ambassador Joseph E. Davies concluded the mission
upon which he served the United States in Russia, he solemnly
pledged to the Soviet officials who honored him in a farewell banquet that he would tell the truth about the U.S.S.R. to all America.   Mr. Davies could not have chosen a better medium than the
motion picture to keep his pledge.   From the book he wrote, titled
Mission to Moscow, has emerged a magnificent, informative and
truly epochal screen document that every American owes himself
the privilege of seeing.   It answers so many questions that have
been only partly answered before about an ally who is fighting our
fight against a common enemy.   And the answers are tremendously
conclusive and of vital importance to us all.

     Mr. Davies' book was widely read.   He went on exhaustive
speaking tours to carry his message about Moscow to the people.
Yet all who have read and heard him previously are not to be compared to the millions that are his audience through the motion picture Warner Brothers have patriotically produced.   It is inspiringly
made in a manner that deserves the vast audience it can reach.   If
Mission to Moscow on the screen is the enormous commercial success it should be, that success will be undebatable proof that motion pictures have come of age.   Here is the most adult document
of its kind ever turned out in Hollywood.

     There is little possibility of properly evaluating the 191 ac-
tors whose names appear on the studio credit sheet, only the first

30 of whom are listed with this review.   Such casting was merely
one of the monumental tasks that faced producer Robert Buckner
and director Michael Curtiz in the screen realization.   Needless to
say, Buckner springs to the ranks of topflight production with this
tremendous work, and Curtiz solidifies his long-established position
as a director of enormous versatility.   Both jobs are admirable in
every respect.

Walter Huston was a great choice to impersonate Davies before the cameras.   He plays without resort to acting tricks and
presents a human, humorous portrait of a man who kept his eyes
open on the mission he was sent to do.   Ann Harding is splendid as
the gracious, charming Mrs. Davies, and Eleanor Parker delightful
as their lovely daughter.   Each of these portrayals is a fine compliment to the real person.

The picture opens with recreations of the League of Nations
meeting when delegations of Germany, Italy and Japan walked out
on Litvinov's speech that followed the plea for aid from Haile
Selassie.   In America, Davies was attempting to take a long-
awaited vacation, only to be halted by a call from President Roosevelt.   He was entrusted with the post of ambassador to Russia because the President wanted to know more about the war talk that
Hitler was stirring up in Europe, and of how Stalin planned to
meet aggression.   What Davies learned and what he saw in U.S.S.R.
are graphically detailed in the reels that follow.   His report con-
tained the information that America had no reason to worry about
Russia taking care of herself--a prediction that has been gloriously
fulfilled.   The things he said in essence upon his return were in-
dictments of the appeasers and isolationists.   The events that have
since taken place show Davies was no alarmist.

It was, however, mainly through the facts Davies brought
back that America was not caught totally unprepared by Pearl Harbor.   He had a hand in the repeal of the neutrality act, and in
putting Russia on the lend-lease program.   The picture closes
courageously with direct answers to those who have still some
thoughts about this war not being our war.   In a foreword, Mr.
Davies appears as himself to establish his authority for the words
Huston speaks for him in the film.

Space prohibits credit to all the players who perform so
capably under Curtiz' direction.   Comment must be made, nonetheless, about Oscar Homolka's Litvinov, Gene Lockhart's Molotov,
Victor Francen's prosecutor, Henry Daniell's Von Ribbentrop, Dudley Field Malone's Churchill, Kurt Katch's Timoshenko, Leigh
Whipper's Haile Selassie, and Captain Jack Young's President
Roosevelt.   Super gems are the moments with Marie Palmer as
the Litvinov daughter and the flash of a serving maid played by
Virginia Christine.

In his photography, Bert Glennon earns a really distinctive
credit.   There is a rousing musical score by Max Steiner, and

executive producer Jack Warner stinted nothing in the technical excellences of the film headed by its stunning art direction by Carl
Jules Weyl.

--The Hollywood Reporter, Vol.
73, No. 7 (April 29, 1943),
pages 3 and 8.

□ MRS. MINIVER (M-G-M, 1942)

The screen at the peak of its eloquence; a portrait of the
war, which, without showing a flag or uttering a word of hate,
graphically reveals the horror of it, its devastating effect on those
behind the lines, the tangle it puts in the narrow fringe that is the
line of demarcation between domestic tranquility and the cruelty of
a world upheaval. As a motion picture, Mrs. Miniver, as long as
our memories last, will be, to us, high on the list of the greatest
achievements of the screen. Yet it is a simple story, simply told,
its people living before the camera, not acting for its recording.

What we see on the screen makes it obvious that in planning
the picture, Sidney Franklin, its producer, felt himself under more
obligation to his medium than to the Jan Struther book. He has
given us a motion picture inspired by a book, not the book itself;
has given us a screen creation of such velvety smoothness I find it
a difficult one to review. While sprinkled through it are inspired
high spots, it is difficult to rate them when the production as a
whole is one inspired high spot in the history of the screen.

Only flawless performances could be responsible for such a
high degree of artistic merit. There is no acting; we see only a
group of people living their lives, doing the things the war has
forced upon them to do, speaking only to one another instead of
bawling at the microphone as they do in so many pictures. Only
inspired direction could produce such results. I have known Willie
Wyler since he was a boy on the Universal lot doing chores for
Carl Laemmle. He had ambitions then to do big things in pictures
and in his direction of Mrs. Miniver he has set himself a mark for
all his fellow directors to shoot at.

Producer Franklin cast the picture with rare discrimination,
and in so doing has given Hollywood something to meditate upon.
Greer Garson has her admirers, but she has had no such boxoffice rating as Hedy Lamarr or Madeline Carroll. Clark Gable and
Spencer Tracy have tremendous followings, but Walter Pidgeon has
been just another actor, a dependable leading man; but no other picture ever produced got such an astonishing reception immediately
upon its release as did this one which presents Greer Garson and
Walter Pidgeon as its leading players.

It suggests that in the picture business, after all, it is the
picture which counts.

In estimating the values of Mrs. Miniver as screen entertainment, there is a group of modest fellows who should not be
overlooked--musicians, cameraman, wardrobe people, sound men,
and, of course, that overlord of visual values, the art director,
and those whose work he directs.   We are prone to take for granted
this group's contribution to a picture, and here are more apt to
credit Mr. and Mrs. Miniver with the good taste they displayed in
furnishing their home, than we are to give it to Edwin B. Willis
who did the furnishing.   But to that outstanding master of visual
values, Cedric Gibbons, Metro's art director, must go to the main
credit for the feast for the eyes provided by the camera of Joseph
Ruttenberg, which realized so fully all the beauty and story-telling
qualities latent in the Gibbons creations.

And the sound recording by Douglas Shearer and his staff
also is to be numbered among the picture's assets.   Sound really
plays an important role in the picture, the screaming sirens, the
heavy guns, the plunging bombs, the crashing buildings being a
story element as indispensable as the lines the players speak.   To
Arnold Gillespie and Warren Newcombe go credit for what is listed
on the screen as "Special Effects."   Editing the film of such a big
production was a responsibility of great proportions, admirably met
by Film Editor Harold Kress.

One word expresses the merit of every performance in the
picture--superb.

> --Welford Beaton in Hollywood
> Spectator, Vol. 17, No. 1
> (September 1, 1942), pages
> 12-13.

*   *   *

During World War I, Hollywood produced not one worthy
dramatic film dealing with the conflict.   To be sure there were
such rococo items as The Kaiser, the Beast of Berlin, Rita Joli-
vet's, Lest We Forget, DeMille's, The Little American, Hearts of
the World, Kultur, To Hell with the Kaiser!, etc. etc., but it was
not until after the cessation of hostilities that the studios made
thoughtful, human studies like All Quiet on the Western Front, The
Big Parade and Journey's End.   Cinematically speaking, we've done
better this time, for out of the Hollywoods have already come This
Above All and the truly excellent Mrs. Miniver.

Mrs. Miniver, unlike the screen sagas projected during the
last war for democracy, is not a song of hate.   It makes its points
without ostentation and is totally devoid of the pamphleteering, adolescent name-calling, of other days.   So certain is it of its thesis
that it is able to eschew obvious melodrama, the declamatory tableau, and the restraint utilized adds infinitely to the dramatic force
and impact.

The cities of the world, no longer immune from the horrors
of combat, have become the firing lines of defense, and today's

civilians shoulder arms hardly less imperative to victory than those used by men in uniform.   The story of the Minivers is the story of an average English family, and how its members emerge from the trivialities of peacetime, gain personal strength and stature when the time of trial arrives.   Tender, genuine, eloquently presented, this M. G. M. photoplay will do more to arouse Americans to their duty than an assortment of parades, and all the lugubrious ballads composed by Mr. Irving Berlin.

The exaltation burrows deep into the heart of the spectator and persists long after one has left the theater.   The thoughtfulness which the work evokes is a credit to the persuasive direction of William Wyler, the supervision of Sidney Franklin, the impeccable playing of Greer Garson, Walter Pidgeon, Teresa Wright, Dame May Whitty, Richard Ney, Henry Travers and Script's own Henry Wilcoxon.

Mrs. Miniver is an emotional experience.   You owe it to yourself to see it, not only as a picture patron, but also as a human being.

> --Herb Sterne in Rob Wagner's
> Script, Vol. 27, No. 634 (Au-
> gust 1, 1942), page 23.

*   *   *

Mrs. Miniver brings the movies abreast of the very moment we're living in.   It is the first war film to talk about "the people's war."

If you've read the book by Jan Struther on which this film is partly based, all you're expecting is a witty picture of a British middle-class family and its small-town social life.   That's how Mrs. Struther wrote the book in early 1940, before the blitz.   But MGM has had the inspiration to shake the Minivers out of their peace-time routine to show you how they must be now: Their home is half-wrecked by bombings; the eldest son is flying with the RAF; the small children go to bed each night in the double-deckers of an Anderson shelter; Mr. Miniver, who took his little pleasure boat to bring British soldiers back from Dunkirk, is now patroling with the Home Guard; Mrs. Miniver, who caught a Nazi aviator in her garden, is keeping house without the servants she used to have--and on wartime rations.

But, as Mrs. Miniver shows plainly, their life still has an imperturbable dignity.   This family steps over the rubble in the drawing-room, ignores the broken window panes, and continues to observe the daily social customs of British middle class society. The war can't interfere with their town's annual flower show, nor does it ever halt the serving of tea.   Their insistence on the nice-ties is as funny as it is heroic.

These and their neighbors are some of the people who are

fighting this war, says <u>Mrs. Miniver</u>, and they're doing a good job
of it.

                              --Louise Levitas in <u>PM</u> (June 7,
                                 1942), page 24.

☐ MRS. PARKINGTON (M-G-M, 1944)

    Greer Garson has never made a severe moral slip on the
screen, and her smug virulence of virtue has become tediously tiresome.   The endless and changeless epithalamiums, her coy hope-
faith-and-charity, pile higher and higher, picture by picture.   As
this department computes it, the Garson saccharin, in quotient, has
so far quite outzigguratted the combined simpering emanations of
June Caprice, Arline Pretty, Bessie Love, Blanche Sweet, Louise
Lovely, Ella Hall, Dawn O'Day, Baby Marie Osborne, Little Mary
McAllister, Virginia Lee Corbin, Shirley Mason, Gladys Leslie,
Lila Lee, Shirley Temple, Evelyn Greeley, Muriel Ostriche, Janet
Gaynor, Jean Parker, Pauline Starke, Mary Miles Minter, Violet
Mersereau, Irene Rich and Mr. and Mrs. Albert Basserman.

    Miss Garson, a few years back on the local stage, played
Coward's <u>Ways and Means</u> with humor that was devoid of archness,
and a sophistication that by no means signified that anyone not on
the guest list of the Duke and Duchess of Rutland was a varlet,
hobbledehoy and general low-life.   As a matter of fact, behind footlights the actress appeared to be just about to slip on the green
hat of Iris March, and there was every indication that it would
prove most becoming.

    But the Garson screen career is very much something else
again.   Her celluloid roles invariably have the texture and aroma
of the titbits sponsored by Awful Fresh MacFarlane, and all the
novelty and excitement to be expected of a rendezvous with one's
wife held in celebration of the golden wedding anniversary.

    In the name part of <u>Mrs. Parkington</u>, the star is not one
whit less noble than was her lot in <u>Random Harvest</u>, <u>Blossoms in</u>
<u>the Dust</u>, <u>Madame Curie</u>, et al.   Again she <u>suffers</u> and <u>forgives</u>
and forgives and suffers with an irritating regularity that caused
this observer to shift and squirm so restlessly as to wear his way
through the seat of his new gray flannel slacks before leaving the
projection room.

    At one time, novelist Louis Bromfield was a reputable writ-
er, with such works as <u>The Green Bay Tree</u> and <u>Early Autumn</u> to
his credit.   For the past several years he has appeared anxious to
usurp the laurels won and worn by Ouida and Ouida Bergère.   <u>Mrs.</u>
<u>Parkington</u> reads and plays as a series of clichés through which one
traces a robber baron founding a dynasty of wealth and respectabil-
ity.   Toney in dialogue and spurious in situation and philosophy, the

film, like the novel before it, takes for granted that Warren G. Harding is still in the White House and finding favor with thinking folk.

--Herb Sterne in Rob Wagner's Script, Vol. 30, No. 692 (November 18, 1944), pages 14-15.

☐ MONSIEUR VERDOUX (Chaplin/United Artists, 1947)

Chaplin's newest comedy, Monsieur Verdoux--his first in more than six years--is his most serious and totally successful. In its social purpose it is bolder and more incisive than anything he has yet made. Furthermore, it signalizes a sharp break with the Chaplin of the past--the traditional romantic who moves uncertain and helpless in a world he does not understand. In this new film Chaplin shows he understands the world only too well. In this sense, Monsieur Verdoux is a new coming-of-age of a significant film maker and a solid contribution to the American screen.

In the past, Chaplin's films were nearly all variations on one theme: protest against the crushing of the individual by social forces. His comedy emphasized the human against regimentation and pleaded for the rights of the individual. In these pictures-- except for the role of Hitler in The Great Dictator--Chaplin was a "little" man, the butt of jests and harassed by poverty, the law, and social forces he can neither understand nor resist. Always this protagonist was confused, bewildered, slapped-about, a poignant symbol of the common man. But in Monsieur Verdoux the protagonist is no longer the fumbling, pathetic little man in baggy pants. That sartorial symbol has been discarded for the natty waistcoat, ascot tie and striped trousers of the new Chaplin character, the modern business man. Verdoux is no "Charlie," the dreamer thinking of pie-in-the-sky, but a hardboiled cynic, an executive, who, as stated by Chaplin himself, is wise to the ways of the world based on a business immorality and acts accordingly. The metamorphosis is evidence of a new intellectual development.

The plot of Monsieur Verdoux is simple and ingenuous, but sharp and eloquent in its social commentary. The depression of 1930 has cost Verdoux, a bank clerk, his job. Since he has a wife and child whom he loves and must support, he resorts to the business of marrying women and killing them for their money. "I am in business," says Verdoux, "and I must do my duty after the classic heroic mode." Nevertheless he considers himself a very moral man; he never lets these women touch him. He hates his work; he hates the women.

Though the story is laid in pre-war France it has meaning to people all over the world today. For, it is obvious from the satirical way Chaplin tells it, the motion picture is not just a funny story of a murderer but a witty travesty on an unethical business-minded society.

A free-flowing cartoon alive with clowning and gags, its humor reaches wild caprice, rowdy slapstick and low burlesque. In a desperate attempt to get fifty thousand francs before morning, Verdoux makes passionate love to a rich victim, who has come to lease the house of a wealthy widow he has just finished off, by playing ring around the trunk with her. Again, later in the film, Verdoux takes one of his wives for a boat ride in order to drown her, having failed to kill her in bed. His ludicrous attempts to throw her overboard, tied to a heavy rock, fail. He then tries to chloroform her only to succeed in chloroforming himself. When she revives him, he attempts to push her overboard again but instead falls into the lake himself and she has to rescue him! During another sequence Verdoux reproves one of his wives for buying a phoney diamond. Angrily he shouts: "It's glass you ass!"

Underneath the film's broad gaiety can be discerned a deeper intention. Daumier-like in its irony. Scenes of charm and sentiment around the family hearth, gardening, polite after-dinner conversation with neighbors, succinctly capture the desultory, half-satisfied life of the middle class. Bombastic and extravagant dialogue of wooing victims for their belongings and nothing else glaringly reveals the "Bluebeard's" life as one of spiritless conflicts and drives, of nerve racking fears of business ruin, of frightened infidelities and forced enthusiasms. Merciless and unceasing attempts at liquidation, none the less ruthless for operating with fine clothes, wide smiles and flattering phrases, exposes the heartlessness and lack of ethics at the core of business.

With the pungent broad strokes of a crusading caricaturist, Chaplin directs each of the six women in the film as pursuing personal ambitions, unaware of the materialistic forces which shape their lives. Lena Couvais, the spinster sister of Verdoux's first victim is a selfcentered, grasping woman, head of the selfish Couvais clan. Marie Grosnay, the wealthy loveless widow who comes to buy Verdoux's house, is a vain, inhibited social snob. Lydia Foray, a wife living alone in a provincial town, is an untrusting greedy woman torn between avarice and fear. Annabella Bonheur, another wife is a lusty, pleasure seeking, insatiable animal. In contrast to the harshness of these women are the soft, sentimentalized etchings of the other two. Monda, Verdoux's first wife and mother of his child, is a cripple forced to get around on a wheel chair. The Girl, an orphan, is a street waif.

To each of these women, Verdoux is a different man, always mysteriously appearing and mysteriously rushing away. To the spinster Lena, he is a scoundrel who married her rich sister instead of her. To the widow Marie, he is an explorer passionately breaking down the barriers of convention and opening up the dark continent of love. To the lonely Lydia, he is an engineer constructing dream castles which someday she hopes to inherit. To good-time Anna-

bella, he is a ship's captain, the proverbial sailor coming into port
only to give her a good time.   To his wife Mona, he is the husband
returning from business trips to dole out sentiment and support.
To The Girl, he is the father offering advice and protection.

Through his relations with these women we discover in Verdoux a complex character, two men at war with each other.   One
is a heartless materialist, a "business" man intent on murder and
rushing across the countryside in a mad effort to secure enough
money to prevent the liquidation of his falling stock.   The other is
a tender husband and father revealing himself in speeches of warmth
and little intimations of love.   Acted by Chaplin in consummate
style, the two-sided portrait lays bare the conflict between good
and evil in the heart of a business-minded society.

The two forces come to a climax in the scene between Verdoux and The Girl.   At first his intention is to murder her.   Not
from any motives of immediate cash--she is penniless.   But simply
to try out his new product, a painless poison that leaves no trace,
which if successful will prove very profitable in his "business."
But when he learns that the girl has lost her lover in the war, that
she has just been released from jail and that she bears no bitter-
ness against the world, that in fact she still retains all the illusions
and faith of a sensitive child, Verdoux is reminded of his own lost
illusions as a poor struggling bank clerk, and, moved, he spares
her life.   He becomes fatherly, telling her the facts of life and
even giving her some money to go to a hotel.   The moral is obvious: the evil in man can be conquered by a return to the ideals
and faith of childhood.

A later twist in the story becomes a brilliant touch of irony.
Verdoux meets The Girl again, but he is now penniless.   She rides
in a luxurious car and wears fine clothes.   But he does not recognize her.   She tells him she was the waif he once befriended and
that she is now the mistress of a munitions magnate.   An ironic
smile is his answer.   Here too the moral is apparent.   His failure
to recognize her is due to the fact that she is no longer the same
girl.   No longer the child with illusions, but a business woman who
has become successful by embracing "the classic code" of the business-minded world.   And though she may not be a murderer like
Verdoux, it is evident that by living with a munitions maker she has
joined herself to one who is.

The Girl takes him to a fine hotel restaurant.   There he is
immediately recognized by Lena, the sister of his first victim who
has been searching unsuccessfully for him until now.   And now she
is able to apprehend him.   It is as though Chaplin were saying: in
a world based on business ethics, the business man who falls from
grace is damned.   The two episodes following one upon the other
also accents the conclusion inherent in Chaplin's theme: that for
the victor as well as for the victim there is no final escape.

Throughout the film, Chaplin makes clear that on the battle-
field of business one is likely to lose all at any moment: Verdoux's

frantic calls to his stockbroker to give him one day, one hour, ten minutes to get additional thousands with which to bolster his sinking securities; Verdoux counting the stolen spoils of his victims with lightening speed, machine-like, inhuman; Verdoux losing everything, his wife and child, his paper fortune in the economic crash; people big and little, not really knowing what hit them, committing suicide.

The crux of the picture's theme is given by direct reference, through the use of actual newsreels, to the rise of Hitler and Mussolini in the period following the economic collapse. People who have lost everything and have no morality to fall back upon, Chaplin points out, will follow "leaders" who offer them uniforms (fine clothes), promises (wide smiles), slogans (flattering phrases) to sterility, slavery, and even war. This is the "tragedy" as Chaplin himself classifies the picture--a "tragedy" which serves as a warning.

The very end of the film, in the nature of an epilogue, contains perhaps some of the most forthright dialogue to come out of the American screen. Verdoux, sentenced to die by the guillotine, accepts his fate calmly. A reporter interviews him:

Reporter: You'll have to admit crime doesn't pay.

Verdoux: No sir. Not in a small way.

Reporter: What do you mean?

Verdoux: To be successful in anything one must be organized.

Reporter: You're not leaving the world with that cynical remark?

Verdoux: To be idealistic at this moment would be incongruous.

Reporter: What's this talk about good and evil?

Verdoux: Arbitrary forces my good fellow. Too much of either will destroy us all.

Reporter: We can never have too much good in this world.

Verdoux: The trouble is we've never had enough. We don't know.

(The reporter goes; a priest enters the cell.)

Verdoux: What can I do for you, my good man?

Priest: Nothing my son. I want to help you. I've come to ask you to make your peace with God.

Verdoux: Father, I am at peace with God. My conflict is with man.

Priest: Have you no remorse for your sins?

Verdoux: Who knows what sin is--born, as it is, from heaven--from God's fallen angel. Who knows what ultimate destiny is served? After all what would you be doing without sin?

(Then, as Verdoux is led out to the guillotine)

Priest: May God have mercy on your soul.

Verdoux: Why not? After all it belongs to Him.

Like a first rate social caricaturist, Chaplin has succeeded in drawing his picture with simplicity and vigor. The major lack in the film is the omission of at least one aspect of the will to struggle against the condition he points out. It would have been more inspiring had there been brought in some challenge to the state of affairs he depicts. Nevertheless Monsieur Verdoux is one of the most significant and unique post-war films and takes its place as a landmark not only in Chaplin's long career but in the progress of the American screen.

> --Lewis Jacobs in Cinema, Vol. 1,
> No. 1 (June 1947), pages 11,
> 12 and 23.

*   *   *

Let it be said at once that Charlie Chaplin has stepped up to a task infinitely more difficult than that which confronted him in making The Great Dictator. There all his great gifts of comedy, satire and charm were directed towards the [exposure] of a man his audiences knew to be as wicked as the devil himself; and they found it supremely cathartic to hate with Charlie, to laugh with Charlie and finally to get down on their knees and pray with him that the world might be delivered from this monster incarnate. Here it's a different story altogether. Charlie has attempted to tell us not that one satanic little German is a disgrace to the human race, but that indeed the entire human race is at the moment engaged in countenancing, in fact in being almost one might say implicated in, the wholesale and general industry of murder--the manufacture of death in a big, big way. His method of conveying this awful fact is through the parable of a little Parisian bank clerk, who after the sudden dismissal from his job, finding it necessary to support a beloved wife and child also, goes into the business of murder--wooing and marrying and then killing off his bigamous partners for the money to be realized from these gentle practices, thus playfully comparing the monstrosity of the general crime with the terrifying but none the less beguiling behavior of Monsieur Verdoux. Charlie seems to shrug his shoulders at the lesser criminal and bring us almost to the point of doting on the delightful little fellow. One can

see at a glance that here is a matter for only the very greatest
satirists--a truly Swiftian theme. With all my admiration for
Charlie's courage and my enthusiasm for a remarkable picture, I
for my part do not feel that he has quite managed to get away with
it.

Why he has not done so I find it difficult to explain. It may
be that he has reserved until his final sequences the expression of
that savage and passionate indignation that should in one way or
another have been animating every stroke of his sardonic little parable, and that Charlie treading the precarious tight rope between
comedy on the one hand and horror and consternation on the other
has weighted his punches too much on the side of laughter--of sheer
delight and charm in his so perfect Charliness and without at the
same time keeping us sufficiently informed of the drift and drive of
the moral issues involved.

He has presented us with a completely new and fascinating
creation. Endowed with the inimitable rhythms and inflections of
a voice hitherto kept up his sleeve, Monsieur Verdoux steps upon
the screen. He has an indescribable hair-do. He wears a variety
of the most excruciatingly funny costumes. All the old perfections
of grace and timing accompany him. He has a whole bag full of
new tricks and dexterities; in short, this debonair (and only oh so
slightly sinister) murderer, who adores his wife and child and an
occasional return to the peace and quiet of domestic bliss after the
excitements and agitations incident on wooing and liquidating of his
bigamous consorts, is absolutely irresistible. He is tender toward
his invalid wife. He reproves his little boy for being cruel to his
cat. It would be difficult to do justice to the felicities of his love-
making. To the poetry of his diction and the choice of his words
("This Endymion hour!" he exclaims as he looks from a window at
the moonlit night just prior to pulling off the most horrific of all
his murders), there is a touch of necromancy. Everybody in his
cast succumbs to the peculiar spell of his demands upon them.
Suffice it to say that in each of the murderous episodes and in the
scenes in which he manages to escape (or to liquidate) his pursuers,
his skill and brilliancy is amazing. To this spectator at least he
appears to have reached the very peak of his genius as an actor and
a director.

Then what is it, I should like to ask again, that is somehow
disturbing about this remarkable picture? Can it be that we find
ourselves shocked at our own delight in the behavior of this macabre
and monstrous character? Had Mr. Chaplin earlier in the film indicated with more pertinent hints and subtler implications the drift
of his satire, might he perhaps have better prepared his audience
to "take" the terrible and passionate indictment of society delivered
by Monsieur Verdoux after the jury has condemned him to the guillotine? One asks. I am not entirely sure of the answer myself.

Tragic it is that this, certainly the most courageous and very
likely the greatest of all Mr. Chaplin's films, has played to empty

houses.   Charlie has fallen from his high position as the popular
idol, caught it would seem in the traps of his own charms and
graces.

--Mary Britton Miller in New
Movies, Vol. 22, No. 4 (Summer 1947), pages 5-6.

* * *

Monsieur Verdoux released in the East several months ago
but only now reaching West Coast screens, is a fascinating film
from one point of view--and an irritating one from another.

In it the great Charles Chaplin, abandoning his classic impersonation of the wistful tramp, plays a dapper, volatile little
Frenchman who is both a bigamist and a murderer.   Since Chaplin
produced and directed the picture, bestowing upon it all the wit,
artistry and movie knowhow of which he is capable, it is worth
seeing.   In fact, no one who is interested in watching a genius at
work can very well afford to miss it.   As Monsieur Verdoux, man
of many aliases, who is at heart a loving husband and father (for
he murders to support his family), Chaplin gives a mercurial, infinitely resourceful performance that is tragic in its implications,
marvelously comic in its manifestations.

But Chaplin has attempted to underscore his story with a
message, which is a dubious one at best.   Monsieur Verdoux gets
out of hand at the end, when the little Bluebeard arraigns society
at large for the sinister life it has forced him to lead.   Chaplin's
social thinking is confused here, and the audience goes away confused, not to say baffled.

--Fortnight, Vol. 3, No. 9
(November 7, 1947), page 30.

☐ THE MOON AND SIXPENCE (Loew-Lewin/United Artists, 1942)

Without sacrifice of the power of W. Somerset Maugham's
dramatic novel, The Moon and Sixpence at last reaches the screen
in a splendid production by David L. Loew and Albert Lewin for
United Artists release.   Predominately adult in appeal, the picture
has a fine chance of being a terrific boxoffice attraction, building
steadily with enthusiastic word-of-mouth.

Hollywood long has tried to film the Maugham book which
was first published in 1919.   A number of different scripts were
prepared by the two studios that previously owned the property, but
it remained for Albert Lewin to work out a filmable adaptation.
Lewin's hand in the success of Moon and Sixpence is large, for he
not only adapted and co-produced it, he took over its direction with
highly praiseworthy results.   His directorial debut is, in many respects, truly brilliant.

His approach to the controversial aspects of the story is basically simple. It is a narrative device that soundly establishes the fictional author's stern disapproval of the character of Charles Strickland, the artist. Yet, although the fellow is far from admirable, he fascinates the author who writes his colorful biography, a fascination the audience will share. It is generally believed that Maugham patterned the tale of Charles Strickland after the life of Paul Gauguin.

We meet Geoffrey Wolfe, the author, as he begins his manuscript about Strickland. He tells of a brief encounter at a dinner party and the subsequent mission he undertook in Paris at the request of Strickland's deserted wife. She thought he had run off with another woman. Wolfe discovers Strickland had merely decided to call quits to his marriage after 17 years because all he wanted of life was an opportunity to paint. He even is willing to starve to satisfy his artistic urge and, when he very nearly does die of malnutrition, he repays his untalented painter friend who saves his life by permitting that man's wife to follow him. She dies a suicide when he deserts her.

The narrative resumes in Java where Wolfe's path again crosses Strickland. He is told by a slattern hotel keeper about a wedding with a native girl. But the tale cannot be finished without the evidence of a doctor who attended Strickland when he contracted leprosy.

George Sanders plays Strickland to mark it as his best characterization on the screen. It is a master performance superbly seconded by the exacting role of Wolfe as realized by Herbert Marshall, who magnificently reads some two-thirds of the lengthy narration. Florence Bates is grand as the slattern hotel keeper who relates the native marriage incident, and Albert Basserman exceptionally fine in telling the doctor's part of the story. One of the effective tricks of the production is the switch from black and white to an off-shade of sepia in the Java sequences and a climaxing touch of rich Technicolor in the scene of the doctor's discovery of Strickland's paintings. The photography by John F. Seitz is a superior job, and wait until you see the stunning paintings contributed by Dolya Goutman.

Steve Geray makes a name for himself in his appealing portrayal of the friend in Paris; Doris Dudley creating arresting moments as his wife. Molly Lamont does well with her role of Mrs. Strickland, and Elena Verdugo projects the charm of the native girl. Eric Blore as a beachcomber amuses, and Devi Dja and her Bali-Java dancers provide a colorful interlude.

Nothing has been overlooked that might add to the atmospheric excellence of the Loew-Lewin production. Stanley Kramer served as associate producer to Loew, and Gordon Wiles did the production design. Art direction is to the great credit of F. Paul Sylos, and music by Dimitri Tiomkin is notable. Also deserving

of mention are the makeup creations of Ern Westmore and the editorial supervision by George Hively.

--The Hollywood Reporter, Vol.
69, No. 43 (September 8, 1942),
page 3.

*   *   *

The Moon and Sixpence, coming to New York next month, has
won the testimonial of no less a show-business intellectual than
Katharine Cornell, who called the script the best she had ever read.
W. Somerset Maugham, who wrote the book in 1919, was so pleased
with the film he said it would probably revolutionize the screen's
treatment of novels.   So The Moon and Sixpence is probably an artistic triumph, which may or may not mean what it usually means in
Hollywood parlance: a movie too highbrow to be a box-office success.

The story of the book and the film parallel the life story of
Paul Gauguin, the great French painter; but Maugham's hero is
named Charles Strickland.   It is the story of a middle-aged stock
broker who, in his overpowering urge to paint, deserts his wife and
children and later abandons others who love and befriend him.
Finally, in Tahiti, free of all normal ties, he finds release for his
great talent.   His paintings made him famous after his death, though
in his life he had scorned fame.   He is brutal, but he is a genius.

First, Warners and then MGM bought the screen rights to
this highly successful novel, and then shelved the story as too tough
to handle.   Albert Lewin, who wrote the script and directed the
movie, was able to meet seemingly insuperable Hays office obstacles by telling the story through a narrator.

The narrator (Herbert Marshall) strongly condemns Strickland's conduct while admiring his painting.   By using this offstage
voice, the screen points two morals.   One is that men who trans-
gress the moral code must pay for it (Strickland lived in terrible
poverty and died of leprosy).   The other is that genius is above
conventional morality.   Which of the two is the right one depends
on the beholder.

--Louise Levitas in PM (September 20, 1942), page 28.

☐   THE MORE THE MERRIER (Columbia, 1943)

If The More the Merrier had been given the satirical stance
of Nothing Sacred, it might well have been a memorable comedy.
Instead, director George Stevens selected to regard his material
with a benign smirk, and so in place of being a sardonic evaluation
of a facet of these abnormal times, it is simply another pleasant

fun film, built about the good old Avery Hopwood high jinks formula.

The More the Merrier greases the Washington roundabout
with the familiar schmaltz of lower-case romance.   When it touches
on political procrastination in the nation's capital it does so only to
reach the conclusion that when the housing situation is difficult, it
is a fine excuse for an unwed lady and two gentlemen to scamper
under one roof, although always remaining well within the requirements placed by the Purity Seal.

The events have considerable charm, due chiefly to the talents of sandpaper-voiced Jean Arthur, and the antics of rotund
Charles Coburn, who pulls every conceivable comedic trick from
the bag of his many years experience in the theater.   Joel McCrea,
rather at a loss in such fast company, sits back, relaxes and permits the competent actors to pull the vehicle to success.

> --Herb Sterne in Rob Wagner's
> Script, Vol. 29, No. 655 (May
> 29, 1943), page 14.

☐ MY DARLING CLEMENTINE (20th Century-Fox, 1946)

John Ford, burdened by hackneyed characters and a scattered
screenplay, still manages to deliver an interesting photoplay in My
Darling Clementine.

This western, it must immediately be understood, is in nowise another Stage Coach.   However, it does have Ford's trenchant
touch in building individual scenes, its scenic attractions are many,
and there is a really rousing action climax which rates high amongst
such things.

The plot, unfortunately, is no better than the film's title, and
My Darling Clementine is something that Republic should have an-
nexed for Roy Rogers if the studio had really been on its toes.
However, Republic need not be too dispirited, for there must be
some consolation in knowing that the same story has been used for
Mr. Rogers time after time.

Henry Fonda, Walter Brennan, Alan Mowbray, Ward Bond
and a high calibre supporting company of character players are of
value to the production.   Victor Mature's Doc Holliday and Linda
Darnell's Chihuahua are something for the book--one's black book.

> --Herb Sterne in Rob Wagner's
> Script, Vol. 32, No. 742 (No-
> vember 9, 1946), page 10.

*   *   *

John Ford's new production comes as reassurance and uplift
to all who believe in the future of the screen as an independent
medium of expression communicating experience in a manner unique
to its own special powers.   On the surface, and to millions of its
audiences, it will appear as no more than a jimdandy Western.
It's all of that.   It is also a sustained and complex work of the
imagination.

Its thin and sometimes preposterous story is no more substantial than those which serve as groundwork for the big gaudy
Westerns we have been getting lately, the Abilene Towns, Rene-
gades, and Canyon Passages.   An incident in the half-fictional lives
of the Western gunmen, Wyatt Earp and Doc Holliday, it centers
throughout around familiar themes--the veteran frontier marshal
drafted by the citizens of Tombstone to clean up the town, his
friendly rivalry with the town's leading gambler and sharpshooter,
his long pursuit of the murderers of two of his brothers, and the
final, climactic gun battle.   What matters is not the plot, moving
as it does from incident to incident without much consistency or
connection, but the manner in which the director has derived from
these materials the portrait of an era and the characters who peopled it.

The "legend" of the film director is frequently exposed in
print these days.   He is, we have been told a great many times,
no longer the dictator of the silent days but merely an artisan whose
secondary function it is to guide the stars through their paces while
spelling out the script exactly as written and as handed to him by
the omnipotent producer.   That this is true as of this month and
year, there can be no question.   Whether it has come about as a
by-product of an assembly-line system of production, or because
there have arisen few talented directors in recent years, is food
for speculation.   But Mr. Ford reveals to us all over again that it
need not be true, and that when a director fully commands his medium he can produce a work whose qualities owe little or nothing to
writing, however fine, acting, however expert, production, however
lavish.   In My Darling Clementine, as in nearly all of the masterpieces of the movies, it is the director's hand and eye which furnish
forth the scene.   And again, as so often in the past, the artistic
process which we see at work reminds us less of writing and acting
and the other crafts of the theatre than it does of music and poetry
and dance, the arts which gain their effects through rhythmic movement.   Every sequence in this film has its own decided tempo, each
of which in measured progression contributes to the tempo of the
whole.   All other elements in the film are subordinated to that developing rhythm.   The aptest analogy is that to music, where notes
form chords, chords harmonies.   As Iris Barry once said of The
Threepenny Opera, "this film has been composed."

How is it done?   In My Darling Clementine by a very interesting process indeed.   The settings of the story are familiar to
banality--the arid plains, the bare Western town, the bar-room, the
cheap hotel.   The ordinary Western uses them merely as backdrops

against which physical action is played. Here they become the
story itself. Consider this: the film opens as four cowboys drive
a herd of cattle over the immense and desolate prairie; we look at
the lowering skies, the charging steers, hear their bellowing and
the cowboys' shouts. A wagon drives up, there is colloquy between
its occupants and one of the cowboys, but we hardly listen to what
is said, we are too immersed in scanning the weatherbeaten faces,
looking beyond them to the cattle, the horses, the endless horizon.
It is the scene and the action that dominate, that communicate, that
give meaning to the slight dialogue. Another time, in a saloon,
when two gunmen take each other's measure at the bar, it is the
silence, and the camera roving over the scared faces of the onlook-
ers, the shining bar, the thrust-back chairs, that knot the tension
and draw the spectator intimately into the scene. Silence and the
roving camera, and the multiple positions of the camera, lend its
intolerable excitement to the final gunfight when four men walk
through town in the dawn toward their enemies ambushed at the end
of the street. Many will exclaim over the beauty of the photography in this picture. Its technical excellence is less to the point
than its functionalism. Again and again the camera seeks out those
details of scene and action which not only clothe the story but actually tell it. It is out of their purposiveness that the illusion of
beauty is created.

All this is far more than an exercise in film direction. Undoubtedly its qualities derive from Mr. Ford's affection for the portrait he is drawing--the portrait of the Old West. It is a mixed
portrait, half-truth, half folklore, but fact or fancy, it is the West
as Americans still feel it in their bones. There is that about the
scene as Ford draws it that brings forth in the spectator some dim
recognizance as of memory or inheritance, remote, perhaps, from
our twentieth-century scene, but whose kinship is not to be denied.
It is in the very look of things, in the clothes the characters wear,
the bone structure of their faces, the tempo of their speech. The
director has been as successful with the people in the film as with
their vast arena. Unlettered, inarticulate men, slow to speak because slow to decide (and how the tempo of the film measures that
slowness of thinking and decision), quick to act because always in
danger. And beyond this, with a sensitive, animal awareness of
the beauty of their surroundings and of the extremes of evil and
good in the humankind they encounter in a land where all are new-
comers and strangers to each other.

Mr. Ford has again had the help of Henry Fonda. Of all
our accomplished players, Mr. Fonda best understands and imagines the Western American, as he has proven three times over, in
The Grapes of Wrath, The Ox-Bow Incident and now in this. This
can scarcely be accidental; Mr. Fonda is as surely the conscious
interpreter of a vanished temperament as though he were a historian
or psychologist. The dominant personage in the whole fascinating
scene, he works on equal terms with the setter of the scene himself. The other players, excellent as they are, seem more nearly
pliable instruments of the director, chosen for some physical trait

or quirk of speech and outlook.   Victor Mature is hardly an obvious
choice for the role of a tubercular gunman concealing under silken
menace his despair at the loss of a Boston medical career, and his
recital of a soliloquy from Hamlet does not suggest college speech.
But the performance comes off amazingly.   Mr. Mature's face is
basilisk, his eyes look inward; in detail of manner and appearance
he successfully suggests the desperate remittance-man.   Other
evocative roles are played by J. Farrell MacDonald--it's good to
see his wise old face again--and Alan Mowbray, who makes the
most of excellent opportunities as a rum-soaked ham, more familiar
with Ten Nights in a Barroom than with Hamlet, but sporting
the assurance of Booth or Irving.   Tim Holt and Ward Bond are
pleasingly right as brothers of Fonda.

        The ladies fare not so well, because their roles are too
much bound up with plot contrivances to seem real.   Cathy Downs
is the colorless Clementine of the title, who's come all the way
from Boston to restore Mr. Mature to his rightful place among the
elite of the Hub.   Linda Darnell has an impossible assignment as
Chihuahua, made up to look like a Hollywood version of a Mexican
dance-hall girl.   The necessity to build her role to stellar proportions tempts Mr. Ford to the film's one aberration, an operation
scene which, though well done, is theatrical and meaningless.

        But, as suggested earlier, it is the environment and the
characters that grow out of it that mean more than plot or event.
Behind the incidents which involve the principal players, one is
conscious all the time of the surging life of the town, the church-
building, cattle-growing, buying and selling, which was building a
new land in this wild country.   There is form and significance to
this, it reaches out to us across the decades.   Seeing it is often
like being a boy in a small country town, ambling along the dusty
street and watching the idlers with their feet up on the hotel porch
railing of a slow Sunday morning.
                            --Richard Griffith in New Movies,
                              Vol. 22, No. 1 (January 1947),
                              pages 6-8.

☐ THE NAKED CITY (Universal, 1948)

        Despite the unreality implicit in Mark Hellinger's wholly
romantic view of New York, The Naked City is good entertainment
and a better example of the documentary type of films now so widely popular.   Based on the routine theme of whodunit, the story unfolds a solution on the level of ordinary police work, a wholesome
variation on the common Hollywood assumption that murders are
often solved by a "private eye" who amazes and confounds the stu-
pid flatfoot by his atomic brilliance.   Since the private detective is
almost nonexistent in real-life crimes of this seriousness, the film
gains mightily thereby.

The picture starts with a case which might have happened many times, and maybe did, of a young and beautiful model, also a tramp, and one of the master minds of a jewel ring murdered by her own operatives in a dispute over the swag. The clues are then carefully worked over by the police, who come upon the identity of the real killer almost simultaneously by two courses of investigation--the gradual breaking down of the victim's co-conspirator Niles (played by Howard Duff), and the hunch of the young, impulsive detective who suspected that the body of a derelict with a criminal record found in the river the morning of the murder had a connection with the case. The young detective is played by Don Taylor. The older, experienced, orthodox homicide detective lieutenant who reaches the same solution in the same time by slowly breaking down Niles, via the unmeshing of a web of lies, is played by Barry Fitzgerald.

The deficiencies of the picture are too obvious. Its overly melodramatic sequences are laid on a framework of documentary reality that makes them even more naked than the title. Some of them are the thin stupidity of the young detective in trying to make the arrest of a murderer by himself when 18,000 men were available on the nearest telephone; the implausibility of Barry Fitzgerald as a detective lieutenant; the cop-and-robber formula of shooting the criminal down from the stark heights of a superstructure on the Williamsburg Bridge (with some good photography as an offset); the assumption that a dead body floats during its first day in the river. Finally is the utter fatuousness of the fadeout line to the effect that there are eight million people in New York and that this is just one of their stories, as though to suggest that all New York steams in a boiling whirlpool of murder, intrigue, jewel robberies, police sirens, etc., and that even this random sample ought to hold the yokels for a while.

For its distinction, the film has some solid achievements. As a documentary, it is an exceptionally close portrayal of the actual type of police work indulged in when the "force" is faced with a "hot" murder and has to solve it before the tabloids begin calling for the removal of the commissioner. Scrupulously thorough in its detail, the investigation follows the generally successful lines pursued when a murderer must be apprehended; the clues are scarce and the publicity extensive. In this respect the film has a marked superiority to the hackneyed product by holding to the theme of patient leg work against the psychic intuition of Dick Tracy or Kerry Drake. Even here the purists may note, however, that it is only an occasional murder that gets the full treatment of Barry Fitzgerald, and that hundreds of small timers are rubbed from the urban scene with hardly a ripple compared to this in the homicide bureau.

The acting as a whole is adequate but not distinguished unless the performance of Adelaide Klein as the victim's mother be noted as such. Otherwise The Naked City on the whole is a good contribution to the demi-documentaries, a reliable epitaph to the

beautiful romanticism of the lamented Mark Hellinger, and a successful and photographically artistic salute to the day-by-day plug-
ging of hundreds of public employees whose efforts make major
crime generally unprofitable from a commercial standpoint in the
great city, and thereby greatly reduces its prevalence.

--Paul J. Kern in New Movies,
Vol. 23, No. 3 (April 1948),
pages 5-7.

*   *   *

How much of the quality of a film can be attributed to a
producer, and how much to the writers and director? No rule can
be laid down, but it seems fairly likely that The Naked City was
pretty much producer Mark Hellinger's baby. The commentator's
voice is Hellinger's; and the yarn combines toughness, humor and
sentiment in proportions that make the brew recognizable Hellinger.

All of this is to the good, for the result is a film of real
distinction. As the movie opens it is 1 a.m. in New York. The
camera roams the streets of the world's greatest city, in and out
of buildings, picking up brief shots of people who are later the
principals of the story. Inside one apartment two men are seen
murdering a woman.

The city awakens, and the story starts. And as the murder
is discovered, the laborious, discouraging, but exciting work of de-
tectives Barry Fitzgerald and Don Taylor commences. From then
on it is a relentless business of sifting evidence, checking clues,
questioning people. (The narrator asks, "Have you ever played
button-button in a city of eight million people--some of whom are
liars?")

Perhaps nothing makes more satisfactory movie entertainment
than a good manhunt--and The Naked City is a first-rate one, cli-
maxed by a hair-raising chase in the superstructure of Williamsburg
Bridge. But The Naked City is more than an expert hunt. Filmed
in the streets of New York, in actual apartments, offices and police
stations, with real citizens peopling its scenes, it is an example of
the documentary technique skillfully adapted to a fictional narrative.
The gloss of studio sets is missing, well replaced by the actual settings.

Hellinger sprinkled this film with newsreel-type glimpses of
the people (without makeup) who compose this conglomerate city--
some of them comical as only native New Yorkers can be, some of
them wistfully sad. By these interpolations, and by his offscreen
commentary, he caught some of the heartbeat of the city, some of
the essence of city life that few film dramas ever capture. His
last film, The Naked City will be remembered as his best.

The odd casting of Barry Fitzgerald as a detective lieutenant
works out well indeed. Fitzgerald plays his role straight, scratch-

ing himself less than usual, and producing a believable character.
He is well assisted by Howard Duff, Dorothy Hart and Don Taylor,
all of whom act as though they had never been nearer Hollywood
than Tenth Avenue.

--Fortnight, Vol. 4, No. 4
(February 13, 1948), page 29.

☐ NATIONAL VELVET (M-G-M, 1945)

The bucolic drama has always had a vast vogue with denizens
of large cities.   Weary and suspicious of mortar and brick and
asphalt-paved canyons, dwellers in congested districts find it pleasant to dream that life adjacent to hillocks and green fields is downright idyllic.   This legend has found wide credence and has caused
a resultant box-office success for such dramas as Quincy Adams
Sawyer, Turn to the Right, Blue Jeans, The Old Homestead.   There
is little doubt that National Velvet will draw much favor from the
same well of misconception.

National Velvet is an excellent motion picture, albeit several
servings too lavish on the side of saccharine.   It is worthily written, particularly in the Anne Revere role of the ex-Channel swim-
mer who foregoes fame after her single exploit and then settles
down to the routine of an average human being.   Miss Revere, an
actress of no mean attainments, makes the assignment ring true as
flicked crystal, and is no slight asset to the film.   Donald Crisp is
good as the father, and Elizabeth Taylor proves quite miraculous as
the mite heroine.   The child has an earnestness absolutely encompassing, gentian eyes that quite atone for Mrs. Kalmus' usual tan-
trums in Technicolor, and an honesty of approach which places her
apart from other under-age Thespians.

So disarming is little Miss Taylor, that by precept she forces
Mickey Rooney to curb his histrionic excessiveness.   Occasionally,
the lad lapses into a synthetic brogue reminiscent of a fledgling
playing a J. Hartley Manners heroine in a grammar school gradua-
tion production, but for the most part he is not the source of the
alarums habitual to his appearances on the screen.

Jackie Jenkins, I have it on irrefutable report, is "a love,"
"a darling" and "a true depiction of the American urchin."   Be that
as it may, like Margaret O'Brien on the same lot, the acting of
Master Jenkins imparts to me a frenzied desire to throw up.

National Velvet is the story of a horse, and has many of the
ingredients usual to a race-track saga, including the climax of the
heroine who masquerades as a boy and rides the nag to victory.
Through some magic which I can't explain, director Clarence Brown
at all times avoids giving the impression that one is watching Anita

Stewart disport in Charles T. Dazey's In Old Kentucky.
                              --Herb Sterne in Rob Wagner's
                                Script, Vol. 31, No. 698
                                (February 17, 1945), page 14.

□ NOTORIOUS (RKO, 1946)

The remainder of the films that have come to my attention
this past fortnight comprise a crime wave of tidal wave proportions,
with more dastardly deeds per foot of Eastman stock than one could
comfortably shake a nightstick at.   While they are all relatively
rewarding, the best of the lot, undoubtedly, is Notorious, an Alfred
Hitchcock stunner, which ranks high among the fright operas he has
staged in Hollywood.

The plot strands of the piece are not devastatingly different
from the ones found in the average I-spy saga, but Ben Hecht has
woven them into a solid fabric of suspense and thrills, and, for
once, Hecht has refrained from ornamenting the dialogue with his
customary verbal moués and grimaces.   The work is straightforward, and Hitchcock, with the aid of Ted Tetzlaff's imaginative
camera approach, thunders the story along through visual surprises
and a series of personality performances that are excellent movie
make-believe.   Ingrid Bergman, the notorious lady of the title, is
consistently fascinating throughout, making even the well-worn drunk
scene appear fresh and unique.   Cary Grant, for the moment without
irksome mannerisms, does the government agent as well as one has
a right to expect.   Two heinous Nazi characterizations are contributed with stealth and consummate villainy by Claude Rains and
Madam Konstantin.   Lenore Ulric's role has been snipped to a few
flashes, but even with no opportunities at all, the lady registers
her old flash and flame.

Notorious is all movie and considerable fun.   The love
scenes between Miss Bergman and Grant are in the Great Tradition,
and to those who have outgrown bobby socks and knickers they will
appear welcome lineal descendents of the memorable romantic moments of the movies contributed in the past by Lillian Gish and
Richard Barthelmess, Greta Garbo and John Gilbert, Norma Talmadge and Eugene O'Brien, Ronald Colman and Vilma Banky, and
Anita Stewart and Earle Williams.
                              --Herb Sterne in Rob Wagner's
                                Script, Vol. 32, No. 739
                                (September 28, 1946), page 12.

□ NOW, VOYAGER (Warner Bros. , 1942)

Bette Davis, eyeing still another Academy Oscar, resorts to

just such a routine in her current foray upon the lachrymal organs, via the gastronomic regions, Now, Voyager. Brewed from a novelistic onion by Olive Higgens Prouty, this has the flavour that suffused the scrivener's Stella Dallas, and while it is obvious that the author has lately been perusing primers dealing with abnormal psychology as well as her customary reading matter--the culinary recipes of Mrs. Georgie Sheldon and Mrs. E. D. E. N. Southworth --the broth is still cayenned to appeal to palates that relish the cuisine of the one-arm luncheries of literature.

Now, Voyager concerns itself with the type of screen neurotic that one would recognize as Davis material even on nights of darkest blackout. In this the maladjustment is caused by the rigid dominance of a mama (played with considerable cane-thumping by Gladys Cooper) and only the efforts of a psychiatrist (this is another appearance of Claude Rains as a benign Belasco) extricates the heroine from a permanent berth in a booby-hatch. Strained, suffering and as beautiful as the Warner makeup department can manage, Bette takes a South American cruise and encounters both love and lust. From then on Life (that Torquemada!) really applies the heat, and the emotional agony becomes so intense as to threaten not only the sanity of the shadow-protagonists but that of the spectators as well. It is all desperately slow, shatteringly inane and violently verbose, but certain ladies at the preview wept and sniffed copiously, thereby conclusively proving that Time has not dimmed the truth of Phineas T. Barnum's most famous observation. Miss Davis repeats the same higgledy-piggledy performance that has been consistently lauded by press and public alike, while Paul Henreid, no longer content to be a competent actor, bursts forth as a sloe-eyed lover and devotes most of his footage to making febrile googoo eyes in the free French fashion that has made Charles Boyer the toast of matinee audiences.

--Herb Sterne in Rob Wagner's
Script, Vol. 27, No. 644 (December 19, 1942), page 22.

☐ THE OUTLAW (Howard Hughes/United Artists, 1946)

The Legion of Decency's Moués at The Outlaw, are a distinct cause for consternation. The film, from this department's orchestra chair, is a moral lesson of no small moment. As a dramatic tract, its influence may well come to vie with certain works of Charles Rann Kennedy, Jerome Klapka Jerome, and Lloyd Cassel Douglas in the number of converts it ultimately collects for the cause of chastity, charity and the other various and sundry virtues.

Rarely in the history of filmdom has a work made Sin such a soporific. If one is to deduce from the sermon of Brother How-

ard Hughes, free-lance love is as inevitably mechanical as the embraces of a Main Street streetwalker; violence is as ridiculously
uncomfortable as appearing at a garden fête arrayed only in nettle
undergarments; and the picture also conclusively proves that, for
conversational prowess, even the company of bankers is likely to
prove more stimulating than the utterances of those who careen
through so-called unconventional careers.   Further, the film firmly comes forth for sexual restraint by its satirical treatment of the
frontal architecture of the heroine.   Viewing what looks like a dire
mammary malady for one hundred and fifteen minutes will, in all
probability, send more males in search of the solitary life than any
other theatrical presentation since Oscar Hammerstein revealed the
face of Mme. Polaire to the American public on the stage of his
Victoria Theater in the year 1909 A. D.

    The Outlaw, as those know who have attempted to attend any
of the four emporiums exhibiting the film in Los Angeles, is attracting phenomenal attendance.   The public is queueing at the box-
offices in numbers far outdistancing the lines at counters which vend
Kleenex and nylon hosiery, and if the photoplay runs as long as is
likely, and if it possesses the wholesale reformative values I suspect, it is only a question of time before our Los Angeles literally
becomes The City of Angels.

    Beyond its virtues as a clarion call to virtue, The Outlaw
has little to recommend it.   An antique visualization of "the West,"
its conception of dramaturgy is lifted from the more rambunctious
melodramas of David Belasco.   Witness such titbits as: a fowl,
tantalized by the stench of blood, about to peck out the eyes of the
wounded helpless hero; the encounter of the hero and the heroine in
the hay, which starts as a fight and ends up as something else
again; the heroine, left suspended by her thumbs in a sequestered
desert spot as a tempting snack for passing vultures; the scene,
obviously considered a lallapalooza by its creators, in which the
heroine, prompted by the fear that the hero is freezing to death,
disrobes and creeps between the coverings in order to stir him
back to life via the warmth of her body.

    Admittedly, these plot figments today would have difficulty
obtaining serious acceptance, even were the heroine to be essayed
by a chick who combines the allure and bravura knack of Mrs.
Leslie Carter, Lenore Ulric and Blanche Bates, and the hero were
to possess the rune to make his performance a pastiche of the
more chatoyant enactments of Hamilton Revelle, William Court-
leigh and Robert Hilliard.   As it is, Mr. Hughes entrusted the
parts to Jane Russell and Jack Buetel, a pair of thespians who are
still disconcertingly moist behind their histrionic ears.   It is lamentable to observe them struggling with the preposterous speeches
and situations; it is agonizing to behold them teeter under Hughes'
inept tutelage.   Whether Miss Russell and Mr. Buetel will ever
develop an aptitude for acting is problematical.   At this point, their
sole talent is one of being able to appear perpetually unpleasant and
petulant.

The Outlaw suffers from lack of professional status.   Ex-
cepting the characterizations vouchsafed by such old hands as Walter Huston, Mimi Aguglia and Thomas Mitchell in the histrionic department, and Gregg Toland's camera work, the film has an ama-
teur air of a kind one might expect in a product confected by some
grammar school cinema class composed of mentally retarded students.   This computation is in no small way aided by Victor Young's
violent musical score, which repeatedly propels the absurd dramatics into the realm of broad burlesque.

However, the public seems more than willing to forgive the
faults of The Outlaw, if one is to draw conclusions from the attendance records.   It would appear that I have never before quite
realized to what lengths motion picture audiences will go, and what
dross they will accept, just so long as it is an inspirational celluloid message that holds the screen.

> --Herb Sterne in Rob Wagner's
> Script, Vol. 32, No. 728 (April
> 27, 1946), page 14.

                              *   *   *

Sitting in cans on a studio library shelf for a couple of years
won't improve the product generally or the acting in particular.
But then, neither will it hurt the appeal of the spectacular Jane
Russell.   Can't think of any other reason for catching this.

> --Fortnight, Vol. 8, No. 3
> (February 3, 1950), page 31.

                              *   *   *

As The Outlaw has already opened in several of the large
cities--in spite of much opposition--perhaps something should be
said about this curious "Western."   It is difficult to take Howard
Hughes's production seriously, since Hughes, who produced, directed and pretty much bossed the whole affair, must have known
what he was doing in including several scenes that are like illus-
trated party jokes.   It must have come as no surprise to him to
discover, when the picture was finished several years ago, that the
Hays Office refused to pass it.   And the advertising campaign being
used now to flaunt the picture is fully aware of what it is trying to
sell.   As a "Western" the film is almost a parody on its genre--
complete with sheriff (Thomas Mitchell), an old, established outlaw
(Walter Huston), a very young Billy the Kid (played with an odd
combination of the naïve and blasé by Jack Buetel), a sultry wench
(provocative Jane Russell) who passes from one outlaw to the other,
and a lot of shooting, posses, Indians.   Some of the action is very
slow and talky, some of it rather silly as if trying to make fun of
other "Western" stories.   The musical score punctuates the action
as if to accentuate the note of burlesque.   The sexy scenes are
done crudely and without imagination, like small boys snickering
over what they don't quite understand.   I suppose, however, that

when you pass a fence on which youngsters have written dirty words,
there is no law that says you have to look at their handiwork.

--Philip T. Hartung in The Commonweal (July 26, 1946), pages
360-361.

☐ THE PALM BEACH STORY (Paramount, 1942)

Preston Sturges offers snappy copy on his three-ringed ec-
centricity: his peculiar sleeping schedule, his tumultuously international childhood, his interest in food and death. But I am more
interested in his attitudes and intentions, and another artist gives
us a clue to these: just as Jean-Baptiste Molière dressed his
themes, often of dangerous leverage socially, in acceptable comic
surfaces, Preston Sturges, in our time, is making a series of
serious, often bitter satires, disguised as slapstick farces.

It is five whole years since various unhappy factors cut off
our regular doses of the Sturges brand of Komic Kathartics. And
the transitory career of even a superior film in the wasteful exhi-
bition channel may have forced us to forget how effective those
doses were. Let us only pray that the unreleased Mad Wednesday
and the unfinished Unfaithfully Yours give us again the jolts we
need.

After pruning away a few of their countless enchanting tan-
gents, the films of Preston Sturges display a remarkable consistency, even unity. His first three films appear as a trilogy on fraud:
fraud in politics (The Great McGinty), fraud in business (Christmas
in July), and even fraud in crime (The Lady Eve). Sturges' last
three films form another trilogy, on hero worship and the nature of
heroism: The Miracle of Morgan's Creek, Hail the Conquering
Hero, and The Great Moment, butchered though this last undoubtedly
was after Sturges' departure from Paramount. Between these two
groups are two of his most brilliant and lucid satires--Sullivan's
Travels and The Palm Beach Story, whose theme is money money
money.

From the opening scene of The Palm Beach Story, where
the money theme is announced simply and unmistakably, to the gag
end of a double mariage de convenance, the thematic material is
given the Sturges treatment. This means infinitely surprising variations and explosive development. The pace remains pretty constant, but the scene switches madly, with a Molièresque alternation
of comedy and farce. Here are money and happiness, too little
money, too much money, money and sex, no money, money and
beauty, money and madness, money to bribe with, money to play
with, MONEY!

Only for one sequence are you allowed to push money into
the background, but it lurks there menacingly in the forms of ex-

travagance, caprice, and waste.   This sequence, the club-car orgy
of the Ale & Quail Club, is expertly placed between the two main
sections of the film, between the New-York-too-little-money first
reels, and the Palm-Beach-too-much-money body of the film.   All
other characters have been drenched in their relation to money (or
to the lack of it) and held dripping before you: John D. Hackensacker (Rudy Vallee) with his pincenez spares, his little account
book that is never added up, and his yacht named "The Erl-King";
Jerry Jeffers (Claudette Colbert), desperate and willing to peddle
her long legs; her penniless artist-husband Tom (Joel McCrea);
the Wienie King of Texas who wants to spend and spend; and the
decorative Toto (Molière's symmetry requires a kept man to balance a kept woman).

   While we await the results of Howard Hughes' recutting of
Mad Wednesday and the Sturges-Zanuck relation, I wish we could
persuade some local revival-house (as close as possible to the Fox
studio) to show us (and Sturges) his highest, bravest, most brilliant
and biting work: Sullivan's Travels.   It might remind him of his
own discerning self-description, "a modern American humorist
working in film," and of Molière's description of his job: "The
correction of social absurdity must at all times be the matter of
true comedy."
                              --F. I. A. in Script (May 1948),
                              page 41.

                    *   *   *

   Ordinarily it isn't proper to go around looking gift comedies
in the mouth.   But with Palm Beach Story you ought to, because
despite its lusty laughs, its quite meaningful sarcasms and its lavish inventiveness, it has an over-all weakness that is disturbing in
a Preston Sturges movie.

   The trouble with Palm Beach Story seems to be that this
time Sturges, who wrote and directed it, simply had too many engaging ideas, with the result that none of them gets quite enough
attention.   For instance he evidently wanted to twit the Hays Office
with his love scenes.   He had an idea about American oil dynasties,
with their divorcing daughters and moralist sons.   He had notions
also about Palm Beach life, sponging Riviera refugees, American
rod and gun manners, yachts, railway club cars, Hollywood movie
plots in general and a new twist on the old twist of twins-and-
mistaken-identity.

   In Palm Beach Story Sturges weaves all these amiably into a
plot which sends Claudette Colbert (who is twins) off to Palm Beach
for a divorce from Joel McCrea (who is also twins), so she can
marry a rich man and finance Joel's booming aeronautical ideas.

   The rest is "business."   There is the business of Claudette's
unmanageable dress hooks, which lead to nifty moments of marriage
bed frankness.   There is the business of Claudette losing her bag

and tickets to Palm Beach, and stowing away with a Florida-bound
"Ale and Quail Club," complete with bird-dogs, shotguns and rich
inebriates.   Then there is the business of the rich and righteous
oil scion, John D. Hackensacker III, who rides in lower berths because he thinks compartments are un-American, grudgingly tips
dimes because he thinks tips, too, are un-American, and has sublime views on the permanence of love, despite his sister who has
had at least five divorces.

This Hackensacker business is really the best thing in the
movie, especially the inspirational casting of Rudy Vallee as the
penny-wise romantic with Mary Astor, herself a multiple divorcee,
as the sister.

Claudette Colbert and Joel McCrea play their respectively
impulsive and diffident selves too, with the bonus for their fans of
both appearing as twins at the finish.

--John T. McManus in PM (January 11, 1942), page 20.

☐   THE PARADINE CASE (Vanguard/Selznick, 1947)

The numerous films produced under the banner of Selznick
International have built for that firm a reputation for opulent production and lavish display of expensive talent.   The numerous films
produced by Alfred Hitchcock have won for this director top honors
as a creator of tense, absorbing murder melodrama.   It is curious,
then, that the Selznick-Hitchcock collaboration, repeated for the
fourth time in The Paradine Case, has not resulted in a more impressive film.   Certainly Selznick has stinted neither on production
values nor cast names, while Hitchcock reveals all his mature
knowledge of filmcraft.   The courtroom scene that comes as the
picture's climax is by far the tightest, most realistic enactment of
a trial that has ever been put on the screen.   Time and again in
the course of the film complicated psychological motivations are
more clearly established by what Hitchcock's camera tells us than
by what the sound-track says.   But the sound track says too much.
Because of it, somewhere along the line interest in the people
themselves and what happens to them begins to diminish.   Somewhere the things they say no longer come as drama but just as
words.

The Paradine Case centers around the efforts of Lawyer
Anthony Keane to free the beautiful Mrs. Paradine from the charge
of poisoning her blind husband.   Although a married man, Keane
soon falls in love with his client, and love blinds him to the possibility that she might be the guilty one.   At the trial he tries to
fix the crime on Latour, Paradine's servant, a young and handsome
Frenchman, discovering too late that it is he whom Mrs. Paradine
really loves.   Latour commits suicide, and the woman freely confesses.   Keane returns home to his understanding and forgiving wife.

It must be obvious even in outline that The Paradine Case is
less a mystery than a drama of psychological compulsions. Indeed,
the mystery which is intended to sustain the film--if Mrs. Paradine
did not poison her husband, who did?--is rather anti-climactically
invalidated by the ultimate disclosure that it really was she.   Even
so, this story might still have served very well as the frame for a
series of acute character studies, studies such as Hitchcock has often given us in the past.

Unfortunately, David O. Selznick in his script has chosen to
elaborate on the murder plot instead of the characters, and in such
extreme detail and with such profusion of aimless dialogue that
eventually the characters themselves are overwhelmed beyond the
ability of even a Hitchcock to extricate them.   Which is a pity, for
in their outlines and suggested interrelationships they all appear far
more interesting than anything they are called upon to do.

To Gregory Peck, of course, has fallen the longest and most
taxing role as the lawyer who loses his heart and very nearly his
reputation in handling the Paradine case.   His work is competent,
sincere, but rarely can we believe that he is really, as we are
frequently informed, one of England's ablest barristers.   Alida
Valli, Selznick's Italian discovery, displays an interesting personality in a role that requires little histrionically.   Far more rewarding are the "bit" parts entrusted to such unaccustomed "bit" players as Charles Laughton, Charles Coburn and Ethel Barrymore.
It is their interpretations of an unusually complex set of subsidiary
roles that give to the film its chief distinction.   Hitchcock works
tirelessly to aid them but the script was just too much.

> --Arthur Knight in New Movies,
> Vol. 23, No. 1 (January 1948),
> pages 4-5.

*   *   *

Director Alfred Hitchcock, who achieved something close to
cinema immortality years ago by his direction of The 39 Steps and
The Lady Vanishes, has in recent years abandoned the breathless
chase type of film of which he is a master.   His latest show is
The Paradine Case, a courtroom drama about the murder trial of a
beauteous, mysterious widow (played by the new Italian actress,
Valli).

Most of the film is set in Old Bailey court, and it has required all the director's ingenuity to keep the proceedings from being static.   Somehow, with the clever camerawork of Lee Garmes
and the frequent interruptions for court recess, the illusion is created that you are observing a show crammed with action--when
actually very little really happens.   This is old stuff, of course,
to Hitchcock, who once photographed an entire film within a lifeboat.   And Hitchcock knows, too, that there is more drama, often,
in the courtroom than in life.

This is a most seductive film in many ways, because, again,
although it is ostensibly courtroom drama, make no mistake: it is
really drawing room stuff. It is less a question of whether the
lovely widow will be found guilty, than whether handsome, patient
wife Ann Todd will lose brilliant barrister-husband Gregory Peck
to the lady he is defending. (What do you think?)

David Selznick has given this affair the most lustrous possible production. His cast is incredibly handsome, superbly groomed,
enormously well-mannered. These wholly attractive people suffer
the sordid court goings-on with aristocratic grace, giving Old Bailey
a glossy polish it is not likely to see again for many a day. Within
the strictures of good behavior, Peck, Miss Todd, Joan Tetzel and
Charles Coburn behave very properly indeed. Judge Charles Laughton goes so far as to do some genuine acting, having himself a rare
time on the bench; and Ethel Barrymore goes farther and indulges
in some ham (high-grade, of course). As the lady on trial, the
new Italian actress, Valli, demonstrates that her beauty compares
with our domestic variety, but she has little acting to do. Another
newcomer, Louis Jourdan, does extremely well with a brief, highly
emotional role.

All in all, this is a wonderfully slick production and a skillful one. It is nothing that will stimulate you mentally to any degree, but it is undeniably a smooth job of popular entertainment.
                              --Fortnight, Vol. 4, No. 2 (Janu-
                              ary 16, 1948), pages 25-26.

☐ THE PHANTOM OF THE OPERA (Universal, 1943)

Universal's remake of Gaston Leroux's The Phantom of the
Opera is a lavish version of the old thriller which goes out of its
way to sear the eyes with raucous color and bludgeon the ears with
completely unmodulated operatic arrangements of Chopin themes and
Tschaikowsky's Fourth. While there is no intention of hailing the
Rupert Julian version as a triumph of art, or the performances of
Lon Chaney, Mary Philbin, Norman Kerry and Virginia Pearson as
anything that could not easily ensnare an Academy Award, the earlier photoplay did possess a quiet charm which this misses completely through an insistence upon visual and aural blatancy.

Motivation has been added to the plot, but this in nowise
makes up for the words placed in the characters' mouths. Dialogue
is not so much of France of an earlier century as it is of a Mono-
gram western of today, and the cast-members read it as though
they at any moment expected to see a posse ride in pursuit of a
gang of cattle rustlers through the doors of the Paris Opera and
right up the Grand Staircase.

Nelson Eddy as a brunet is much as he was as a blond, and
judging by Susanne Foster's perpetually peevish expression she

wasn't enjoying his company any more on the screen than was this
department from its orchestra chair.

--Herb Sterne in Rob Wagner's
Script, Vol. 29, No. 665 (Octo-
ber 23, 1943), pages 14-15.

□ THE PICTURE OF DORIAN GRAY (M-G-M, 1945)

MGM's The Picture of Dorian Gray is remindful of nothing
so much as a Grosset and Dunlap edition of the Oscar Wilde work,
editorially fumigated by Lloyd C. Douglas, and ornamented with il-
lustrations from the brush of Maxfield Parrish.

In view of the current intellectual standards of film production and the further curtailing gyves of the Hays Office, the mere
possibility of depicting a theme of aberration with any degree of
sense or sensibility is preposterous.   The Code amply provides for
fidelity in filming the moralistic samplers of Louisa M. Alcott, but
anyone sufficiently optimistic to believe that he can even approxi-
mately reproduce the fulminations of a Wilde, Huysmans, or Louys
on celluloid under these conditions is himself a subject for psychiatric probings.

Sex, according to contemporary celluloid, is solely an unin-
volved matter of a heroine (in a sweater snug as her own epidermis)
and a hero (whose salient charms are a pair of tight trousers) meeting in a moonlit glade to indulge in chaste osculation.   Pathology,
on the screen, is limited to mad scientists who possess superfluous
sets of dentures, and who expend their sexual span on this sphere
among elaborate laboratory retorts seeking an elixir of longevity.
Between these libidinal antitheticals there is only total vacuum, if
one is to credit the film.

With very, very few exceptions, the Hollywood motion picture today has all the erotic sophistication of a Midwestern adolescent whose only source of glandular stimulation has been a complete file of Captain Billy's Whiz Bang.

The bones of The Picture of Dorian Gray are essentially
those of the Wilde novel, but the flesh belongs to Joe Breen.
Aside from the vulgarization of Sibyl Vane in converting her attractions from those of a composite of Shakespeare's heroines to
those of a barroom thrush--thus blasting the entire motivation of
Gray's aesthetical and sexual philosophy--the addition of several
conventional amours, and the malformation of the climax which
switches Gray's demise from the sardonic to a transposition of
Marguerite's himmelfahrt in Faust, the film is a literal, if illiter-
ate, limning of the printed plot.   Both in his script and direction,
Albert Lewin seems to suffer from a fulsome miscomprehension of
what the Wilde work is about, for in both capacities Lewin appears

determined to interpret the curious, emotional dance macabre as a
simple Boy Meets Ghoul routine.

The sets, grandiose, well aired and streamlined, do much
to negate the stifling, patchouli-clotted atmosphere which Wilde
managed to make so poisonously inferential in print.   Only George
Sanders' Lord Henry Wotton has rudiments of the original intent,
even though the actor handles the rapier epigrams as though they
were a cricket bat, and sedulously avoids any suggestion that he is
portraying a Britisher with marked Greek inclinations.   Hurd Hatfield essays Dorian throughout the entire film with the same lack
of facial animation which Clara Kimball Young employed in char-
acterizing those moments of the screen transcription of the Du
Maurier novel when Trilby was totally under the spell of the hyp-
notic prowess of the Svengali of Wilton Lackaye.   Further in the
direction of novelty, young Hatfield dubiously enhances Dorian, de-
scribed in the text as "... a young man of extraordinary personal
beauty...," with as unfortunate an affliction of acne as a make-up
department has been called upon to conceal.

Aided by the several distressing portraits of Ivan Le Lorraine Albright, Dorian Gray in the fillums, emerges as a fin de
siècle dame chaser whose primary predicament lay in having been
born before the discovery of the Wassermann test and penicillin.

Mr. Wilde, are you chuckling?
                                    --Herb Sterne in Rob Wagner's
                                    Script, Vol. 31, No. 701
                                    (March 31, 1945), page 14.

*   *   *

The Picture of Dorian Gray, based upon the Oscar Wilde
story, represents an interesting and daring experiment by Metro
in view of the subject matter.   What it may do at the boxoffice,
something not as easy to foretell as with most pictures, also makes
it an intriguing piece of merchandise for analysis.   It's a critic's
picture.

In the advertising, exploitation, publicity, etc., may lie the
answer from a gross point of view.   However, the ad approach is
something exhibitors may have difficulty in deciding upon.   The
Wilde name may mean something, but the cast names do not.   It
would seem, especially in view of the fact that the horror and
murder cycle is now enjoying popularity, that the best way to merchandise Dorian Gray may be to stress that angle; also, perhaps,
to try to arouse the public on controversial aspects of the film.

Pandro S. Berman has invested the picture with much production value.   It is reported to have cost over $2,000,000, raising
the question of whether the negative cost will be returned.   That
again may depend a lot on the selling and how much talk about the
film and its theme may count in arousing interest in seeing it.

Five persons, including Dorian Gray, go dead in the picture. That
might be played up, too. The first is the saloon singer who kills
herself over Gray, the second his friend who did his portrait and
is murdered by Gray, the third a chemist who suicides, fourth a
sailor out to get Gray who's accidentally shot by a hunting party
and, finally, Gray himself. It's his painting, horribly disfigured
and bloodied up by Gray, which, in line with fantasy, turns on him.

The morbid theme of the Wilde story, carefully but also
somewhat boldly adapted to the screen, is built around Gray; his
contempt for the painting that was made of him, the fears of not
retaining youth and, of course, the unregenerate depths to which
Gray sinks and the evil rumors about him that have become widely
circulated. His utter indifference to them, his troubled mind, the
weaknesses that make him an interesting character and, on the other hand, his sadistic tendencies, all combine to make Gray a subject any psycho-analyst would like to lay his hands on. In the
adaptation, Albert Lewin, who directed, has very subtly but unmistakably pegged Gray for what he was, but it may go over the heads
of a lot of people anyway. Also, much of the offscreen narration,
explaining among other things what is going on in Gray's mind,
plus the epigrammatic slants, might be too much for most to grasp.

Hurd Hatfield, who had a minor part in Metro's Dragon Seed,
is pretty-boy Gray. He plays it with little feeling, as apparently
intended, but does it well, though he should have been aged a little
toward the end. As Hatfield does the Gray part, he's singularly
Narcissistic all the way. Sanders, misogynistic of mind and a
cynic of the first water, turns in a very commendable performance.
It's he who upsets the romance, ostensibly serious on Gray's part,
which has developed with a cheap music hall vocalist. She's Angela
Lansbury, who registers strongly and very sympathetically. Miss
Lansbury sings "Goodbye, Little Yellow Bird," a haunting old English music hall number which is reprised several times. Another
sympathetic character is Donna Reed, who also falls in love with
Gray but is brushed aside. Peter Lawford plays the man she jilts,
while Lowell Gilmore is the murdered painter, Richard Fraser the
brother of Miss Lansbury, and Douglas Walton, the chemist suicide.
All are well cast, together with numerous minor characters.

--"Char" in Variety, Vol. 157,
No. 18 (March 7, 1945), page
20.

☐ PINKY (20th Century-Fox, 1949)

Two years ago the Darryl F. Zanuck production of Gentleman's Agreement marked a significant motion picture milestone.
Today, with his brilliantly compelling presentation of Pinky, Zanuck
again writes motion picture history. He is not the first producer
to emblazon the screen with a daring and progressive story of the

Negro problem in our United States.   All credit is due the gallant
independent pioneers whose foresight and imagination sparked a new
concept of boxoffice values in relation to socially important subjects.
Pinky comes then as the masterly punctuation of these inspired efforts.   For the Zanuck dramatization of the Cid Ricketts Sumner
novel is a more accurate expression of the dramatic form.

Its power is drawn from purely creative forces rather than
the realism of documentation or the crutch of psychiatric exploration.   Pinky is the kind of story the screen does best, a pictorial
novel with a factual basis and with which there is that all-important
element of self-identification.   Neither white man nor Negro can
appraise Pinky without thinking earnestly: "What would I do under
the same circumstances?"

The screenplay, written with rare sincerity, draws the spectator into the orbit of the story and holds him there rooting for the
good people and scorning the evil.   It is the traditional motion picture technique, equally important to the social drama as it is to the
Western.   The difference is the trick of application, and Zanuck,
plainly, is a showman who has mastered it.   Pinky points a moral,
yes, and it is a devastating indictment of bigotry and prejudice.   Its
fine purpose, however, is accomplished without preachment and
without sacrifice of entertainment.   It is not necessary to agree
with Pinky to enjoy it.

The meticulousness of his supervision of the screenplay is
also found in Zanuck's intuitive casting and his choice of director.
The performances, from stars to bit players, are extraordinary and
every one the expression of the enormous talents of director Elia
Kazan.   His courtroom scene may be submitted as one of the finest
suspense episodes ever created for the screen and made so by the
spine-tingling abruptness of its conclusion.   The minimum of gesture, the simplicity of Ethel Barrymore's death scene, the delicate
handling of the touchy love story--these are the accomplishments
of a director who follows no prescribed course, but chooses his
own unerring way.

Pinky inevitably will cause comment, consternation and controversy as it wends its way into release.   What happens to it in
the South will be front page news.   What the critics say and what
the next door neighbor thinks will also be considered.   Pinky, if
she wanted to, would have a difficult time being a retiring young
lady, and the heroine who can provoke such interest and comment
can't go wrong at the boxoffice.   She's a natural ticket seller.

Pinky is the story of a light complexioned Negro girl, sent
North by her washerwoman grandmother, Ethel Waters, to be educated.   A love affair with a white doctor brings her back to the
South.   From the moment of her arrival she feels the bitter sting
of prejudice and segregation.   Her quick reaction is to return to
the North, but Ethel Barrymore, the imperious dowager who has
been served for years by Ethel Waters, falls dangerously ill.

Waters no longer has the health to help her.   Moreover, Pinky is
a graduate nurse.   Reluctantly the girl makes her choice.   She
works faithfully until the end.   She comes to love and understand
the acid-tongued old woman, and her patience is rewarded when
Miss Barrymore's will makes Pinky her heiress.   The community
rises in resentment, and a cousin fights the will, charging that the
girl used pressure.   Justice triumphs, however, and Pinky resolves
the purpose of her life by sending away the white doctor and opening a nursery school as a wise, gifted and beautiful woman proud
of her Negro heritage.

You are going to hear a great deal about this ending, that it
is too pat and comfortable, that it is telegraphed in advance and
somewhat unrealistic in view of the record of Southern courts in
matters of Negro property rights.   The opinion of your Hollywood
Reporter reviewer is that it is logical and consistent with the characters, and that enough judicial and legislative progress has been
made in some Southern states to give hope that a story such as
Pinky's can end honestly on a note of optimism.   Those who dis-
agree will make more lively and interesting the discussion about
this splendid motion picture.

Jeanne Crain's warm, sensitive and appealing performance
of the title role adds such stature to her career that the worry is
whether she will find the part to top it.   The young actress is
superb.   Ethel Barrymore's Miss Em is made skilfully sympathetic
by the fine trouping of the distinguished actress.   The grandmother
of Ethel Waters is warm and vibrant--a wonderfully conceived characterization of a woman whose lack of book learning has only augmented her vast store of human understanding and innate sense of
dignity.

William Lundigan, in the extremely difficult role of the doctor, plays the part with needed directness and straightforwardness.
Basil Ruysdael is exceptionally fine as the judge who takes Pinky's
case.   Frederick O'Neal is decidedly effective as a cunning ne'er-
do-well who lives on the sorrows of his people.   Kenny Washington
is excellent as a young Negro doctor, and Nina Mae McKinney
stands out as O'Neal's high living wife.   Evelyn Varden, the avar-
icious cousin of Miss Barrymore, lifts the action with her every
appearance as the chattering matron.   Griff Barnett's small town
doctor has charming appeal.   Raymond Greenleaf, as the judge,
rates commendation for his stirring delivery of the brief speech on
American justice.   Dan Riss, William Hansen and Arthur Hunnicutt
complete the fine cast.

Technically Pinky is everything that motion picture craftsmanship should be.   The photography of Joe MacDonald catches the
full flavor of the fascinating art direction of Lyle Wheeler and J.
Russell Spencer.   One can almost feel the sticky heat of the languid
Southern clime.   Alfred Newman's score has impact without being
obtrusive, and the editing by Harmon Jones contributes much to the

fast, suspenseful pace of the picture.

--The Hollywood Reporter, Vol.
105, No. 47 (September 30,
1949), page 3.

□ THE PIRATE (M-G-M, 1948)

The Pirate originally was a minor, featherweight gambol that
literate playwright S. N. Behrman scribbled for the Theatre Guild's
lustrous Lunts. For the movies, MGM has given it the full-dress
works--a dazzling Technicolor production, fetching songs by Cole
Porter, breakneck direction by Vincente Minnelli, and an exceedingly energetic cast headed by Judy Garland and Gene Kelly singing and
dancing like dervishes.

The result is one of the liveliest, loudest, most colorful and
generally over-powering musical romps ever to reach the screen.
Sparked by Gene Kelly's immense vitality and the most sensational
dancing he has done for the movies, The Pirate is bursting with
vitality. Director Minnelli has created an irresistible spectacle
that combines visual opulence with carnival gaiety. It may just be
that there is an excess of sound and fury in the production, and that,
like an opium dream, it will leave the beholder entranced but exhausted. More likely, though, audiences will applaud the tireless
zest of the high-spirited cast and the directorial artistry with which
Minnelli puts them through their paces. For robust, colorful musical entertainment plus some extraordinary dancing, The Pirate
will give you your full money's worth. That's something, these
days.

--Fortnight, Vol. 4, No. 13 (June
18, 1948), page 30.

*   *   *

*If Lynn Fontanne hadn't been taken ill in the spring of 1943,
S. N. Behrman's satirical comedy The Pirate might have been good
for more than 177 performances on Broadway. But it would never
have rated as one of the Lunts' more spectacular successes. The
current film adaptation, however, has been given a shot in the arm
in the form of some new Cole Porter songs and a script souped up
by Albert Hackett and Frances Goodrich. With Judy Garland and
Gene Kelly pitching energetically into the lead roles, the new Pirate
is one of the most delightful musicals to hit the screen in a month
of Sundays.

It concerns Manuela (Judy Garland), an outwardly demure

---

young maid of Calvados (a city somewhere in the Caribbean), who
is scheduled in true loveless Spanish tradition to marry an old
fuddy-duddy named Don Pedro Vargas (Walter Slezak).   But before
the wedding she becomes entangled with Serafin (Gene Kelly), the
leader of a group of itinerant players who, with the help of his old
friend Mesmer's magic mirror, persuades her to reveal her secret
love for "Black Mack" Macoco, an erstwhile pirate of rather sinister repute thereabouts.   Serafin, who hasn't been able to get to
first base with her in his own identity, naturally assumes the role
of a swashbuckling Macoco and sweeps her off her feet.   In this he
is grudgingly abetted by solid citizen Don Pedro, who is anxious to
disguise the fact that he himself is the real pirate in a very unro-
mantic state of reformation.

The Pirate is a rare and happy combination of expert dancing, catchy tunes, and utterly unbelievable plot which manages to
achieve pure escapism without becoming either sentimental or corny.
In tastefully handled Technicolor it is as appealingly frivolous as a
new Easter bonnet.

--Newsweek (June 7, 1948), page
83.

☐ PORTRAIT OF JENNIE (Vanguard/Selznick, 1948)

Throughout the centuries poets have sung of the timelessness
of love; and have dreamed of a beautiful existence on some astral
plane, in which time and space would merge so that predestined
lovers might meet, and be joined in bliss through all eternity.

Poet-novelist Robert Nathan's delicate and fragile little story
related, in tender and moving prose, such a love.   Artist Eben
Adams, strolling through Central Park late one winter afternoon,
comes upon a strange little girl who suddenly appears out of nowhere.   Jennie is dressed in a long out-moded fashion, and Eben
is charmed by her elfin ways and ethereal beauty.   She replies to
his questions elliptically, but promises they will meet again.   During the following months, she grows older by leaps and bounds;
Eben falls in love with her, paints her portrait and it is this painting that brings him his first success.   It also soon becomes apparent even to him that Jennie is not altogether of this world.   Like
the haunting little song she sings, "Where I come from nobody
knows, and where I'm going--everybody goes."   Their strange love
bridges time and space but it obviously cannot, even in poetic fantasy, be long reconciled with reality.

Nathan's theme--that an ageless love can cross the frontiers
of life and death, and that neither time nor space need be a barrier
to those who refuse to find them so--was the basis of his gentle
whimsy, as it is of the filmplay by playwright Paul Osborn and
Peter Berneis.   But the result onscreen is not by any means as

satisfying.   Snaring elusive fantasy is difficult under the best of conditions, and Nathan's novelette, left between its book covers, is far more likely to make a lasting impression than it does when transposed into celluloid upon a harshly realistic screen.

The second half of the episodic and rambling film--as the lovers realize their predicament and become desperate with the knowledge that they can never be united in this life--is superbly dramatic and touching.   But the tremendous hurricane sequence, at film's end, as a gigantic tidal wave roars (in green tint) across the screen to separate them, is, for all its power, harshly out of key with the wistful tenderness of most of the other scenes.

Joseph Cotten and Jennifer Jones play their leading roles with restraint and ingratiating appeal; with fine support from Ethel Barrymore as a spinster art dealer,   David Wayne (of Broadway's Mr. Roberts), Albert Sharpe, Cecil Kellaway and Lillian Gish. William Dieterle (Love Letters) directed.
                                        --Cue (April 2, 1949), page 22.

                        *   *   *

The late Percy Hammond, reviewing for the N. Y. Herald Tribune, used to employ the phrase "a brave and tender play" to describe a drama that showed sensitivity but failed to provide a valid dramatic experience in the theatre.   Portrait of Jennie is brave and tender, wrapped protectively in the wispy dress of fantasy.

Its gossamer story concerns a painter (Joseph Cotten) inspired by an ethereal figure (Jennifer Jones) who appears to him from time to time but who never materializes--except in his portrait of her.

At times director William Dieterle succeeds quite well in translating this elusive tale to the screen, and a sort of dreamy, poetic mood is temporarily achieved.   But the mood is transitory, for no matter how well Mr. Cotten plays his difficult role, he cannot for long make it believable; nor can Miss Jones' wraith seem anything but make-believe.   Lastly, a tempest of unparalleled fury is unleashed on the screen, completely out of keeping with the fragile nature of the fantasy and serving as a final disenchantment from whatever spell has been created.
                                        --Fortnight, Vol. 6, No. 1
                                          (January 7, 1949), page 31.

☐   THE POSTMAN ALWAYS RINGS TWICE (M-G-M, 1946)

The Postman Always Rings Twice bears little of the true mark of Cain.   The screen transcription of the novel is less may-

hem than moral values, and as an osculatory opera its merits are
strictly those of the kiss of death.   John Garfield is excellent type
casting, but he hasn't much chance against a dull script and ditto
direction.   Lana Turner, it is my guess, drew the inspiration for
her heroine from recent runnings of Norma Shearer's single performance in Her Cardboard Lover, We Were Dancing and Romeo
and Juliet.

> --Herb Sterne in Rob Wagner's
> Script, Vol. 32, No. 729 (May
> 11, 1946), page 23.

*   *   *

James M. Cain has not only turned over a whole series of
fictional stones, but he has also trained a powerful microscope on
the beings he found crawling around underneath them.   The Postman Always Rings Twice is every bit as good as the rest of his
stories in which he works like a magician as well as a scientist.
However, as much as one regrets to say it, his formula, like all
others, becomes standardized with familiarity.   The spectator's interest is no longer concerned with the "why" and "wherefore" of the
characters, interesting as they are, but rather with the "how" of
the story.   No matter how infinite the variety of a formula, repetition stales it.

It's no fault of Carey Wilson's slick production that The Postman doesn't make with special delivery.   Tay Garnett handles the
emotional scenes with his usual ability, but is too explicit in his
staging of the action scenes, which demand a fast pace.   Nevertheless, it's an absorbing and frequently exciting picture.   The lack of
impact is partly due to the fact that it follows Double Indemnity.

Upon still closer inspection, The Postman's leading characters engender even less sympathy than those in it and Mildred
Pierce.   For instance, the husband in Double Indemnity was so
thoroughly distasteful that the plotting of his death didn't place undue opprobrium upon the conspirators.   In The Postman, Cora
Smith's husband, also marked for speedy dispatch, is an ingratiating personality in Cecil Kellaway's casting.   The ratio between
sympathy for the murdered man and sympathy for the murderers
changes in direct proportion to our growing interest in Nick Smith.
This matter of sympathy would be relatively unimportant if the picture could shock an audience unused to this type of story.   But,
cushioned against shock, and their sympathies divided, the audience
has no choice but to regard it as an exercise in dramatic chess,
played much too leisurely.

Frank Chambers, a personable young vagrant, takes a job at
Nick Smith's roadhouse, and promptly goes on the make for his
employer's luscious wife.   After some preliminary sparring, they
decide they love each other enough to run away together.   However,
Cora thinks better of it.   Unwilling to give up her soft berth, and
yet searching for a way out of her dilemma, Cora finds the idea of

murder born in her mind. The first attempt goes awry. The surrounding circumstances excite the curiosity of the police, but since
Nick recovers from his injuries, and believes it was an accident,
there's nothing they can do about it. Driven by desperation, Frank
and Cora succeed with their second plan for murdering Nick. They
are caught red-handed, but through miscarriage of justice, engi-
neered by a smart lawyer, they are acquitted. At last, when all
their troubles seem to be over, and the pair have made peace between themselves, the irony of fate makes both pay for their guilt.
There's a terrific joker in the cards, and the way it's dealt will
satisfy all manner of belief, whether it springs from religion or
philosophy.

A bare outline cannot begin to do justice to the clever invention which carries the story to its smashing finish. There are
many good things in it, but two are outstanding. First, the rivalry
between the lawyer and the district attorney, which results in the
acquittal, is corrosive comment upon our ways of justice. Second,
the fact that Cora becomes a kind of celebrity illuminates for a
moment the darker recesses of our national mind. Harry Ruskin
and Niven Busch have, for the most part, retained the bite and
pungency of the novel, at the same time making it a well-articulated,
if rather verbose, screenplay. Their prolixity is most apparent in
the final scene, which labors the point of retribution.

It was to be expected that Lana Turner would demonstrate a
highly saleable commodity as Cora. No one will quarrel with the
story for giving her so many opportunities to appear in bathing
costume. She fills out her character as well. It's a sound, three-
dimensional performance. Her wardrobe alone strikes a false note.
Irene ought to know that simplicity is divided from elegance by no
more than a seam.

John Garfield is a tower of strength as Frank. He imbues
his part with rugged virility. Unfortunately, the slow-paced direction to a certain extent dissipates the effect of what ought to have
been a crackling characterization. Even so, Mr. Garfield comes
through with a large share of honors.

Cecil Kellaway comes close to stealing a great many scenes
away from the stars. His Nick is a pleasant old cuckold, adroitly
played for comedy as well as drama. Hume Cronyn as the lawyer,
and Leon Ames as the district attorney, provide mordant humor in
their sharp characterizations. Alan Reed makes much of a menacing role, but Audrey Totter barely has time to register in a bit.

The Wilson physical production puts upon the screen with
amazing fealty the studied indolence of southern California, a spirit
also captured deftly by Garnett. Anyone who ever lived or visited
the clime will recognize it here. The spirit also is carried out in
the excellent art direction and set decoration. Sidney Wagner's
photography is always stunning, often brilliant.

The picture, with its highly-publicized story background and its two potent star magnets, should have sensational openings. But, with Double Indemnity still fresh in audiences' mind and remembered by most exhibitors as something of a boxoffice flop, what happens after opening is a sizeable question. Anything the exhibitor can dream up in the way of sensational exploitation will not be wasted. The film's success will depend upon it.

--Hollywood Review, Vol. 37, No.
2 (March 19, 1946), page 20.

☐ RANDOM HARVEST (M-G-M, 1943)

Love, the commodity which reputedly makes the world go 'round, bestows much the same practical swivel-activity upon the turnstiles of motion picture theaters. Let it once be noised about that a movie is chock-full of female self-sacrifice, and the ladies immediately coerce the males of their acquaintance into viewing the attraction with them--thus providing additional credence to their age-old contention that there is nothing Eve wouldn't do for her man.

Random Harvest is just such a tidbit, and though the bonnets, shawls, crinolines and dark blue spectacles of Mrs. Henry Wood's Lady Isabel are plainly evident, director Mervyn LeRoy has kept the stock company dramatics well under control by italicising the story's characters rather than the antiquated plot predictions. A less reticent screenplay and unrestrained manipulation could have converted the film into an experience as moist as the Johnstown Flood. Fortunately, tact was lavished on the depiction of the amnesia victim of the last war and some importance is granted the account of his bi-world travails through the genuinely consummate performances of Ronald Colman, Greer Garson, and that of a brilliant new star in the Hollywood heavens, Susan Peters. Philip Dorn is excellent as the psychiatrist, and other interesting figures are created by Elizabeth Risdon, Una O'Connor, Reginald Owen and Aubrey Mather.

Best moments: Susan Peters proposing to Colman; Susan Peters rejecting Colman; and Miss Garson's expert selling of the song, "She's Ma Daisy." Worst sequence: Greer Garson, as the music hall entertainer turned Lady, suffering as her husband-in-name-only places an emerald pendant ("--reputed to have been the property of the Empress Maria Theresa--") about her throat, while her heart yearnsyearnsyearns for the costume jewelry of the days when love ruled all.

--Herb Sterne in Rob Wagner's
Script, Vol. 29, No. 645 (January 9, 1943), pages 14-15.

*   *   *

There is positively nothing random about Random Harvest. It is shrewdly and meticulously dollar-crafted in every particular.

Its British accent is as captivating as <u>Mrs. Miniver's</u>. It is cast
with pearly players in every part. Its <u>pedigreed plot</u> is savored
with just the right mixtures of ups and downs, ecstasy and well-
bred anguish, implausibility and psyche. And it moves toward its
climax with the measured tread and nicely-timed emotional bumps
of a Hearst Cosmopolitan serial.

In short, <u>Random Harvest</u> is custom-built to evoke all the
customary rave adjectives, yet not to stir any weighty ones. It is
a super-colossal commonplace.

The story, which is probably pretty much as James Hilton
wrote it, introduces an English soldier (Ronald Colman), invalided
out of the last war with shock and loss of memory. As just John
Smith, he marries a music hall singer (Greer Garson) who helped
pull him together. They are just beginning to make a go of it
when a taxi hits him, jogging the music-hall idyll out of mind and
returning him to his pre-war identity as heir to Random Hall and
a Vickers-style industrial combine.

From then on <u>Random Harvest</u> settles down to an involved
hour of what might be called cinema psycho-therapy, designed to
discover without any blunt, un-psychiatric questions whether His
Worship's John Smith marriage was love or just amnesia. The
obvious flaw in all this, which it is probably not cricket to mention, is that all the forgotten wife needed to do at any point, as
far as I can see, was to walk up to the guy with a pleasant "Hey!
Remember me?" and <u>Random Harvest</u> would have been all over but
the fadeout.

<u>Random Harvest</u> probably cost upwards of $2,000,000, and
it is perhaps the clearest example of the year of how a studio pos-
sessing lion's shares of movie-making capital and ingratiating talent
can mate these two to synthesize a magnificent neuter, which will
predictably bring in vast box office returns with which to produce
more neuters.

In the course of <u>Random Harvest</u> several of MGM's pre-
flight players get workouts paced by the polished leads. One of
these, young Susan Peters, seems pretty definitely marked as a
girl of the future, although her part in <u>Random Harvest</u> leads her
into emotionally over-deep water before she bows off. Another,
Philip Dorn, has a part so unnecessarily distended that you can bet
he is being built up for something mildly colossal on his own.
                              --John T. McManus in <u>PM</u> (De-
                                cember 18, 1942), page 20.

☐ THE RAZOR'S EDGE (20th Century-Fox, 1947)

Perhaps if 20th Century-Fox had not ushered in its scenari-
zation of W. Somerset Maugham's novel, <u>The Razor's Edge</u>, with

so many searchlights on the red carpet that guided its ermine-clad
guests to the world premiere at the Roxy in New York, one might
have viewed this highly-touted film more judicially.   But the show
was all on the outside.   Half a hundred foot and mounted police
tried to control the shoving, hysterical mob roped off Seventh Avenue between 50th and 51st Streets.   Loudspeakers blared the approach of Tyrone Power and Annabella, Gene Tierney, Clifton
Webb, Secretary of State Byrnes, the Duke and Duchess of Windsor
and sundry celebrities in an audience wearing formal dress by request of the producers.

The Razor's Edge, one of Maugham's lesser novels (which
at least one literary critic suggested left readers up a tree on its
publication two and a half years ago), emerges as a pedestrian motion picture.   Although the author purported to probe Larry Darrell's quest for salvation and resolution of faith, actually he merely
discussed it through his observation of various characters in the
post World War I period in Chicago and Europe.

The film follows Maugham's pattern respectfully, but it fails
to translate his talents as a master story teller--which is the novel's only excuse.   At least, Larry wrote a book of his own to justify his vagabonding.   In the film, he is colorless and confused.   He
won't work in Chicago so that he can marry his boyhood sweetheart;
he slums in the dives of Paris and talks quaint platitudes with a
bearded Yogi on a Shangri-La mountain of studio canvas, supposed
to represent a hideaway in the Himalayas.   After all this, he's set
for a career as a taxicab driver back home.

To make The Razor's Edge moving drama and release it
from its specious exploration of a man's soul, the scenario might
better have eliminated the character of Maugham as an ubiquitous
commentator and concentrated on how life really affected Larry
Darrell.   The people of the photoplay are all stencils; the story
takes too long getting underway, because of brief, cluttered scenes
at the beginning, and there is a strained artificiality of settings and
atmosphere.

As Isabel, Darrell's boyhood sweetheart, Miss Tierney shows
no perception of this vicious siren; Mr. Power as Larry is the conventional "good" hero; Herbert Marshall's Somerset Maugham is a
wan observer.   Anne Baxter and Clifton Webb have the meatiest
roles and make the most of them.   Miss Baxter effectively depicts
Sophie's progress in alcoholism, and Mr. Webb, as the snobbish
Elliott Templeton, does his best acting in a death scene.

The film should have a successful showing.   Many people
may be attracted by its superficial treatment of a vague philosophy.
                    --R. R. in Rob Wagner's Script,
                        Vol. 33, No. 746 (January 4,
                        1947), pages 13-14.

*   *   *

The Razor's Edge is a pretentious attempt, as was Somerset Maugham's original novel, to juxtapose two ways of life--the worldliness of the rich and the simplicity of the pure in heart.   For a central character it presents us with a guileless young man who has been profoundly affected by his nearness to death during World War I, who rejects all his high-society friends (including a girl passionately in love with him) and goes off to the Himalayas in search of some vague, mystical revelation.

Although this is Darryl Zanuck's most ambitious effort of the year and has been filmed with enormously careful attention to detail, The Razor's Edge misses fire.   Just what is this spiritual message that Mr. Maugham's hero brings back to Paris with him? It has something to do with Vedantaism and with looking at the dawn from a mountain top; it gives him the power to cure friends of headaches (a neat parlor-trick if you can get away with it); it inspires him with the curious yearning to become a New York taxidriver.   Except for these evidences, the hero is merely Tyrone Power, looking exceptionally healthy and agreeable, but never once suggesting (as Jennifer Jones did so convincingly as Bernadette) any miraculous inner compulsion.   He is not only a baffling character; he is an incredible one.

This tale of saints and snobs is unquestionably a handsome picture.   It moves gracefully, in its cosmopolitan way, through Paris bistros and salons, Chicago country clubs and Riviera drawing rooms.   Moreover, it has a high degree of technical finish, thanks to the extraordinary fluidity of Edmund Goulding's direction. But it remains a lot of pother about very little.

Gene Tierney plays the Chicago society girl whom Mr. Power would love, did he not love the Absolute more; while she is undoubtedly fetching to look at, she is unable to convey the basically sensual impulses that drive the girl to cruel acts.   Clifton Webb's caricature of her uncle, a waspish, middle-aged snob, is just that --a caricature.   Herbert Marshall (as Maugham himself), John Payne and Lucile Watson are also in it.

The film's one memorable performance is contributed by Anne Baxter as the degraded young woman whom the hero offers to marry but never does.   Miss Baxter's dipsomania is as alarming as Ray Milland's and it gives The Razor's Edge a momentary spark of reality that the film otherwise lacks.
                         --Fortnight, Vol. 1, No. 5 (December 30, 1946), pages 41-42.

☐ RIO GRANDE (Argosy/Republic, 1950)

Rio Grande is filmed outdoor action at its best, delivered in the John Ford manner to attract a strong play at the boxoffice.

While dealing with a familiar subject--Indian fighting in the early
west--the Ford treatment insures entertainment and the marquee
worth of the cast names.

A Ford-Merian C. Cooper-Argosy production for Republic
release, it features big, brawling mass action clashes, mixed together with a substantial portion of good, honest sentiment, ingredients that, when as well done as in this, practically always meet a
good reception in the general market.

John Wayne trods familiar story paths in his role of a cavalry officer who lets nothing stand in the way of martial duty.   This
devotion to military oath had led him, some 15 years back, to destroy the plantation home of his southern-born wife during the war
between the states.   He is now a lonely man, fighting Indians in
the west.   To his fort comes his young son, Claude Jarman, Jr.
whom he has not seen in 15 years.   Youngster is an ordinary
trooper, enlisting after flunking out of West Point.

Into this setup of rugged living, endangered daily by marauding Indians, comes Maureen O'Hara, Wayne's estranged wife, determined to take the son back for another attempt at being an officer
and gentleman.   Jarman is just as determined to see his new life
through and has ample opportunity to prove he is a man in the
savage tests of courage that ensue.   Plot's windup finds Miss
O'Hara seeing her husband's duty in a new light, and the family is
reconciled.

Among the vivid action sequences staged by Ford that stand
out are the Indian raid on the cavalry outpost and the troopers'
foray across the Rio Grande into Mexican territory to rescue a
group of children from the blood-thirsty Indians.   Sharpening the
sentiment in the James Warner Bellah Satevepost story, scripted
by James Kevin McGuinness, is the Victor Young music score and
the eight songs that are woven in the background as well as neatly
vocaled by the Sons of the Pioneers.   "I'll Take You Home Again,
Kathleen," reprised, is especially effective, and there are several
Stan Jones numbers, such as "My Gal is Purple," "Yellow Stripes"
and "Footsore Cavalry" that fit aptly.   Vocals are used in a manner that does not slow the movement.

Wayne is very good as the male star, and Miss O'Hara gives
one of her best performances.   Ben Johnson, Texas member of the
cavalry, scores as do Jarman, Harry Carey, Jr., and Chill Wills.
J. Carrol Naish's role of General Sheridan is small but excellently
delivered.

Comedy touches are introduced by Victor McLaglen as the
top sergeant, a role he has performed in other Ford pictures, and
general audiences will find plenty to laugh at in the familiar antics.
Grant Withers, Peter Ortiz and the others carry their footage capably.

The photography by Bert Glennon plays an important part in portraying the movement, as well as giving the film the pictorial dress that usually marks a Ford production. Other technical assists are of the best.

--"Brog" in Variety, Vol. 180,
No. 9 (November 8, 1950),
page 6.

□ THE ROAD TO MOROCCO (Paramount, 1942)

Like the previous peregrinatory ventures of Bing Crosby and Bob Hope, The Road to Morocco is solidly paved with hilarity. The lads are off again on a highway of captivating comedy, and the antics, which provide the impression of being ad-libbed, make this one of their top travelaughs.

The Road to Morocco lampoons itself, as well as all other harem-scarum movies, from the opening shot of Bing and Bob astride a camel warbling the facetious title tune which boasts an incisively humorous set of lyrics by Johnny Burke. Not a cliché of the camel operas escapes unlambasted, and before the fadeout is screened the usual yashmak yardage is thoroughly shredded into comedic strips.

Crosby and Hope are in great form, and their talents are given a lively workout by the energetic Frank Butler-Don Hartman script. Songs by Burke and Van Heusen are easy on the ears, and while Dotty Lamour is easy on the eyes, she comports herself in a lethargic manner no whit different from that of "The Sixty Most Beautiful Girls in The World" who nightly parade, like so many cataleptics, for Maestro Earl Carroll's customers.

--Herb Sterne in Rob Wagner's
Script, Vol. 27, No. 642 (November 21, 1942), page 18.

□ ROPE (Transatlantic/Warner Bros. , 1948)

One director who knows the virtues and possibilities of screen techniques has thrown them all away and made a play look something less than a play and not at all like a motion picture. Alfred Hitchcock has taken Rope, with its continuous action in a single setting, and photographed it in one long camera movement without a break except for two cuts that look like accidents in editing. In this macabre story of two young men who give a tea party over a chest which contains the body of a boy they have murdered, there are no sudden close-ups of apprehension, no sharp reaction-shots of horror, to whip up the excitement of his little exercise in

sadism.   Thus Rope gains nothing from the artifices of the screen,
while it seems sapped of the sinister vitality it had on the stage as
we watched the action across the top of the sepulchral chest.
                                    --Kenneth MacGowan in Script,
                                       (September 1948), page 42.

                              *   *   *

        Alfred Hitchcock, who used to make films that never stood
still, has of late been experimenting with movies that stir but fit-
fully, if at all.   In The Paradine Case, Mr. Hitchcock took his
camera into a courtroom and confined it there so long that he
wound up with a kind of shambling documentary on trial procedure
instead of the lively melodrama he had presumably set out to create.   Now, in Rope, he is working in even smaller quarters--a
middle-sized apartment in Manhattan--and this time his photography
is only slightly more animated than that of Daguerre.   In addition
to the fact that it has little or no movement, Rope is handicapped
by some of the most relentlessly arch dialogue you ever heard.
The picture, rather freely adapted from a twenty-year-old play by
Patrick Hamilton, undertakes to describe how a pair of very peculiar young men do in a friend of theirs, dump him in a chest, and
then, the rascals, invite relatives and friends of the victim to a
buffet supper, during which the bier is used as a serving table.
The young men are obviously patterned after Leopold and Loeb, and
their conversation smacks of the same sort of adolescent nonsense
about Nietzsche and supermen that the Chicago boys went in for.
Their chatter is tedious, Lord knows, but it's no worse than that
of the other characters.   "What would you say to some champagne?"
one of the killers asks a young lady at one point.   "Hello, champagne," she answers.   This young lady, who is the wittiest person
in Rope, salutes everybody as "Chum" and likes to point out that
"Everything is ginger-peachy."   Another witty type is the headmaster who got the young men interested in becoming Übermenschen in
the first place.   He talks waggishly during what seemed a good part
of Rope about the necessity of having superior people kill inferior
people, and if Miss Ginger-Peachy doesn't drive you into the streets,
he will.

        Among those involved in this slow-motion Hitchcock are John
Dall and Farley Granger, who play the mauve young men; James
Stewart, who is cast as the headmaster; and Sir Cedric Hardwicke
and Constance Collier, who serve as relatives of the victim.   They
all enunciate distinctly.
                                    --John McCarten in The New
                                       Yorker (September 4, 1948),
                                       page 61.

☐   ROXIE HART (20th Century-Fox, 1942)

        Remember the Turbulent Twenties, when Prohibition and

speakeasies flowed side by side, when flappers first astounded their
elders, and themselves, by rolled stockings and corsetless torsoes,
when male flaming youth wore Valentino haircuts and carried hip-
flasks? Ah, those bad, good old pre-Depression, Charleston-
dancing days in which the only war talk pivoted about the Battle of
the Sexes.

Roxie Hart strives to re-create that rash, brash era.
Based on Chicago, the Maurine Watkins play that satirized its own
period, the story of Roxie, who gunned her boy friend with her
little .45 and then rode high on the front pages of every newspaper
in the nation, is told in flashback form. It opens in a modern bar
as a newshawk, on another murder assignment, relates the yarn
while a player-piano grinds out the vintaged "Brokenhearted";
("There she goes, my best gal, there he goes, my best pal, and
here am I, broken-hearrrrrted...").

The spike-heeled, bowed dancing pumps of Roxie fit Ginger
Rogers perfectly, and she doesn't spare venom in creating the cheap
little slut who uses homicide as an excuse to make a name for herself. To placate the censors, this transcription insists that the
damsel only pretends to be guilty, and so much of the cold irony
of the original is dissipated. This, and other factors, cause the
film to lose much of the punch which the stage show and the Phyl-
lis Haver movie possessed. The absurdities depicted are no longer
pertinent and situations that once had hot, topical appeal are now
just so much costume stuff that is diffused history to the mature,
and utterly incomprehensible to the youngster generation. The characters, too, are severely self-conscious, finding short skirts
"quaint" and reading slang of two decades ago as though recognizing
it as definitive corn.

Miss Rogers' work has a note of authenticity (see any past
or present issue of The American Weekly). Sara Allgood is superb
as the prison matron, while Adolphe Menjou, Lynn Overman, and
Spring Byington each manage a factual portrait. George Montgomery
is woefully ill at ease. He seems to regret the sagebrush atmosphere that surrounded so much of his studio career and gazes
steadfastly into the distance as though sustained by the fond hope
that, possibly, he will catch sight of a pinto pony.
                                    --Herb Sterne in Rob Wagner's
                                      Script, Vol. 27, No. 623
                                      (February 28, 1942), page 10.

☐ SAMSON AND DELILAH (Paramount, 1950)

This, friends, is an epic; a tremendous, stupendous Cecil
B. DeMille production with no holds barred. Victor Mature as
Samson is at his peak when cracking Philistine skulls with the jaw-
bone of an ass. Hedy Lamarr as Delilah, dressed in a succession

of 50-Girls-50 costumes is easily one of the most beautiful women in the world. She alone is worth the price of admission or a haircut.

--Esquire, Vol. 33, No. 1 (January 1950), page 146.

*   *   *

You have probably heard the expression "a DeMille Production"; when you see Samson and Delilah (from the Biblical characters of the same name) you'll know for sure what the term means. It has everything but subtlety.

From the prologue when we learn that since the beginning of time people have been striving for freedom, to the grand finale when Samson destroys the evil powers that keep his people from freedom, it is a spectacle of magnitude.

The Technicolor is brilliant and beautiful, the sets are stupendous, the costumes (there were 5 costumers) fabulous, the battle scenes awesome, the love scenes tantalizing and the religious message as delicate as a sledge hammer.

Victor Mature as mighty Samson excelled himself in interpreting the power of the Lord, but his prayer scenes are less mature, more Mature.

Hedy Lamarr breathes the fire of Eve into her part. Delilah herself couldn't have been sexier, meaner or more repentant than her modern counterpart.

Angela Lansbury plays a radiantly lovely Semadon, Samson's first love.

During the entire two hours and ten minutes of Samson and Delilah DeMille's genius for detail is always evident. Even in his gigantic mob scenes there is reason for every movement, every actor. He balances these scenes with quick flashes of individual reactions to the momentary situation. His sense of design is wonderful, he groups and moves people with the artistry of an expert choreographer.

Applause to a long list of artists, actors, decorators, make-up men, costumers and photographers for their part in this magnificent DeMille production.

--Fortnight, Vol. 8, No. 3 (February 3, 1950), page 31.

☐ SANDS OF IWO JIMA (Republic, 1950)

From Tarawa to Mt. Suribachi, this is a brutally effective

film about the Marine Corps in action.   It may contain a lot of the
stock war-movie elements, but for realism and full-throttle fighting,
this film has it all over the war stories told on the screen in the
last few years.   John Wayne, as the soft-hearted sarge with armor
plate for skin, plays his part to the hilt though he is faked out of
position a few times by some pretty slip-shod scripting.   But he is
the key to the battle scenes that mix actual documentaries with well-
framed fiction.   They are the most terrifying and honest we've seen
in a long time.   Unfortunately, there is a love story tacked on to
the plot as well as a few tried-and-true movie crutches.   Totally
unnecessary (and happily brief) these scenes back in the training
areas must have been conceived in a silo.   When this picture is
good, however, it is really good.   And maybe you'll be able to
forget the in-betweens, as we're trying to do.

--Esquire, Vol. 33, No. 4 (April
1950), page 48.

*   *   *

Sands of Iwo Jima is a real war story.   There is no half
way about it.   The picture uses footage actually shot during combat and weaves it, with tremendous effect, into a gripping, dramatic and tragic story.   The script is a vibrant, realistic narrative--
contrived in a sense, but never to the point that its heroics are
phoney or its characters more or less than normal human beings.
These marines of Iwo Jima worm their way into your heart before
the footage has gone very far along, and by the time the last note
of the Marine Hymn has died away, you know that you have seen a
very fine and inspired motion picture.   By far it is the best thing
Republic has ever done and one in which the studio can take real,
honest pride.

For Edmund Grainger, whose production chores embraced
the enlisting of the Marines' co-operation, getting the tremendous
government film, and supervising actual shooting, the credit is undoubtedly the most important to date.   His supervision of the story
is distinguished by extraordinary good taste, and his casting will
make stars of quite a few young men in the troupe.   Allan Dwan,
likewise, rates commendation for the intelligence and dignity of his
direction.   The human comedy touches in which the picture abounds
breathe welcome lightness into what is, essentially, a grim and
horrifying story.

War is not a pleasant thing to contemplate, but, if another
is to be prevented, recollection is important.   So a film like Sands
of Iwo Jima serves the twofold purpose of providing superlative
drama and reminding people of history they are too inclined to forget.   When a film like this one issues from Hollywood it is obvious
that the picture industry is not shirking its responsibilities.   To
meet the public halfway it is necessary to camouflage documentation
and social content as entertainment.   Sands of Iwo Jima accomplishes this to near perfection, and consequently it can anticipate
nothing less than top boxoffice response.   Its emotional appeal is
tremendous.

A platoon of marines, of which John Wayne is the sergeant, are the heroes of Sands of Iwo Jima.   We meet them at a training camp in New Zealand and go with them through the capture of Tarawa and on to the frenzied battle for Iwo Jima, through to the historic raising of the colors on Mount Suribachi.   Fragments of their personal lives are unfolded in the course of these two actions. These characterizations of the men against the background of the battle action account for the impact of the drama.

John Wayne, long in a class by himself at the job of playing military characters, makes the tough sergeant his personal triumph. It is a great role, a strong, unrelenting, but humble man, and Wayne gives it the full measure of his commanding talent.   John Agar, heretofore a likeable if unspectacular actor, shows the fullness of an important screen personality in a part that makes real demands.   He is the scion of a long line of Marines who is in the Corps simply because of tradition, but who learns from Wayne the greatness of his calling.   Forrest Tucker impresses vividly as the nearest thing to a heavy, and Wally Cassell's flip delivery of the platoon comedian is a delight to hear.

Adele Mara, playing Agar's bride, and Julie Bishop, in the striking role of a deserted mother, are the two lone feminine members of the cast, and in their brief assignments do just as well as the men.   James Brown, the older marine who stays close to Wayne to keep him out of trouble, is excellent.   Others who impress particularly are James Holden, Peter Coe and Richard Jaeckel.   The film also makes effective use of several Marine officers and the three survivors of the Suribachi flag raising.

Reggie Lanning's photography, with its grim, realistic flavor, matches artfully with the documentary footage.   James Sullivan's art direction is equally authentic.   Victor Young supplies an impressive musical score.   The intricate editing is the outstanding work of Richard L. Van Enger.

--The Hollywood Reporter, Vol. 106, No. 49 (December 14, 1949), page 3.

□   THE SECRET LIFE OF WALTER MITTY (Goldwyn/RKO, 1947)

Two years ago word went 'round that Hollywood might be interested in filming James Thurber's tender and fragile short story, The Secret Life of Walter Mitty.   Immediately an aroused and cornered Thurber blazed: "I'll pay $10,000 to any producer not to touch it!"

But Progress (if that is the proper word) is not so easily blocked.   Movie mogul Samuel Goldwyn looked longingly into the heart of Thurber's timid, yet valorous, little hero who escaped his

nagging wife by daydreaming himself into a never-never land filled
with wondrous adventures--and saw in the mousy but magnificent
Mitty the perfect movie role for his star performer.   That, of
course, would be the lightning-tongued, rubber-faced, git-gat-gittle
Danny Kaye--the blond young man whom many today consider, not
without some justification, to be the screen's most talented comedian.

        Goldwyn is one of the most persuasive as well as obstinate
entrepreneurs on the Celluloid Coast.   He sold Thurber on his idea
of immortalizing Mitty on film, then cajoled him into journeying to
Hollywood to lend personal aid and counsel to perspiring scriptwrit-
ers Ken Englund and Everett Freeman, who labored somewhat more
than a year and a half on the script.

        There were not too many difficulties in their way.   But
there was one bleak moment during the screening of the $3,000,000
Technicolored comedy opus when there was some talk of abandoning
the story's original title for the more sensational I Wake Up Dreaming.   After some argument, saner minds prevailed.   Mr. Goldwyn
was calmed down, Mr. Thurber breathed again, and Thurber fans
(reputedly preparing with pen and gun for war) relaxed.

        However, it is still rumored that, come Thursday August
14th, when the new Goldwyn-Thurber-Kaye picture opens at the
Astor, the Battle of the Thurberites will be joined.   Having heard
(at fourth or fifth hand) that Mr. Mitty's original vignetted daydreams have been translated into gigantic neon-lighted, million-
dollar Technicolored nightmares, an army of Thurber fans has
threatened to march on the Astor and rend it from proscenium to
projector.

        This may, of course, merely be publicity talk from the
Goldwyn-RKO offices.   In any case the Thurberites may save their
ammunition, put away their fountain pens and conserve their tem-
pers.   For Mr. Thurber's fictional gem, now lengthened, broad-
ened and filled-out to nearly two hours of sparkling Technicolored
fact-and-fancy, turns out to be grand movie entertainment as well.
Mild little Mitty's daydreams--which occupied a brief five-and-a-
half paragraphs in Thurber's 2,200-word sketch--have been extended, high-lighted with uproarious comedy sequences and rounded
out with rich invention and lively dialogue.

        In addition, the film has been given a solid base in a run-
ning real-life melodramatic spy-and-secret-papers plot, which--
whether or not it is authentic Thurber--is howlingly funny Danny
Kaye.   And several merrily mad daydreams in the true Thurber
idiom have been added, so that even Mr. T. himself could not have
been too displeased, since he remarked: "I think the picture with
which I tampered will be an interesting one."

        From a movie-going entertainment viewpoint, the word "in-
teresting" is an outrageous understatement.   The Secret Life of

Walter Mitty, for all that it may be a bit overlong, is what the movie trade terms a "wow"--which suggests that both the public and Mr. Goldwyn may expect to be equally pleased by it.
                              --Cue (August 9, 1947), page 9.

                              *   *   *

Danny Kaye's characters have always been inorganic, super-natural and strange, but until now they've been presented as bread-and-butter real-life people. In Walter Mitty, however, no holds are barred on his imaginative flights, and his schizophrenic character-izations run the gamut from a salty sea captain to a Parisian mil-liner. Walter is a chap who finds the world too much with him and slips off into the most preposterous daydreams at odd moments. With him, daydreaming is almost an occupational hazard.

At home, Walter is no hero. Dominated by his mother, Fay Bainter, patronized by his flighty fiancée, Ann Rutherford, and browbeaten by her mother, Florence Bates, he finds refuge only in his dreams. In all of these, the same beautiful girl--Virginia Mayo--appears.

In retrospect, the plot dwindles until it is hard to believe that it was spread out to consume a couple of hours, but Danny does a couple of his double-talk specialties, written by his wife, Sylvia Fine, and, in the Irish sequence, sings "Molly Malone"--the only number he has sung "straight" in his screen career.

George Jenkins and Perry Ferguson have achieved wondrous sets by blending literal realism with ebullient fantasy. The paddle wheel of the riverboat, for example, leaves a wake of silver bub-bles.
                              --Fortnight, Vol. 3, No. 6
                              (September 26, 1947), page 30.

☐ SERGEANT YORK (Warner Bros., 1941)

There isn't much that Jesse Lasky doesn't know about mak-ing motion pictures. One of the pioneers of the industry, Lasky has mined and lapidaried many of the finest celluloid gems to come out of the Hollywood shafts. It is pleasant to report that, during his recent spell of inactivity, the producer has kept abreast of the times, that his comeback film, Sergeant York, is a contribution of unusual luster.

Striking its story roots deep into the soil of America, the photoplay possesses the integral optimism that one likes to believe typical of those who inhabit our forty-eight states. It is an honest, heartening account of simplicity that blossoms as valour, of the struggles, hopes and indomitable courage of plain, everyday people.

Presented with lyricism and poetic insight, this study of the mar-
row of a nation is as engrossing, as encompassing, as anything the
screen has presented.

Gary Cooper's portrayal of the name part is likely to become
legendary. Reticent, certain, at all times dimensional, York
emerges from the mists of the past and becomes, during the unreeling, as close and understandable as a chum one has known
since childhood. The tale of the mountain boy who so firmly believes in peace that he goes to war to fight for it, could easily
have been given a synthetic, Guy Empey aura. But there isn't a
frame of mock heroics and no attempt has been made to wave the
flag of professional patriotism. Instead, the film unveils the love
of freedom that exists in the hearts of men and permits the spectator to draw his own conclusions.

It has been some time since a motion picture has compelled
such complete affiliation. When York works night and day to obtain
a bit of farmable land, the idea that he may not get it is too ex-
cruciating to contemplate. And when it is discovered that he has
lost out and that his efforts have been in vain, one has a definite
feeling of agony.

York, of course, was a real-life hero of World War I. He
started out as a hell-raising lad in the Tennessee hills, turned to
religion when a bolt of lightning almost ended his earthly existence.
The conversion scene is a masterly welding of sight and sound.
With the aid of Walter Brennan (who gives a stirring show), Cooper, and a choir, the moment becomes a telling cinematic achievement. When the United States enters the war, York refuses to fight
on the grounds that it is against Scripture, registers as a conscientious objector. He is torn between his love of God, his love of
country. The sequence in which he struggles to adjust the question, high in his own Cumberland mountains, is something you are
not likely to forget. Finally, York goes overseas, and re-enacted
in hair-raising manner is the routing of a German machine gun unit
and the capture of one hundred and thirty-two prisoners, which
York accomplishes practically single-handed.

Performances, without exception, are genuine and moving.
Margaret Wycherly is amazingly effective as the hillwoman, while
Joan Leslie makes a substantial bid for prominence as the heroine.
Tykes June Lockhart and Dickie Moore furnish superlative portraits
and bows are certainly earned by George Tobias, Stanley Ridges
and Harvey Stephens. Beautiful direction (Howard Hawks), an
imaginative screen play, and the remarkable lensing of Polito and
Edeson all have a place of merit in making the Lasky production a
hit you will want to see.

> --Herb Sterne in Rob Wagner's
> Script, Vol. 27, No. 610 (Au-
> gust 30, 1941), page 14.

☐ SHADOW OF A DOUBT (Universal, 1943)

Alfred Hitchcock takes another turn in the dark garden of psychopathy with Shadow of a Doubt. This time murder whirls to the strains of a Lehár waltz, and into its cadences are drawn an interesting variety of people who thread this distinctive killer-chiller.

Gordon McDonnell has fabricated a really original original story, and Thornton Wilder, Sally Benson and Alma Reville have cloaked it in a dressy screenplay that flatters the intelligence, rather than belabors it, as is the case with most chill-fests.

Numerous canny directorial "touches" succeed in giving the film a sizing of suspense, and there are praiseworthy acting contributions by Patricia Collinge, Edna May Wonacott, Henry Travers and the lovely Teresa Wright. Joseph Cotten, as the strange gentleman around whom the plot spins, is good too, except in such instances when he does Trilby to the Svengali of Orson Welles, and apes the sepulchral vocal tricks of his mentor of The Mercury Theater Group. McDonald Carey, pleasantly devoid of the tortured widow's peak and the other Arrow Collar idiosyncratic stigmata of the average screen hero, is impressive as the detective, and Wallace Ford does capably as an assisting minion of the law.

Shadow of a Doubt is one of the top spine-tinglers to come from Mr. Hitchcock's well-stocked chamber of horrors. It is recommended to those whose blood-pressure can stand being maneuvered into the higher brackets.

> --Herb Sterne in Rob Wagner's
> Script, Vol. 29, No. 650
> (March 20, 1943), pages 14-15.

☐ THE SHANGHAI GESTURE (Pressburger/United Artists, 1942)

Although The Shanghai Gesture recently opened in New York to quite as many critical catcalls, lampoonings, and derisive comments as any major movie has received, the paying customers have fallen all over themselves in an attempt to purchase tickets. That an ill-wind, on occasion, blows a box-office gale is well known. In this instance the draft is due, no doubt, to the film's high sex-content.

In the yesteryears, The Shanghai Gesture was a stage shocker that made considerable mazuma by escorting the audience through an expensive bordello, at just a fraction of the cost that a bona fide tour would entail. It gave the peep-show maniacs of the corn belt the opportunity of seeing sin without sinning. It further provided the yokels with a vicarious glimpse of soigné arcana which, upon

the return to Burlington, Iowa, could be palmed-off as the real Mc-
Coy of personal experience, to the startlement of under-travelled
cronies.

Of course the locale of the flicker transcription has been
shifted to a glittering gambling hell, and though Mother Goddam
has become Mother Gin Sling, the lure of the piece remains much
the same.   While Poppy no longer raucously delights in acclaiming
herself a nymphomaniac, and strict censorship has silenced all
suspicion that the lass has a predilection for opium, a whimsical
use of feathers, and the more abstruse forms of sadism, she is
still no Elsie Dinsmore.   As a matter of record, Poppy is the
most torrid trollop the camera has caught in many a long day and,
for extra-temperature, Victor Mature gives a hot-pants performance
that has had no counterpart since Rudy Valentino crooned "When an
Arab sees a woman he wants he takes her!" to Agnes Ayres in
The Sheik.

Stacked to the rafters with clichés, the film is lamentably
slow and dull.   It lacks anything resembling structural development
and the characters totter on the brink of, and frequently fall into,
the abyss of burlesque.   Even the famous dinner scene where
Mother relates how she "survived" the flower boats and the coolies,
has been hacked and mutilated by the adaptor (Josef von Sternberg),
the director (Josef von Sternberg), and the power-behind-the-lens
(Josef von Sternberg, ASC).

It was to be hoped that von Sternberg's long, enforced rest
from studio activity would have given the gentleman perspective
on himself, and that his come-back would have been in the nature
of a return to the vigor and ingenuity which he displayed in Underworld, The Blue Angel, and Shanghai Express.   Instead, he repeats
the errors of monotony, formlessness, and arty antics which caused
him to lapse into professional limbo.
                                    --Herb Sterne in Rob Wagner's
                                    Script, Vol. 27, No. 620 (Janu-
                                    ary 17, 1942), pages 16-17.

□ SINCE YOU WENT AWAY (Selznick/United Artists, 1944)

David Selznick, one of the masters of the movies, has
scored again with Since You Went Away.

The film has the same distinction, taste and sense of drama-
turgical contour which stamped such of his past productions as
Rebecca, Anna Karenina, The Garden of Allah, What Price Hollywood? and Nothing Sacred.   In the precision and restraint which his
films disclose, Selznick is the Charles Frohman of Hollywood.   And
that is a compliment in an industry which most generally genuflects
toward the David Belasco tradition.

Since You Went Away runs two hours and fifty-six minutes.
At no time in its unreeling was I inclined to writhe and squirm,
for the film is so carefully balanced and counterbalanced in its
drama and comedy, that time flies, making the old Mutual trade-
mark at long last come true.

The picture is a picture of Today. Of what the average
American family is undergoing and fearing and hoping. The treatment is sentimental, but it seems that sentiment is something this
hour needs as an antidote to the terrible reality of a world at war.
There is a wholesale fidelity in the Hilton family that this department has never quite encountered in life. There is a twenty-four-
hour-a-day compatibility between characters, also never personally
encountered. Sweetness, too, is completely unrationed and exists
as it never exists in the world we live in. Something of Saroyan's
apotheosis of humanity is encountered in the story, but without the
fanciful extremes which abound in the work of the Fresno Armenian.

Selznick's personally-penned screenplay is deft in dramatic
design. It lingers briefly on plot, long and lovingly on incident and
character. The dialogue is easy and natural, at no time putting a
strain on the intelligence. The characters speak as ordinary folk
do, and it is that very quality that makes the woes, worries and
joys of these people highly personalized problems to the spectator.

We meet the Hilton family just after the father joins the
service. He leaves a wife and two growing daughters behind, and
the ways they attempt to readjust their lives to new conditions
makes up the framework of the film. We encounter the Hilton's
friends, servant and pet, and spending an evening in idealized surroundings is not a bad thing at this time.

John Cromwell's direction is fluid and fluent, gently guiding
the characters through their paces to maximum impact. He utilizes
the camera to superb effect, etching in background characters in a
way that is most unusual in a talking film, and is extremely satisfactory. The employment of the closeup (as witness the sweetshop
scene), is most dramatically adroit, as it brings the actors into
close proximity to the audience, and at no time is a fear disclosed
of playing important sequences with a similar sense of intimacy.

The cast is quite remarkably worthy. Claudette Colbert essays the mother with a new depth of emotion, plus her customarily
apt acting technic. The two daughters are Shirley Temple and
Jennifer Jones; they are both fresh, charming young girls, and
never resemble photoplay actresses. Miss Jones seemed particularly encompassing. If her impersonation of the heroine of The
Song of Bernadette won her an Academy award, there is no sensible
reason why her current acting contribution should not garner her a
pair of Oscars the next time the esteemed organization convenes to
dispense its gold-plated benedictions.

Joseph Cotten displays a recently acquired assurance, pitching the character of the genial wolf in just the correct key. Robert

Walker, like Van Johnson, is inclined to choke a bit on his own
charm, but when he really gets into the role he does it exceptionally well. The Walker tendency to scuff his boot and twirl his hat
in embarrassed hands should be restrained, or he is likely to become too coy for comfort--and that would be a pity for he has the
makings of a good actor. Guy Madison makes a hit of a bit, and
Alla Nazimova, as usual, is wonderful.

The production design of William Pereira is artful without
being ostentatiously arty, and there is fine camera work by Stanley
Cortez and Lee Garmes. The musical score of Max Steiner is
worthy of note. A bow, too, to Selznick and his staff for their
consideration for those who acted in the production and the members of the press in furnishing an unusually complete index to guide
reviewers. The program breaks the film into clearly defined and
labeled sequences, with the performers designated so that each, if
he merits it, can be excavated for printed applause. I, for one,
am grateful, because through the years, the credits of motion pictures have been about as vague and confusing as their production
methods.

Since You Went Away bids for tears and laughter, and does
very well in obtaining its objectives. It has a number of notable
sequences, a thoroughly beguiling charm. It is very likely to prove
as popular, despite its more lilting leanings, as any of the heart-
throb hits the screen has had in the history of silence and sound.

--Herb Sterne in Rob Wagner's
Script, Vol. 30, No. 684 (July
29, 1944), page 14.

☐ THE SNAKE PIT (20th Century-Fox, 1948)

Mary Jane Ward's The Snake Pit comes to the screen in its
Darryl F. Zanuck presentation for 20th-Fox as a picture so compelling, dramatically exciting, and frankly courageous as to defy
comparison. Nothing like it has ever been done before in films.
Certainly The Snake Pit will go down in Hollywood annals as one of
the most unusual subjects ever attempted, and what is more to the
point, successfully accomplished. It is bold and original--a defiant
answer to those who say that our American motion picture creators
cannot evolve a mature dramatic subject. The difference lies in the
fact that our native craftsmen additionally provide also the highly
necessary ingredient called entertainment. Zanuck has created a
masterpiece, took a terrific gamble and won.

The Anatole Litvak-Robert Bassler adaptation of Miss Ward's
story about an insane asylum is intelligently geared for the mature
mind. It makes no compromise with the shocking facts as presented in the novel. The result is a drama that builds to a fever
pitch of tension and holds itself there with superlative artistry.

The tempo Litvak achieves in his direction literally takes the spectator's breath away as he moves his story relentlessly from one
dramatic peak to another. It is an extraordinary directorial feat
for which the greatest credit must be given.

Evidence of the meticulousness which governs The Snake Pit
is found in the excellence of its cast. From Olivia de Havilland
down the line to the selection of cabaret star Gracie Poggi and
musical comedy leading woman Jan Clayton to perform mere bits,
painstaking effort to make The Snake Pit truly outstanding is vividly
discernible. Such craftsmanship and integrity should be rewarded
at the boxoffice with top flight business, for The Snake Pit, besides
being one of the most fascinating pictures of the year will also be
among the most discussed. Talk sells tickets, and The Snake Pit
will provide plenty of conversational fodder.

The taut, suspenseful screenplay stays close to the pattern
of the novel. It uses first person narrative to tell the dramatic
account of a girl who, soon after her marriage, becomes hopeless-
ly insane and is sent to a state institution for treatment. Only the
personal interest of a kindly doctor and the affection of her husband
prevent the worse tragedy of permanent confinement. Grimly she
fights her way back to mental health but not without tragic setbacks
induced as much by the seriousness of her condition as the fact that
the overcrowded asylum produces its own terrible hurdles for her to
overcome.

Olivia de Havilland, in the role of the unhappy girl, gives a
performance that is as exciting to watch as it must have been
strenuous to play. It is one of the greatest performances we have
ever seen on screen or stage. The deftness with which she balances hysterics and the sly touches of humor that relieve the part,
shows magnificent mastery of the acting art. Mark Stevens is well
spotted as her bewildered husband who, despite his understanding,
still makes blunders that impede her recovery. Leo Genn, the
psychiatrist who probes her past to learn the reason for her mental
aberration, reads with patience, strength and conviction. Celeste
Holm is outstanding as a patient who knows her way through the
strict rules of the institution, and Glenn Langan is seen advanta-
geously as another wise doctor. Helen Craig proves admirably
suited to the role of a cynical nurse.

All the vivid performances of The Snake Pit are not in the
upper division of the cast. There are outstanding moments by
Beulah Bondi, an elderly lady who imagines herself wealthy; Ruth
Donnelly, another inmate; Betsy Blair, a girl who never speaks;
and Howard Freeman, playing a doctor whose thoughtless ways
harass the unhappy victims.

Leo Tover's photography catches the flat ugliness of life in
an institution and tells its own grim and somber story. Lyle
Wheeler's art direction gets right to the heart of the drama as it
faithfully depicts the uncarpeted corridors, the huge, cold assembly

hall, and the visiting rooms of the asylum. Alfred Newman's musical direction matches the motivation with vibrant chords. Dorothy
Spencer's editing is brilliantly attuned to the sweep of Litvak's direction.

--The Hollywood Reporter, Vol.
101, No. 15 (November 4, 1948),
page 3.

*   *   *

The Snake Pit, as everybody must know by now, is set in an
insane asylum and is based on actual experiences of its author,
Mary Jane Ward. Unusual material for a motion picture it certainly is--as striking a deviation from formula movie entertainment
as we have had this year.

For bringing such unconventional material to the screen honestly and for refusing to go overboard on the gruesome side, or to
cheapen a sombre theme with comedy, the producers are entitled
to due credit. They have played down Mrs. Ward's frightful experiences enormously in a sincere effort to avoid the macabre.
Indeed, despite the commendable purpose of this underemphasis,
they have gone almost too far in the opposite direction, so that
The Snake Pit, while immensely interesting clinically (it describes
hydrotherapy, narco-synthesis, etc.), actually lacks emotional force.
Its heroine's illness and cure comprise a case history. One follows her progress with interest but without gripping concern: emotional tension is somehow lacking. Probably it is director Anatole
Litvak's fault that the film is not the overwhelming experience it
might have been, for the script is lucid, the acting excellent, the
photography graphic--but the film does not build.

For Olivia de Havilland, however, The Snake Pit is a full-
scale triumph. With her beautiful soft voice and her own quality
of quiet persuasiveness, this gifted actress captures expertly each
difficult phase of the sick heroine. Working through all the mental
stages from rationality to raving mania, she handles a flamboyant
emotional assignment with amazing virtuosity. It is a superb job,
technically and artistically, undoubtedly the finest acting Miss de
Havilland has done in films.

As her doctor, patiently raising her from tragic mental
abysses, Leo Genn complements the star brilliantly. And supporting the pair are vivid bit performances by practically every character actress in Hollywood. The list includes Celeste Holm, Helen
Craig, Beulah Bondi, Natalie Schafer, Ruth Donnelly, Minna Gombell, Betsy Blair, Dorothy Neumann, Isabel Jewell and dozens of
others.

--Fortnight, Vol. 5, No. 14
(December 31, 1948), page 29.

☐ SONG OF THE SOUTH (Disney/RKO, 1946)

If you want to get your fill of good, old-fashioned Southern corn, just dash right out and see Walt Disney's Song of the South. The film, an adaptation of Joel Chandler Harris's Uncle Remus stories, is a coagulation of cartoon sequences and orthodox screen drama employing live actors. The cartoons, which take up a third of the picture, are, unfortunately, a lot less inspired than many that Disney has turned out in the past, and the rest of the piece consists of the purest sheepdip about happy days on the old plantation. In portraying in cartoons the antics of Br'er Rabbit, Br'er Fox, and Br'er Bear of the Harris stories, Mr. Disney has not only made the action a little too jittery to watch for any length of time but has also accompanied the drawings with almost incessant crescendos of a maniacal laughter from Br'er Fox that is nerve-racking to listen to. When the camera investigates those merry darkies singing around their cabins and on their way to the cotton fields, you begin to wonder if Disney doesn't think Lincoln was wrong in signing the Emancipation Proclamation. As Uncle Remus, James Baskett is as sweet and kind and contented a slave as you would want to meet, and Bobby Driscoll, as the boy to whom he tells his tales, seems fairly satisfactory, despite a tendency in some of the scenes to look as if he had a precocious hangover.

--John McCarten in The New Yorker, (November 30, 1946), page
88.

☐ A SONG TO REMEMBER (Columbia, 1945)

This glorious picture is a major event in film history. It is one of the finest and most beautiful screen productions yet given to the world, and in the field of music films of its kind it stands alone. This extraordinary presentation of the works of the great Polish composer, Frederic Chopin, who still is without a peer in the creation of piano music, through the medium of a fascinating story based on his life, is the first venture in this field by American film makers and is a magnificent success. Heretofore, European producers have given screen glorification to Beethoven, Schubert, Tschaikowsky and Handel; but this Sidney Buchman production so far surpasses those efforts as to set a new standard.

The actual presentation of the music itself is a thrilling triumph, particularly as the major medium of musical expression employed is the piano, admittedly the most difficult of all instruments to record. But here the recording is so perfect that there is no sense that it is recorded. The flooding waves of melody, now thunderous, now softly rippling, are vibrant, alive and compellingly real, again and again rising to exalted heights of enthralling beauty which set the spine tingling. Nor does one have to be a classicist

to be enraptured, for Chopin was a supreme melodist. His haunting strains are for everybody, and everybody will sit entranced
through A Song to Remember, just as it is certain that virtually
everybody will see it. It's that kind of picture.

It took the vision, understanding and great writing talent of
Sidney Buchman, who wrote the screenplay and followed through on
the production, and the vision, understanding and great directorial
ability of Charles Vidor, who interpreted it, aided by the finest of
technical talent in every department, to bring about this superb result. It is a masterpiece worthy of the master's music which is
offered so generously and so intelligently that every number becomes an integral part of the story. The brilliant cast and its interpretation of the action also are fully worthy of their subject.

The story introduces Chopin at the age of 11, already a vir-
tuoso and composer, also already an underground patriot in the
struggle of the Poles against their czarist oppressors. His good-
humoredly garrulous and ambitious teacher, who is the guide of his
life, aims for a Paris career for his protege but it is not until
Chopin is 22 that he leaves Warsaw for the French capital, fleeing
as a fugitive from the tyrants he has publicly defied. After a
faltering start, his Paris career finally is launched through the aid
of Franz Liszt and the trousers-wearing, convention-defying author-
ess, George Sand. Then he falls completely under the spell of the
writer, who persuades him to shut out the world--with her, of
course--give up patriotic causes and devote himself entirely to composition. His success as a composer is spectacular but he has
neglected everyone, particularly his able mentor, the professor,
and has forgotten the needs of his own people. He is brought back
to himself by a tragic jolt, breaks with Sand and, despite failing
health, embarks on a great concert tour all of whose proceeds go
to the liberation of Polish prisoners. His success is tremendous
but the too-great effort brings about his untimely death.

In all honesty, it must be stated that the film story takes
extreme license with the facts of Chopin's life but this is of small
moment. Buchman's script tells a powerful, deeply moving tale
and, above all, it has captured the real soul and personality of
Chopin, who was one of the most sensitive artists in musical history.

Every performance in the film is outstanding. Paul Muni's
delineation of the professor is one of the finest of his screen characterizations, brilliant in its delicate shadings. He lives the role,
at times delightfully amusing, at others movingly powerful. His
reading of the rebuke which reawakens Chopin is superfine. Merle
Oberon gives to the unlovable George Sand role a brilliant strength,
never yielding from the crisp, cold, selfishly dominating personality she assumes, hers a telling, memorable portrait. Cornel
Wilde's performance of Chopin raises this young player to the
heights. He achieves the difficult feat of making dramatically alive
the portrayal of a man whose scope of action is confined almost

exclusively to the piano bench, using his sensitive features with consummate artistry and restraint to convey the emotion of Chopin's tortured soul.

George Coulouris gives another of his splendid, polished characterizations as Pleyel, the impresario and music publisher. Howard Freeman makes his sharp etching of the obese, irascible music critic, who long was Chopin's foe, one of the most memorable in the picture. Nina Foch scores decisively as the Polish girl who arouses the composer to a new sense of his responsibilities after he has long neglected her. The role of the effulgent Franz Liszt is played with a finesse and charm which makes it delightful. Sig Arno, George Macready, Claire DuBrey, Frank Puglia, Fern Emmett and Sybil Merritt all are splendid in lesser roles.

The magnificent production quality of A Song to Remember makes this for producer Louis F. Edelman the outstanding credit of his career. It would be impossible to praise too lavishly those who brought the music of this picture to the screen. The musical direction by Morris W. Stoloff, the adaptation of Chopin's music by Miklos Rozsa and the supervision by Mario Silva are almost spectacularly great, while the work of sound engineer Lodge Cunningham and William Randall, who recorded the music, constitute one of the greatest triumphs of the film. In all respects it is one of the finest recording jobs ever done and in the recording of piano music it has never been equalled. The amazing passage covering the lengthy montage of Chopin's final tour is an unforgettable achievement not only in film but in musical history.

The art direction by Lionel Banks and Van Nest Polglase is of Academy Award caliber, providing beautiful, often sumptuous but always tasteful settings throughout. Equally notable is the exceptional film editing by Charles Nelson. To Travis Banton, high praise is due for the costuming of Miss Oberon in both masculine and feminine garb. Tony Gaudio and Allen M. Davey achieved a masterpiece of Technicolor photography, perfectly keyed to every mood of the film, always vivid, warm and rich in beauty.

--The Hollywood Reporter, Vol.
81, No. 47 (January 18, 1945),
page 3.

☐ SORRY, WRONG NUMBER (Paramount, 1948)

From a radio play by Lucille Fletcher which was so good it still is repeated occasionally on the air, Miss Fletcher and Paramount have contrived a pulse-pounder good enough to scare the pants off moviegoers so clad. With extremely tense direction by Anatole Litvak, a clever, taut script by Miss Fletcher, and an impressive exercise in bravura emotional acting by Barbara Stanwyck (who plays almost all her role in bed), <u>Sorry, Wrong Number</u> can be counted among the most effective suspense films of the year.

Its terrifying story is about an invalid (Miss Stanwyck) who overhears a phone conversation between thugs planning to murder a woman.   Sometime later, when plot pieces have fallen into shape-- and after Sol Polito's camera has had a sinister field day gliding around Miss Stanwyck's bedroom, turning innocent shadows into hor- rendous monstrosities--Miss Stanwyck comes to the shocking reali- zation that the intended victim is herself.

With the action centered almost entirely in one room, and the leading character playing her role from her bed, <u>Sorry, Wrong Number</u>, of course, can be called a trick film.   And to develop the story's background and advance the action, elaborate use of cut- backs was necessary, which at times gives the drama a choppy ef- fect.   Nevertheless, the climactic buildup in this movie is im- mensely powerful, likely to leave you limp and pop-eyed.

Besides Miss Stanwyck, who does a remarkable job as the hysterical invalid (it is the best acting of her career), Burt Lan- caster appears as her husband, and the supporting cast includes Ann Richards, Wendell Corey and Harold Vermilyea--all very good. Better see this one.

--Fortnight, Vol. 5, No. 7
(September 24, 1948), page 30.

☐   THE SOUTHERNER (Loew-Hakim/United Artists, 1945)

Probably it would have been commercial folly to send a movie out into the Broadways and Main Streets under the title <u>Hold Autumn in Your Hand</u>, the novel from which this picture was made.   What in the world does it mean, people would ask, a few perhaps would guess that when a farmer starts out with his seed in the spring, all the possibilities of the fall harvest are there for him to look forward to.   So it was easy to think up something short and simple like <u>The Southerner</u> to call it, which has the double disadvantage of say- ing too much and not saying enough, besides probably annoying those who may find the film an unsatisfactory picture of the South as they know it.

The title does fit in its limited way the young hero, who is a cotton planter who doesn't want to be a share-cropper but to build up independence and eventually have a place of his own.   The condi- tions under which he starts out, and the things that happen to him, are also southern in that they would not have been the same any- where else.

But essentially this is a story of a man and his family, and the spring, summer and autumn of one year in their lives.   Sam is

the man, and Nona his wife, and they have two children and a bitter, querulous old grandmother. Sam has found some land he can
rent--under stringent terms--because it has been neglected for
years and the owner is glad enough to let someone clear its rich
soil: he knows all too well the chances are it will be turned back
to him again, worth more than ever for the toil Sam will have put
into it.

But Sam has got one step beyond being a migratory worker;
he has become a tenant farmer, and he can dream of eventually
owning his own place. He is no "poor white": he is intelligent,
ambitious, his heart is in farming and his mind knows how to cope
with a farmer's problems. His young wife is in the truest sense a
helpmate, and his kids--they are the kind who not only go to school
with eager minds but take back home what they have learned there,
and make it part of their lives. A family of the character you can
call the salt of the earth. They have only nature and human nature to contend with.

The house they get is not much better than a hen-coop after
it has been struck by a hurricane. The land has to be cleared by
the most back-breaking labor. The well doesn't work and they have
to borrow water from a neighbor. The children need fresh vege-
tables and milk to keep them from getting the "spring-sickness"
(the local euphemism for pellagra) and the boy actually does fall
victim to that disease of malnutrition. Their neighbor is not help-
ful--he is a bitter and envious man, made so by his own poverty,
and even grudging of water from his well.

A dreary enough set-up, but it is never sordid or morbid.
Sam and his family are courageous and cheerful, and wise with the
patient wisdom of those who live close to the soil because they love
it. The nagging old grandmother is what they might become in time
if they give up, but give up they never will. If there is no meat
Sam can catch a possum or a big fish. If life is too monotonous
there is an outing in town with his town friend and a fine fracas in
the bar-room, or a wedding with its dancing and pranks and drinking. Even a cloudburst that wrecks all the promise of the arduous
spring planting is not a knockout blow. The town friend argues for
going to work in the factory, where wages are regular and certain
and life reasonably secure. But Sam knows what his inner nature
demands: he will stay on being a farmer in spite of everything.
(There is a hint, not too belabored, that a kind of salvation lies
in the farmer and the factory worker understanding each other and
helping each other to a better life.)

Not since The Grapes of Wrath has an American film got so
close to the lives of the struggling poor, and The Southerner is
nearer to that life because it has more of what might be called the
eternal verities in it. It gets a lot of its power from being put into
natural settings: the outdoors in which so much of it happens gives
it a tremendous impact of being fact, not story. Yet it is fact illuminated by the spirit of poetry. Jean Renoir, who fashioned the

novel into a movie and directed it, brings something of the French
tradition to the handling of it, but the director whom he most recalls is Dovzhenko, the Ukrainian poet of the film, who stands in a
magnificent niche all his own. Renoir has a remarkable cameraman to help him visualize the spirit in which he has worked, Lucien
Andriot, who has turned out some of the most beautiful photography
you will see in many a day.

This comparison with French and Russian ways of film-
making shouldn't give the impression that there is anything but pure
America in this picture. The actors would attend to that, were
Renoir seven times a foreigner. Zachary Scott is a Sam right out
of our native soil, and Betty Field and the children are as real as
real can be. Beulah Bondi, J. Carrol Naish, Percy Kilbride,
Estelle Taylor (and a fine bit it is she contributes!) are vivid parts
of a vivid whole.

This film may not be an accurate overall picture of the
South (it doesn't aim to be) or a signpost to ways ahead (it doesn't
pretend to that except inferentially). But it is rarely beautiful and
moving, with human people in it that will be long remembered by
those with eyes to see and hearts to feel.

> --James Shelley Hamilton in New
> Movies, Vol. 20, No. 4 (May
> 1945), pages 3-4.

*   *   *

The Southerner is at once a rare and rewarding motion picture and a challenge to those agencies and elements in our society
who believe in full freedom of democratic expression.

This is the film, produced by the great and thoughtful French
director, Jean Renoir, from George Sessions Perry's Hold Autumn
in Your Hand, which was banned by the Memphis (Tenn.) film censors. The Memphis ban has since been lifted but the film will undoubtedly be excluded from other areas in the South because it is a
story of sharecropping.

Yet it is not a Tobacco Road, leering at human grotesques,
nor is it The Little Foxes, directed at predatory owners spoiling
the vines, the people and all human values in their avarice.

It is, instead, a simple, straightforward story of a migratory
farmer who turns hopefully to tenant-farming on a neglected piece
of bottom land alongside a treacherous, flooding Texas river.

It offers no preachments, even though it might have talked
crop insurance and flood control as a means to a happy ending for
all people of such land. Beyond a fleeting reference to the choice
between share-cropping and "six bits a day" working for the big
planter, it hints at no class differences.

It does, however, dramatize some other deep-rooted ills which beset people destined to the land with no security against its treacheries, no means of fulfilling its lacks.   It is a story of bleak and hungry Winter in a wind-swept shack; of hard, hard work clearing the land for cotton; of pellagra in the Spring with no health-bringing milk and green things for children's needy bodies.

It starts with a glimpse of broad cotton fields, black hands and white, olive-skinned and oriental, picking the cotton, hauling it in huge white bags to the weigh-master, discussing where to go next along the worn paths of the American migratory farm worker.

One of these workers, rangy Sam Tucker (Zachary Scott), with wife and two kids and his aged grandmother to fend for, decides to stay on the plantation as a sharecropper.   It is a dignified decision, born of resolution, not defeat--the natural choice of a man of the soil seeking the best future within his means for a growing family.

The piece of neglected floodplain they choose is "rich as mud," Sam knows, but with a season of clearing to do and a winter to live out before a crop can be put down.   The gaunt shack on it is woefully ramshackle.   Granny rebels at the prospect instinctively, almost like a horse balking at an unsafe bridge.   Without knowing the reasons, she senses disaster, remembering the hardship and privation of her own young years, of the "spring-sickness" which took three of her children.

But the Tuckers confidently tackle the job, with borrowed mules, seed on credit and even borrowed water, harshly lent by an embittered neighbor, resenting new hands and enterprise along the river which he had come to regard as his own domain.

In honest, straightforward storytelling, The Southerner spins the tale of the Tucker family's fight to make the land produce. There are terrible conflicts, moments of bursting happiness, times of dread sickness and finally, after the crop has been brought to snowy ripeness, the sickening devastation of a flashflood, wiping it all out.   Sam Tucker, viewing the ruined crop, is ready to quit the land for the certain $7 a day of the factories.   But at the end it is the womenfolk who display the deeper staunchness, retting up the flood-torn house, getting the stove to working again, and one unforgettable sequence of the ancient grandmother patiently hanging the children's teddy bear on the line to dry.

Jean Renoir is the searching director who made The Lower Depths and The Grand Illusion, among other famous works, before fleeing his native France for America when the Nazis came.   With the detachment of a visitor, but clearly with the guidance of sure American hands in guaranteeing the authenticity of his story, Renoir lets us see our own land through the cameras much more clearly than our own eyes sometimes permit.   The cast he has chosen is uniformly excellent, especially Betty Field as the wife, Beulah

Bondi as Granny and J. Carrol Naish as the flinty neighbor. And, of course, Zachary Scott as Sam Tucker.

Renoir's Tucker family are not the down-beaten, hopeless people we are prone to imagine our sharecroppers, although they are spared none of the hardships. They are a people of faith in the land and hope of security and peaceful living, wanting little more. They are indeed the salt of the earth, the Tuckers, and their story as told in The Southerner cannot fail to bring wider understanding of their problems and the necessity for providing them guarantees of security, just as the nation has been assuring, step by step, social security and welfare guarantees to the other wage-earners of the nation. It is a film not to miss, nor to let your friends miss.

                                        --John T. McManus in PM (Au-
                                    gust 27, 1945), page 16.

☐ SPELLBOUND (Selznick/United Artists, 1945)

David O. Selznick's productions invariably indicate a lavish expenditure of time, thought, dramatic tact, a gentlemanly taste in décor and design, and no parsimony in purchasing the more costly talents in the realm of motion picture making.

All this, as must be apparent, is most commendable, for it results in films that have sheen and texture only too rare on the contemporary American screen. But these factors, admittedly admirable, cannot conceal that Selznick's past several profferings have been lamentable in their lack of vitality. Since You Went Away, I'll Be Seeing You, and the current Spellbound all are without the dash, the life, that made the producer's earlier efforts, such as What Price Hollywood? and Nothing Sacred, vividly alive creations. Possibly the lethargy results from Selznick's current perfection-fetish, which councils extensive retakes, excessive collaboration, and minute personal interference with the expensive minds he hires. Whatever the causes, the recent celluloid results that Selznick has released predicate some process of erosion during production which wears away the very qualities which engrossing cinema should contain.

Spellbound, although its apathy engendered considerable apathy in this spectator, is still a superior photoplay when compared with the average product on view. It benefits by Alfred Hitchcock's adroit style of presentation, by that lambent quality which is Ingrid Bergman's most salient asset, and the supporting character performance by Michael Chekhov which adrenalins the proceedings whenever the camera hovers on his work. Further, the film has the inestimable advantage of Ben Hecht dialogue, and this intermittently crackles in the best metaphorical manner of that craftsman.

As a thesis on psychoanalysis, Spellbound is no more trust-
worthy than a brochure on the subject such as may be purchased at
most cut-rate drug stores for the sum of twenty-five cents. As a
matter of fact, the treatment here afforded the alleged science is
as superficial, as banal, as that which Moss Hart utilized in Lady
in the Dark. The only major way in which this is superior to the
Hart versions is that it neither reveals Ginger Rogers in Technicolor, nor reveals a necessity for the spectator to play peek-a-boo
with Gertrude Lawrence's varicose veins as displayed in her rendition of "The Saga of Jenny" specialty on the stage.

Spellbound, it seems to me, is Hitchcock's least noteworthy
goose-pimple photoplay since Saboteur. The "mystery" is cumber-
somely wrought, passively developed, and the denouement in which
the murderer is revealed is quite as irritatingly pat as though Nick
Charles were the "private eye" involved in the case.

Several sequences of the film demonstrate that Hitchcock has
a knowledge of, and appreciation for, cinema history. Witness the
counter-motion filming and cutting of the scene in which Miss Bergman ascends the stairs to Gregory Peck's room at night, a device
first employed by Mr. Griffith in the Babylonian court scenes of
Intolerance, and later utilized by DWG in the court ballroom sequences of Orphans of the Storm. The climactic close-up of the
revolver exploding into the face of the spectator is a thrilling
melodramatic trick, but no more so now than when Edwin S. Porter
first presented it, without hand tinting, as the dynamic tag to The
Great Train Robbery, in the year 1903.

--Herb Sterne in Rob Wagner's
Script, Vol. 31, No. 717 (November 17, 1945), page 14.

*   *   *

A frantic chase through hospitals, hotels, stations, trains
and consulting rooms, culminating on a ski run, is the route Alfred
Hitchcock takes, armed with Ben Hecht's Freud-slanted script. It
is a very simplified Freud, to be sure--simplified to the point of
being rather incredible if you can stop long enough to think about
it. But Hitchcock doesn't give much time for critical contemplation
what with his dazzling use of pace, mood, camera and detail.
Psychoanalysis is not exactly a new ingredient for a movie. In 1937
a Swiss film called The Eternal Mask made it the solution in its
plot of a doctor who suffered from a split personality brought about
by a guilt complex. And as in Spellbound the treatment was simplified to a point where according to practitioners it would not have
been effective as a cure. In the February 1937 number of the National Board of Review Magazine, Dr. A. A. Brill, a famous American psychiatrist, discussed the professional aspects of The Eternal
Mask and several things that he said are applicable to Spellbound.

"I think that the picture was overdone in one place and
underdone in another. The authors put everything that one

sees in such mental cases into this one picture. ...   The
treatment as depicted here is the worse part of the presentation judging it psychiatrically.   The average onlooker
gets the impression that it took about a half an hour or
so to cure Dumartin.   The fact of the matter is that it
takes months and sometimes longer to cure such a case.
To unite the split off elements is not so simple as the
authors would make one believe.   I feel they could have
shown in some way that in actual practice such treatment
consumes more time than is here shown.

Both these objections apply rather neatly to Spellbound as a
study of a mental malady and a demonstration of psychiatric treatment.   The hero of the film suffers from amnesia, a guilt complex, split personality and a form of paranoia that not only makes
him believe he killed a man but on several occasions gives the impression he intends to commit murder again.   With all that the matter with him, his psychiatrist sweetheart, who takes on herself to
cure him, snaps him out of it in what appears to be little more
than three days.   In behalf of dramatic clarity perhaps the author
could tell his story in no other fashion.   Certainly no other picture
in the class known as fiction film so far made has overcome the
difficulties mentioned by Dr. Brill in the above extract.   If psychiatric material is to be used in movies perhaps we must accept its
oversimplification as a necessary dramatic form and cease worrying
about clinical accuracy.

Essentially Spellbound is melodrama with a strong and luminous love element in it.   When the false Dr. Edwardes arrives to
take over as chief in the sanitarium, he and Dr. Constance Peter-
son, a woman member of the staff, fall deeply in love with each
other.   It soon becomes apparent to her that he is not only an imposter but that he is very sick mentally.   Suspicion also grows
among the other doctors that the new chief is not Dr. Edwardes and
that he may be criminally involved in Edwardes' disappearance.
Constance, banking on the instinct of her love, believes him innocent and determines to save him.   Just a lick ahead of the police
the impostor takes flight to New York whither Constance pursues
him and tries to initiate his cure.   From there they fly to Rochester where her old teacher is persuaded to help her dig into the sick
man's subconscious and save him from the chair or the mad house.
A dream sequence (constructed by Salvador Dali in his well-known
cliché) gives them the essential clue that saves the man's mind.
But he is not out of the woods yet.   The real Dr. Edwardes has
been found murdered and the hero is accused of the crime.   The
climax of the film takes up the warm devotion that keeps Constance
on the trail of the murderer to clear her lover.

To those who recall Hitchcock at his best--even the fabulous
pre-Hollywood Hitchcock--Spellbound offers much to please and excite in its adventure, in the virtuosity of its passages of tensity.
But more than in his earlier films he has woven into Spellbound an
entrancing love story.   Through the hectic sequences Ingrid Berg-

man and Gregory Peck carry it with maturity, delicate insight and
even moments of what may be called poetry. Objections that the
romantic elements slow the melodrama can be sustained but they do
enrich the whole picture with a warmth and humanness somewhat
rare in Hitchcock. The other characters are well realized too,
especially that of Constance's teacher played with humorous subtlety
by Michael Chekhov and that of a persistent masher played by Wallace Ford. All make for drama rich in flesh and blood.

--Arthur Beach in New Movies,
Vol. 20, No. 8 (November
1945), pages 5-6.

☐ THE SPIRAL STAIRCASE (RKO, 1946)

The Spiral Staircase, the action of which takes place somewhere around the Lizzie Borden territory of New England in 1906,
concerns itself largely with the activities of a finical strangler engaged in eliminating young ladies who don't measure up to his ideas
of physical perfection. He has the eye of a basilisk, the strength
of a gorilla, and the enthusiasm of an S. S. Übermensch, and the
picture is only a few minutes old when we see him (face hidden, of
course) throttling a handsome blonde whose gimp leg annoys him.
After that he becomes preoccupied with the murderous pursuit of a
pretty little mute who serves as companion to the bedridden mistress of a spooky mansion decorated with the hides of various wild
animals and full of creaking doors, gates, and shutters. Since the
maid of the establishment is a drunk, the English bulldog, Carlton,
is a rather lethargic type, and everybody else around the place is a
possible murderer, it often seems as if the mute is headed for an
inarticulate doom. And what with the rain bucketing outside, people
meandering mysteriously through the cellar, and the reflection of
the strangler's eye popping up in a mirror every now and then, the
business gets rather exciting, even though the villain's identity isn't
much of a puzzle by the time about half of the film has gone by.

The Spiral Staircase is fortunate in its cast. Ethel Barrymore, as the bedridden mistress of the manor, is full of gruff authority, and if she rolls her eyes too frantically at times, it's
probably because she has to stare at a dead tiger that lies on the
floor beside her bed during most of the picture. In the role of
the mute, Dorothy McGuire has a wistful, ingratiating charm.
Sara Allgood is also on hand, and as usual is a pleasure to watch.
In picking the killer, you can take your choice of George Brent,
Kent Smith, Gordon Oliver, and Rhys Williams. The constable,
played by James Bell, definitely didn't do it.

--John McCarten in The New
Yorker, (February 9, 1946),
page 80.

*   *   *

If one were to ignore the fact that Dore Schary's The Spiral
Staircase is the most gripping, spellbinding and intensely thrilling
motion picture seen in many, many years; if one were to set aside
the indisputable fact that its dramatic punch is so solid that it
leaves its audiences feeling as if they had been wrung through a
wringer; then the fact still remains that this eerily fascinating
film should be seen by every last person engaged in the production of motion pictures as the one perfect example of the literacy
the screen can attain in creating entertainment.   It is a classic,
not alone of its kind, but of absolute perfection in production,
writing, direction, acting and to the end of its splendid technical
accomplishments.   Seldom has the motion picture achieved such
exquisite perfection of expression.   Words are as nothing to the
impact with which this picture smashes its beholder.   You are
pitched headlong into it with the unusual opening sequence immediately the printed titles are gone; for the next 83 minutes you
are held glued to your theatre seat and no eye wavers even mo-
mentarily from the screen as you sit terrifyingly thrilled by its
bewildering and mounting succession of morbid drama.

The Spiral Staircase is indeed a classic of its kind.   It
should and will be held up as an example of the perfect mystery
film.   In its plotting toward a dizzying and staggering climax and
in the keen use of an absolute minimum of dialogue to terrify, the
Mel Dinelli screenplay is as brilliant a one as has been written.
The direction of Robert Siodmak stands alone without equal as the
best that has ever been displayed in mounting mood upon mood for
the sole purpose of terrifying an audience.   Yet what makes the
drama so perfect is that it is not forced, it builds simply and skillfully to bludgeon you with its eroticism.   You terrify yourself from
the film's cold logic and devastating understatement.   If there has
ever been direction of a mystery film more thoughtfully and cold-
bloodedly worked out than this it does not come to mind.   You will
wish some member of the cast somewhere in the story would cut
loose with a blood-curdling scream in order to free you from the
cold sweat in which the picture imprisons you.   Yes, this is classic
film mystery.

Dore Schary has pioneered something here.   His production
is a blueprint.   Study it after you have seen it to think if there was
one moment in its construction and final edited print that was not of
vital necessity to its whole.   You will find there was nothing missing and nothing yet needed to mar its perfection.   The picture seems
short even as you think back on all that has gripped you for its 83
minutes.   That is because it moves so fast, from one shocking sequence to another as destiny--the calculated cunning of its murderous, motivating mind--pursues relentlessly the cast upon the screen.
Even when you know the human shape and face at last of the cruel
power moving the swift parade of sudden deaths, you remain fas-
cinated.   Seldom--almost never--has a movie achieved illusion so
perfect and so near reality.   That this is a triumph of cannily perceptive direction none can deny.

Dorothy McGuire is excellent as the story's heroine, a deaf mute who speaks exactly three words in the entire film, and these the three units of a telephone number when her life is the next on the murderer's time table.   The story opens as an old silent movie is being exhibited (and what an opening sequence is there, my friends!) and a murder taking place on the floor above in a furnished room.   Only the chilling eye of the fiend do we see as he lurks in an afflicted girl's closet.   We follow the heroine home to her duties of serving maid in the household of a bedridden old woman and her son and step-son, children of the same father. On her way, she is given a lift by the new, young doctor of the village and her romance with him is established.   He enters the house to visit the invalid at her request and a quarrel with one of the sons ensues, after which the doctor begs the mute girl to take immediate leave of the house.   No character in the story is above suspicion and therein lies its greatest strength as superb mystery plotting.   Next on the murder list is the pretty girl secretary of the elder, learned son and it takes place in the sombre atmosphere of the wine cellar in Siodmak's masterfully staged action.   And when the mute, thinking she knows at last the foul fiend behind all the crimes, locks in a cubby the one person physically able to save her in the fear-ridden house, the actual murderer is free to come out in the open, and in as coldly cunning and fearfully-staged a scene as has ever been, the killer prepares to add her to the list of victims.   When you, as audience, have given up the last hope, help appears from a source wholly unexpected.   The ending is a happy one and you are free of the spell which has chained you steadfast for an hour and 23 minutes.

Besides Miss McGuire's intelligent study of her demanding role, there is high praise to be heaped upon the rich talents of Ethel Barrymore and George Brent in other leading roles.   Rhonda Fleming shines briefly as one of the victims.   Such always good character performers as Elsa Lanchester, Sara Allgood, Rhys Williams and James Bell enter the story briefly, spin their webs of suspense with cleverly striking performances, and quit the scene. Kent Smith makes a memorably lasting impression upon a role that is too brief for the fine talent he displays.

But the lion's share of acting honors, as much as can be wrested by one performer in a story as overall gripping as this one, falls to the magnificent Gordon Oliver with a delicately shaded interpretation of the younger son.   In the forced gaiety of his brash talk and the earnestness of purpose inherent beneath, he succeeds in creating an added undercurrent of suspense.   It is a splendidly unusual job that will at last secure for him a place he inherited several performances ago.   A handsome figure of a man, Oliver also amazes here with the quiet dignity of a beautifully rounded piece of acting.

In Nicholas Musuraca's and Vernon Walker's photography, in the art direction by Albert S. D'Agostino and Jack Okey, in Roy

Webb's music and its direction by Constantin Bakaleinikoff, in the
editing and every other last facet of its technical and creative production there is exemplified the handiwork of masters of their
crafts. Masters of these masters are Siodmak and Dore Schary,
who have taken their contributions and forged them into a brilliantly
terrifying motion picture that spells fascinating entertainment for
millions of picture audiences and a devilishly enjoyable special holiday for those specialists of film horror who have kept Hollywood
grinding out ghoulish subjects these many years. For exhibitors
and for RKO, The Spiral Staircase spells millions of dollars in
grosses. The Schary production is unparalleled as eerie entertainment.

> --Hollywood Review, Vol. 36, No.
> 18 (January 7, 1946), pages 1
> and 2.

☐ THE STRANGER (International Pictures/RKO, 1946)

     The Stranger is the type of horrendous melodrama that woos
and glues pre-puberty listeners to the family radio. Orson Welles,
as director and star of this fright wig opera, capably visualizes
the standard ingredients of thriller broadcasts, though never for
a split second can one credit the frenetic events that revolve
about a fat Nazi spider that weaves his noxious web in a small
Connecticut town. A visit to the film will disclose that Mr.
Welles struts and storms in his customary style; that Loretta
Young's appearance has begun to belie her surname; and that Edward
G. Robinson remains one of the more reliable actors working before
the cameras.

> --Herb Sterne in Rob Wagner's
> Script, Vol. 32, No. 734 (July
> 20, 1946), page 13.

☐ SULLIVAN'S TRAVELS (Paramount, 1942)

     The New York critics robustiously applaud any type of en-
deavor that takes a blow at Hollywood's solar plexus. Even so indifferent a lampoon as Sullivan's Travels is greeted with hurrah-
ing and a tossing of adjectival top-hats. Though the metropolitan
gentry found the film to be "great art," this reporter believes
it to be no more than an inept, carelessly manufactured jibe
that is no-end dull. After three phenomenal hits in a row, Preston Sturges proves he is no more than mortal, a quotient that
will relieve many of his competitors, who were really beginning
to worry.

Sullivan doesn't travel so much as merely wander about.   It changes its theatrical attack with a frequency causing suspicion that the photoplay was shot off the cuff.   Satire, slapstick, melodrama, romance, and sociology each has an inning, with the net result a patchwork, completely without pattern, in which the colors jar. Fault must be placed with the screenplay, and if Director Sturges wishes to invite Author Sturges into the alley for a good, sound thrashing, I hereby offer to donate my services as referee.

The initial premise is promising: a Hollywood director, who has made his reputation on such objets d'art as a series of Ants in Your Plants of ... films is nibbled by the sociological termite and aches to do a low-life saga.   When his producer convinces the chap that he knows nothing of existence in the raw (except, maybe, sleeping without pyjamas) the megaphoner takes to the road in a tramp outfit furnished by the wardrobe department, with only a dime in his pocket.   So far, so swell.   Then a chase sequence, followed by one in which an elderly, lecherous widow makes passes, an in-you-go-out-you-come pool stanza, all of early Sennett vintage and quite as novel as the classical chestnut which queries, "Who was that lady I seen you with last night?"   Then on, and abruptly, to the horrors of a deep-south chain gang; this footage appears to have been intro-duced merely because the studio had a chance of picking-up some Warner Bros. stock shots at bargain rates.   It all ends well for the actors, if not for the spectators, when the director (the character, not Mr. Sturges) is exonerated, returns to Celluloid City, convinced that what the public needs is laughter.   The moral is something which Sturges and Paramount may well take to heart after scanning the grosses on this effort.

Veronica Lake finally breaks down and shows us the right side of her face.   Joel McCrea is competent in a part that is short on opportunities.   Only Jimmy Conlin manages to really score, as the kindly convict in the prison camp.

--Herb Sterne in Rob Wagner's
Script, Vol. 27, No. 622
(February 14, 1942), pages
14-15.

*   *   *

Sullivan's Travels is a curious but effective mixture of grim tragedy, slapstick of the Keystone brand and smart, trigger-fast comedy.   Being unusual and satisfying entertainment, it is surefire audience material and will do from good to big business.

Beyond the draught of Joel McCrea and Veronica Lake, film calls for selling, advertising and exploitation.   Among other things, the title may cause some confusion, especially where fans remember Gulliver's Travels and think carelessly that this may be a repeat of that or a cartoon sequel.

Written and directed by Preston Sturges, he goes against many of the rules, but gets excellent, refreshing results.   Sturges springs a flock of surprises as he flits from slapstick to stark drama, from high comedy to a sequence of the Devil's Island prison type of stuff, into romantic spells, some philosophy and, in effect, all over the place without warning.

He ties it all together neatly, however, and with the possible exception of the chain gang sequence which is a little long, he keeps his audience on the go and on edge.   Sturges' dialog is an enormously important factor.   It is trenchant, has drive, possesses crispness and gets the laughs where that is desired.   There are plenty of the latter, but good ones.   Sturges even shakes the ribs at the expense of the Music Hall, Pittsburgh and Lubitsch.

McCrea plays a Hollywood director.   The titles given to two pictures he has turned out, Ants in Your Plants of 1939 and Hey, Hey in the Hayloft, are typical of the Sturges sense of humor that trickles through the film.   Incidentally, those cracks about income tax are laugh outstanders.

Premise of the story may be believable or unbelievable; it doesn't matter.   McCrea, anxious to produce Oh Brother, Where Art Thou?, an epic of hard times and troubles, disguises himself as a hobo and goes out to look for troubles, finding plenty for himself.   He picks up Miss Lake on the way and they travel the rails together, she in boy's clothes.

The circumstances of their adventures are unique, being comical and grim in turn, with some romance poured into the cauldron to stew it up.   Scores of clever little touches, in action, dialog and directions, make it all highly palatable regardless of the plot.   However, the plot construction has much to recommend Sturges as a writer.

A very effective sequence is the one in the Negro church somewhere down south where convicts are invited as guests to view a picture being shown the colored congregation.   Cut into Sullivan's Travels is a Mickey Mouse short, most of which is screened, with the film cutting back and forth between it and the strange audience.

A fine cast has been assembled around McCrea and Miss Lake.   Latter supplies the sex appeal and does a good acting job. This is her second picture, first having been I Wanted Wings, also Par.   McCrea, in the lap of luxury as a Hollywood director one minute, and a bum the next, turns in a swell performance.   Large company of players includes Robert Warwick, William Demarest, Franklin Pangborn, Porter Hall, Byron Foulger, Margaret Hayes, Robert Greig and Eric Blore, most of whom are attached to the Hollywood studio where McCrea is a director.

Paul Jones has given the film good production and backgrounds, while the photography of the John Seitz-Farciot Edouart

team adds excellence to a job which in every other way is close to
tops.

> --"Char" in Variety, Vol. 145,
> No. 1 (December 10, 1941),
> page 8.

* * *

Preston Sturges, writer and director of Sullivan's Travels,
has played a trick on Veronica Lake's legion of admirers. Since
I Wanted Wings, her first movie, Veronica's frankly outlined glamour has been impressed on the nation's locker rooms. So instead
of following a successful precedent, Mr. Sturges has chosen to
cover his star in the sackcloth and ashes you see at the left with
the dog. The grimy tatterdemalion is Veronica as she appears
through two-thirds of the movie.

But Mr. Sturges has a reputation for getting away with almost anything he does. The more he has turned movie formulas
upside down, the more he has wrung golden tribute from the box
office.

The story of Sullivan's Travels, which will open at the Paramount on the 28th, seems like a familiar parable; it's about a
movie specialist in comedy who wants to do tragedy. Though he
has larded his film with slapstick, Mr. Sturges for the first time
strikes an unexpectedly serious vein. Hollywood is waiting to see
whether he gets away with this new sort of trick.

> --Louise Levitas in PM (January
> 18, 1942), page 46.

☐ SUNSET BOULEVARD (Paramount, 1950)

The return of Gloria Swanson was the occasion for much
ballyhoo--and she earned every bit of it. Her performance in this
long yarn about a washed-up silent movie queen and her young,
parasitic lover is nothing short of sensational. The picture itself
goes from improbability to reality and back again, but Miss Swanson holds it all together with her classic screen creation of Norma
Desmond, the mad heroine.

> --Esquire, Vol. 34, No. 6 (De-
> cember 1950), page 74.

* * *

Sunset Boulevard sets out to impale some Hollywood values
and roast them over some burning bright coals of observation. It
further attempts to do so in a particular style that may best be de-
scribed as Hollywood Gothic. The style, which is effective if not
original, is more successful than the content, for somewhere along

the line Sunset Boulevard turns into the very sort of goods it attempts to discredit.

Stripped of low-key photography and stagey personalities, the
film seems to want to say that the Hollywood success standard of
values is warped. But it says so in such soft and sometimes coy
terms that the young heel played by William Holden turns out an
ineffectual heel-hero. Morbid psychology is not to be dabbled in,
at least not to any dramatic effect. Every effect in Sunset Boulevard is hollow for that reason.

On a superficial level there are many arresting moments,
chiefly those dominated by the theatrics of Gloria Swanson as the
aging star who shines in morbid seclusion. But even this character
is merely presented, never probed or developed, as a symbol.
The screenplay wavers between artful craftsmanship and the poor
taste involved in dragging in "realistic" Hollywood references.

Documentary technique is one thing, and merely photograph-
ing an authentic place or a person another. And when Cecil B.
DeMille is hailed into proceedings to proclaim a script within the
script as unworthy of him, "realism" has been carried beyond
the point of coyness.

Somewhere along the line, the scripters make obeisance to a
film that combined style with integrity, Great Expectations. In a
purely visual and superficial way, Sunset Boulevard occasionally
touches the quality so richly present in the fine British picture.
The tragedy is that Sunset Boulevard could have been the devastating commentary it set out to be.

--Fortnight, Vol. 9, No. 5
(September 1, 1950), page 32.

*   *   *

Not the least unfortunate aspect of Sunset Boulevard, a pretentious slice of Roquefort starring Gloria Swanson, is the fact that
the narrator is a corpse. He is one of the more remarkable
corpses in cinema history. Right at the beginning of the film, we
are shown a body floating face down in a pool adjoining an elaborate
Hollywood mansion. In a crisp, detached tone, the narrator in-
forms us that we are gazing at none other than himself. For the
next hour and a half, we are privileged to witness flashbacks of the
events leading up to his fatal immersion. He is (or was, since
the chap is evidently dead) merely a struggling screen writer in
Hollywood, and we see him in his simple quarters, pounding away
at his typewriter. A couple of credit men knock at the door and
tell him they have come to take away his automobile. He eludes
them in his car, has a flat tire, and swerves into a huge private
garage, overgrown with moss and cobwebs, on Sunset Boulevard.
It is the garage of an aging star of the silent screen, the celebrated
Norma Desmond, who lives in a huge, mossy, and cobwebbed mansion alongside, dreaming large, maniacal dreams of a successful

comeback in the "talkies." Spying our narrator, and thinking him
an undertaker come to bury her recently deceased chimpanzee, she
summons him to her establishment, where she lives surrounded by
hundreds of pictures of herself and attended only by a mysterious
German butler (the first of her three husbands). Apprised that our
narrator is a writer and not an undertaker, she installs him as a
permanent house guest, buys him countless suits with padded shoulders, and puts him to work editing a screen version of Salome,
which she has written with herself in mind for the leading role.

To cut a dismal story short, Miss Desmond gets no further
with her dreams of a triumphant return than an interview with Cecil
B. DeMille, played by Cecil B. DeMille. During the interview,
DeMille--wearing, so help me, directorial puttees--says to her,
"Norma, you must realize that times have changed in pictures. "
Her house guest, with whom she has now fallen madly in love,
takes to sneaking out nights to collaborate on another screen play
with a writing chick at Paramount. Our narrator finally tells Miss
Desmond off and starts to leave the premises. Insane with jealousy,
Norma Desmond plugs him in the back. He staggers across the
lawn and flops into the pool, face down. Being an all-round
corpse, however, he continues to narrate the story until the final
scene--Miss Desmond being led away by the police and making a
last, desperately poignant appearance before the newsreel cameras.

Since Sunset Boulevard contains the germ of a good idea,
it's a pity it was not better written. The Messrs. Charles Brackett, Billy Wilder, and D. M. Marshman, Jr., who fashioned this
tone poem, substituted snappy photography and dialogue for what
could have been a genuinely moving tragedy. It seemed to me that
the authors never quite made up their minds whether they were
with Miss Desmond or against her. There are moments when they
appear to have a healthy cynicism toward Hollywood, past and
present, but before the film is over, it is quite evident that they
have a pretty unhealthy contempt for aging stars. Sunset Boulevard
has engrossing scenes, to be sure, since it is peopled with splendid
actors, notably Miss Swanson as Norma Desmond, Erich von Stroheim as the zombie butler, and William Holden as the corpse/writ-
er, but their combined highly skilled efforts cannot cover up the essential hollowness of the enterprise.
                                        --Philip Hamburger in The New
                                        Yorker, (August 19, 1950),
                                        page 70.

☐ SUSPICION (RKO, 1941)

Despite certain acrimonious correspondence from fledgling
actors that, on occasion, reaches this desk, homicide is not my
hobby. Murder, even as a fine art, provides me with no more
stimulating pleasure than would a walking tour of the Chicago stock-

yards, and the current vogue for fireside necrology seems to me to be a ghoulish, grisly pursuit. However, many an acquaintance has turned his attention from such intellectual weightliftings as Semantics, the Great Unshowered, Technocracy, and Mah Jong to devote his leisure hours to the astounding number of gore-tomes that, each month, appear in fresh array on booksellers' shelves. And rare is the gin soirée, these days, at which heated discussions do not occur on subtly poisonous brews, erudite motives, esoteric means of disposing of The Body. At such gatherings, this reporter confines himself to the grog and silence, hoping that the latter will hide the fact that only a single cause célèbre has ever captured his interest. In explanation of this instance may it be added that the allure was engendered by the curious clinical anecdote that leads one to infer Evelyn Nesbit first learned to love her husband, Harry K. Thaw, when he shot White.

Although admittedly indifferent to sonatas of violence, I found Suspicion a most engrossing photoplay. A literate and ingenious mystifier, it disdains the customary comic constables, sliding panels, bat-masked culprits, and replaces such shenanigans with inferential dread. An air of naturalism pervades the opening and the introductory reels are light, good humored, gay. Then slowly, unobtrusively, Alfred Hitchcock evokes a vague uneasiness. A calamitous mood threads its way through the casual happenings until suddenly the worst suspicions of the spectator are confirmed. Those with "nerves" are in for a grand and horrent time.

Carefully contrived, the film builds the relationship between a rather plain and wealthy spinster and a dashing, picaresque young man who drifts into her life. They marry; things go well until the bride suspects that her mate has murdered his best friend. Next, she has reason to conclude that he is preparing to get her out of the way in order to obtain her life insurance sum. But so strong is the fascination of guy for gal that she permits the man to have his way ... in the novel, "Before the Fact." The adaptation, however, becomes weak-kneed, and at the last moment concludes the suspicions were quite without foundation. Audiences are likely to feel cheated, for the theme is so well documented that the belated whitewash job is wholly unconvincing.

Under the Hitchcock aegis, Joan Fontaine performs with beautiful virtuosity. This young lady is a highly individualized actress, possesses a poise and patrician charm the screen has lacked since the retirement of Elsie Ferguson, Florence Vidor, and Alice Joyce. The past twelvemonth has not seen a worthier screen delineation and this department heartily concurs with those who believe Miss Fontaine deserves an Academy Oscar. Cary Grant, too, is at his very best as the genial rascal and there are striking characterizations supplied by Nigel Bruce, Sir Cedric Hardwicke, and the late Auriol Lee. A surprise is Gavin Gordon's expert bit as a professor of criminology; the figure is straight from The New Arabian Nights and The Three Imposters.

Suspicion pretty nearly scared the gray flannel slacks off
this reporter. It is diversion recommended to those who enjoy an
intelligent shocker-saga.

--Herb Sterne in Rob Wagner's
Script, Vol. 27, No. 621 (January 31, 1942), page 14.

☐ THE TALK OF THE TOWN (Columbia, 1942)

The Talk of the Town takes a sociological theme and (wonder!) develops it without rancour or headlines from The Peoples'
World. It states its case in restrained, dramatic terms and employs none of the odetseries which, invariably, make this department see every color but red. Actually, one hero is a chap who
is educated and worldly and still has a heart! Much of the delightful charm of the picture comes from the polished writing talents of
Irwin Shaw and Sidney Buchman, who do not disdain the casual epi-
gram, even though their plot deals with the injustices of society.

George Stevens maintains a balance of power between drama
and comedy with uncanny ease. A long opening sequence tells its
tale in pantomime, establishes mood and motivation long before a
word is uttered. Then the photoplay swings into the details of the
factory hand who is made the patsy for higher-ups and has been
framed on an incendiary and murder rap. The lad breaks jail and
where he hides, with whom, are fragments of a mosaic that is
gradually filled in with bright bits and pieces.

Ronald Colman, as the law pedagogue who is ruled by his head
until he learns to use his heart, steals top honors. Stiff competition
comes from Cary Grant as the lad whose heart rules until he learns to
use his head, and Jean Arthur who is seen to better advantage than ever
before; Edgar Buchanan and Glenda Farrell are mighty good, too.
The all 'round fine acting competition finds Colman winner, and
this performance should certainly convince David Selznick that he
is the one, and only logical choice, for Rochester in Jane Eyre.

Lovely lensing, by Ted Tetzlaff, and an adroitly amusing
musical score (Frederick Hollander) aid in making The Talk of the
Town something to shout about.

--Herb Sterne in Rob Wagner's
Script, Vol. 27, No. 636 (August 29, 1942), page 21.

☐ THIS IS THE ARMY (Warner Bros., 1943)

There isn't as much of the Army in This Is the Army on
the screen as there was on the stage, for the Brothers Warner have

pretty well shunted the enlisted men into the background in order
to make room for nonservice performers.

A plot has been injected into what was a straight revue, and
the tedious story and the usual movie faces manage to dim the exuberance which was the show's greatest asset. Irving Berlin has
much more merit as a patriot who has worked assiduously and well
for Army Relief than he has as a penman of reminiscent melodies
and infantile lyrics, and his talent as a popular tunesmith is devoid
of the inventiveness and taste of such clef-specialists as George
Gershwin, Cole Porter and Noel Coward. In addition to the "original" show's score, Mr. Berlin proffers "What Does He Look Like?"
which is undoubtedly the most outrageous bit of slushful sentimentality to be heard since that worthy unloosed "Since I Lost You" on
a defenseless public.

The best numbers of the footlight entertainment--the dream
ballet and "Russian Winter"--have been omitted for some obscure
reason, and the finale, "Dressed to Kill," loses most of its dramatic point by being retitled "Dressed to Win," for the benefit of such
movie audiences as refuse to believe that combat occasionally ends
in something unpleasant. Sergeant Robert Shanley impresses with
his singing, Private James Cross gets his tapping across in fine
style, and the rest of the old-line khaki-clad boys score whenever
the camera infrequently gets around to providing them with an opportunity.

--Herb Sterne in Rob Wagner's
Script, Vol. 29, No. 661 (August 28, 1943), page 14.

☐ TO BE OR NOT TO BE (Lubitsch/United Artists, 1942)

Since the halcyon days of The Marriage Circle, Ernst Lubitsch's films, with but few exceptions, have been sardonic investigations of the connubial couch and its immediate environs. To
many he is the supreme pundit of the epithalamium, and there are
those who contend that his dictates on matters marital possess a
larger, and even more faithful clientage than the bulls sponsored
by Judge Ben Lindsey, Mademoiselle Beatrice Fairfax and Mrs.
Estelle Lawton Lindsey.

However, the director's latest enterprise, To Be or Not to
Be, only tentatively dallies with peekaboo-peerings at such events
as exist betwixt the sheets of matrimony. True enough, the central protagonists are gyved in wedlock. And we have the jealous
husband, the comely wife a roving eye for well-filled military uniforms in the best, and most repetitious tradition of Continental
fare. Still, the boulevardier humours are but a single facet of this
comedic jewel and Lubitsch devotes his more meticulous lapidary
talents to cutting, and polishing-off the Nazis.

In a sense, the photoplay is a companion piece to Ninotchka. The director found a valid target for satire in the shirt-sleeved satellites of Comrade Stalin and their inordinate passion for the commonplace; he now looses vitriol-tipped arrows at Hitler and his Germaniacs. The results are largely amusing, and while the picture is one you surely won't want to miss, its score is somewhat less high than that achieved by its forerunner. The wind that keeps some of the missiles from reaching dead-center is an accent on plot, the slighting of psychological factors. While Ninotchka explored the proletarian vitals of the borschtites and disclosed the gnawing amoeba of mediocrity, this contents itself with superficially ridiculing the symptoms of Nazism and bothers not to investigate the virus of the disease.

Lubitsch and his highly touted "touches" are at their best in the film's intimate sequences. Where the script accents the byplay and interplay of individuals, the direction has distinction. But when the moments of plot progression arrive they are presented in so bald a manner as to suggest that the Master, impatient with sheer mechanics, abruptly passed these sequences into the calloused hands of a second unit.

The subtle jibes, the illuminating bits of caricature showered on the actors who portray actors, are certain to be relished by those familiar with backstage life. Carole Lombard gives a beautifully modulated performance as the Polish star caught in the vicissitudes of the German invasion of Warsaw. Jack Benny (he dons an Edwin Booth makeup as Hamlet!) is better than even his most ardent enthusiast had any right to expect. Heretofore strictly a vaudevillian, Lubitsch has transformed Benny from comic into comedian. A large supporting cast is excellent, with Sig Rumann deserving a very special salvo of applause.

Despite its background of war-torn Europe, there is nothing depressing about To Be or Not to Be. If it is possible for you to lay aside the Ninotchka yardstick, you will probably find it very good indeed.

--Herb Sterne in Rob Wagner's
Script, Vol. 27, No. 623 (February 28, 1942), page 10.

                          *   *   *

Carole Lombard's last comedy is certainly nothing to weep over. It is, as a matter of fact, something to laugh over from start to finish. The laughs come a little lugubriously at times, not because you're seeing a greatly beloved actress scheming, cutting up, laughing and storming at you from the screen when you and all about you know she is dead, but rather because of To Be or Not to Be's background and characters.

Its scene is laid in Warsaw, at the outbreak of war in 1939, and comedy, no matter how purposeful, played out against a back-

ground of grim reality like the scarred skeleton of Warsaw, is apt
to make you think more about the war than about the comedy, even
though the Nazis are the stooges.

The comedy is a drama acted for keeps by a company of
actors caught in Warsaw, to outwit the Gestapo. The actors wear
Gestapo uniforms, impersonate all degrees of Nazis, including Hitler himself (Tom Dugan). And by the time they whisk out of Warsaw in an official airplane and head for England, the audience and
the Nazis have been treated to about the grimmest curtain gag of
all time.

The gag is played on the two Nazi pilots of the last-act airplane by the play-acting Fuehrer. He summons the two away from
the controls, and points to an open hatch, at 2000 feet or so.

"Jump!" he barks.

They jump. No parachutes either. What a double-take
laugh the Rivoli audience did on that one!

As for Carole (who died in an airplane crash on Jan. 16, on
her way back to Hollywood after a Defense Bond campaign in her
home state, Indiana, ten days after she finished this picture), she
is really a terrific trouper in To Be or Not to Be. As the calm
and seasoned actress wife of a whopper of a ham actor (Jack
Benny)--they are billed as the Lunt and Fontanne of Poland--she
has to play what was probably a very tough assignment--a subdued
role.

She enters in white satin, traditionally her most flattering
cloth. Next thing you know she is trotting back to the dressing
room, on orders from her ham husband, to change into a costume
more suitable for Gestapo, the satire they are rehearsing and which
they finally play out grimly for their lives.

As prescribed by the slick Ernst Lubitsch direction, Carole
has to let her ham-actor husband steal practically every scene.
And some of the scenes of Jack Benny hamming for his life are
among Benny's, and Lubitsch's best.

--John T. McManus in PM (March
8, 1942), page 23.

☐ TO EACH HIS OWN (Paramount, 1946)

In theme, To Each His Own is the type of sob saga that today still seeks to rape the lachrymal ducts between the hand-lotion
advertisements and the cake recipes of the women's magazines.

It relates, in considerable detail, the emotional plight of a
girl who bears an infant out of wedlock, loses her child to another

woman and lives to learn that the world, without love, is but a
garden of weeds.

Hmmmm!

From this synopsis it should be evident that the film includes every heart-throb cliché familiar since Lady Isabel and
Jacqueline Floriot were the favorite heroines of the ten-twenty-
thirty circuits, but the old plot has been plumed, polished and
presented as though it had been spawned not earlier than this very
hour.

Considering the film will undoubtedly net several millions to
Paramount, and about half that sum to the Handkerchief Makers of
America, Inc., it is idle to ponder why Charles Brackett, Mitchell
Leisen and a capable cast should be disgraced with carrying such a
sorry string of situations.   Once the plot has been accepted for
what it is, it should be immediately admitted that those concerned
with the enterprise have done very well indeed with it.

The tale stretches its woe between World Wars One and
Two.   The atmosphere is carefully sustained at all times, and the
texture of the earlier period of carnage is beautifully managed,
mainly through the relatively authentic period costumes by Edith
Head and the F. Scott Fitzgerald technique of recalling the near-
past via the popular songs of the day.

Olivia de Havilland is wonderfully effective and effecting.
She trips the gamut from youth to middle age with no perceptible
effort, and, surprisingly, it is in the stanzas of maturity that she
manages her best impression as a legitimate actress.   Roland
Culver, Phil Terry, and newcomer John Lund are most satisfactory
in support.   Mary Anderson, it may be noted, occasionally becomes
so excessive in her presentation of a neurotic as to entice titters.

--Herb Sterne in Rob Wagner's
Script, Vol. 32, No. 735 (August 3, 1946), pages 12-13.

*   *   *

The heroine of To Each His Own is neither wife nor widow;
for the father of her child flew away to the war and was killed before there was any talk of marriage.   All this is told in an exceedingly long flashback which shows how the woman suffers and
pays.   What keeps the sentimental story from being just an orgy
of lavender and old lace are the first-rate performance of Olivia
de Havilland in the lead, the good supporting cast and the sincere
direction of Mitchell Leisen.   Middle-aged in 1944, Miss Norris
(de Havilland) sits in a London railroad station, waiting to get a
glimpse of her son, remembering the years since the last war.
Producer Charles Brackett (who also wrote the script with Jacques
Thery) has faithfully reconstructed the atmosphere of a small 1918
American town, and we are made to feel the excitement of a girl

with two suitors (Bill Goodwin and Phillip Terry) who falls for the
attentions of a handsome airplane pilot (John Lund).   But when the
bond rally is over and her lover gone, Miss Norris realizes her
awkward position in this town where everyone knows everyone.
Her son is adopted by a couple whose baby has just died; and Miss
Norris learns (through years of yearning) that "just bringing a child
into this world doesn't make you its mother." The picture's final
scenes in wartime London will tear the hearts out of all women,
particularly mothers (and I suspect fathers and even stony bachelors
will sniffle too).   Griff Barnett, as the erring girl's father who
says, "We don't judge each other; we love each other," and Roland
Culver, as Miss Norris's English friend, give moving portrayals.
But this is really Olivia de Havilland's picture.   Her smooth, honest performance as the young girl, the efficient business woman,
the heartsick, rather frustrated spinster-type, stands with the best
acting that cinema has to offer today.   The men's characterizations
are by no means neglected in this film, but since events are seen
mainly through Miss Norris's eyes and from her viewpoint, To Each
His Own must be called a woman's picture, a label however, that
does not detract from its interest.

                                        --Philip T. Hartung in The Com-
                                             monweal (June 7, 1946), page
                                             193.

☐   TO HAVE AND HAVE NOT (Warner Bros. , 1945)

          Sex, according to the inditements of my critical confrères,
is Lauren Bacall.   And in the poesy of these same pundits of the
press, Lauren Bacall is Sex.

          So, at the first opportunity, your scrivener bee-lined to the
nearest celluloid emporium showing To Have and Have Not, plunked
some silver, plus a knowing wink, at the cashier's disposal, and
sauntered into the darkness of the theater bent on a clinical investigation of this new dazzler reputed to possess the allure of Lilith,
Chrysis, and Evelyn Nesbit at the hour Harry K. Thaw confused
Stanford White with a clay pigeon.

          It required not more than ten minutes to convince this ob-
server that the boys who bat out learned critiques on the drama
had been hoodwinked by an ersatz siren, a robot confected by the
Messrs. Warner from the more salient mannerisms of several
highly individualistic screen charmers--plus a King's Size set of
Gay Deceivers added to cause talk that, in view of the circumstances, is just so much mammary palaver.

          Lauren Bacall is a pastiche of many a famous face, figure
and personality.   To generate Mystery, la Bacall is given mono-
syllabic dialogue, a device which harks back to the Dietrich of any
Josef von Sternberg opus, and one which launched Hedy Lamarr to

attention in Algiers.   Her hair is coiffed in the manner originated
by Veronica Lake.   The Bacall eyes bat bountifully in the Dietrich
tradition, and her sultry speaking and singing are frenetic filchings
from the Misses Dietrich, Bankhead, and Bennett (Constance).
Lensed so that her cheek bones are accentuated, that her face has
all the mobility of a Benda mask, Miss Bacall, in appearance,
vacillates between Kate Hepburn, the Garbo of silent films, Jeanne
Eagels of The Letter and Jealousy and the Emily Stevens of Metro
movies, circa 1917.

After sitting through To Have and Have Not, I defy even the
shades of Alan Dale and William Winter to gauge Miss Bacall's
abilities or potentialities as an actress.   Obviously, her reading of
the single words which are her "lines" has been so coached as to
totally erase originality.   Her movements at all times indicate that
she has an infernal machine secreted somewhere about her person.
The studied glances, meant, no doubt to be provocative, only succeed in making one fear that the lady is the victim of a myopia
third only to that possessed by Laurette Taylor and Theda Bara.

Lauren Bacall has the acquired attributes of an all-star cast
of established glamour gals.   Attempting to portray a woman with a
past, Miss Bacall appears to have had an affair with no man not
employed by the research division of The Museum of Modern Art
Film Library.

> --Herb Sterne in Rob Wagner's
> Script, Vol. 31, No. 698 (Feb-
> ruary 17, 1945), page 14.

☐ TOBACCO ROAD (20th Century-Fox, 1941)

No excuse for it.   Practically no story, just a series of episodes in the lives of people in whom you are in no way interested
and can not be made interested by the manner in which they are
presented on the screen.   One demented youth screams his way
through the picture, takes delight in smashing a new motor car,
marries a woman--also a halfwit--old enough to be his mother,
and neither of them contributes anything to the forward progress of
the ghost of a story.   The settings are squalid, the landscapes
bleak, the roads rivers of mud, the whole thing depressing.

One can see how the Hollywood mind functioned in selecting
Tobacco Road for transference from the stage to the screen.   As a
play it has been running in New York for almost a decade, gaining
the long distance record and still attracting profitable business.
Any play which can do that automatically becomes screen material,
so thinks Hollywood.   It is the unlovely ruggedness of the play,
profane dialogue, sex in the raw which continue to attract theatre
audiences, but all are elements which the screen is prohibited from
presenting.   What is left is nothing of value, and that is what is
presented to us as motion picture entertainment.

The picture does not even make the best of what material it
has. The screaming of the demented youth which makes such assaults on audience ears, is entirely unnecessary. He could have
been presented as a sullen, morose half-wit who mumbled his lines
just loudly enough to be heard. But even a better suggestion would
be that Twentieth Century-Fox should have picked something else
off its story shelf, something which would have permitted John Ford
to give us another Long Voyage Home.

> --Welford Beaton in Hollywood
> Spectator, Vol. 15, No. 5
> (March 1, 1941), page 8.

*   *   *

Despite the lack of acclaim on the part of the New York
drama critics, Tobacco Road is, currently, in its eighth consecutive year on Broadway. Because of John Ford's superior handling
of the 'way-down-south theme, the cinematic transposition is likely
to be more cordially treated by those who write about motion pictures. Whatever worth this tale of worthless people possesses is
due solely to Ford's directorial genius, but it is doubtful whether
the film will be able to match the play's wholesale vogue.

By this time it is an open secret that the screen version resembles the novel more than it does the Jack Kirkland dramatization. Nunnally Johnson (who did a similar laundry chore on The
Grapes of Wrath) carefully scrubbed the situations and dialogue.
Despite the liberal applications of yellow naphtha soap, water and
good old elbow grease, the characters remain poor white trash.
In an effort to please the censors, if not the paying patrons, the
Lesters and their friends have shed their bleak sexuality; with that
change Tobacco Road loses the very pivot of its popularity and becomes just an uninspired and uninspiring folk tale that shifts un-
easily from comedy to drama and back again. Due to the lack of
a definite viewpoint, it is neither farce nor good red preachment.

Without a single exception, the dwellers on Tobacco Road
are lazy, shiftless and entirely unprepossessing. Young and old
have the I. Q. of a not-too-bright brat of six. Vicious, willfully
destructive, there isn't one good reason apparent as to why they
deserve any type of salvation--or audience sympathy. The Joads,
of the Steinbeck volume and film, wanted work, security and happiness. Consequently, their plight had poignancy. The dilapidation
of these people is a result of wanton degradation and there is a feeling that if Jeeter and Ada were to receive the money which would
keep them off the poor farm, they'd probably use it to light a pipe,
or employ it in place of the James Whitcomb Riley corncob.

Ford, like Alfred Hitchcock, has a more certain touch with
dramatics than with humour. Consequently the latter reels have a
stamina which the early footage lacks. As in the recent "Road-
show," there is reason to complain of the archaic methods of en-
ticing laughter, for the points of derivation are similar. The first

two gags are plainly of early Keystone vintage and the sprinkling scene was hilariously projected by Mary Pickford in The Poor Little Rich Girl, circa 1917.

Charley Grapewin, Elizabeth Patterson, Ward Bond, Gene Tierney, Marjorie Rambeau and William Tracy establish characters that are sharply defined. But they can't do the impossible: make them appealing or interesting. Dana Andrews has the best break of his career; in appreciation he proves Mr. Goldwyn's faith in him and gives a likable show that should do an appreciable amount for his popularity.

Tobacco Road is controversial material. Some will laud it; others will find it definitely distasteful.

Heartbreak-moment: The single shot of Mae Marsh, peering through a window. Remember her as the really great actress of The Birth of a Nation, The White Rose and Intolerance? It does seem as though she deserves more than a brief flash in today's motion pictures.

--Herb Sterne in Rob Wagner's
Script, Vol. 25, No. 590
(March 8, 1941), page 16.

☐   THE TREASURE OF SIERRA MADRE (Warner Bros., 1948)

We have become so accustomed to motion pictures based upon the amatory emotions that whenever a film motivated by something other than sexual attractions and repulsions comes from Hollywood we are like a convict who, inured to the prison yard, is allowed an hour in the meadow of the prison farm. On such rare occasions gratitude often dissolves our discrimination, or our hats are in the air even before we have seen the brave new picture that is sans sex, sans glamour, sans everything b. o.

About twenty years ago one of the most curious writers of our day--he calls himself B. Traven--wrote a novel about an old gold prospector and two American derelicts in the mountains of Mexico which resembled, in theme, Frank Norris' McTeague from which Erich von Stroheim had made the motion picture Greed. The theme: men can be so affected by the discovery of gold that they lose their souls and sometimes the gold as well. Traven called his novel The Treasure of Sierra Madre, and Walter Huston's son John has made an exceptional photoplay out of it. Its action, like that of Greed, derives from actual human motivations, not the usual rationalized ones.

B. Traven's old prospector is a bloody but unbowed veteran eager to risk his last stake in one final gamble. His two companions are chance encounters in a Tampico flophouse. One of them has honor and one has not. The reactions and interactions of these three after they find gold in the remote Sierra Madre comprise the subject matter, as well as the plot, of the film. The dishonorable man, after stealing the gold, is killed by Indian bandits who, thinking the saddle bags are filled with sand, spill them out upon a windy ground.

This bitter fable is told with cinematic integrity and considerable skill. True, there is some unnecessary melodrama, for which Herr Traven is to blame. Occasionally there is Hollywood hyperbole, as when Mr. Huston assembles hundreds of Mexican Indians for an effect Sergei Eisenstein achieved with a few dozen. And Humphrey Bogart is miscast. Mr. Bogart can exhibit grace under pressure incomparably, but he cannot successfully be mean. Moreover, his part has atrocious lines. But these flaws are in the shadow of some outstanding virtues. First, the basic subject matter of this picture is valid, not synthetic. Second, the exposition of this subject matter is forthright, not bowdlerized, and it is possible to learn from the screen that morality is still skin deep. And third, Walter Huston portrays the old prospector with the creative élan that sometimes comes over actors who are truly great.

--Henry Hart in New Movies, Vol. 23, No. 2 (February-March 1948), page 6.

* * *

The Treasure of Sierra Madre was something of a family affair. John Huston wrote the screenplay and directed--and acted a bit. His father, Walter Huston, played one of the leads. Another lead was handled by Tim Holt, and in one sequence keen-sighted observers may identify a disreputable-looking extra as his father, Jack Holt. Humphrey Bogart is starred in the film, but so far as this reviewer could note there was no trace of Lauren Bacall anywhere.

Whether it was domestic felicity, or just skill and zest, they have made of Treasure a highly entertaining and rather unusual film. Shot partly in Mexico, the film is a rough-and-ready yarn of gold prospecting in the Sierras. But more than an outdoor epic, it offers some reflections on the curious traits gold can arouse in men. Nothing very profound is added to our knowledge of human character, but the film does toy bewitchingly with this philosophical problem.

Tatterdemalion clothes and unkept whiskers evidently had an exhilarating effect on Walter Huston, for he acts his role with enormous relish and runs jauntily away with the show. As in The Fugitive the cast was supplemented by nonprofessional native Mexicans, who appear to be the finest natural actors a director could wish for.

--Fortnight, Vol. 4, No. 3 (January 30, 1948), page 30.

☐ A TREE GROWS IN BROOKLYN (20th Century-Fox, 1945)

A Tree Grows in Brooklyn is about as credible and creditable a depiction of American tenement life as has been seen on the
talking screen. The Betty Smith novel is transposed with tenderness and restraint by writers Tess Slessinger and Frank Davis, and
director Elia Kazan has contoured the characters with considerably
more veracity than one has come to expect of "people" in Hollywood
pictures.

Brooklyn, that city just adjacent to the United States, is depicted with a minimum of habitual whitewash. Incident, rather than
plot is accented against this background, and through this method
the spectator becomes quite thoroughly acquainted with the Nolan
family. Here we have poor people resigned to their plight, expecting very little and receiving just about that in the way of happiness,
security and the fundamental decencies of life. There are none of
the usual clichés concerning poverty being ennobling, that want
breeds Wonder. The very resignation of the people makes their
plight the more pathetic.

The treatment vouchsafed the theme is neither so direct nor
so lacerating as that which Griffith devised for the modern story of
Intolerance and Vidor created for The Crowd. In the conventional
conception of the weak and genial Johnny, and the expurgated portrait of Aunt Sissy the film fails to meet the general high quality of
the rest of the presentation.

However, the photoplay hits heights in the projection and
playing of Katie and Francie. In this film, as well as in the still
unreleased The Enchanted Cottage, Dorothy McGuire proves herself
a distinguished actress. Incisive and authoritative, she grasps a
character with ease, and condescends to none of the superficial
hankypanky all too customary to the current crop of young celluloid
cuties. In this department's opinion, Miss McGuire is one of the
more salient histrionic talents revealed by the talking screen.
Peggy Ann Garner is downright superb as the imaginative younker
of the family. Ted Donaldson, although his assignment is less imposing, is excellent too, and he makes a thoroughly understandable
boy of Neeley.

Worthy of note is the harrowing realism with which the child-
birth sequences are presented. Not since Griffith first exploded the
stork myth on the screen two decades ago by showing Anna Moore
in the throes of hideous labor in Way Down East has a movie so
had the courage to announce motherhood as anything but a most
beautiful and delightful experience.

--Herb Sterne in Rob Wagner's
Script, Vol. 31, No. 700
(March 17, 1945), pages 14-15.

*   *   *

A tree that has become one of the near-legends of these times--a tree that grew in Brooklyn--has been transplanted from the printed page to achieve distinction on celluloid. A bestseller for many months, Betty Smith's novel about the Brooklyn of a generation ago has emerged as one of the fine film dramas of the year.

The earthy quality of Brooklyn tenement squalor, about which Miss Smith wrote so eloquently in A Tree Grows in Brooklyn, has been given a literal translation to the screen by 20th-Fox to become an experiment in audience restraint. There have been few pictures to tug at the heartstrings as this one does.

This is the story of that Brooklyn locale called Williamsburg and of the poverty-ridden Nolan family. Katie, the young mother, had to scrub down the tenement steps to help defray the family expenses. Johnny, her husband, had more zest for fun-loving than the capacity to support his brood. Francie, their daughter, dreamed of becoming a writer. Neeley, the youngest, had a desire for food greater than the family coffers could afford. And there was Aunt Sissy, Katie's sister, with her perpetual flair for new husbands.

Around these are woven a story that is lengthy but never tedious, a yarn whose propensity for minor details looms forever importantly as the tale develops.

Tree recalls an absorbing period of a colorful tribe, of a Brooklyn neighborhood that was tough in its growing-up, where kids fought or were kicked in the slats; where on Saturday nights fathers and husbands, more often than not, loped uncertainly from the corner quenchery.

Some of this might have acquired the tinge of travesty in hands less skilled than those of Miss Smith--or director Elia Kazan --but never does the serio-comic intrude on a false note; never does this story become maudlin.

This may be fiction but there's no disguising the basis of truth for this story. The dramatic power it possesses seemingly could never have been attained from imagination alone. Miss Smith, herself, through one of the characters, professes that stories are little lies that never have their basis on truths.

The Nolans--and the characters forever lending strong background--make for superb studies. Katie Nolan, penny-pinching, her brow forever furrowed with worry over whether the family would have enough food--or about the new baby to come--was sometimes too circumspect in her family decisions. Katie felt she had to be. Johnny meant one day to be the best darned singing waiter in all Brooklyn--even Manhattan--but Katie--and Johnny did too, down deep--knew that he didn't have a ghost of a chance. Everything was against them. And when Katie figured that Francie had to quit school, so she could go to work and help out because of the new baby, that incited Johnny to tramp the employment agencies so that his little girl could continue her schooling. Johnny couldn't get a job, but he got pneumonia and died trying.

To Dorothy McGuire, who has appeared in only one other film, in the title role of Claudia, also for 20th-Fox, went the prize part of Katie Nolan. For the first reel or so it's difficult to associate the girl-wife of Claudia with the almost-calloused character of Katie, but soon Miss McGuire develops with the part, and the part with her. It is a role that she makes distinctive by underplaying.

Johnny Nolan is a comeback part for James Dunn. The role has a greater depth than any he has ever played, and Dunn plays it excellently. Peggy Ann Garner is the teen-aged Francie and this character must certainly have been the author's favorite. Upon Francie, Miss Smith has lavished much of the story's sympathies, and the young actress performs capitally.

Young Ted Donaldson, as Neeley, also contributes importantly. Joan Blondell as Aunt Sissy has considerable of the hoyden quality intended by Miss Smith, and Miss Blondell also gives an impressive performance. Lloyd Nolan, as a policeman, is another outstander.

The adaptation has been carefully made by Tess Slessinger and Frank Davis, with particular attention paid to the original.

Where Tree is frequently slow, it is offset by the story's significance and pointed up notably by the direction of Elia Kazan. This film runs two hours and 12 minutes, but Kazan's direction has paced the story admirably. The production values are evident all the way, and that includes the fine photography and musical score.

Oh, yes--the tree! Bent and twisted, it grew, somehow, amid debris and clotheslines in the backyard of the tenement where the Nolans lived. Bent and twisted--but beautiful to Johnny and Francie Nolan. As bent and twisted--and as beautiful--as the people Betty Smith has written about.

--"Kahn" in Variety, Vol. 157, No. 7 (January 24, 1945), page 10.

☐ UNFAITHFULLY YOURS (20th Century-Fox, 1948)

Sturges the writer offers the original outrageously comic material that exactly suits Sturges the director and producer. A great conductor suspects that there's an affair going on between his wife and his secretary. During the three numbers he conducts at a concert (Rossini's "Semiramide" overture; the Tannhäuser Venus-

berg music and the overture to Francesca da Rimini) he imagines
himself carrying out three sorts of revenge, each conditioned by
the character of the music.   His attempts later to reenact these
plans in actuality result in a melee of sophisticated slapstick.   A
little too wordy, its slapstick a little too prolonged, the film nevertheless has moments of Sturges at his funniest.   The score and its
performance are worthy of a separate hearing.

--New Movies, Vol. 23, No. 5
(November-December 1948),
page 15.

*   *   *

It has been a nightmare-filled year in Hollywood--one that
film-makers would like to forget.   Foreign grosses, which in 1947
accounted for 94% of the industry's net profits, are off an estimated
$20 million.   Restrictive agreements in Britain alone have cut the
take there 40%.

Not only that, but domestic business has declined alarming-
ly.   Company earnings are 'way down, employment has been cut,
frantic economy measures have been instituted.

The two-year-old labor dispute between CSU and IATSE still
is unsettled.   Antitrust actions now pending in court threaten to
wreck the film distribution setup (most large film-producing cor-
porations own their own theatre chains, whence come the big profits).   The Red scare threw Hollywood into a dither last spring,
and investigations may be renewed.   The growing spectre of tele-
vision has given filmmakers fearful ulcers, as producers envision
millions of potential theatregoers sitting home watching the video
screen....   And then there was the marihuana scandal.

Some insistent voices have claimed that there is nothing
wrong in Filmland that good movies won't correct.   There is plenty
wrong with pictures besides the quality of the output.   But unless
Hollywood improves its product it might just as well forget its other worries.   Not more than a handful of films produced this year
have been worth adult attention--and an embarrassing number of
these were foreign made.

Fortnight's reviewer, who sees films well in advance of their
release date, feels that the outlook for the next few months, as far
as the quality of pictures goes, is better than it has been for some
time.   Outstanding among the new releases is Unfaithfully Yours,
the year's best comedy, written, produced and directed by Preston
Sturges.

Unfaithfully Yours is about a symphony orchestra conductor
(played with rare wit by Rex Harrison) who returns from tour and
comes to wonder if his wife has been unfaithful during his absence.
As his imagination works, he fabricates a grand passion between
his wife and his secretary--which has no factual basis whatever.

During a concert, as Sir Alfred conducts his program, in his mind's eye he conjures up diabolical plots to solve this ugly triangle.

The daydreams or "prospects" are violent, gentle and dramatic, according to the music that inspires them. They gave Sturges an unusual opportunity to indulge in literary horseplay. For these prospects are not Sturges', as it were, but Sir Alfred's --and as in all dreams, the dreamer's role is notoriously over-written, with all the action and all the sententious speeches given to him. It is exactly the sort of thing a bad playwright would write with himself in mind for the leading role.

But the film comes to its climax after the concert, when Sir Alfred goes home alone, sets about staging one of his little dramas, gets dreadfully tangled in props, stumbles over furniture, is seized by a humiliating sneezing fit. Wife and secretary burst in, frantically worried, see this mess, and, like little Audrey, just laugh and laugh. And Sir Alfred realizes he has made an ass of himself!

The idea for Unfaithfully Yours goes back to 1937, when Sturges was working on Easy Living for Paramount. Writing a scene one day, he found that it came out quite differently from what he intended. Puzzled, he realized his mood had been affected by radio music pouring in from the next room. Since then he has been kicking around the notion of doing a film to illustrate the effect music has on the emotions. (One famed director told him it could never be done: "Too subtle for a general audience.")

It does sound like a difficult theme for comedy hijinks. But it is Sturges' particular talent to blend sophisticated comedy with prattfalls. He is gifted with the rare ability to conceive a witty idea, develop it into a literate screenplay, stage it with insane slapstick--yet make it retain its incisive, witty point.

Dialogue, comic business, sound (which Sturges uses more imaginatively than any other movie-maker except Disney) make this movie a superlative treat. And the performances are sheer delight. Suave Rex Harrison, whose eyes have always had a comic twinkle, abandons all vestiges of British reserve and comes through with a rip-snorting comic performance that sparkles with titillating touches. He will look pretty silly in stuffy British roles after this. Screen wife Linda Darnell lets down her lovely black back hair, and old reliables Rudy Vallee, Julius Tannen, Edgar Kennedy are in there pitching for laughs--as well as Barbara Lawrence and Kurt Kreuger. It's immense fun.

Sturges, a man who has left his distinctive stamp on a long string of superior films, first achieved fame in another ghastly year, 1929--when his play, Strictly Dishonorable, hit the jackpot in New York. In the same year he started writing for films, came to Hollywood in 1932. Like most oldtimers (it startles him to hear the term applied to himself) he has made the rounds of the studios.

Since 1940 he has been his own producer as well as director and writer, a triple-threat arrangement enjoyed by few film-makers.

He lives in hopeless clutter in a modest manse in the Holly-wood hills, spends a good deal of time yachting, is an ardent fight fan and a gourmet. (He owns The Players, a restaurant on Sunset Strip frequented by film people.) When he is busy on a picture, he works prodigiously. A lot of clowning goes on during shooting, for Sturges is a man of great good humor. And yet, he has a serious turn of mind. Unlike some film artisans, he has a re-freshing esteem for the movie-going public, believes it is generally underrated. There is no danger of being too subtle, too precious for one's audience, he feels; the danger is in being too condescend-ing.

More than anything else, talent like Preston Sturges', and films like Unfaithfully Yours, can help Hollywood out of its current doldrums.

--Fortnight, Vol. 5, No. 9 (Octo-ber 22, 1948), pages 28-29.

☐ WHITE HEAT (Warner Bros. , 1949)

White Heat takes the successful cops and robbers formula of the '30's, adds psychopathic complexes and scientific sleuthing by T-men, brings back James Cagney as the tough guy gang leader and proves again crime never, never pays, except at the boxoffice.

Cagney, as ruthless killer "Cody" Jarrett, scores again in a violent melodrama of a homicidal paranoiac with a macabre lust for money. Beauteous Virginia Mayo as the unfaithful anthracitic wife and Margaret Wycherly as crafty "Ma" Jarrett are thoroughly con-vincing in their roles, as is sinister Steve Cochran and the rest of the cast including Edmond O'Brien, John Archer, Wally Cassell and Mickey Knox.

The photography and music are particularly effective and veteran director Raoul Walsh even gives time-worn clichés such as "dead men won't talk" and "we'll be on top of the world, baby," a refreshing touch, to make White Heat high-voltage entertainment in the detective story pattern.

--Fortnight, Vol. 7, No. 5 (September 2, 1949), page 31.

*   *   *

White Heat is a return to the Cagney of old, Cagney at his best, cast as a ruthless, brutal gangster leader in a picture so dramatically-compelling that it will be one of Warners' top grossers of the year. In point of suspense buildup, it has seldom been ri-

valled and presents star, in his first picture since rejoining his
old studio, in what will be regarded by most as his most rugged
and dynamic characterization. Producers have drawn upon surefire
plot ingredients which will keep any audience on the edge of its
seat.

Yarn follows the exploits of a homicidal paranoiac, in his
pulling a train holdup and his going to prison on a minor charge to
avoid any connection with the crime in which four trainmen are
murdered. Treasury agent Edmond O'Brien is assigned task of
learning whereabouts of the $300,000 in newly-printed federal bank-
notes which holdup netted Cagney, and is committed to prison with
him as an undercover man. Cagney, with a mother complex despite
his toughness, escapes when he learns that the mother has been
killed, and T-man goes with him. Climax occurrs in a huge chem-
ical plant in Los Angeles as law catches up to gangster.

Star delivers an unforgettable portrayal which will stand high
in this or any year's performances. Character is without a single
redeeming quality, and Cagney plays it to the hilt. One of most
memorable sequences in film is when he learns in prison dining
hall of death of his mother, and he goes temporarily insane. A
perfect foil for Cagney as his wife is Virginia Mayo, playing a
hard-boiled, brittle moll, a lovely interpretation. Highlight in their
scenes together is moment when Cagney kicks chair she is standing
on out from under her and she takes a hard tumble.

O'Brien likewise scores with a punchy performance, and
Margaret Wycherly, as Ma Jarrett, Cagney's mother, breathes
quiet menace into a strong role. Steve Cochran also is outstanding,
as Cagney's henchman, John Archer lends authority to top Treasury
agent part, and balance of supporting players generally are well and
know-how from a top screencast.

Raoul Walsh directs with drive play by Ivan Goff and Ben
Roberts, adapted from a story by Virginia Kellogg. Louis F. Edelman packed film with appropriate values in his production helming
and technical departments are expertly handled throughout. Standing
out here in particular is music score by Max Steiner, camera work
by Sid Hickox, art direction of Edward Carrere and Owen Marks'
editing.

--Daily Variety, Vol. 64, No. 58
(August 25, 1949), pages 3 and
10.

☐ WILSON (20th Century-Fox, 1944)

Serious screen biographies have almost exclusively stayed
away from hotly controversial ground by sticking to scientists, artists, musicians and writers, and ventured into the portrayal of

figures that could be called, more literally, "historic" only when
their lives fell comfortably within the field of costume drama. To
attempt an account of the career of so nearly a contemporary figure
as Woodrow Wilson was much more of a challenge: how far could
it go without treading on living toes, offending or failing to satisfy
the friends of people not long dead, or stirring up controversies
not too deeply buried still to contain heat that might flare up again?
How much could it tell, what concessions would it have to make,
how honest and impartial could it be? How near would it dare to
come to the truth, if indeed the exact truth could be discerned as
a goal?

The picture Wilson is a surprisingly successful answer to
all these challenges, besides being an engrossingly interesting
drama. It achieves its success by a canny arrangement of emphasis: it makes an ideal its central theme--the ideal of world
peace, which is timeless in its appeal--and embodies it in the person of the man who died fighting for it. That, at a stroke, sim-
plifies the whole manner of presenting Wilson's life. It can begin
with how he came to get into politics, follow him along broad lines
from being governor of New Jersey to becoming president, then
through the war to the domestic fight over the League of Nations.
All along it can highlight the idealistic qualities of Wilson as a
statesman, and culminate in the noble and heroic crusade against
future wars that ended--certainly for him and by implication for
the whole world--in tragic defeat.

The result is a portrait of a man which has been warmed up
considerably as a private person--as professor and husband and
father a much more ingratiating figure than Wilson's even most ardent public ever saw any evidence of, amusing, very much a simple
home-body, tender in his family relationships, touchingly lonely after his first wife's death. Alexander Knox is ideal for this kind of
a portrait, with enough indication of sturdy mind and character to
keep it from seeming soft. The delicate matter of his second marriage is handled with impressive dignity and fine feeling.

This is the personal thread that is woven into a remarkably
vivid and exhilarating picture of the America of which Wilson became the national leader. The political conventions and campaigns
are extraordinarily good--the development of Wilson's "New Freedom" is sketchily but adequately suggested--the entry of the United
States into world affairs and its emergence as a great world power
is sufficiently shown to point up the main theme: our responsibility
in helping maintain world peace.

The political struggle that defeated our becoming one of the
League of Nations and our retreat into a short-sighted dream of
"normalcy" and isolation is--perhaps necessarily--over-simplified.
Senator Lodge is given the whole burden of villainous opposition--
no hint of Borahs or Hiram Johnsons, for instance--and even he
has to be presented with careful regard for the feelings of family
and friends. The elements in Wilson's own temperament and char-

acter that had a part in defeating his purposes--his "one-track
mind" and his stubbornness in going his own way--are indicated but
their results not stressed. But his great dream and his great
fight--that for which history will chiefly remember him--are power-
fully presented. And the picture reverberates with echoes and re-
echoes of significance for the America of this day and this very
hour.

> --James Shelley Hamilton in New
> Movies, Vol. 19, No. 6 (Octo-
> ber 1944), pages 4-5.

*   *   *

In the field of motion picture biographies, Wilson towers as
a tremendous film achievement of world-wide importance to our
present generation. It is deserving of the warmest possible acclaim for every single individual who had a hand in its making, for
Darryl F. Zanuck's great production brings into impressive play all
of the vast resources at the command of master screen craftsmen.
What has been accomplished dwarfs comparisons in nearly all respects. Its stature cannot be properly summarized even by a
statistical survey of the three years the picture was in preparation,
the close to four million dollars it cost, the 13,000 players it employed to reenact vital modern history in 162 stunning sets and
probably the most realistic Technicolor photography ever filmed.
None of these statistics gives appropriate emphasis to the driving
power and emotional impact of the dramatic story told, a courageously true story, the telling of which fills almost three crowded
hours on the screen.

Zanuck took as his premise to the depiction of Woodrow Wilson, 28th President of the United States, the assumption that "sometimes the life of a man mirrors the life of a nation. The destiny
of our country was crystallized in the life and times of Washington
and Lincoln, and perhaps too, in the life of Wilson. " These are
the words of the foreword.

When an audience first meets Woodrow Wilson, he is the
prexy of Princeton University, author of several tomes on democratic government and of a number of social reforms in the school's
student body. Invited by boss politicians to become a candidate for
governor of New Jersey, he accepts upon the advice of his wife and
family, only to repudiate publicly boss rule and, after election,
actually carry through the repudiation. Thus does a gentleman and
scholar enter the political arena.

In 1912, Wilson's name was placed before his party at the
national convention in Baltimore, and he went on to his first term
in the White House. That the sensitive writing of Lamar Trotti
frequently highlights the human element of the Wilson saga is
pointedly demonstrated by the scene of the family's introductory
inspection of the Presidential home, a family that had "never even
owned a horse and buggy" delighted by the state automobiles at its

disposal. They remained essentially homey folk, often gathering
with their three daughters around the piano to sing simple ballads
until tragedy visited the happy household when Ellen Wilson died.

The clouds of World War I broke in Europe before Woodrow
Wilson came up for the 1914 nomination in the Chicago convention.
He was reelected to the Presidency on the slogan that he "kept us
out of war." But shortly after assuming office for a second term,
keeping out of war became impossible, and he rose in righteous
wrath to denounce militaristic German Kultur in a dramatic encounter with Ambassador von Bernstorff, and subsequently delivered his
famed "champion of mankind" speech in asking Congress for a dec-
laration of war.

Among the many excellences of Zanuck's production is the
inspired use of historic newsreels as a montage of the years of
World War I and a repeat of that technique after the Armistice
brought about League of Nations meetings. In one of these, Alexander Knox, the actor who masterfully impersonates Wilson, is
stripped in to make the illusion perfect.

Wilson's dreams of world peace as embodied in his 14 points
were denied fulfillment by Congressional reactionaries and isolationists, chief of whom was Senator Henry Cabot Lodge. Accompanied
by his second wife, Edith Galt Wilson, the President took his warn-
ings of the danger of a World War II to the American people in an
exhaustive speaking tour, a trip from which he returned broken in
health. The implication is unmistakable that Wilson literally gave
his life in the cause of world peace, a question that has again confronted all civilized mankind.

Direction of such a powerful document of America demanded
a skilled and meticulous hand. The responsibility is admirably un-
dertaken by Henry King in the most commanding work of his career.
He is aided by the Academy Award photography of Leon Shamroy, a
past master of the Technicolor camera, who outdoes his previously
celebrated attainments. Superlative technical merits are headed by
the arresting art direction of Wiard Ihnen and James Basevi, who
executed monumental sets in exquisite taste and contrasting riots of
color which capture the tasteless hurly-burly of political conventions.

Evaluation of the performance of the title role by Alexander
Knox has been purposely delayed until the exacting nature of his
portrayal could be clearly stated. His part is before the camera
almost continually and is one of the longest ever written. He was
given a reasonable resemblance to Wilson and, with true dignity and
magnificent diction, the actor brings it to life. Never once does
he err by trying to become spectacular.

The Wilson family is becomingly played by Geraldine Fitzgerald as Edith Galt Wilson, Ruth Nelson as the first wife, and
Mary Anderson, Ruth Ford and Madeleine Forbes as the daughters.

Leading the supporting cast is Charles Coburn as "Henry
Holmes," a fictional composite of Wilson's professorial friends.
Another composite is the role William Eythe draws as a college
student called "George Felton." But there is nothing fictional about
the part of Joe Tumulty which Thomas Mitchell plays with relish.
He is the man who became Wilson's trusted secretary and continued
to address him as Governor even after he became President. Sir
Cedric Hardwicke's Senator Lodge is excellent.

Amazingly accurate are the portraits drawn of Colonel House
by Charles Halton, William Jennings Bryan by Edwin Maxwell, Jo-
sephus Daniels by Sidney Blackmer, Clemenceau by Marcel Dalio,
and Lloyd George by Clifford Brooke. Not much is made of William Gibbs McAdoo, impersonated by Vincent Price, but there are
outstanding moments from the contributions of Stanley Ridges,
Thurston Hall and Tonio Selwart, the latter as von Bernstorff.

Especially noteworthy is the music by Alfred Newman, and
mention must be made of the Technicolor direction by Natalie Kalmus and Richard Mueller, the editing by Barbara McLean, the
costuming by Rene Hubert, and the makeups by Guy Pearce.
> --The Hollywood Reporter, Vol.
> 79, No. 30 (August 2, 1944),
> page 3.

□ WOMAN OF THE YEAR (M-G-M, 1942)

Somehow or another, this department is unable to flagellate
itself to the pitch of enthusiasm about Woman of the Year achieved
by the New York scribes and the audiences which jampacked the
Music Hall for weeks on end. To me the most amusing thing about
the venture is that Kit Hepburn read the original script and considered it such a novelty that she prevailed upon the studio to buy it
for her use. If the star and the executives got around to seeing
movies, instead of just acting in and producing them, they would
have realized that the piece, in substance, has already been filmed
twice within a twelvemonth as You Belong to Me, Appointment for
Love. This knowledge, undoubtedly, would have whittled the reputed purchase price of one hundred and ten thousand American
dollars. Which, as the boys at the corner pool emporium are
wont to observe, ain't exactly Yen.

Hepburn appears as Laura Harding, a career gal who marries a career guy. They have a hell of a time getting privacy on
their wedding night, their interests conflict, and the marriage almost ends on the rocks of Reno. Suddenly, the lass realizes that
although she is the woman of the year (see title), she has been
less than Woman to her man, turns over a new leaf (that of a
cookbook!), and proceeds to feminize herself by preparing breakfast
for hubby--according to the precepts laid down in "Mack Sennett's

Maxims for Willing Brides. " If you can credit that any modern
miss, no matter how haute monde, is utterly confused by a Silex
coffee-maker and an automatic toaster, and that a balloon inserted
in a waffle iron (in emulation of too much yeast in the batter) is
ingenious humor, you'll probably cackle as convulsively as did spectators at the local preview.

Hepburn contributes a crisp, ingratiating performance, which
finds an excellent foil in the utter naturalness of Spencer Tracy.
Fay Bainter, as always, lends superior support, and two new-to-
me faces (owned by Dan Tobin and Edith Evanson) score.   Dialogue
is bright, George Stevens' direction spontaneous, and Joe Ruttenberg's photography is strictly major league.

--Herb Sterne in Rob Wagner's
Script, Vol. 27, No. 627 (April
25, 1942), pages 26-27.

☐ WONDER MAN (Goldwyn/RKO, 1945)

Wonder Man is wonderful.   A merry, mad melange of music
and mirth, this Samuel Goldwyn production for RKO Radio release
is a fantasy done in splendorous Technicolor, loaded with gals and
gags, all wrapped up in as neat a package of film entertainment of
the musical comedy type ever to come out of Hollywood.   It was
made strictly for enjoyment by the widest possible range of film
patrons.

The picture is tasteful and lavish film fare, splashed with
technical and personal beauty.

The second picture to reach the screen to star Danny Kaye,
the film offers a wide range of chances to exploit the talents of the
new star.   His double role gives him opportunity for a wide range
of comedy and his unusual song style, in addition to what might in
the zany Kaye manner be "straight" matter.

The story, more than a framework for the musical numbers,
opens with Kaye, brash cafe entertainer who witnessed a gang murder, being killed himself and his "spirit" entering the body of his
book-worm brother, a meek, learned character.   With the information given him by his brother and the talent infused in him, the
meek one gets himself involved with two girls, the gangsters and
others in a hilarious sequence of events, winding up in a hysterical
opera number in which he conveys to the district attorney the information needed for the arrest of the killers.

Bruce Humberstone comes through with a fine directorial
job, taking all in easy stride to turn out a well-leavened cinema
offering.   When Kaye went into straight acting, he guided him; but
he wisely let Kaye have his head in the musical numbers.   It marks
one of the director's best productions.

The two feminine leads are played by Virginia Mayo and
Vera-Ellen, both of whom carry out their assignments exceptionally
well in addition to looking lovely.   Vera-Ellen makes an auspicious
film debut, both as an actress and dancer-singer.   Donald Woods,
as the night club owner; S. Z. Sakall, in a comedy role as a be-
fuddled delicatessen proprietor; Allen Jenkins, Edward Brophy and
Steve Cochran as the gangsters all deliver ably.   The new set of
"Goldwyn Girls" is unbelievably beautiful.

Technically, the picture is superb.   The orchestration of the
musical numbers by Ray Heindorf, the photography by Victor Milner
and William Snyder, special photographic effects by John Fulton,
the Technicolor direction by Natalie Kalmus and Mitchell Kovaleski,
art direction by Ernst Fegte and McClure Capps, musical direction
by Louis Forbes, editing by Daniel Mandell are all top examples
of their respective craftsmanship.

Sylvia Fine did a grand job of the "Otchi Tcherniya" number
and the music and lyrics for the "Bali Boogie" and opera numbers,
all of which are solid.   The song, "So in Love," by Leo Robin and
David Rose, seems hit material.   John Wray did the creditable
dance direction.

--The Hollywood Reporter, Vol.
83, No. 16 (April 25, 1945),
page 3.

☐ YANKEE DOODLE DANDY (Warner Bros. , 1942)

Two hours of delightful entertainment; a feast of music
sprinkled with mirth; a story of a family which has earned for itself a lasting place in the history of the American theatre.   Jim-
mie Cagney, as George M. Cohan, gives a magnificent performance, and the acting support given him by all the other members
of the long cast leaves no room for criticism.

As a matter of fact, the even excellence of the production
robs me of an opportunity to devote much space to it.   Spectator
reviews get their bulk from the points in pictures it feels could
have been improved, and I failed to detect in this imposing Warner
production one such point, one weakness or one moment when it
sagged.   Hal Wallis, producer, and Michael Curtiz, director, never
turned out better jobs.

The leading players, all of whom are to be credited with
fine performances, are James Cagney, Joan Leslie, Walter Huston,
Richard Whorf, Irene Manning, George Tobias, Rosemary DeCamp,
Jeanne Cagney, Frances Langford, George Barbier, S. Z. Sakall,
Walter Catlett, Douglas Croft, Minor Watson, Eddie Foy, Jr.

Technically the production is a cinematic triumph which is
to be credited to the following: Screen play, Robert Buckner and

Edmund Joseph; film editor, George Amy; photography, James
Wong Howe; art director, Carl Jules Weyl; montages by Don Siegel;
dance numbers, Leroy Prinz and Seymour Felix; sound by Everett
A. Brown; makeup, Perc Westmore; gowns, Milo Anderson; orchestral arrangements, Ray Heindorf; musical director, Leo F. Forbstein.

--Welford Beaton in Hollywood
Spectator, Vol. 17, No. 1
(September 1, 1942), page 15.

*   *   *

Yankee Doodle Dandy, the Warner Brothers' credit sheet in-
forms the Press boys and girls is "based on the story of George
M. Cohan." The truth of the matter revolves about what is meant
by "story." If the statement refers to the professional accomplishments of Old Glory's celebrated son, well and good. However, as
a personal reflection of the actor-composer-playwright-producer,
the piece conceals more than it reveals. Cohan's romances and
marriages with Ethel Levey and Agnes Nolan are replaced by a
fabricated Mary, and all reference to his children is avoided as
carefully as though the showman were Pope. His anti-labour attitude in the Equity strike is deleted, as the actual reasons for his
managerial abdication from Broadway and his split with Sam Harris
in the '20's. As far as the present account is concerned, Cohan
never so much as smelled Eastman stock, but unless memory is
awry this reporter recalls seeing him in three silents (Broadway
Jones, Hit-The-Trail Holiday, Seven Keys to Baldpate) and two
talkies (The Phantom President, Gambling).

Those willing to accept Yankee Doodle Dandy as pure and
adulterated musical comedy will find it an entrancing affair. It
captures the atmosphere and attitude of a past theatrical era with
considerable skill and is one of the rare films able to transpose a
salient stage personality to the screen. Here is entertainer Cohan
with all his brash theatrical necromancy--from the soft-shoe stepping to his voiceless singing--quite marvelously projected by James
Cagney. Cagney doesn't merely imitate or impersonate Cohan; he
really gets under the man's Thespian skin, evaluates his attributes
as an entertainer and supplies a trenchant commentary on the actor's footlight salesmanship.

Considerable bunting-waving is rightfully present and there
are such patriotic songs as "Over There," "You're a Grand Old
Flag," "Yankee Doodle Boy," plus a number that mention "Mary,"
to stir nostalgia. Walter Huston is superb, and there is a truly
fabulous enactment of his dad by Eddie Foy Jr. Joan Leslie, S. Z.
Sakall, Patsy Lee Parsons and Odette Myrtil score individual hits,
but if Irene Manning bears the slightest vocal or visual resemblance
to Fay Templeton, I'm "Bozo" Snyder!

While George Cohan remains behind footlights, Yankee
Doodle Dandy is authoritative; whenever he leaves by the stage

door the fictional meanderings become agonizing to those who like a
bit of authenticity in their entertainment.

> --Herb Sterne in Rob Wagner's
> Script, Vol. 27, No. 635 (Au-
> gust 15, 1942), page 24.

☐ THE YEARLING (M-G-M, 1946)

The Yearling, as it has been screened under the direction
of Clarence Brown and the production of Sidney Franklin, is an
emotional experience seldom equalled in the theatre.   This is a
tale from American folklore that, because of its captivating simplicity, will live forever.   Few who read the book will ever forget
it.   In the motion picture, enlivened by superb performances and
breathtaking Technicolor, the Baxter family of three who struggle
for existence on a last frontier of American pioneer life will never
be forgotten.

Statistics and facts surrounding the making of The Yearling
at MGM are among the most voluminous known to Hollywood.   The
Pulitzer Prize novel of 1938 by Marjorie Kinnan Rawlings took
nearly eight years in its filming.   Talent scouts interviewed close
to 20,000 eleven-year-old boys for the role of Jody before Clarence
Brown found Claude Jarman, Jr., in Nashville, Tenn.   Six separate
expeditions were made to Florida to film scenes.   A total of 126
deer were trained, to be used or discarded because they grew too
fast, before the fawn Jody named "Flag" completed its role.   The
rest of the difficulties encountered would take several hundred pages
to list in detail.   But the finest thing that can be said of this motion picture work of love is that the result is eminently worth every
bit of the trouble.

The story picks up eleven-year-old Jody at the time when he
first starts hinting to his Pa and Ma that he would welcome an animal to pet and care for.   He casually "suggests" that a baby rac-
coon would be acceptable, or maybe something else.   But Pa Baxter
is having trouble enough eking out a bare existence in the Florida
forest clearing where he brought his bride and where they buried
four children before Jody grew "old enuf to live."   Ma will have
none of this truck about pets to eat what they need to feed themselves.

Not until after Pa takes Jody hunting the marauding bear,
"Slewfoot," and the cowardice of one of their dogs is discovered,
does Pa decide to make a trade with neighbors that will rid him of
the dog and get him a better gun.   The trade is expertly made, and
Jody meets again the crippled boy, Fodderwing, who has lots of
pets.   Jody becomes doubly anxious to have one of his own.

An accident, when Pa gets bit by a rattler and his life is
narrowly saved, gives Jody his pet, a fawn that survived the killing

of its mother. Despite the protests of Ma, the boy is allowed to
raise the little deer until it becomes a "yearling" and a menace to
the livelihood of the Baxter family. Flag, as Jody named him,
eats the growing corn crop and tramples the precious tobacco plants.
The survival of the Baxters depends upon the disposal of a beloved
pet, as Jody is at last brought to realize.

Such a story demanded the ultimate in sensitive direction,
which is exactly what the skill of Brown provides. It is his finest
screen work, an observation any member of his craft can appreciate. His handling of Claude Jarman, Jr. in the role of Jody is a
thing of beauty. The boy had never before acted, but no one would
know it from the performance delivered.

Gregory Peck scores an amazingly vigorous hit with his playing of Pa. The camaraderie between father and son when confronted
with the natural antagonism of womankind is deftly presented. The
understanding that Peck gives his boy and his role is deep.

Jane Wyman is literally a revelation as Ma. Although her
makeup is anything but glamorous, she has never been lovelier in
films. Here is an actress in every sense of the word, as the acclaim she should win will unquestionably prove.

Franklin exerted splendid care in casting all down the line,
as he did with arresting production excellences. Outside of the
Baxters, the rest of the parts are bits. Yet the neighboring For-
rester clan is portrayed by such character experts as Chill Wills,
Clem Bevans, Margaret Wycherly, Forrest Tucker, Matt Willis,
Dan White, George Mann, Arthur Hohl, and little Fodderwing by
appealing Don Gift. The storekeeper is none other than Henry
Travers; his daughter, Joan Wells; the romancing Oliver, Jeff
York, and pretty Twink Weatherby, June Lockhart.

The screen credits three directors of photography, Charles
Rosher, Leonard Smith and Arthur Arling. But the name that is
printed the largest is Rosher. The music score by Herbert Stot-
hart, utilizing themes from Frederick Delius, is superb. Chester
M. Franklin is named as director of the second unit, and Harold
F. Kress for the film editing.

--Jack D. Grant in The Hollywood
Reporter, Vol. 91, No. 21
(November 27, 1946), page 3.

*   *   *

The Yearling is Metro's bid for the Academy Award. Based
on the Pulitzer Prize novel by Marjorie Kinnan Rawlings, it is a
thorough and earnest regional study, a strong tale of a simple,
forthright pioneering people. Technically, it is one of the finest
films ever produced, and there seems little doubt that Gregory
Peck, Jane Wyman and 11-year-old Claude Jarman, Jr., will be
strong contenders for acting honors. Their portrayals of the lead-

ing roles add stature and dignity to the drama.   And if there were
some way to count the number of tears shed, and if awards were
based on a tear-quota, certainly this movie would win hands down.

Much of the comedy and pathos of the picture revolves
around Flag, the pet deer of 11-year-old Jody Baxter.   As the
deer grows, it threatens the very existence of the little Baxter
family by trampling the corn crop and the precious tobacco plants.
The Baxters--father, mother and son--typify the pioneering farm
family in the South who were forced to battle against nature, wild
beasts, and other humans in order to eke out a bare existence from
the land.   Every foot of tillable soil had to be productive in order
that the family might eat.   And money for such luxuries as a three-
yard piece of alpaca (for Ma's best dress), or for the seed for the
"money crop" (tobacco), represented years of saving.   With barely
food enough to nourish the family, it is only natural that Ma should
be adamant in her refusal to permit Jody to keep a pet.

From the moment when Jody overcomes her objections and
adds an orphaned fawn to the household, tragedy hangs high over
the horizon.   The unhappy ending, even to those who haven't read
the book, comes as no surprise.

The illusion of the family's relationship to the beasts of the
forest, who are both friendly and menacing, is beautifully maintained.   One of the tenderest episodes concerns Fodderwing (Don
Gift), an imaginative crippled child, son of the aging Forresters
(Clem Bevans and Margaret Wycherly), who shares his bed in a
treetop with Jody one night.   Jody's grief at Fodderwing's death is
well enacted; and the five roistering Forrester sons are well cast.
The story is packed with gentle charm, albeit a trifle too exhaus-
tively.   Director Clarence Brown must be credited with having
turned out an impressive picture.

--Fortnight, Vol. 1, No. 4
(December 16, 1946), page 42.

☐ CREDO

Thirteen years ago this department-to-be, with the dust of
the world on its shoes, first stamped into the old Script offices on
Dayton Way and was appraised by that delightful dragon, Molly
Lewin, who then guarded the outer editorial fortress of Rob and
Florence. I had just returned to California from a several-year
vagabond quest through China, Cochin-China, Siam, Burma, India,
Mesopotamia, Syria, the Holy Land and Egypt, during which, when
cash ran low, I impaled jobs on sundry daily papers of the East and
conducted film reviewing pages for the multi-colored multitude.

Armed with cuttings of my printed accomplishments, and
dreams of the mighty future of the cinema based on the evidences
of such superb films as Intolerance, Greed, The Crowd, The Blue
Angel, All Quiet on the Western Front and Cavalcade I talked my
way past Script's drawbridge and convinced Rob and Florence that
I had a fondness for, a respect for, some knowledge of, the drama,
and that I was just the chap to do reviewing chores for them.

A veritable Niagara of celluloid has poured through motion
picture projectors since that time and this, when the final issue of
Script appears under the Wagner aegis. In the interim, I have witnessed the almost complete triumph of the standardized photoplay
in America. Mediocrity, in considerable measure, has vanquished
worth. The indifferent have flourished, while such titans as Griffith, von Stroheim, von Sternberg and Rex Ingram have ceased con-
tributing to the art they helped create, and these days, King Vidor
is "credited" with having directed Duel in the Sun. I have seen
Academy Oscars for "acting" accorded Luise Rainer, Greer Garson, Jennifer Jones and Joan Crawford. Julian Johnson, Richard
Watts, Jr., Vachel Lindsay and Wolcott Gibbs no longer are available to pen considered critiques in terms of aesthetic standards
that are superior to those of today's fan publications. And Script
has received numerous petulant letters each time this department
has ventured to demonstrate that it possessed a few illusions about
what the film should be. However, I still assume that a single
film is not to be judged entirely by itself but, too, in relation to
the entire accomplishment of the art's existence.

The motion picture in America, for several reasons--includ-
ing the present staggering production costs--has become a composite
medium. Spending millions in order to appeal to millions, it is no

longer feasible for a Griffith to spin from himself a Broken Blossoms. Nor is it possible for a von Sternberg with six thousand dollars to take a camera to San Pedro and come back with a Salvation Hunters, a Charles Brabin to take to the Kentucky mountains with a camera and return with a Driven. Individuality in the American photoplay of 1947 is sporadic, and survives only in rare instances, with the names of John Ford, Preston Sturges, Billy Wilder, Chaplin and Orson Welles coming most readily to mind. Perhaps the present success of the distinctive British film on this side of the Atlantic will again prove to those who remain unconvinced that there is an American audience for motion pictures that are not cerebrally and artistically bankrupt. For my time and attention, there have been few better photoplays ever than the recent importations, Henry V and Odd Man Out.

During the years with Script I have seen domestic films of worth, but the record discloses that of late such have appeared with alarming infrequency. With no attempts at computing their relative merit, and with memory solely as roadmap, the following list of accomplishments during this period remains warmly in mind.

There is Slim, an unpretentious venture about a high-tension wire linesman, which starred Henry Fonda. Trouble for Two, an extraordinary atmospheric adaptation of Stevenson's Suicide Club, with remarkably accurate delineations by Robert Montgomery as Prince Florizel and Louis Hayward as The Young Man with the Cream Tarts. Sturges' Menckenian treatment of American small-town foibles, The Miracle of Morgan's Creek and Hail the Conquering Hero, remain unforgettable. John Ford contributed at least three notable dramas: The Informer, The Long Voyage Home and Stagecoach. Ernst Lubitsch, who gave us such ingenious musicals as The Love Parade and Monte Carlo in the early days of sound, supervised the entrancing Marlene Dietrich comedy, Desire and imparted his best "touch" all the way. In addition, Lubitsch directed Ninotchka, for which Charles Brackett and Billy Wilder wrote one of the best satirical scripts to reach the screen. Later, Brackett and Wilder on their own made the excellent Major and the Minor and The Lost Weekend.

Chaplin's Modern Times seems to me to rank with such of his earlier great comedies as Easy Street and The Kid. Wellman's The Ox-Bow Incident and Lang's You Only Live Once were powerful documents. William de Mille and Arthur Hopkins collaborated on a charming adaptation of Arnold Bennett's Buried Alive which, though released under the insane title of His Double Life, gave Lillian Gish the chance to prove her talents as a comedienne. Borzage, a different man from the one who recently gave me the collywobbles with I'll Always Love You, was responsible for the very fine A Farewell to Arms and Little Man, What Now?

Von Sternberg proffered at least two excellent melodramas, Morocco and Shanghai Express, plus two notable experiments in the bizarre, The Scarlet Empress and The Devil Is a Woman. Orson

Welles's venture into screen archaeology, Citizen Kane, was certainly worth viewing, as was his curious conception of Tarkington's
The Magnificent Ambersons.   Odets' None But the Lonely Heart
impressed me considerably, as did Stevens' Alice Adams which had
a superlative performance from Katharine Hepburn.   David Selznick,
one way or another, had a hand in delivering the meritorious What
Price Hollywood?, David Copperfield, A Bill of Divorcement and
Nothing Sacred, the latter from a superbly nippy Ben Hecht script.
Hecht, in collaboration with Charles MacArthur, produced, directed
and wrote the intriguing The Scoundrel, which featured a titillating
fancy-pants performance from Noel Coward.

She Done Him Wrong possessed a lustiness that both the
screen and Mae West have since lost.   Sam Goldwyn produced the
moodful Wuthering Heights, and revealed major performances from
Ruth Chatterton, Walter Huston and Mary Astor in Dodsworth.
Blood and Sand, under Mamoulian's direction, made the most dramatic use of color yet seen on the screen.   Cukor and Garbo contributed the perfect visualization of Camille in motion pictures--and
the Dumas fils heroine had been played for the cameras previously
by Bernhardt, Theda Bara, Clara Kimball Young, Nazimova, Norma
Talmadge, and Yvonne Printemps.

In the way of musicals, Fred Astaire and Ginger Rogers led
the parade with a half dozen honies, my favorite being The Story of
Vernon and Irene Castle.   Cover Girl later captured an equal radi-
ance in the same genre.   Despite the mass of misinformation about
the personal life of George M. Cohan in Yankee Doodle Dandy, the
film presented an apt impression of him as a performer, with James
Cagney doing a mighty job as G. M. C.   The musical sound track of
The Jolson Story is one of the most exciting to be recorded, for it
re-creates Al's magnetism to an astonishing degree.   Yolanda and
the Thief had a delicate charm that seems to have been generally
missed by the multitude.   Screen glamour, it seems to me, has
pretty generally become a lost art since the von Sternberg-Dietrich
partnership was dissolved, but it returned in all its chatoyant glory
in the Ouidaesque Gilda, which had a creature of utterly disturbing
beauty in Rita Hayworth.

Looking over the partial list of the American films I have
appreciated during my life with Script, I find that my attitude
towards the motion picture is at variance with that of Wolcott Gibbs,
who, when he absconded from the film reviewing chores of The
New Yorker, gave as his reason that he finally realized he had
been writing for the information of his friends about entertainment
plainly designed for their cooks.

In the main, of course, Mr. Gibbs's evaluation of the average film is correct.   It requires a long view to select a few examples of superior picture making from the many dreadful mistakes,
and so it requires strong nerves, a patient temper, and a strong

stomach to retain an enthusiasm for, and a belief in, the photoplay, year following year.

--Herb Sterne in <u>Rob Wagner's</u>
<u>Script</u>, Vol. 33, No. 751
(March 15, 1947), pages 14-15.

☐ BIBLIOGRAPHY OF ANTHOLOGIES OF FILM CRITICISM

Aside from the books listed below, there have been a number of attempts through the years to publish periodicals of collected film criticism, most notably Motion Picture Review Digest, published from 1936 through 1939 by the H. W. Wilson Company; New York Motion Picture Critics' Reviews, published from 1944 through 1946 by Critics' Theatre Reviews; and Film Review Digest, published from 1975 through 1977 by Kraus-Thomson.

Adler, Renata. A Year in the Dark (Random House, 1969).

Agate, James. Around Cinemas (Home & Van Thal, 1948).

_____. Around Cinemas, second series (Home & Van Thal, 1948).

Agee, James. Agee on Film (Grosset and Dunlap, 1967).

Alpert, Hollis, and Andrew Sarris, eds. Film 68/69 (Simon and Schuster, 1969).

Anstey, Edgar; Roger Manvell; Ernest Lindgren; and Paul Rotha, eds. Shots in the Dark (Allan Wingate, 1951).

Brownstone, David M., and Irene M. Franck, eds. Film Review Digest 1976 (KTO Press, 1976).

_____. Film Review Digest 1977 (KTO Press, 1978).

Cocks, Jay, and David Denby, eds. Film 73/74 (The Bobbs-Merrill Company, 1974).

Cooke, Alistair, ed. Garbo and the Night Watchmen (McGraw-Hill Book Company, 1971).

Crist, Judith. The Private Eye, the Cowboy and the Very Naked Girl (Holt, Rinehart and Winston, 1968).

Denby, David (editor). Film 70/71 (Simon and Schuster, 1971).

_____. Film 71/72 (Simon and Schuster, 1972).

_____ . Film 72/73 (The Bobbs-Merrill Company, 1973).

_____ . Awake in the Dark: An Anthology of American Film
    Criticism, 1915 to the Present (Vintage Books, 1977).

Hardy, Forsyth, ed. Grierson on the Movies (Faber and Faber,
    1981).

Kael, Pauline. I Lost It at the Movies (Little Brown and Com-
    pany, 1965).

_____ . Kiss Kiss Bang Bang (Little Brown and Company, 1968).

_____ . Going Steady (Little Brown and Company, 1970).

_____ . Deeper into Movies (Little Brown and Company, 1973).

_____ . Reeling (Little Brown and Company, 1976).

Kauffmann, Stanley. A World on Film (Harper and Row, 1966).

_____ . Figures of Light (Harper and Row, 1971).

_____ . Living Images (Harper and Row, 1975).

_____ . Before My Eyes (Harper and Row, 1980).

_____ , and Bruce Henstell, eds. American Film Criticism:
    From the Beginnings to Citizen Kane (Liveright, 1972).

Lejeune, C. A. Chestnuts in Her Lap (Phoenix House, 1948).

Lorentz, Pare. Lorentz on Film (Hopkinson and Blake, 1975).

Macdonald, Dwight. Dwight Macdonald on Movies (Prentice-Hall,
    1969).

Morgenstern, Joseph, and Stefan Kanfer, eds. Film 69/70 (Simon
    and Schuster, 1970).

The New York Times Film Reviews: 1914-1968 (The New York
    Times and Arno Press, 1970).

The New York Times Film Reviews: 1969-1970 (The New York
    Times and Arno Press, 1971).

The New York Times Film Reviews: 1971-1972 (The New York
    Times and Arno Press, 1973).

The New York Times Film Reviews: 1973-1974 (The New York
    Times and Arno Press, 1975).

The New York Times Film Reviews: 1975-1976 (The New York
    Times and Arno Press, 1977).

The New York Times Film Reviews: 1977-1978 (The New York
    Times and Arno Press, 1979).

Pratt, George C. Spellbound in Darkness (The New York Graphic
    Society, 1973).

Reed, Rex. Big Screen Little Screen (The Macmillan Company,
    1971).

Sarris, Andrew. Confessions of a Cultist (Simon and Schuster,
    1970).

Scaramazza, Paul A., ed. Ten Years in Paradise (The Pleasant
    Press, 1974).

Schickel, Richard. Second Sight (Simon and Schuster, 1972).

_____, and John Simon. Film 67/68 (Simon and Schuster, 1968).

Simon, John. Movies into Film (The Dial Press, 1971).

_____. Reverse Angle (Clarkson N. Potter, 1982).

Taylor, John Russell, ed. Graham Greene on Film (Simon and
    Schuster, 1972).

Wilson, Robert, ed. The Film Criticism of Otis Ferguson (Temple
    University Press, 1971).

Winnington, Richard. Drawn and Quartered (The Saturn Press,
    1948).